Angels
in the
Machinery

Angels in the Machinery

* * *

*Gender in
American Party Politics
from the Civil War
to the Progressive Era*

Rebecca Edwards

New York Oxford • Oxford University Press 1997

Oxford University Press

Oxford   New York

Athens   Auckland   Bangkok   Bogota   Bombay   Buenos Aires
Calcutta   Cape Town   Dar es Salaam   Delhi   Florence   Hong Kong
Istanbul   Karachi   Kuala Lumpur   Madras   Madrid   Melbourne
Mexico City   Nairobi   Paris   Singapore   Taipei   Toyko   Toronto   Warsaw

and associated companies in
Berlin   Ibadan

Copyright © 1997 by Oxford University Press, Inc.

Published by Oxford University Press, Inc.
198 Madison Avenue, New York, New York 10016

Oxford is a registered trademark of Oxford University Press

Library of Congress Cataloging-in-Publication Data
Edwards, Rebecca (Rebecca Brooks)
Angels in the machinery: gender in American party politics
from the Civil War to the progressive era / Rebecca Edwards.
p. cm.
Includes bibliographical references and index.
ISBN 0-19-511695-X; ISBN 0-19-511696-8 (pbk.)
1. Women in politics—United States—History—19th century.
2. United States—History—19th century.
3. Political parties—United States—History.
I. Title.
HQ1236.5.U6E39 1997
306.2'082—dc21   97-10594

3 5 7 9 8 6 4 2

Printed in the United States of America
on acid-free paper

For Mom, Dad, and Tim

Acknowledgments

The fortunes of historians, like those of politicians, lie largely in the hands of their friends, and I offer heartfelt thanks to a number of people who made this book possible. Among the friendly archivists and librarians who helped me in countless ways, I am especially grateful to Brita Mack and Jennifer Watts of the Huntington Library, Darrol Peirson of the Indiana State Library, Lisa Backman of the Denver Public Library, Edith Mayo and Denise Meringolo of the Smithsonian Institution, and the interlibrary loan staff at the University of Virginia and Vassar College libraries. I received research support from Phi Alpha Theta, through its John W. Pine Memorial Award; the American Heritage Center at the University of Wyoming; and the Smithsonian Institution. The University of Virginia extended aid through its Department of History, Graduate School of Arts and Sciences, and Commonwealth Center for Literary and Cultural Change. Vassar College provided research funds to complete the project. My dedicated Vassar research assistants, Shira Jacobs and Heather Harmon, deserve special mention for their hard work.

I owe thanks also to a series of insightful readers, including Eileen Boris, Jo Freeman, Robyn Muncy, Elisabeth Israels Perry, and Sheri Holman. At the University of Virginia I received sage advice from Brian Balogh, Ann Lane, Nelson Lichtenstein, and Anne Schutte. Michael Holt's suggestions both shaped the initial project and refined the conclusions. Participants in the Southern History Seminar—especially Hannah Rosen, Scot French, and Brad Mittendorf—challenged me to clarify my analysis of the South. Alan Berolzheimer, Melanie Gustafson, Kristin Hoganson, Lisa Severson, Elizabeth Varon, and Jonathan Zimmerman generously shared their insights and their works in progress. I am also indebted to Drew VandeCreek for our many debates on economics, partisanship, and policymaking.

My colleagues at Vassar have been wonderfully supportive. In addition to helpful critiques in the History Department seminar, parts of the manuscript received additional attention from Bob Brigham, Miriam Cohen, Clyde Griffen, and Anne Constantinople. Where flaws and errors persist, they do so in spite of all these critics' generous advice. Editor Thomas LeBien, production editor Jessica Ryan, and their colleagues at Oxford have been a joy to work with during final revisions and publication. Most of all, I thank my parents and my brother Tim for their encouragement throughout. This book is for them.

When I began this project with two dissertation advisors, I worried about receiving conflicting advice. Since those advisors were Cindy Aron and Ed Ayers, I should have known better. Their insights have been harmonious as well as wise. Both read untold drafts with extraordinary patience and good cheer; both supported me through the rough patches while challenging me with hard questions. I am deeply grateful for their guidance and friendship. If this book reflects even a small part of their scholarly subtlety and generosity of spirit, it will be a great success.

Poughkeepsie, New York
December 1996

Contents

A section of illustrations appears after page 116.

Chronology of Key Elections and Other Events

D = Democrat, R = Republican, P = Populist; numbers in parentheses indicate official popular votes

1856 James Buchanan (D, 1,832,955) elected president over John C. Frémont (R, 1,339,932) and Millard Fillmore (American Party, 871,731); first presidential campaign in which Republicans field a candidate

1860 Abraham Lincoln (R, 1,865,593) elected president over three opponents: Stephen Douglas (Northern D, 1,382,713), John Breckinridge (Southern D, 848,356), and John Bell (Constitutional Union, 592,906)

1861–65 Civil War

1865 13th Amendment to the Constitution abolishes slavery

1868–70 14th and 15th Amendments establish national citizenship and universal male suffrage irrespective of race

1868 Ulysses S. Grant (R, 3,598,235) elected president over Horatio Seymour (D, 2,706,829)

1869 Wyoming Territory grants women full suffrage, the first state or territory to do so

1876 Rutherford B. Hayes (R, 4,034,311) elected over Samuel Tilden (D, 4,288,546) and Peter Cooper (Greenback Party, 75,973); contested election followed by secret agreement for withdrawal of last federal troops from southern states

1877 Depression hits; nationwide railroad strike; Farmers' Alliance founded in Texas

1882   National Prohibition and Home Protection Party founded

1884   Grover Cleveland (D, 4,874,621) elected over James Blaine (R, 4,848,936) to become the first Democratic president since 1860; Prohibition candidate John St. John (147,482) attracts support in swing states

1888   Benjamin Harrison (R, 5,447,129) elected president over incumbent Grover Cleveland (5,537,857), winning a majority in the electoral college but not in popular votes; organization of National Women's Republican Association

1890   Republican-dominated Congress passes McKinley Tariff, approves new pension appropriations, and debates Lodge Bill in the "Billion-Dollar" session; Democrats win sweeping victories in fall elections

1892   Strike at Carnegie steelworks in Homestead, Pennsylvania; Knights of Labor and Farmers' Alliance merge at St. Louis Convention to form national People's Party; Cleveland reelected (5,555,426) over incumbent Harrison (5,182,600) and James B. Weaver (P, 1,029,846)

1893   Women win full suffrage in Colorado, the first such victory in a state referendum; severe economic depression hits the United States

1894   Republicans win sweeping victories in Congressional and state elections

1896   William McKinley (R, 7,102,246) elected president over William Jennings Bryan (D, P, and Silver Republican, 6,492,559); Populist Party fragments

1898   Spanish-American War

1890–1908   State constitutional conventions disfranchise black men throughout the South

1901   McKinley assassinated; Theodore Roosevelt becomes president

1912   Woodrow Wilson (D, 6,296,547) elected over incumbent William Howard Taft (R, 3,486,720), Theodore Roosevelt (Progressive Party, 4,118,571), and Eugene Debs (Socialist Party, 901,873)

1913   16th and 17th Amendments, respectively, authorize Congress to levy income taxes and provide for direct election of U.S. Senators by popular vote

1919   18th Amendment prohibits sale of liquor (repealed, 1933)

1920   19th Amendment establishes national woman suffrage

Angels
in the
Machinery

Introduction

As witnesses to an industrial revolution, nineteenth-century Americans were fascinated by the power and complexity of machines. In political debate they used machines as a metaphor for both the electoral system and for parties. A convention of freedmen, for example, urged southern blacks to organize "as a political unit, looking towards equal rights, with decided political machinery." "Party machinery," declared a Republican leader in 1868, "is the only possible method by which a free republic can accomplish the purpose of its existence." Other references were negative: one New York Democrat protested convention rules that made a delegate "a mere cog in the wheel of a machine," and *Harper's* scoffed at the "usual machinery" of electoral campaigns.[1]

Party structures found their ideal opposite in the gentle domesticity attributed to women. Like their English Victorian counterparts, leaders of American opinion hailed the home as "woman's sphere," a place where wives and mothers conserved family bonds and religious devotion. Both men and women of the era described women as "angels of the home." To many, women's selflessness and purity were the very qualities that unfitted them for politics.

Politics, however, could not function without the virtues women represented. The institutions of political life might resemble machines, but each party fought for deeply held values. At a fundamental level, elections were disputes about faith and family order, and campaigns rested on opposing views of the family's relationship to the state. "If politics means anything, it concerns women," wrote a Populist author, and most Americans would have agreed.[2] The question was, should men manage politics in the interest of women and families, or should women join the debates and exercise power themselves?

3

In 1886, New York politician John Boyle O'Reilly expressed his abhorrence at the idea of woman suffrage. "It would be no more deplorable," he declared in a public letter, "to see an angel harnessed to a machine than to see a woman voting politically." O'Reilly's words hinted at ambivalence toward both women and political affairs. If harnessing women's virtue would be cruel and degrading, what did that say about the values of the electoral machine? By 1900 Henry Adams wrestled with the same problem, contrasting the new energy of industrial dynamos with the fading religious forces represented by the Virgin. Adams and his circle believed the women they knew were morally superior to the men; they would make better legislators and presidents. What, then, should be their political role? Without women's moral force, was the political machinery not empty of higher purpose?[3]

Like Adams's ideal Virgin, O'Reilly's angel bore little relation to the lives of real American women. Women had loyalties of region, race, and economic interest, as well as views on religious and family order, all of which translated into beliefs about government policy. At the time O'Reilly wrote, many women were busy harnessing themselves to party and electoral machinery. They proved to be no angels, but were keen strategists who deployed the language of womanhood, as men did, to further their own causes and denounce opponents as immoral and corrupt. Hardly a heavenly band working for common purposes, women disputed each other's priorities, virtue, and presence in the political sphere.

I have borrowed O'Reilly's words for my title, not because they describe the activities of real women but because they capture a fundamental tension in nineteenth-century thought. Americans described their political institutions as they did industrial machinery: both were inventions of great power operating on a vast scale for good or ill. Seeking to use them for good, partisan Americans defined their goals in domestic terms. On all sides they claimed their policies would preserve domesticity and true womanhood. The "angel of the home" legitimized the machinery of politics, and the machine validated the angel. This gender-based ideology shaped both the limits and possibilities for women in the political arena.

NINETEENTH-CENTURY AMERICA was a place of intense political loyalties and hard-fought elections. Most states adopted universal white male suffrage in the 1820s and 1830s, prompting party leaders to organize mass meetings, barbecues, and parades. Voter turnout was massive by today's standards. In every county, town, and city ward, party supporters mobilized to bring neighbors and friends to the polls. Arguing that broader suffrage rights would prevent the class conflicts that haunted Europe, Americans proudly quoted John Greenleaf Whittier's "The Poor Voter on Election Day":

> The rich is level with the poor,
> The weak is strong today,
> And sleekest broadcloth counts no more
> Than homespun frock of gray.
> Today shall simple manhood try

The strength of gold and land;
The wide world has not wealth to buy
The pow'r in my right hand![4]

Party leaders often described campaigns in the language of worship. They urged citizens to visit party "shrines" and bring their principles "to the polls as punctually as to church." Such metaphors reflected a widespread view of the parties as communities of shared faith. The challenge for politicians was to confirm old loyalties, probe for conflicting priorities, and apply the most effective levers of persuasion.[5]

At the root of each coalition's agenda were deeply held beliefs about the nature of family and state. Over and over, Americans argued that the fundamental unit of society was the family; government's first duty was to preserve proper relations within the home. Exactly what this meant was a fiercely disputed question. For centuries, justifications of monarchy and patriarchy had intertwined: masters ruled their households as kings ruled their subjects. In the eighteenth century, when they established the United States as a republic with no state-supported church, American Revolutionaries opened a series of questions on the relations of family, church, and government. Though the link was acknowledged very slowly, rejection of monarchy helped undermine husbands' and fathers' authority in the home. In the United States, the political roles of women and the relationship of government to the family were increasingly contested. The republic would decide these issues, not through royal decree or the doctrines of an established church, but by law as determined through politics.[6]

Debate intensified in early nineteenth-century America as women's economic and social positions underwent rapid change, especially among the prosperous classes of the industrializing Northeast. Influential Americans of both sexes began to argue that women were more spiritual and morally pure than men. This ideology of female moral superiority offered a rationale for women's involvement in a host of reform activities, and it quickly led them into politics. Northeastern middle-class Protestant women joined men of their class in a variety of projects to uplift America—an impulse I will loosely call "northern evangelicalism."[7] Among their activities, these reformers gradually turned to government as an instrument to regulate family life.

By 1860, northern evangelicals and their opponents formed the cores of the two major parties that battled for federal power. Both Republicans and Democrats built broad coalitions that contained internal tensions and competing themes. Among many ways of describing the parties, one is this: Republicans accepted the ideology of women's moral superiority and placed new emphasis on maternal influence, while Democrats defended white men's patriarchal control over their households. Partisan debates on a host of issues were, at a deep level, conflicts over relations of power within the family, and over government's potential to enforce, protect, or undermine them.

Such debates were especially heated in the three decades following the Civil War, a period famously described by Mark Twain as a corrupt but glittering "Gilded Age." By the late nineteenth century, Americans were transforming their agrarian society into a modern industrial nation. The drive to unify the country politically, resolved by Union victory, had produced the beginnings of a modern federal government. Not coincidentally, the postwar decades witnessed the emergence of an independent movement for woman suffrage, accompanied for the first time by broad public debate over women's claims to political equality. In the same years, Republicans and Democrats found themselves in such close competition for national control that they exhausted themselves in virtual stalemate. For all these reasons, Gilded Age Americans engaged in bitter public struggles over the definitions of family and government power.

The Civil War built fervent Republican allegiances among many northern, western, and black voters while reinforcing the Democratic convictions of most ex-Confederates. The war took 600,000 lives and mobilized soldiers and civilians on an unprecedented scale. It also entrenched in Washington a new party with domestic and evangelical purposes. Republicans styled themselves "the party of the home"; they celebrated women's moral influence and praised men who recognized the Christian example set by mothers and wives. "Free Hearts and Free Homes," proclaimed an early Republican campaign banner in 1856.[8] By no means all voters shared these values at the time; in fact, a majority probably opposed them. But by the end of the Civil War, Republicans had won a loyal following. During Reconstruction and beyond, party leaders defended their innovative policies in gendered terms that became familiar to every American. From Union widows' pensions to the transformation of southern "slave pens" into model households, Republicans described their achievements as victories for the American family.

Democrats attacked this ideology as destructive to patriarchal authority, and its proponents as effete aristocrats. The war weakened the Democratic Party but intensified diehards' conviction that they must protect American homes from an intrusive federal government. Because most Democrats, northern and southern, defined slavery as a household or family institution, they viewed Emancipation and black male suffrage as threats to patriarchal as well as racial order. When Union victory brought black freedom, Democrats around the United States reacted with a race-based appeal for white women's protection, warning of the sexual threat allegedly posed by black freedmen. From the secession movement of the 1850s to disfranchisement campaigns of the 1890s, southern Democrats drew a strong connection between expansions of federal authority and the sexual violation of white women. Both were encroachments on the patriarchal home; rape and seduction served as consistent metaphors for the perils of excessive government force.

War wounds did not heal overnight, and campaign arguments based on Union victory or Radical Reconstruction remained salient well into the twentieth century. During the postwar decades, however, economic transformations forced Republicans and Democrats to address urgent new concerns. Rapid settlement brought nine western states into the Union between 1867 and 1897. By the latter year, five railroads linked the Atlantic to the Pacific and prominent Americans lamented the passing of the frontier. With diffusion of new technologies, mines and factories produced staggering outputs. Young men and women from rural areas led a migration to the cities, taking new white-collar and pink-collar positions in growing corporations. Thousands of immigrants arrived each year, speaking tongues as diverse as Hungarian, Norwegian, and Chinese. City dwellers marveled at streetcars, telephones, and electric lights, while rural folk perused mail-order catalogues for amenities they had never before seen.[9]

Industrialization created enormous pressures in American society as rich and poor, farmers and city dwellers expressed anxiety about deteriorating labor conditions and unequal distribution of wealth. Party leaders struggled to address these issues with only partial success. Abandoning Reconstruction, Republicans faced a resurgent national Democratic Party whose leaders denounced GOP economic policies, especially the high protective tariff. North-South rifts threatened to reopen, and northeasterners discovered to their dismay that new sectional interests had developed in the West. Within the South, Democrats faced challenges from insurgent movements that sometimes crossed racial lines. During the period of flux between 1876 and 1894—in which the House of Representatives changed hands five times, and four presidents squeaked into office by absurdly narrow margins—Republicans, Democrats, and third-party challengers sought frantically to invent appeals that would guarantee lasting victory.[10]

To meet new circumstances, the major parties reshaped their old gendered arguments. Democrats, attacking high tariffs as the source of economic woe, articulated a new political identity for women based on their household duties as shoppers and consumers. Republicans responded with warnings about the degraded state of female labor in Europe, claiming tariffs offered protection to the American home and to female wageworkers. Since its first appearance in the late 1850s, the party had translated a Protestant vision of domesticity into politics; by the 1880s, "protection of the family" became less a religious imperative and more an economic argument. Republicans struggled for the next decade to hold the loyalties of the northern working class, who apparently decided that wages and prices were more important matters than a war that had ended a quarter-century before. Only after a massive depression, which hit while Democrats and Populists were in office, did Republicans manage to rebuild a winning coalition and regain a firm grip on national power.

In the meantime, third-party insurgencies advanced more radical proposals along gender lines. Carrying Republicans' evangelical impulse in new directions, the Prohibition and Home Protection Party emphasized the duty of Christian mothers to protect American families. The Woman's Christian Temperance Union (WCTU) helped create this party in the 1880s; WCTU members held direct power in it as delegates and candidates, and its platforms repeatedly called for woman suffrage. Western Populists, focusing instead on economics, offered the most egalitarian vision of men's and women's roles advanced by any party in the Gilded Age. As a result of Populists' temporary electoral successes during the 1890s, women won full suffrage in several western states.

The Gilded Age thus produced a series of political experiments, some initiated by the major parties and others by third-party challengers. As the postwar economy deteriorated, various factions vied for the support of angry farm families and working-class men and women. Regional economic grievances drove the parties' agendas, but at the same time limited their national appeal: Republican pledges to protect northeastern textile operatives, like farm women's political mobilization in the West, met unexpected reactions in other parts of the country. New proposals failed to bridge growing divisions of region and economic interest, and between young and old. As the Civil War generation faded from leadership, young men and women began to seek their own motivations for political action. Gilded Age campaigns thus produced multiple, overlapping searches for effective models of political manhood and womanhood that would meet the needs of a new age.

In all the era's partisan experiments, men and women worked together. Of course, they brought different social identities into politics; gendered arguments drew their very force from Americans' contrasting views of manhood and womanhood. But I find no evidence of a separate "women's political culture" in the Gilded Age. On the contrary, women who enlisted in a variety of political projects—even the most radical suffragists—repeatedly worked through party mechanisms and cooperated with male allies who shared their views. Until their disillusionment and exclusion in the late 1890s, thousands of women tried to achieve their goals through the electoral system, or as reformer Florence Kelley once called it, "the machinery at hand."[11]

Most politically active women demonstrated female consciousness. They believed their gender identity was a useful political tool—probably the most powerful available to them—and they deployed it in the service of their goals. Few, however, gave top priority to the cause of women's political rights. The suffrage movement languished as various coalitions of women and men fought to protect Catholic schools, defend black communities, disfranchise black men, secure government aid for farmers, and resolve class conflict through tariffs, free trade, labor laws, or silver coinage. Even those who gave first priority to women's advancement disagreed profoundly on the means to this end. Many believed that Republicans' protective tariff was the key to women's elevation, because it offered male breadwinners a family wage and allowed women leisure for self-cultivation. Others argued that prohibition of liquor would secure the greatest happiness for the greatest number of women; still others, that Republicans' currency deflation had driven thousands of women to the misery of prostitution, and the most urgent task for women of all classes was to stop the sexual oppression of the poor.[12]

Over the course of long public careers, many women altered their strategies and priorities in response to the rapid changes they saw around them. Even Elizabeth Cady Stanton, one of the few who consistently named suffrage as her chief aim, worked for Republican candidates in the 1870s and early 1880s, later endorsed the Prohibition Party, supported Democratic and Populist nominee William Jennings Bryan in 1896, and finally declared herself a Christian Socialist, disavowing party ties. Throughout, she weighed suffrage against competing goals, including abolition of slavery, religious toleration, and remedies for economic injustice.[13] Gilded Age party politics hardly excluded women. Rather, it offered women, as it did men, a bewildering choice of identities and objectives.

Men, like women, justified their party loyalties by reference to gender, deploying what we might call "male consciousness." Reading contemporaries' constant exhortations to manhood, manliness, and manly honor, one can only conclude that the public identities of nineteenth-century men were as strongly gendered as those of women. To make things more complicated, women and men used each other's gender identities as instruments of persuasion. The gubernatorial candidate who begged women to use their divinely ordained influence "for the good of the Democratic Party," and the women who threatened to mail petticoats to legislators who did not fulfill their protective masculine role, show that men's and women's political identities were mutually dependent and intertwined.[14]

By now it will be obvious that I am defining politics narrowly, offering the warp to the woof of recent feminist scholarship. While I appreciate that expanding the meaning of politics enables women to see personal relationships as part of a larger system of power relations, nineteenth-century Americans did not think this way. To them, politics was the system by which factions and parties won control of government through elections. In an era when government services were scarce and party affiliations the key factor in legislative votes, elections dominated the public's understanding of political structure. Women's rights advocates shared this view: they repeatedly sacrificed other concerns to focus on winning the franchise, which they believed would convey direct, authentic power. Until the late 1890s, mass-based parties had overwhelming visibility and breadth of appeal, and suffragists, like other men and women, sought their victories largely by partisan means.

In the following pages I will return frequently to suffragists and their engagements with the electoral machinery. These women and men joined one of a number of Gilded Age movements that championed specific legislative goals without forming their own political parties. The partisan negotiations of civil service reformers and Mugwumps have been extensively explored elsewhere; suffragists' have not.[15] Of the many Gilded Age political experiments, the suffrage movement was the most female-controlled and the most self-consciously devoted to women's rights. Its fortunes offer insight into a key question: how did gendered campaign arguments shape access to political institutions?

Three aspects of the political system have proved particularly important in answering this question. First, outside political offices themselves, parties were the most important political structures of the era. Second, the two-party American system functioned differently from parliamentary arrangements in other countries, where multiple small parties could build governing coalitions.

Two-party politics forced political discourse into binary channels, most notably, in the late nineteenth century, into evangelical and anti-evangelical camps. The need to construct broad appeals hampered both major parties in their efforts to design new solutions to the nation's problems. At the same time, the system's stability blocked new parties from mounting effective challenges to Republican and Democratic control. A third, related aspect of political structure was the winner-take-all rule. In a given district or presidential race, arguments that persuaded 51 percent of voters secured 100 percent of power.[16] Victors controlled the engine of government and could use it to build up their arguments and tear down those of discredited opponents.

Ultimately, this is what happened in the partisan realignment of the 1890s. In a new regional accommodation, southern Democrats won "home rule" and white supremacy while Republicans regained control of the presidency and Congress for fifteen years. The men who won the crucial elections of 1894 and 1896 based their appeals on militarism and physical force. These arguments first appeared prominently in northeastern and midwestern Republican campaigns against labor interests, socialists, and the alleged threat of anarchy. In southern Democrats' fight against Populism in the region, self-styled white supremacists used similar appeals, calling on voters to protect white women by disfranchising black men. In both cases, party loyalists used aggressive masculinity to bridge class and regional gaps that Populism and socialism had exposed. Of course, not all Americans agreed with these gendered appeals and the uses to which they were put. Electoral victory conferred, however, direct and lasting power on the new ideology and those who employed it.

Party realignment explains why certain female political roles, recognized by men in Gilded Age campaigns, became temporarily unavailable in the first decade of the twentieth century. Women of the early Progressive Era could claim public identities based on Protestant faith, motherhood, and their positions as consumers and workers, but not as party decision makers or voters. The latter options were closed off by the defeat of third-party challenges and by a widespread association of woman suffrage with Populism. Between 1897 and 1910, suffragists won no more state victories and the movement spent "a decade in the doldrums," as its leaders later recalled.[17] Under these conditions women—especially those seeking woman suffrage and remedies for poverty and the exploitation of labor—found that the most effective tactic was to style themselves nonpartisans. They invented effective new techniques for lobbying, grassroots organizing, and otherwise exerting pressure from a "disinterested" position outside the parties. Women did not choose these tactics as a separatist strategy during their first forays into politics. Rather, after decades of work in partisan campaigns, they had become disillusioned and excluded.

Meanwhile, aggressive masculinity validated dramatic new forms of state activism. Though President Theodore Roosevelt became the most popular symbol of the "manly virtues" in politics, many others—including southern demagogues like Benjamin Tillman and James Vardaman—put the rhetoric to their own uses. With Republicans' national dominance assured and Democrats in control of a solid South, the men in power reached something of a bipartisan truce. Democrats approved greater levels of government authority, most notably to enforce racial segregation. Republicans reclaimed older models of masculinity and adapted them to new objectives, including regulation of industry at home and supervision of overseas "protectorates." Aggressive manhood united North and South, East and West in shared military projects. Celebrating its muscle, America plunged into adventures in Cuba and the Philippines and assumed a new presence on the world stage.

Men's reassertion of political authority, based on ideals of soldierhood and sexual honor, had its limitations. Republicans and southern Democrats had not bridged domestic chasms between classes or races. Realignment created a new climate of political stability, but the gold standard, high tariffs, and white supremacy were at best partial and limited solutions. After the crisis of the 1890s, many Americans no longer saw the GOP and the Democratic Party as communities of shared faith. The parties' desperate attempts to cope with economic dislocation had exposed them as outdated machines whose wheels and gears could not cope with the new tasks at hand. Disaffection was most acute in cities, where the gap between party machines and constituents' needs was obvious, but it extended to state and national affairs. Everywhere, women and men turned in disgust from the "mere machines" of party and sought new political projects that seemed more authentic and useful. Yet in developing new techniques of voter education and lobbying, they continued to emphasize ballots as the fundamental units of political power.

The parties have weakened in twentieth-century America. Voter turnout has slowly declined, and politics has lost its central place as a social activity and popular entertainment. At stake in politics today, though, are many of the same issues raised by a New York reformer in 1838, when he described American homes as "ten thousand little republics." Americans continue to describe the family as our most important social institution. In politics, we still propose and dispute policies designed to strengthen marriage, assist mothers and fathers in fulfilling their proper roles, and protect "family values" that are defined in many different ways. Conservatives still associate women's rights with expansions of the federal government's power, and they still link patriarchal authority in the home with resistance to government intrusion. "We are a nation and not a mere confederacy," wrote a convention of woman suffrage advocates in 1880. "The theory of a masculine head to rule the family, the church, or the State is contrary to republican principles and the fruitful source of rebellion."[18] Their assertion remains contested, not only in its claim of women's equality but in its definition of the American nation.

1

The Political Crucible
of the Civil War

One who is brave as a lion and gentle as a woman: such is the hero of the hour.
—Republican Text-Book for the Campaign of 1880

In October 1868, a giant campaign rally in Alabama featured a flag presentation by "the fair and noble ladies of Mobile" to local Democratic candidates. Honorable John R. Tompkins read a statement on behalf of the women's committee, who declared that "our conquerors do not expect us to forget, our natures would not permit us to forget" the glory of the Confederacy. They pledged "earnest cooperation in the great cause you advocate." In the same year, young white women marched in an Indiana Democratic parade under a banner demanding "Save us from nigger husbands." Meanwhile, New York abolitionist Lydia Maria Child exhorted men to vote Republican and uphold the principles of the Union and Emancipation. A year later, former slave Mary L. Hall was at the polls in Savannah, assisting voters who could not read. "I saw the advantage that the white people were taking of my people," she recalled later, "giving the colored voters Democratic tickets and the Negro men did not know any better. I saw that I could be of use."[1]

As these accounts suggest, the wrenching events of the Civil War opened many political prospects for women. They did so, in part, because war issues deepened the connections made by each party between government power and a particular ideal of family life. In the crisis, Republicans used federal power to intervene forcefully in household affairs, most notably to end the "domestic," family-based institution of slavery. In doing so they drew on a new Protestant middle-class model of family order. Northern Republicans displayed growing commitment to a maternal family ideal; the chief danger to the nation, they claimed, lay in Democratic men's propensity for violence and rejection of female moral influence.

To Democrats, their opponents' uses of the state threatened the authority of independent white men, upon which rested both civic and household order. Democrats labeled their enemies weak and effeminate, but the legacy of battlefield victory temporarily shielded Republican men from these attacks. A particular configuration of gender ideals helped Republicans justify expansions of government power. The party's brave military heroes were Christian men who accepted the influence of pure and pious mothers and wives, and thus exercised an enlightened form of paternalistic authority. Throughout the war and Reconstruction, Democrats vehemently disagreed. They argued that Republicans' illegitimate use of federal force resulted in political and sexual corruption.

On both sides, these arguments reached a high pitch during Radical Reconstruction, bringing Republican and Democratic women increasingly into politics. On the basis of domestic ideology, Republican women claimed new roles in the public sphere. Democratic women responded to the challenge, but never in the same numbers and with much less support from men in their party. The question of the postwar era was not whether women had party loyalties, but in what ways they ought to express them. Should women organize partisan clubs? Speak from the stump? Serve as convention delegates and influence party platforms? Vote at the polls?

For the few suffrage advocates, two decades of Republican power in Washington created headaches as well as opportunities. Many suffragists argued that the progressive wing of the GOP was the only body of men sympathetic and powerful enough to enfranchise women, and that they would do so after the war. The moral "influence" of mothers and wives, hailed by almost everyone in the party, did suggest to some Radical Republican leaders that women should join in political decision making. Their numbers were few, however. After the war, suffragists in the North and black women in the South quickly discovered the limits of the new Republicanism. The party helped women advance into politics, but its leaders declined to endorse women's direct political power.

Whig and Democratic Women Before the War

The deepest roots of women's party loyalties lay in republican values, widely held by Americans in the decades after the Revolution. Citizens of the new United States began to recognize women's claims to republican motherhood: women needed to acquire a basic education and take note of public affairs so they could instill civic virtue in their sons. As parties developed, politicians claimed that only their own doctrines would sustain the republic, denouncing opponents as aristocrats or potential tyrants. Both men's and women's commitment to the republic shaded easily—sometimes, at first, unintentionally—into party loyalty. Women should be patriots; parties declared their goals to be patriotic; could women be disinterested when the nation's future was at stake? By casting themselves as defenders of the republic, party leaders provided from the start a rationale for women's partisanship.[2]

During the social and economic upheavals of the early nineteenth century, a new domestic ideology reinforced some Americans' belief in female republican virtue. The United States remained overwhelmingly rural. In most families men and women accomplished different tasks, but they cooperated in running farm households. In the early nineteenth century, especially in the Northeast, towns and cities grew rapidly and the economy began to diversify. As a result more and more men worked away from their homes. The ideal middle-class woman, though she raised children and managed a household, no longer "worked." Instead she protected the sanctuary of the home, and to a large extent religious faith, from the values of an aggressive market economy. The result was an ideal of domestic life centered on motherhood. Women, some Americans came to believe, were physically weaker than men but morally and spiritually purer. They were better parents and better Christians.[3]

In keeping with patterns of industrialization, the maternal family model won its earliest and strongest adherents in the Northeast, in towns and cities, and among the middle class. Its influence spread to some working-class and farm families, southerners, and non-Protestants; observers of the day, however, widely viewed it as an invention of prosperous Protestant Yankees. Many other Americans still conceived of the family as firmly patriarchal and emphasized the primacy of fathers over mothers within the home. In national politics, Americans who resisted the policy implications of the maternal family did so through the Democratic Party.[4] Up until the Civil War, they largely won.

The ideal of the "maternal family," however, offered increasing numbers of women a rationale for political activity. Recognized for superior moral qualities, women could make a stronger claim to republican virtue than they had in prior decades. As in other spheres of life, women needed men's protection and intellectual guidance, but they could rival men in patriotic sentiment. Thus Henry Clay told a group of women in 1844, "I hope the day will never come when American ladies will be indifferent to the fate and fortunes of our common country, nor fail on rare and critical occasions, to demonstrate their patriotic solicitude, in a manner suitable to the delicacy and dignity of their sex."[5] As the Whig candidate in a close presidential race, Clay clearly intended his audience to conclude that the occasion was "rare and critical," and that patriotic women should use their influence—within strict limits—on his behalf.

The absence of female voting rights reinforced the utility of women in party campaigns. Since they could not vote or hold office, their party loyalties appeared selfless, even though by their family, community, racial, and economic ties women gained and lost by election results. Men in politics faced frequent accusations that they were permitting self-interest or ambition to outweigh patriotic duty. For women, domestic ideology masked this tension: a woman's motives must be pure because she allegedly had no political self-interest at all. Of course, this applied only to *woman* in the abstract; the intentions of individual women quickly came under attack. As early as 1840, a female Democratic pamphleteer was accusing a Whig counterpart of having transformed herself "from an angel of peace to a political bully."[6]

In a series of close national campaigns after 1840, Whig and Democratic politicians began to appropriate women's virtue. They urged women to attend campaign meetings, flattered them profusely from the podium, and boasted afterward of their attendance. By 1844 speakers and editors on both sides had developed formulaic descriptions of women's presence that remained in use for the next half-century. These accounts praised women's "bright eyes," their cheerful faces, and the handkerchiefs they waved in approval. Editors often described women, like the Cheshire cat, as nothing but smiles. Orators greeted "the approving smiles of the fair," editors bade women "give the inspiration of your presence and your smiles to the glorious cause," and headlines reported "Ladies Smiling Cheer Into the Canvass." A Maine Republican wrote after one meeting that "the crowded galleries contained a goodly number of ladies, whose beaming faces told of an enthusiasm for the cause not a whit less intent than that of their male escorts."[7]

Such references began to appear in almost every account of campaign events, suggesting that women's presence held compelling advantages for partisan men. In the words of one Florida Democrat, "ladies in full force" represented "the beauty, virtue and refinement of this community," who lent "the sanctity of their presence to the occasion." Women contributed to the parties a purer form of republican virtue than men in the canvass could claim, since the latter sought patronage and public office. By embodying "beauty, virtue, and refinement," or "good order, beauty, and grace," women affirmed their parties' high ideals.[8]

From the 1830s onward, the advent of universal white male suffrage intensified politicians' need for both masculine self-assertion and feminine expressions of support. Americans had often called their political foes effeminate aristocrats; with a dramatic expansion of the white working-class male electorate, such appeals became more frequent and flamboyant. Politicians abandoned classical speaking techniques in favor of popular appeals, which one Illinois man denounced as "slang, low jokes or unwholesome puns, and scurrilous attacks upon personal character." Men described politics through metaphors of warfare, cockfighting, and boxing. Editors derided opponents as "grandmas" and "eunuchs." Campaign speakers found themselves dismissed as feeble, weak, and shrill.[9]

Such accusations took their toll, and oratorical skill was a source of great anxiety to political aspirants. Future president James Garfield rated each of his speaking efforts and reproached himself for weakness and lack of talent. After nervously agreeing to give his first Democratic speech, young William Jennings Bryan expressed relief when no one showed up. Upon listening to an 1884 speech by North Carolina's governor, young Woodrow Wilson wrote, "I had expected a good deal of him; but I received more than I had expected. In the first place he looked like a man, which is almost half the battle with a public speaker; in the second place, he had the voice of a man, full, round and sonorous; and in the third place, he spoke the words of a man." In contrast, Wilson told his future wife that he felt "sadness when you declare your desire to hear me speak. . . . Not until I have freed myself from the accursed bonds of self-consciousness can I be an orator."[10]

Loyal editors showed no such doubts; they praised speakers and candidates as "powerful," "forcible," and the highest embodiments of manhood. Some invoked bare-knuckle fights, countering charges of elitism by identifying their parties with a working-class pursuit. One Republican "handled his subject without gloves"; a Democrat "proceeded to handle the July ticket with the gloves off." Conspicuously masculine rhetoric also accompanied pole raisings, in which men affixed a party banner to a post and installed it in a prominent location. Men on both sides proudly reported the length of their poles and the quickness with which they raised them. Local partisans accused each other of not being able to raise their poles, or in one case of "failure to keep it in an upright position." The only recourse against such attacks was victory. After election day, men hoped their favorite newspaper could depict their party as a crowing rooster, facing an opponent shown limp in defeat.[11]

Such conflicts betrayed underlying vulnerability. A fair-minded man acknowledged the honor of worthy opponents, but in a deeper sense campaigns set men against each other in bitter contests over masculinity. Rejection at the polls undermined one's manhood, and in every election one side lost. Party leaders' insistence on the manliness of supporters and their appeals to partisan ladies were complementary strategies, both addressing the need to affirm masculine honor. By representing pure virtue, women who attended campaign meetings substantiated men's claim that high ideals were at stake, not just personal gain. Women also confirmed men's proper place as leaders and protectors. Their supportive smiles eased the anxiety of those whose manhood would be gauged, all too publicly and numerically, when the ballots came in.

It is not surprising, then, that politicians recruited women most energetically in periods of upheaval and partisan realignment. The first widespread appearance of women at political rallies occurred in the heated campaigns of the 1840s, when Whigs challenged the Democrats' grip on national power. The second coincided with the rise of Republicanism in the late 1850s.[12] Parties needed women's presence in these years because claims to republican virtue were particularly unstable. Old associations crumbled, and men who joined new coalitions faced charges of treachery. Elections were unpredictable, and the possibility of defeat loomed large.

In these eras of realignment, though, the parties were not Tweedledums and Tweedledees offering voters interchangeable arguments simply to win control. During the 1840s both Whigs and Democrats invoked womanhood to signify republican virtue, but their definitions of that virtue rested on conflicting beliefs about the nature of government power. Whigs—and later, much more clearly, Republicans—tended to view state authority as a potential source of good, while Democrats eyed it suspiciously as a source of evil. Whigs often argued that weak government would lead to anarchy and mob rule. To Democrats, centralized power was an invitation to tyranny.

Opposing conceptions of family life were engines that drove these beliefs. Americans had long looked to family relations as a political model. Puritan

domestic ideology
not created
by all politics

theologians, for example, had conceived of the family as a "little common-wealth" and government as family writ large. In rejecting monarchy during the Revolution, Americans had strengthened the home as a political unit, vesting less power in the central state and more in individual citizens who were both masters and representatives of their households. In the Jacksonian era, with universal white male suffrage and dramatic changes in domestic life, political speakers and candidates referred constantly to the family. Good government depended on proper household order; tyranny or anarchy, as threats to the republic, appeared in the guise of sexual sin.[13]

By the 1840s, perhaps even earlier, Democrats and Whigs grounded their worldviews in contrasting reactions to the new domestic ideology. Whigs celebrated the influence of wives and mothers and counseled men to rely on women's moral guidance. They offered a model of gentle, virtuous authority that would slowly, over decades, translate into a vision of benevolent government. Democrats, on the other hand, tended to describe extensions of government power as usurpations of the rights of white men. Only grudgingly did they accept the idea that men should defer to the influence of either centralized government or feminine authority in the home.

Thus Whig men and women sang "Home, Sweet, Home" at campaign rallies for more than sentimental reasons. Consistent with their view of themselves as benevolent reformers who sought power for God's good purposes, they were willing to use state governments in limited ways to enforce proper family behavior. Some Whigs, over strenuous Democratic protests, prohibited drinking and business activity on the Christian Sabbath and banned liquor sales altogether. They established public schools in most parts of the North, hoping to instill not only literacy but also the values of hard work, sobriety, and self-control. Whig men were, on the whole, more likely than Democrats to believe in women's moral superiority and to welcome their public influence. The humorous character Petroleum V. Nasby poked fun at this tendency when he claimed that "I wuz born a Whig. My parents wuz a member uv that party, leastways my mother wuz, and she alluz did the votin, allowin my father, uv course, to go thro the manual labor uv castin the ballot, in deference to the laws uv the country."[14]

Whig women made a more rapid and dramatic political appearance than did their Democratic counterparts. Whig men were the first to invite women to campaign meetings, during the famous Hard Cider and Log Cabin campaign of 1840. (Virtuous ladies abstained from the cider, but some remembered baking desserts in log-cabin shapes.) Whig newspapers were the first to praise the "approving smiles of the fair" and urge women to exert political pressure on their husbands, suitors, and sons. As early as 1844, Whigs organized dozens of female campaign clubs that pledged support for Henry Clay. Whig leaders like Clay and Daniel Webster appealed for women's aid at special "ladies' lectures." In a few rare instances, Whig women even gave stump speeches. These developments were most striking in midwestern and border states where election results were most in doubt. A combination of intense party competition, new mass-based tactics, and domestic ideology offered women their first major opening into political campaigns.[15]

Democrats' response to Whig innovations betrayed a certain perplexity. At first they ridiculed Whig men for "dragging women into politics" and forecast dire results for female purity. Forbearance toward the ladies themselves seemed, however, the wisest course. Attacks on women might provoke a gallant defense that would call Democratic honor into question. Male Democrats were reluctant to invite women to their own meetings, but after the 1840 campaign they paused to reconsider. They had just lost the White House for the first time in twelve years, to a skilled opposition campaign. By 1844 Democrats in some areas copied the Whig approach. They invited women to meetings and praised their loyalty; Democratic women even formed campaign clubs, though not in numbers equal to those of Whigs. They, like Whig women, were most visible in areas where competition was fierce. In the Midwest, especially, the 1840s ushered in bipartisan acceptance of women's campaign presence.[16]

From the first, women's partisanship contained a potential invitation to share power. "I can remember political campaigns since the days of Jackson and Van Buren," an Iowa suffragist wrote in 1884. "It made my young pulse thrill when women were first permitted to attend campaign meetings." Abigail Scott Duniway, later a prominent advocate of women's rights, made her maiden speech in 1840 at age six. She gathered "the village children together under the shade of a sycamore tree, where I climbed to a horizontal limb and harangued them about 'Tippecanoe and Tyler too.'" Susan King of New York, another suffragist, recalled:

> I was nine years old when Jackson and Clay were the opposing candidates for the presidency. At that time I did not know why a girl should not hurrah for a president as well as a boy, and my candidate was Jackson. . . . I was chosen leader of about a hundred of the ragged riff-raff of the town, and one day at a grand political meeting when Sargent Prentiss was making a speech for Clay, we marched up the street with our Jackson banner.

She requested "'three cheers for Jackson,' which the crowd gave with tremendous effect." Many suffragists like these fondly recalled childhood party loyalties.[17] From an early date, they learned the value of the vote as a tool for partisan victory.

In the 1850s, adult Whig women were already following their party's logic to further degrees. Some lobbied legislatures; others pressured individual politicians for anti-liquor laws and funds for charitable institutions. In more than an idle grumble, one opponent warned in 1852 that women's political work "cannot often be repeated without serious effects upon the delicate harmonies of the family and social structure."[18] In the next two decades, this Democrat must have been appalled by national campaigns. Whigs had advanced a new gendered ideology of state power and justified women's political influence; their Republican successors would far outdo them.

Infringing upon Our Rights: Democrats and the Patriarchal Family

Lincoln's election, southern secession, and Republican rule were a series of terrible shocks to the Democratic Party. Its southern wing withdrew into the Confederacy; most northern Democrats remained loyal to the Union, but were dismayed by Republicans' conduct of the war and Reconstruction. The rift plagued Democrats for decades afterward as party leaders tried to satisfy an eclectic constituency of Catholics and Protestants, immigrants and natives, Union and Confederate veterans. A frustrated New Jersey Democrat once called his party "a veritable omnium gatherum of odds and ends," while a Californian compared it to "the prairie-dog villages, where owls, rattlesnakes, prairie-dogs, and lizards all live in the same hole." Between 1860 and 1883, the loss of six consecutive presidential elections aggravated disharmony.[19]

Democrats shared, nonetheless, a defensive ideology linking white men's political rights to their household authority. Whenever opponents pressed for extensions of federal power, Democrats issued impassioned calls for "manly resistance" against such intrusion. Like Whigs and Republicans they hailed the family as both exemplar and foundation of republican virtue, but they assigned different roles to women and men. Women's virtues, associated with domestic morality and religious faith, were to Democrats matters of personal conscience; to impose them in the public sphere was to interfere with others' liberty. Social and political order rested on white men's authority over wives and children, and in the South over slaves. The most extreme pro-slavery advocates argued that "no social state, without slavery as its basis, can permanently maintain a republican form of government"—that is, that the nation's fate hinged on noncitizens knowing their place as dependents and on citizens being masters. Few white men owned slaves, but in the Democratic view all were masters in their homes.[20]

The many issues addressed through this argument reflected the ethnic, religious, economic, and regional concerns of a diverse coalition. Catholics opposed efforts by "high steeple" Protestants to force all children into Protestant-run public schools. Other Democrats suspected that anti-liquor forces in the Whig and Republican camps would interfere with men's drinking rights. On behalf of working-class constituents, Democratic leaders denounced taxes as a burden on the laboring man, an encroachment on his masculine claim to his full wages, and an interference with his ability to support a family. During the war these grievances multiplied along with the new taxes and federal debts that Union victory required. The military draft won widespread enmity for reasons of both class bias and encroachment on civil liberties. It forced men into service, and wealthier men could purchase substitutes. One northern Democrat denounced conscription as "infringing upon our rights" and "insulting our homes."[21]

The rise of Republicanism focused Democrats' attention most closely, though, on the religious and moral dimensions of male freedom. Events of the early 1850s were already worrisome; Maine's passage of a stiff anti-liquor law in 1851 seemed to many Democrats an ominous sign. Before the Republicans, several other parties appeared fleetingly in the Northeast and Midwest to advocate prohibition of liquor, anti-Catholic legislation, and measures to prevent the spread of slavery. When Republicans emerged in the late 1850s, their murky position on slavery was only one of their disturbing traits. As a Democrat warned in 1857, "abolition is but a small part of their programme and probably the least noxious of their measures."[22]

The most noxious Republicans seemed ready to strike directly at the institution of marriage. Democrats watched in horror as Massachusetts, Iowa, and Kansas legalized interracial marriage. Controlled by new anti-Democratic coalitions in the 1850s, several states liberalized their divorce laws. Massachusetts, led by the nativist American Party, relaxed restrictions on remarriage, strengthened alimony rights for women, and for the first time authorized judges to attach the wages of divorced men. New York's legislature faced pressure from women's rights advocates on the same issues. Six months before Lincoln's election, the state passed a law dramatically weakening men's right to claim the earnings of their wives. In stark contrast stood South Carolina, soon-to-be leader of the secession movement and the only state that still entirely prohibited divorce.[23]

Republican leaders insisted they were not abolitionists or women's rights advocates and would not interfere with "domestic institutions" of any kind. Democrats were suspicious nonetheless. Many associated the new party, despite its disavowals, with the radical wing of the antislavery movement. Abolitionists like Elizabeth Cady Stanton and Angelina Grimké were, in fact, claiming a link between black and female emancipation. These women, a southern Democrat observed, went about "haranguing promiscuous assemblies of men, lecturing in public on infidelity, or religion, or slavery." Some abolitionists endorsed the new party, a move unwelcome to many Republicans and not lost on Democrats. The logical end of Republicanism, its opponents warned, was that husbands would lose authority over wives. If any man needed further proof, he could look to the northern legislatures that were meddling with their marriage laws.[24]

Republicans' attack on the Mormon practice of plural marriage held particular foreboding for Democrats as they tried to discern the new party's intentions toward slavery. Settled in Utah territory by the 1850s, leaders of the Mormon church were marrying multiple wives and authorizing the practice for certain men of the faith. Republicans seized on this sensational issue; their first national platform, in 1856, denounced in one breath "those twin relics of barbarism, Polygamy, and Slavery." Congressmen from the party's radical wing launched efforts to intervene in Utah and impose fines and jail sentences on polygamous families. Newspapers with Republican sympathies offered lurid tales of Mormon "harems," and party speakers appealed for women's support on the basis of Democratic pro-Mormonism.[25]

Defending plural marriage was a thankless job, and some Democrats re-

lnr. of religion

fused to do it. Many, however, saw anti-Mormonism as part of a broader evangelical attack on both religious freedom and men's prerogatives, and thus deserving of denunciation. One Democratic editor asked Republicans to review the U.S. Constitution and explain "under what clause [Congress] finds jurisdiction over the relation of the sexes." "We do not wish," declared another, "to see the Federal government legislating on the marriages or morals of domestic life."26

In a reversal that presaged his shift on Kansas slavery issues two years later, northern Democratic leader Stephen A. Douglas first defended plural marriage, then gave in to rising public outrage and denounced it as a crime. Democratic President James Buchanan wished the issue would go away and considered resettling the Mormons in Alaska. In the end, he seized the initiative and sent troops to Utah. They engaged in a brief, bloody fight with Mormon defenders and established partial federal control. Buchanan may have calculated that preempting the polygamy issue would undermine support for the fledgling opposition party. If so, he was wrong. Battles over the structure of the American family only intensified in the coming years.27

Almost all Northern and Southern Democrats of the antebellum era supported slavery, an institution that influenced their ideology long after the Civil War. Party spokesmen identified both marriage and slavery as "domestic relations" in which government had no right to interfere. Like Mormon polygamy, slavery was a household matter. "The principle of Republicanism," claimed one Democrat, was "to meddle with the domestic institutions of other States, and to meddle with family arrangements in their own states—to force their . . . creed down the throats of other men, and compel them to digest it." Another argued that if Congress could dissolve slavery, it could also abolish marriage.28

In the slavery debate, as on other issues, Democrats' constant references to coercion, submission, and resistance bespoke a fundamental defensiveness, a desire to maintain power as both masters of households and independent citizens. Most seem to have rejected the central tenet of domestic ideology, that women's virtue gave them a moral authority to which men should defer. They agreed with a New York minister from early in the century who argued that "all government originated in patriarchal authority."29 Democrats preserved this view longer and more widely than Whigs and Republicans, insisting that the submission of wives, children, and slaves was divinely ordained.

This argument contained profound tensions, based in its view of women and slaves as voluntary subjects of male rule. When pressed, as they often were during the Civil War and Reconstruction, Democrats described household relationships as based at their core on force and obedience. Humane men should not need to use coercion unless dependents rebelled, but the power to do so remained available as the fundamental source of domestic and political order. Danger to the republic lay in usurpation of this power by excessive centralized authority. In warning of this threat, party spokesmen invoked a sexual vocabulary: they spoke of federal "rapacity" and opponents' "insatiable lust." In the secession crisis, a typical appeal from Georgia labeled Republicans an assembly of "the vile, the licentious, the profligate." Democrats regularly described submission to corrupt authority as moral "degradation."[30]

Nowhere was this argument more important than on the issue of race, which at the end of the war united northern and southern Democrats in zealous opposition to Emancipation and black male suffrage. Horrified by these policies, Democrats around the country described them as a source of sexual corruption and especially of danger to white women. During the war northern Democrats introduced songs and images from minstrel shows into political campaigns. Skits of "emancipators' balls" featured lecherous black men dancing with Republican women; Lincoln appeared as "the great miscegenator," and campaign wagons showed black men leading white women into the White House. Democrats circulated broadsides with cartoons of such couples locked in passionate embrace.[31]

In the Reconstruction years, the most extreme southern Democratic newspapers extended the same themes. If Emancipation had threatened white women, black men's political power heightened the peril. In the 1868 campaign, one Savannah paper accused a black legislative candidate of leading a brutal gang rape of a "young and beautiful widow." The paper called this "Radicalism in its Full Development." Three weeks later, the same paper claimed a white man in Indiana had compelled his daughter to marry a black husband—"a little victory of Republican principles."[32] To Democrats, Radical policies forcibly rearranged the natural order of sex and race relations; sexual violation was the ultimate metaphor for tyranny. If enfranchised black men were guilty of rape, Republican officials were the surrogate rapists.

Perhaps the most revealing aspect of this argument was the conflation of rape and consensual sexual relations. In Democratic rhetoric white women were often victims who resisted black men's aggression, but at other times they appeared as willing partners. Invoking what one Republican called "the bugbear of amalgamation," Democrats also ignored relations between black women and white men, whether consensual or not. The issue at stake was clearly not rape in any modern sense, but violation of the white household.[33] In Democrats' patriarchal view, blacks were dependents and had no rights of citizenship to assert. White women's consent was also largely irrelevant, though presumably no "true" woman would submit willingly to a black man's advances. What mattered was the opinion of white men concerning incursions on their authority over the home.

Though white women were most vulnerable, white men claimed they themselves faced forcible marriage at Republican hands. A black editor in New Orleans, exasperated by such arguments, offered a witty solution in 1868:

> For the benefit of suffering Democratic humanity, we propose that the colored ladies throughout the county shall draw up and sign a pledge that under no circumstances will they marry a Democrat. As soon as this is accomplished, the harrowing fear that now disquiets the souls of the Democracy will be destroyed. . . . When a Democrat has exhausted all his other arguments

against political equality, he always yells out, "Would you have me to marry a nigger?" If the colored girls, then, will promise never to marry a Democrat, we will hear no more of this cry.[34]

Democrats' warnings of black men's sexual aggression, then, were part of a broader connection they drew between sexual coercion and abuse of government power. During Reconstruction, anti-Republican newspapers printed a striking number of sexual accusations against Reconstruction leaders. The charges included rape, bigamy, prostitution, extramarital and interracial liaisons, and the use of sex for political persuasion. If not alleging the acts themselves, Democrats implied them. The *Charleston Mercury*, for example, referred to Franklin J. Moses, white speaker of the South Carolina legislature, as "a bought political prostitute—taken, *flagrante delictu* with this negro body at Columbia, [in] shameless infidelity and gross association."[35]

Such charges were more muted outside the South and after Reconstruction, but they persisted. In 1880 Democrats attacked presidential candidate James Garfield for allegedly taking bribes during the Grant administration; they called him "debauched" and nicknamed a damning piece of his correspondence "the Scarlet Letter." When Republicans began wearing "329 badges" to show their rejection of charges that Garfield had taken $329, one Democrat likened them to "a shameless prostitute who publicly parades her dishonor." Reporting on the investigation that cleared Garfield of wrongdoing, an Alabama paper insinuated that "the most important witness . . . Garfield manipulated was a black woman named Amy Mitchell. . . . All that occurred in that dark room in the Custom House, between the pliant Amy and the versatile statesman is not, and will never, be known. But this much is known: this black angel of Republicanism was so accommodating to the tender Garfield that her testimony was changed."[36] In such stories, Democrats suggested that black and white Republican women played a role in the corruption of power. Virtue in both family and state was based on hierarchical relations between white men and dependent women and blacks; outside this order lay the allied evils of sexual and political illegitimacy.

With women implicated in Republican corruption, what role should Democratic women play in public campaigns? Many privately shared male party leaders' views, including those on women's proper sphere, without becoming public speakers, though some took up their pens to defend Democratic principles. In the 1850s, South Carolinian Louisa Susanna Cheves McCord defended "God-given distinctions of sex and race" and attacked abolitionists and woman suffragists as "would-be men" and "petticoated despisers of their sex." In the secession crisis women around the South published letters and petitions urging men to stand up for southern honor. A group of forty Virginia women showed they could appropriate Democrats' defensive language and use it as a challenge to men. "However weakly the fire of noble pride is flickering in the bosoms of Virginia's sons," they wrote, "it yet glows with its pristine vigor in the hearts of her daughters." They predicted that "degeneracy" would result from "submission to [the] tyranny . . . of Black Republicanism." If their "beloved State is insulted with impunity," the letter concluded, "the dastards who cause her to submit to such degradation are not countenanced at home."[37]

In keeping with Democratic philosophy, these women did not become public speakers or canvass wards during the secession crisis. Rather, secessionists turned to an older model of women's public action drawn from Revolutionary precedent. To punish the North, southern Democratic women formed groups to sew homespun as a substitute for northern-made cloth. They pledged a boycott of jewelry, silk, and other items made in northern states. Some groups declared themselves official associations, like the Lowndes Ladies for the South in Lowndes County, Alabama. Others threw informal parties to display their new clothes as emblems of southern patriotism.[38]

The actions of secessionist women reflected their commitment to an economic role for women within the household. Unlike Whigs and Republicans, who idealized women's moral purity rather than their productive household labor, southern Democrats harked back to an older view of the ideal housekeeper, seated at her loom or spinning wheel. This image was not necessarily in keeping with women's real lives; the revival of homespun invoked, conservatively, the virtues of an agrarian past when each household had produced its own commodities. By dusting off their spinning wheels women could combat "luxury" and moral vice. The secession crisis was an extreme demonstration of the view, but it reflected larger patterns in both northern and southern Democratic thought.[39]

Democratic men attacked Republicans, in fact, for embodying the sins of extravagance and corruption. Continuing a strategy that had proved useful since the Jacksonian years, postwar Democrats ridiculed Republican men as effete and womanly. This view was particularly popular among working-class men, one of whom commented during the war years, "there are but two parties in the country—Aristocrats and Democrats." In Indiana, Democrats praised a local candidate by waving a banner proclaiming, "no kid gloves or silk stockings on ours." *Puck,* a popular Democratic weekly, printed caricatures of Ulysses Grant, James Garfield, and other Republicans as women in fashionable dress. When cartoonist Thomas Nast abandoned the Republicans in 1884, he quickly adopted the same approach. His cartoons portrayed GOP leaders Whitelaw Reid and William Walter Phelps as the "New York Daisy" and the "New Jersey Lily."[40]

Like race-based arguments, these Democratic attacks were ambiguous: undue power made men both sexually dangerous and sexually weak. The link appeared far back in the 1820s and 1830s, when both parties accused each other of aristocratic designs, associated with "dandyism," excessive "delicacy," and "effeminate indulgence." By the postwar years Democrats leveled such charges far more often than Republicans did, conflating effeminacy and femininity. An Ohio paper declared that if an opposing candidate were sent to Congress, he "would be of about as much consequence as a eunuch in a harem." In the 1870s, when William Mahone led a successful challenge to Democratic rule in Virginia, an editor claimed that ladies in the national capital were curious about Mahone's attire. He wore "ruffles covering his wrists" and "skirts" on his coat that hid, the paper hinted, petticoats or a corset.[41]

By contrast, Democratic men asserted an aggressive racial manhood. They often referred to themselves as "the white man's party," while Democratic veterans of the Union Army distinguished themselves from Republican "Boys in Blue" by organizing as "White Boys in Blue." More often than Republicans, they used metaphors of physical confrontation that drew on workingmen's rough street culture, and in the South on a pugnacious code of honor. During a rousing speech, Democratic audiences might shout "Don't spare him" and "Hit him again!" The *Lynchburg Virginian* claimed a speaker who made a telling point had "killed the gamest cock in the pit." Amid incidents of campaign violence directed against blacks, both northern and southern Republicans worried about large-scale riots.[42]

Though practices varied by region and community, Democratic men's rough campaign culture proved, on the whole, much more resistant than Republicans to the participation of women. In keeping with their more tolerant view of liquor, the saloon figured prominently among Democrats as a locale for political activity. One Nevada editor reported in 1884 that the "principal Democratic campaign speaker" did not "run the round of the saloons and give the boys a drink." "There is no hope," he added, "of his ever getting elected for anything after such conduct." When Democrat Tom Watson stumped Georgia in the 1880s, he expected some all-male audiences and carried a notepad to remind him of racy jokes: "the definition of adultery," "why Joseph didn't sleep with Potiphar's wife," and a tale about a man who when asked, "why did you beat this man up?," answered that he was "drunk and thought it was his wife." It is hard to imagine such jokes being told (at least publicly) by a Republican like Rutherford Hayes, whose campaign biographer claimed that Hayes had "never uttered a profane word."[43]

In response to their opponents, Democrats did begin to include women in limited ways. By the postwar era the party's midwestern branch rivaled Republicans in its enthusiasm for women's campaign glee clubs and marching units. From at least 1864, New York City campaigns featured the occasional woman as a Democratic stump speaker. A reporter noted in 1880 that at least five prominent New York women had supported the Democrats' presidential nominee "with the pen and from the platform"; one was organizing campaign clubs in Italian-American wards.[44]

Southern Democrats were unwilling to go so far, but men often spoke on women's behalf. A typical event took place in Bartow, Georgia, when the Democratic governor passed through on an 1880 campaign tour:

> While the train stopped for a few moments the ladies, through a gentleman of this place, presented Governor Colquitt with a handsome bouquet, who said he was authorized to say it was an evidence of their esteem for him personally and an indorsement of his administration. The governor replied, saying: "These flowers are fragrant and refreshing to a weary traveler. It is not their

fragrance for which I esteem them, but for the expression of confidence in me and in my administration that the fair ladies in their presentation express, and also for their well wish."[45]

White women's presence often served as a racial reminder to white men. In another Georgia town, a Republican candidate appeared one day earlier than his opponent. "Though invited, not a lady heard Norwood yesterday," the Democratic paper reported. "Many of them turned out to-day and shook the general's hand. . . . Norwood will not get two hundred white votes in the county. He seems to have turned his attention entirely to the negroes." After a Florida picnic, Democrats reported that their candidate had been "surrounded by our fair daughters, to many of whom he had been personally presented."[46]

Women, however, made slight appearance in Democrats' popular campaign biographies, in which party heroes demonstrated hardy masculinity. Biographies of Winfield Scott Hancock, the party's presidential choice in 1880, were typical. The candidate had grown up as a leader "in all the manly sports and enterprises of boyhood." His running mate had a childhood of "adventure and reckless daring." Hancock received little praise for intellect. One biographer wrote that "the boy was by no means a prodigy either of studiousness or learning. He grew to be a rugged, large-boned lad, fond of gymnastic exercises and wild sports." Another claimed that by choosing a military career, Hancock had lost an inheritance from a wealthy Quaker relative, Miss Polly Roberts. The incident showed Hancock rejecting wealth, pacifism, piety, and female authority in favor of manly independence and battlefield honor.[47]

Hancock's wife and children were virtually invisible in these biographies, which celebrated the candidate's heroism in the Mexican and Civil Wars. Almira Russell Hancock remained publicly faceless; campaign biographies printed dozens of military portraits and battle scenes, but almost no sketches of the Hancock family. One poet summed up his party's praise with this dubious tribute:

> In the days when MANHOOD rose,
> Answering unto FREEDOM'S throes;
> And the womb of Freedom yielded
> UNION with her Stars enshielded;
> In the days when MEN were MEN—
> Sword with sword, and pen with pen,
> . . . Then, to witness Freedom's claim,
> MANHOOD wrote that deathless name—
>   'HANCOCK!'

Other presidential candidates, with or without war records, were portrayed in the same aggressively masculine terms.[48]

The ideal Democrat, then, was an independent white man, master of his home, quick to defend his interests, and vigilant for signs of corrupt government power. In Democrats' vision, threats to the nation lay in concentrated government; compared with Whigs and Republicans, they took a grimmer view of the nature of political power, and perhaps of human relationships in general. Maintenance of proper order required white men to assert their rights. More broadly than in the defense of slavery, and long after the Civil War, Democrats' ideology rested on male household mastery.

It is tempting to see this ideology as older than that of Whigs and Republicans—a patriarchal holdout from previous eras. Certainly nineteenth-century Democrats harked back to old models of republican virtue when, for example, secessionist women took up their spinning wheels to emulate Revolutionary housekeepers. As the more conservative party, Democrats found themselves dragged along in protest during periods of rapid political change, when opponents captured control of government and used it for new purposes. Eighteenth-century ideals of manhood, though, differed markedly from the new Democratic model, which was, like domestic ideology, a product of the Jacksonian era. The self-made white man, armed with a ballot and ready to fight his way upward in a competitive marketplace, was a figure as new as the morally superior "angel of the home."[49] In the realm of politics, a bipartisan system provided the mechanism through which these ideal personages would clash.

Democrats' constant denunciation of state "paternalism" linked all their chief grievances through their assertion of independent manhood. As one stump speaker observed, his party opposed "High Daddy" policies: he ridiculed Republicans' vision of broader state power, in which "the Government is to rock the cradle and drive the hearse, weep over the grave and sit up with the widow, and pay every man for cracking his own lice."[50] The double gendering of this critique—which assailed paternalism but also implied opponents' *maternalism*, or feminine soft-heartedness—was itself a reaction to the new domestic ideology. In this view, Radical Republicans who upset domestic order were effeminate men and licentious women; they cooperated in sexual and political corruption. Viewing them in disgust, Democrats raised an important question: in a political house built on foundations of gender difference, how would Republicans employ domestic ideology? Did they envision government power as masculine, feminine, or some complicated combination? The Civil War, by temporarily removing from the Union a substantial portion of its Democrats, gave Republicans a decade of national control in which to begin answering this question.

An Impression of Domestic Harmony: Republicans and the Maternal Family

The Republican Party's appearance in the late 1850s brought a rush of campaign excitement in the North. As the issue of slavery's expansion in Western territories came to dominate party debates, first Whigs' and then Democrats' national coalitions collapsed. The new party was, as Democrats charged, sectionally based; its 1856 and 1860 presidential candidates did not even appear on the ballot in most southern states. More clearly than Whigs', Republicans' power bases lay with those committed to the new domestic ideology. If the party's exact direction was unclear before 1860, its organizers' proclivity for holding meetings in Protestant churches spoke volumes to potential foes and friends.[51]

In the Midwest, where women's bipartisan activities had been widespread in the 1840s but diminished in subsequent years, Republicans built on this tradition. By 1860 young women were marching in Republican parades, giving stump speeches, and organizing as Republican Young Ladies. In one Michigan parade they rode horseback, wearing Wide-Awake uniforms to show vigilance against the southern slave power. "Westward the star of empire trails its way," announced a campaign sign. "The girls link on to Lincoln, their mothers were for Clay." A Republican editor praised "the brave and true hearted girls of the West" who were "doing their utmost for the cause of freedom."[52]

Young men shared this generational impulse; commentators noted the large numbers of youthful Republican voters. Republicans of 1856 contrasted the Democratic presidential candidate, aging bachelor James Buchanan, to their own dashing young explorer John Frémont and his beautiful wife Jessie, daughter of Missouri Senator Thomas Hart Benton. The prospective first lady was widely rumored to be an abolitionist; in campaign songs she was not only a "sweet bright lady" but also "our lovely Jessie, the pride of the free" who "shall be our Liberty's queen." Frémont's running mate, John Dayton of New Jersey, was largely neglected by midwestern Republicans, whose banners endorsed "John and Jessie," "Frémont and Our Jessie," and "Jessie's Choice." Republican women in the Northeast were less bold than their midwestern counterparts, according to regional precedent, but they attended campaign meetings in large numbers, wearing "Jessie" badges and waving her picture enthusiastically. Democrats, contemptuous of women's participation and the masculinity of Republican men, called the two presidential campaigns "shrieks for freedom."[53]

Republicans looked promising to evangelical and reform-minded women, who had become publicly active over the previous three decades in a variety of religious and benevolent causes. Aside from the slavery question, some Republican leaders expounded on the alleged evil influence of the Pope; others supported temperance; their 1856 platform promised to end Mormon polygamy. As Democrats noted with alarm, the new party and its antecedents had a propensity for revising state marriage laws, offering greater protection to mistreated and abandoned wives. A few Republican men even indicated their willingness to consider woman suffrage.[54]

To the extent Republicans moved beyond Whigs, though, in their vision of women's public influence, it was largely due to their wartime conversion to abolitionism. During the 1850s thousands of women signed antislavery petitions to Congress and raised money to assist former slaves. Many who had been disgusted by Whig inaction quickly championed Republicanism, following the lead of such prominent abolitionist women as Lydia Maria Child, Elizabeth Cady Stanton, and—most famous of all—Harriet Beecher Stowe, author of *Uncle Tom's Cabin.* Not all abolitionists supported the new party, whose leaders disavowed antislavery intentions with increasing vigor as their prospects for victory grew. Stowe herself admitted that Republicans "are far from being up to the full measure of what ought to be thought and felt on the slavery question." But she and others worked for the party nonetheless, convinced that it offered the best hope for change. Clarina Nichols, possibly the first American woman to undertake a partisan stump-speaking tour, did so in Kansas where the slavery issue raged. A paid lecturer for a New England antislavery group, she spoke fifty times for Republicans in 1856.[55]

Though not "up to the full measure" of abolitionists, prewar Republicans did offer a gender-based critique of slavery. In demanding its geographic limitation, they emphasized the threat it posed not only to free white labor in the North but to white families in the South. Republicans described the southern domestic order as morally degenerate. As in antipolygamy diatribes, they considered "luxury and licentiousness" the results of unwholesome family relations. Slaveholders, they said, had too much personal power and no traditions of honest labor or self-control. One Republican argued that slavery made "mother and daughter, for successive generations . . . the unresisting prey of degrading passions." Like Democrats, Republicans associated excessive power with sexual corruption and lust, warning of slavery's "rapacious" power in Washington. From the beginning, though, they located sexual depravity more within private households and viewed federal power in positive terms. Democrats sought to protect private homes from the potential corruption of centralized government; Republicans wanted, at the least, to use federal power to block the spread of an immoral family order into the West.[56]

These tendencies became far more pronounced during the war, as the Emancipation Proclamation of 1863 transformed all party loyalists, however reluctant, into abolitionists. Following the example of Lincoln and former slaves, white Republicans began to find in black freedom a justification for the war's horrors. By the late 1860s the antebellum vision of abolitionist reformers had been validated; they were no longer troublemakers but visionaries. Their most radical proposals on gender relations—as on race relations—did not come to pass, but Reconstruction opened doorways in these directions.

From an early point in the war Republican leaders demonstrated their regard for women through an innovative pension law. Generous and prompt by standards of previous wars, the Pension Act of 1862 offered unprecedented protection not only to invalid soldiers but to women whose male relatives had sacrificed their lives for the Union. For the first time not only widows but also mothers and "orphan sisters" could claim monthly payments; in the first decade they were the chief beneficiaries of the law. At war's end, three-quarters of pension payments went to widows and dependents rather than to former soldiers. As late as 1875, well over half of the $28 million allotted for pensions went to dependents, most of them in female-headed households. Because Republicans' pension system set a precedent for future relief programs, its commitment to women's support is particularly notable. In effect, Republicans were willing to use the federal government as a surrogate breadwinner. "The widows and or-

Money Interest -

phans of the gallant dead," argued a party leader in 1868, "are the wards of the people—a sacred legacy bequeathed to the nation's protecting care."[57]

More broadly, the Civil War enabled Republicans to describe God's purposes for the nation in religious terms. The United States was a reunited family of states; the war had produced a "purified Constitution." In a typical Reconstruction appeal, future GOP vice president Levi Morton of Indiana declared that "the first act of nullification was when the fallen angel rebelled against God" and "the second was when Adam sinned." Reverend Henry Ward Beecher endorsed Republicans in an 1868 stump speech, praising the party for overcoming "the sin and weakness" of the old party system. Democrats, he said, were "looking back toward Babylon and Egypt."[58]

This vision of the party as an agent of God's purposes was, perhaps, not so different from that of Whigs when they passed Maine's temperance law in 1851. Republicans, though, had mobilized the nation on a vast scale and won the Civil War at a cost of 600,000 lives. They had abolished slavery, and they freely appropriated black Americans' view of this deliverance as akin to that of Moses and the Jews. As late as 1880, the *Chicago Tribune* celebrated electoral victory with the headline, "BABYLON IS FALLEN, and Union Men is Gwine to Occupy de Land." An Indiana editor urged Republicans to bring "the old mothers of the Republican Israel" to the next rally for "the party that saved the land from destruction."[59] Evangelical issues like temperance had never won a majority of voters' loyalties, and in the antebellum years the Whig Party had failed to secure lasting federal power. Union victory, however, solidified a Republican majority in the North, for whom the crucible of war had imbued the party with the sanction of God.

The gender dimensions of this religious impulse were especially clear during Reconstruction. In the South, some Radical Republicans discarded statutes outlawing interracial marriage. Most retroactively declared that slave marriages were legally binding and the children of such unions legitimate. Southern courts began to recognize the rights of black and poor white women to bring suit against men, whether white or black, for sexual assault. Around the nation, the Reconstruction years were a heyday of liberal divorce laws, many of which were later amended in a more conservative climate. Many northern states also began to recognize equal custody rights for divorced mothers. A Philadelphia court summed up the new tendencies of Republican jurists and legislatures. "We do not," the judges wrote, "look upon the wife and the children as mere servants to the husband and father, and, as therefore held, subject to his will."[60]

As the Radical tide receded it left behind an intensified allegiance to domestic ideology, born of the war and abolition. Presidents Ulysses Grant, Rutherford Hayes, and James Garfield, for example, continued Lincoln's efforts to eradicate Mormon polygamy through federal legislation. But to the consternation of women's rights advocates, the vast majority of Republican legislators did not endorse woman suffrage. On this, as on other issues, Republican momentum slowed to a halt by the late 1870s. Exhausted by the struggles of Reconstruction and by scandals during the Grant administration, party leaders settled into a comfortably limited agenda.[61] In their commitment to domestic ideology, they nonetheless continued to articulate views far different from those of Democrats. The implications of this for women's role in politics would become clear only gradually, but it was a marked departure from antebellum norms.

Like Democrats, Republicans spent a great deal of time defining a type of manhood they rejected. To them, the aggressive masculinity celebrated by Democratic men was the antithesis of domestic morality and an embodiment of drunkenness, violence, and lust. Republicans often attacked their opponents through reference to these vices. In a typical example, the *Chicago Tribune* reported after a Republican parade that "of course, the nasty, drunken, brawling Democrat was around, and made himself obnoxious." A Philadelphia editor contrasted two parades: "the morning of Sunday, September 19th, after the Democratic parade, was until four or five o'clock, made wretched and detestable by vulgar rowdyism, profanity and blackguardism." Republican clubs, on the other hand, "were determined upon order and sobriety . . . and the Sabbath was not profaned." An 1884 campaign song embodied Republicans' view, focusing in this case on Irishmen:

> My name is Mike Dolan, I'm one of the boys,
> I'm fond of good whiskey and plenty of noise.
> I voted for Tilden from morning till night,
> I killed a dutch tailor that day in a fight,
> I scared the black nagers most out of their coats,
> And so the Republicans lost all their votes.
> . . . I'm a roaring repeater of Democrat fame
> And just from the state penitentiary I came,
> For when the election is coming about,
> The Democrats' Governor pardons me out.[62]

Other Republicans denounced Democratic "roughs" and "hoodlums" for throwing rocks at GOP parades. Republican women echoed these criticisms. Young Mattie Van Orsdohl of Kansas wrote in 1884 that she was "at school. Very little studying tho', as it is Election Day, and teachers & pupils alike— being almost every one, Republicans—are very much interested. . . . God grant the Republicans may gain a grand victory." Later she recorded that a local black Republican had been killed while "hurrahing" by a Mr. Burghe, "who is a Democrat & was drunk." Van Orsdohl noted with apparent satisfaction that the victim "shot Burghe badly before dying."[63]

Republicans regularly leveled charges of lewdness and sexual depravity. One editor condemned Democrats as "gamblers and keepers of houses of ill fame." A New York paper gleefully took note when, in the midst of a Democratic parade, a wagon appeared "advertising the delights of the burlesque as interpreted at Haverly's Fourteenth Street Theater." Another Republican paper noted with distaste that brewers' wagons in the parade contained "young women in uncomfortably scant clothing." These criticisms were not limited to opponents in the North. Accusations continued that southern masters had been corrupted by sexual access to slave women; black Republicans were particularly adamant in charging such sins to the Democratic Party. "Every unbiased man," wrote a black Kansan in the campaign of 1880, "sees a rebel horde . . . again sweeping down like a pack of hungry wolves upon the Union sheep-fold. In the composition of this vast throng may be found every pimp who can boast of having insulted a woman, every bummer who has injured a negro, every overseer who has violated female chastity."[64]

Thus Republicans accused all their male opponents of the same transgressions: intemperance, violence (including political interference at the polls), hatred of blacks, sexual misconduct, cruelty to women, and a loud, cursing, swaggering style. This depiction of Democratic men enabled republican leaders to combine class, ethnic, and regional concerns in addressing a particular type of male behavior. Unlike their opponents, Republicans viewed sexual corruption as anarchic, a corollary not of concentrated power but of individual male rebellion. The chief charge against Democratic men was that they did not subscribe to the tenets of domestic manhood: temperate habits, self-control, and deference to the moral guidance of Christian mothers and wives.

Acknowledged battlefield heroism gave Republican men more leeway to claim these virtues for themselves. Between 1868 and 1896, almost every Republican presidential candidate was a former Union officer. (Most had been generals, but young William McKinley had only reached the rank of major before the war's end.) All but one were from the Midwest, where women's public partisan influence had first emerged; these candidates lent to national campaigns a combined military and domestic sensibility. They presented themselves as devoted family men, while their brave war records shielded them—at least in Republican eyes—from any taint of effeminacy. In the clearest expression of this impulse, Republicans moved their presidential campaigns into candidates' homes. Garfield ran the first front-porch campaign in 1880; Benjamin Harrison and McKinley continued the tradition between 1888 and 1896. These candidates spoke from their porches to male and female visitors while their wives welcomed the crowds and distributed lemonade. Newspapers around the country printed sketches of the candidates' houses, portraits of their wives, mothers, and children, and reports on their "Home Lives."[65]

From Democrats' point of view, the heroes of Republican campaign biographies were disgustingly feminized. A biographer presented this account of Rutherford Hayes' childhood: "He naturally shunned the coarse and rude boys upon the street, being as timid and nervous as a girl. This disposition, together with the cautious and unceasing oversight of his anxious mother, kept him free from all the little vices and mischievous traits which characterize nearly every boy. . . . He did not splinter his desk with his penknife, nor throw paper balls or apple-cores. . . . He was a model boy." Four years later, biographers called James Garfield "exceedingly temperate in all things, save brain work" and "a devoted husband and father."[66]

Republicans described their candidates as transformed by the moral influence of mothers, sisters, wives, and schoolteachers, in tribute to the maternal family ideal. "Virtuous wives and Christian mothers are the safeguards of the nation," proclaimed a Hayes biographer. "Without their potent influence, a republic is not possible." Several treatments of Hayes mentioned his admiration for his deceased sister, and one quoted the candidate's tribute to her: "I loved her as an only brother loves a sister who is perfect. Let me be just and truthful, wise and pure and good for her sake." One of Garfield's schoolteachers was said to have exercised a large influence over his future life. An 1884 biography of James G. Blaine included portraits not only of his mother but of "Matilda Dorsey, Blaine's First Teacher."[67]

Democrats attacked the wives of Republican presidential candidates, from Jessie Frémont and Mary Todd Lincoln to Lucretia Garfield and Harriet Blaine, as shrewish and powerful women who controlled their weak husbands. Perhaps for this reason, Republican leaders were at first reluctant to say much about their proposed first ladies, even when grassroots supporters waved their portraits and wrote their names into campaign songs. GOP leaders eventually sang the same tune, and by the 1880s the moral influence of presidents' wives had become an established part of Republican ideology.[68]

Rutherford and Lucy Hayes played an influential role in this transition. Only forty-four years old when she entered the White House in 1876, Lucy Hayes held a degree from Ohio Wesleyan Female College, an unusual level of education for a woman of her day. A faithful Methodist, she dressed plainly and gathered her family in the evenings for hymn singing. One campaign biographer praised Lucy Hayes's "ennobling" influence on her husband; another wrote that if the Hayes family moved to Washington, "the pure and elevating influences radiating from such a home would pervade and purify the social life of the National city, if not the land."[69]

Soon after Hayes's inauguration, the purification took a tangible form: the new president announced that alcohol would no longer be served at White House functions. The ban was widely and correctly thought to be Lucy's doing, and it won effusive praise from temperance leaders. Republican journalist Mary Clemmer wrote that Lucy Hayes's "devotion to principle is a talisman to hold all women steadfast to higher things." Author Laura C. Holloway was inspired to write the first collective biography of first ladies, in which she declared that "Mrs. Hayes was the most widely known and universally popular president's wife the country has known."[70]

After this pathbreaking appearance, Republicans showed more confidence in presenting Lucretia Garfield to the public in the next presidential campaign. One noted that she had studied Greek and "shares with her husband his thirst for learning, and his ambition for culture." He concluded that "much of General Garfield's success in his subsequent career may justly be attributed to his fortunate marriage." James Garfield's assassination further strengthened the domestic ideal and enhanced first ladies' celebrity. Shot by an office seeker in July

1881, Garfield lingered until September with his wife constantly by his side. After his death, door-to-door peddlers sold thousands of biographies stressing Lucretia Garfield's heroism, devotion, and self-sacrifice.[71]

Lucy Hayes and Lucretia Garfield were ideal subjects for Republican biographers. They were young and progressive, yet as mothers of eight and seven children, respectively, they fulfilled a reassuring domestic role. A theme of sentimental domesticity now pervaded GOP campaign literature. In a statement typical of the genre, a friend of Hayes's running mate William Wheeler recalled afternoons at the Wheeler home, where visitors paused

> to hear the sweet melody of those household hymns we all love so well, floating down from their parlor above us, where Mrs. Wheeler would be, sitting at some light, dainty feminine work, and her rich voice would half unconsciously begin,—"Shall we gather at the river?" or other kindred strain; and Mr. Wheeler, pausing at his busy writing-desk, would always join in with his deep, clear bass, giving an unconscious impression of domestic harmony.[72]

Such a scene affirmed a key foundation of party ideology: respectable Protestant domesticity shared by women and men.

Republican men often used marital fidelity as a larger metaphor for their devotion to the party. In a speech to young men, James Garfield proclaimed that "twenty-five years ago the Republican Party was married to liberty, and this is our silver wedding, fellow-citizens. A worthily married pair love each other better on the day of their silver wedding than on the day of their first espousals." Republican newspapers worried over young voters' choice between virtuous and seductive doctrines, stressing the seriousness of a young man's "maiden ballot" or "virgin vote." The *Cheyenne Sun* of Wyoming warned, "Young men, ye who cast your first vote to day, record it on the side of the Republican Party and you will not be forced to say in after years that you lost your maiden ballot."[73] Implicit in such appeals was the hope that boys would end their political virginity through marriage to Republicanism. Democratic men, by contrast, rarely implied that first voters were virgins. Nor did they associate straight-ticket loyalty with male marital fidelity, which was not on the list of virtues they endorsed on the stump.

Though they drew on domestic ideology, Republican leaders did not define government as a maternalistic enterprise. Power lay in the hands of military men, heroes who had crushed a slaveholders' rebellion and upheld the nation's honor. The political role of Republican women was indirect and consisted mainly of influencing boys and men. The party did, however, condemn unlimited and uncontrolled male power, in the form of Democratic manhood, as a political threat that good men should defeat at the polls. To Republicans, Democratic men were a danger loose on the streets because they lacked the self-control they should have developed with the aid of mothers and wives. Whether or not they intended it, Republicans had issued women an invitation to direct power. If women were morally purer than men, why should they merely wield indirect influence? Could they not, themselves, make political decisions for the greater public good? By the postwar years, the stage was set for a conflict between Republican men who held power and coalitions of women and men who sought to use it for new domestic ends.

Black Women in the South and the Limits of Republicanism

By the postwar period, women around the country were visible in electoral campaigns. Much more than the activities of elite women who wrote pamphlets and pressured influential male relatives, female participation was mass-based. Women gathered in small towns for campaign suppers, receptions, and dances. Party leaders in rural districts organized thousands of family picnics and barbecues, held in pleasant groves and beside county courthouses. A British visitor recalled that during the 1880 campaign, "in the rural districts in the Southwest the women of the farmers' families drove into town with the men for the meetings." He found more women attending rallies in Texas than in New York. An orator in Chicago reported that his "country audiences" were "composed largely of women."[74]

For both women and men, these events offered a chance to socialize with friends, share food and entertainment, and show party loyalty. For women they offered very little say in Republican or Democratic affairs. Conventions were closed to women except as observers. Men were delegates and decision makers; in the vast majority of campaigns, only men could vote and run for office. Republicans, though more willing than Democrats to praise women's influence and accept them as stump speakers and campaign organizers, offered them no direct power.[75]

During Reconstruction, black southerners offered a challenge to this arrangement, revealing the limits of Republicans' willingness to accept women's support. Passage of the Fifteenth Amendment delivered to the party a vast new constituency, staunchly loyal, who had never before voted or engaged in partisan campaigns. Though the amendment specifically enfranchised black men, freedmen and freedwomen shared distinctive priorities born of slavery and white racial prejudice. The need for race loyalty was urgent and obvious, and blacks' means of asserting it did not immediately draw upon white northern models of political action.

After ratification of black suffrage in 1867, black women became active in southern Republican campaigns. Observers noted their presence at party rallies; white women complained of having to find their own lunches when maids and cooks disappeared to meetings. Whites in Yazoo County, Mississippi, were startled to find in 1868 black female employees wearing Ulysses Grant buttons. Black women often marched with men in campaign and victory parades and a few gave Republican speeches. Clubs of Georgia freedwomen pledged weekly donations to pay a male orator to tour their district. Others used more personal forms of leverage to persuade black men. Some freedwomen voted to expel Democrats from their churches, or withheld bed and board from husbands and sons who voted Democratic. During a North Carolina gubernatorial race, a cook in Charlotte told her white employer she would no longer work for him if he voted for an ex-Confederate colonel. He did, and she quit.[76]

Some observers claimed black women were more loyal Republicans than were men. Speaking in New York, black author Frances Harper hailed the GOP as an "evangel of freedom" and claimed that not a single southern freedwoman was a Democrat. Another black writer, Anna Julia Cooper, later claimed that black men grew "more apt to divide" as Reconstruction faded. She reported that "it is largely our women in the South to-day who keep the black men solid in the Republican Party. . . . Black women in the South have actually left their husbands' homes and repudiated their support for what was understood by the wife to be race disloyalty, or 'voting away,' as she expresses it, the privileges of herself and her little ones." In the absence of woman suffrage, it is impossible to gauge the accuracy of such assessments. Women's lack of voting rights was the very thing that allowed a party to claim their unqualified devotion: at the time Harper made her speech, ex-Confederate president Jefferson Davis was also declaring that there were "no reconstructed women in the South," meaning of course white women. Clearly, though, many black women ardently supported the Republican Party.[77]

In an unstable political arena, this support included physical defense. Groups of black South Carolina women guarded muskets while Republican meetings were in progress. When vigilante groups threatened violence, both women and men picked up axes and hoes and rushed to the rescue. Some black women risked their lives on behalf of political leaders, hoping violent Democrats would hesitate to hurt a woman. John P. Green, a black politician from South Carolina, recalled being threatened when he arrived to speak in Moorefield, West Virginia. A black schoolteacher and his wife, Mr. and Mrs. George Strauther, invited Green to their home. When he told them of the threat, Mrs. Strauther said, "Don't fear, Mr. Green. I will go to the courthouse with you, and if they harm you they will have to harm me, too."[78]

At first, black women's political action included voting in conventions and rallies. Often held in churches, mass meetings drew few distinctions between delegates and observers. Leaders asked audiences to show support for a measure by rising; the votes of women, and sometimes older children, counted with those of men. Black women at some Radical conventions engaged men in heated debate. In these decision-making bodies, black communities chose a course of action based on majority will, including both women and men in that majority.[79]

Thus freedwomen in Richmond, Virginia, began to attend mass campaign meetings at First African Baptist and participated in the Republican state convention of 1867. The wife of Robert Elliot, a prominent black legislator in South Carolina, sat on the speaker's dais and consulted with her husband and other leaders. Predictably, state Democrats dismissed her and other black women who participated in the session as "mulatto prostitutes." Democratic papers frequently denounced the political interference of "negro wenches." Other editors invented epithets for the crowds at Republican rallies, such as "the brethren and sistern" and "the dusky sons and daughters of Afric's sunny clime."[80]

These attacks may have played an indirect role in limiting black women's power, but for the most part Republicans began, from the inside, to police their own gender boundaries. The Fifteenth Amendment officially established black men as voters, denying black women equality at the polls. Attitudes held by white Republicans quickly translated to their black allies, as shown by a revealing report from Laura Towne, a white schoolteacher in South Carolina's Sea Islands. At a Republican meeting on St. Helena, a local white man "got up and said women and children ought to stay at home on such occasions." Towne reported that "the idea took." Planning the next meeting, a black leader asked whether "the females must stay at home"; a white man answered that "the females can come or not as they choose . . . but the meeting is for men voters." The black man "immediately announced that 'the womens will stay at home.'"[81]

Moving into politics required black men to accept the gender norms of the white party system. Many did so eagerly; Virginia Republican Thomas Bayne denounced the idea of woman suffrage and declared that "it is a woman's right to raise and bear children, and to train them for their future duties in life." Even if they found such views troubling, black men and women found them an important tool in their struggle for respectability and acceptance. Southern freedmen's papers exhorted men to protect their wives and children by voting Republican, and more broadly to "GET A HOME," which "will promote virtue and build up strong family ties." Women, on the other hand, should "learn to make good bread" and provide "perpetual sunshine in the home." On election day, their first duty was not to work the polls but to "pray . . . that we may have peace and order, and that no violence or bloodshed may, to-day, occur in our midst."[82]

Black women's political power served the interests of none of their allies. It interfered with black men's claim to "full manhood rights" analogous to those of white men, and it undermined Republican definitions of Christian womanhood. There was no precedent for women to denounce a male delegate's views from the balcony of a political convention. Republicans' ideal of the maternal family, though innovative from a white perspective, limited black women's claims to political power. Southern black communities quickly adopted more indirect standards of female "influence," and black women, like their white counterparts, spent decades pressuring for suffrage rights.

National Republican campaign literature more often portrayed black women as helpless victims. In 1876 Eliza Pinkston of Louisiana watched her husband and child murdered by Democratic night riders and testified in court, showing open wounds; her name became an emblem of ex-Confederate cruelty. Campaign biographies, recounting Republicans' deeds as young lawyers, noted their success in winning damages for "colored women of good character and reputation" who had suffered slander or assault. To white voters, black women served as more sympathetic victims than did black men, especially in light of Democratic warnings about the threat posed by black men's sexual aggression.

Black women appeared not as active party loyalists, but as foils for the evils of Democratic manhood.[83]

Whether Republican women were black or white, then, male party leader assumed their influence would not extend to voting, choosing candidates, or disputing platform planks. Annette Hicks Lord discovered as much in the 1880s. A wealthy New York widow, she met Iowa Senator William Allison at a dinner party and joined the crusade to nominate him for president. On an elaborate pretext she attended a GOP convention and tried to assist Allison's faction, but she found herself ridiculed and ignored. The one politician who consulted her observed that "money was the ticket." Allison's manager accepted a three thousand dollar contribution from Lord but refused to meet with her. She ended up watching from the balcony as the convention chose a different man.[84]

On both Republican and Democratic sides, men did not want female decision makers (though they might accept a cash contribution). They showed a decided unwillingness to view women as part of factional or policy debates. Republican men spoke of themselves—as did Democrats—as "Grant men," "Garfield men," or "Blaine men." Confronted with the anomaly of a woman backing an individual candidate, men's language overrode the contradiction. An enthusiastic judge wrote to Lucy Hayes that "my wife is a great Hayes man." A woman attending a Republican convention found herself labeled "a Sherman man." In few other circumstances did men so confuse the gender of women, whom they both revered and patronized as distinct beings.[85]

War issues had entrenched women's party loyalties; the Republican experiment provided opportunities for women to claim new roles in political campaigns, especially on the Republican side. But it had not yet offered them direct power within the parties or at the polls. The Republican model, based as it was on men's self-control and women's moral authority, pointed in this direction, but the promise remained unfulfilled. As Americans of the Gilded Age turned to new issues and reforms, the ambiguities of this situation would become apparent both to Republicans and to new coalitions of women and men. When Rutherford Hayes deferred to his wife's judgment on temperance, some Republicans as well as Democrats saw it as an ominous sign. Female influence was a fine thing, but what if Republicans lost the next election on the liquor issue? It was delightful to hear a woman give a rousing Republican stump speech, but what if she concluded with a pitch for woman suffrage? Increasingly, men and women with different interests and priorities would contest the limits of domestic ideology in politics. The issues at stake would be women's right to a share of power, and the willingness or unwillingness of Republican leaders to transform their view of the maternal family into a vision of a benevolent state.

2

Suffragists, Prohibitionists, and Republicans

The quiet, silent, powerful forces of Christian energy and the noisy machinery
of practical politics may or may not work well together.
—Topeka Capital

Gilded Age Americans looked back on abolitionism as one of the boldest and most effective movements in the nation's short history. Whigs and Democrats had ridiculed abolitionists in the 1840s; the targets of these jibes had responded that politicians were ignoring slavery at their peril. In little more than a decade, the prophecy had been fulfilled. The Whig Party vanished, Democrats' national coalition collapsed, and a new party with antislavery leanings captured the White House. Of course, Republicans only ended slavery as an extreme war measure, and historians no longer believe that abolitionists caused the demise of the second party system. In the decades after Emancipation, however, many Americans argued that those who had aroused public opinion deserved the credit (or the blame) for ending slavery. As an Indiana woman wrote in 1884, abolitionists could feel in retrospect "the tremendous power of the political lever within their own grasp."[1]

This interpretation was a key legacy of the Radical Republican era. As former abolitionists turned to other projects, their understanding of Civil War politics profoundly shaped their strategies. Like any successful cause, antislavery attracted hundreds of thousands of admirers once the hard work was done. Few Americans had shared abolitionists' early hardships but many claimed their legacy and sought to learn from their triumph. The result was that many self-described "reformers," though pursuing varied goals, collectively endorsed partisan tactics. Most were northeasterners and westerners who were predisposed to view the GOP as the party of progress. They were, however, ready to demand realignment if Republicans behaved like recalcitrant old Whigs and refused to budge on key issues.

In the 1870s and 1880s, reformers who broke from the Republicans promptly encamped with other parties. In doing so they extended the logic of Republicanism in directions the party itself was unwilling to take. Like GOP leaders, these men and women used domestic ideology to legitimize their aims, extending the political applications of female moral authority. The new parties, however, began to advocate woman suffrage and to nominate women as convention delegates and candidates for office. As in the Republican model, women inspired men and exerted indirect moral influence. But the new coalitions also began to argue that women should have direct political power.

Having freed a class of chattel slaves, many abolitionists turned to the problems of industrialization and poverty in the North. In the early 1870s such famed antislavery advocates as Frederick Douglass, Wendell Phillips, Susan B. Anthony, and Elizabeth Cady Stanton joined the National Labor Union, a new association that sought federal measures to alleviate terrible conditions suffered by the urban poor. The coalition was torn by internal conflicts among both labor leaders and their middle-class allies. Douglass and others argued for remaining with the Republicans, exerting pressure on those in power; Phillips sought a separate labor party. Anthony and Stanton, disgusted by Republicans' refusal to enfranchise women, endorsed third-party action but wanted platform recognition for women's rights. The new Labor Reform Party raised issues that would reemerge nationally in the 1890s, but its existence was brief.[2]

Ten years later the Greenback Party took up related themes amid a nation-wide depression accompanied by desperate strikes. The party's name suggested its chief goal: continued circulation of paper dollars, which the Union government had issued to finance the war. Republicans were withdrawing greenbacks and returning the nation to a gold standard, a deflationary policy that benefited investors but not debtors or workers. Greenback supporters denounced the plan as beneficial only to Wall Street. At their peak in the late 1870s, Greenbackers elected fifteen congressmen and forced a partial modification of Republican financial plans. The GOP-dominated Congress agreed to support paper dollars with limited purchases of silver as well as gold, providing a somewhat larger currency supply. With this decision and with rising prosperity in the 1880s, the third party faded.[3]

Like the National Labor Party, the Greenback Party attracted many reform-minded women. Several workingwomen's associations sent voting delegates to the 1880 national convention; in a few states, Greenbackers were the first ever to nominate a woman for statewide office. Marion Todd and Sarah Van De Vort Emery, later famous Populists, began studying economics when they joined the Greenbackers. Todd served on the California Greenback-Labor platform committee in 1882 and in the same year received the party's nomination for state attorney general. While the national Greenback platform never contained a suffrage plank, a number of state platforms did.[4]

More broadly, the party echoed Republican descriptions of ideal manhood and womanhood. The 1880 Greenback presidential candidate, James B. Weaver, was a former Union general. His wife won praise for her "womanly heroism" during the war years, while Weaver himself was "thoroughly temperate, zealous in good works," and noted for "benevolence and Christian charities." Greenbackers equated their cause with abolition, denouncing the "shackles" that held laboring men in a state of "wage slavery." Invoking the language of evangelicalism, Sarah Emery described her new party as "people chosen by God."[5]

A longer-lasting experiment began in 1881, just as the Greenback presence began to fade. The Prohibition Party also drew on Republican precedent, emphasizing the problems of liquor rather than finance. Male Prohibitionists had been fielding candidates for over a decade, but their successes had been few and the party was almost moribund. The Woman's Christian Temperance Union, led by young and dynamic Frances Willard of Illinois, was largely responsible for its resuscitation. Willard convinced many WCTU members that the cause of "home protection" required women to work for Prohibition victory at the polls. In turn, Prohibitionist men offered women unprecedented power inside a party structure, and the party's national platforms called for woman suffrage.[6]

Prohibitionists challenged Republicans' claim to the legacy of evangelical domestic ideology. "THE SALOON MUST GO!," wrote party supporter George C. Hall in 1888. "Until it goes money, time, character, self-control, home happiness, home itself, children and wives, yea, and immortal souls, are through it forever lost." Prohibitionists accused men in *both* major parties of the intemperance, violence, and sexual corruption that GOP leaders charged to Democrats. In place of such debauched manhood, the third party presented men of pure character and "manly tenderness" and women of "the most exalted virtue." Endorsing woman suffrage, a male Prohibitionist at an Ohio convention told party supporters to "count me with the angels."[7]

In part, Prohibitionists' vision of female political power resulted from their status as outsiders. As Susan B. Anthony observed, third parties "in their weak state . . . are ready to grasp at straws."[8] With no patronage to distribute and prospects of victory distant, a new party needed the volunteer time and energy women could bring. More important, though, was Prohibitionists' conviction that liquor was the source of domestic misery, and that Democratic and Republican leaders—like hopeless alcoholics—lacked the self-control necessary to change. America needed the moral guidance of women, who would use the power of the state to prevent the tragedy of alcohol abuse in the home.

Even more than Greenbackers, Prohibitionists created immense headaches for the dominant party. By 1880 Republicans had lost their edge as representatives of progressive reform. Notorious corruption in the Grant years had tainted the party's image even among the faithful. In the wake of depression the GOP faced renewed challenges in northern states, while southern Democrats were recapturing state governments one by one. With national competition tightening, upstart voters who joined third-party movements became far more important even if they could not win. By attracting votes in key states, Prohibitionists helped deny Republicans the White House in 1884. Furious GOP loyalists were forced to watch the inauguration of Grover Cleveland, the first

Democratic president since before the days of Lincoln. Cleveland's election served as final notice that Republicans' decades of dominance were at an end.9

Prohibitionism also threw the woman suffrage movement into turmoil. Though some suffragists were Democrats, the vast majority were loyal Republicans and former abolitionists. For twenty years their efforts to persuade their party to enfranchise women had failed. They now faced shifting political sands and new partisan divisions in their own ranks. To some suffragists, the Prohibition Party was a promising experiment and a source of leverage against inflexible Republicans. To others it was a futile movement with no chance of success. Though Prohibitionists persuaded more Americans to endorse ballots for women, most of the new suffragists considered anti-liquor work their top priority. Loyal Republican women argued, meanwhile, that continuation of their party's policies must take precedence over women's votes. Suffrage leaders found it difficult to plot strategy amid these developments. Was the party in power the only engine for change? If not, where should women turn?

The Home Protection Party

Temperance had been a social and political issue since the evangelical revivals of the early nineteenth century. Before the Civil War the movement had been led by Protestant men, who organized clubs to pledge voluntary abstinence from liquor. Temperance advocates in the postwar years turned more and more to government, believing the social costs of alcohol were high enough to warrant its prohibition. Ohio women initiated a series of saloon raids in 1873 and organized the WCTU; from then on, women were visible leaders of the movement. They promoted temperance as a personal choice but also advocated political solutions, convinced that only state and national law could prevent the insidious spread of alcohol abuse. Frances Willard, an astute strategist and charismatic leader who became WCTU president in 1880, spent the next dozen years trying to shepherd her followers into the Prohibition Party.10

Willard traced her political roots to her childhood. "I always found a fascination in politics," she recalled later, "and I always reached out with a perfectly democratic grip to get hold of a newspaper, and most of all liked to turn to the editorials and see about the Whigs and Democrats." She absorbed political ideas from both her parents:

> I was a farmer's daughter, and got this idea of politics through father's and mother's talks together, as much as from the newspapers. I remember so well sitting by and listening to their talk, and mother was a very motherly woman, and a tremendously potential politician. . . . I never knew quite what was the matter with her, but she was born to be a senator, and never quite got there. Then my brother came to be twenty-one. . . . He dashed off and got into the lumber wagon with father, and the two of them, dressed in their best Sunday-go-to-meetings, because we thought election day was a kind of Sabbath, went off together and voted for John C. Frémont.11

Willard's beloved father had won a seat in the Wisconsin legislature in 1848 as a member of the Free Soil Party, and Willard later recalled her excitement over his campaigns. Like her father she transferred allegiance to the Republicans, but she never forgot the role her father's third party had played in forcing politicians to take up the slavery question. In her autobiography Willard noted that her father had been one of only thirteen Free Soilers in the Wisconsin legislature, but they had "held the balance of power." She believed another third party could do the same.[12]

Willard attended the 1881 Lake Bluff Convocation of Prohibition leaders in Chicago and helped organize a new party, called the Home Protection Party in recognition of a WCTU slogan. One year later it merged with the older body to form the Prohibition and Home Protection Party. Four Union women promptly became paid campaign lecturers. Between 1884 and 1900 eleven women, mostly from the Midwest, served on the party's national committee. At national conventions the number of female delegates sometimes exceeded 30 percent. Willard served on the executive committee as a respected strategist, and national Prohibition platforms repeatedly endorsed suffrage.[13] No party had ever offered women so many possibilities for direct power.

Like Willard, male Prohibitionists looked back on Republicanism as a precedent for their own movement. "Note how anxiously the politicians consider and study the prospects and possibilities of the 'Third party vote,'" argued one campaign tract. Its author predicted that the new party would grow to national success: "1888 will be the Frémont year and 1892 will be the Lincoln year." Urging prohibition advocates to desert the GOP, Minnesota pastor W. W. Satterlee declared that "the reformation of an old party or church is a thing unknown in history. . . . Such an organization *must die*, to give place to a new, and better form of life, and work. Such is God's plan." Responding to arguments that the movement should be nonpartisan, Satterlee wrote:

> The government is a machine.
> *The party in power runs the machine.*
> THE RESPONSIBLE POWER IS THE PARTY, AND NOT THE MACHINE.
> The party is the fountain of governmental policy on all live questions.
> Change the party policy, and the government is changed.

In a two-hundred-page campaign handbook, Satterlee repeatedly compared anti-liquor work to the abolition of slavery. The accomplishment of both goals, he argued, required the creation of new parties.[14]

With their emphasis on Christian principle, Prohibitionists' arguments and campaign rituals were more overtly evangelical than those of Gilded Age Republicans. Willard observed that no smoking, spitting, or cursing was allowed at conventions. Rather than hiring brass bands and shouting hurrahs, third-party delegates celebrated nominations by singing hymns. Prohibition candidates, though, received praise similar to that enjoyed by GOP nominees. The 1888 Prohibition ticket consisted of "noble, self-sacrificing men and generous knights of the new chivalry." A campaign biography of presidential nominee Clinton Fisk was a story of "humble Christian faith, devoted consecration to good works and loyalty to the principles of right, of temperance and truth." The biographer dedicated his work to Fisk's "worthy wife and daughter."[15]

Prohibitionists contrasted the virtues of these faithful family men with the behavior of politicians in the major parties. A typical campaign report described bacchanalian scenes on Capitol Hill after the last day of the session:

> I saw an aged Senator pass into the private dining room with two hilarious "peaches" on his arms. . . . Two old men in an advanced stage of inebriety were plying a young girl with liquor. . . . Hearing songs and laughter issuing from an adjacent committee room, I peeped in as I went by. A woman, with her daintily booted foot elevated on a committee table and a glass of champagne elevated in her hand, was singing a merry song, while a dozen members and their friends sat around smoking.[16]

Like Republicans who attacked Democratic manhood, the new party condemned drunkenness, violence, and lust. The lives of congressmen mirrored the corrupt society their permissive laws allowed; the remedy was federal prohibition, which would curb abuses in both House and home.

Prohibitionists asserted a logic of male obligation based on the slogan "a father's constituency is his family." One of Willard's favorite stories was of a Kentucky man, a former alcoholic, who at his wife's request voted against county liquor licensing. When friends ridiculed him at the polls the man replied, "Boys, I've always joined with you before, but by the grace of God here goes a vote for Sallie and the children." The story reappeared from Texas to Maine, and "voting for Sallie and the children" became Prohibitionist watchwords.[17] The phrase had a double meaning. A man who voted for Prohibition put his family in place of his old party. And in the sense that he "voted for" his family rather than "voting for" a major candidate, he invested his wife and children with political power.

Women as well as men justified Prohibitionism by reference to the sacred trusts of family and faith, cloaking partisan and suffrage advocacy in the rhetoric of motherhood and Christian obligation. Willard declared that "the Ten Commandments and the Sermon on the Mount are voted up, or voted down, upon election day." "When it is a question of preserving the Sabbath itself," she said on another occasion, "and guarding the homes which are the sanctuaries of Christ's gospel, we women believe that no day is too good, no place is too consecrated for . . . the determining of votes." The Illinois Union declared that its members "seek the ballot for no selfish ends. . . . There is no clamor for 'rights,' only prayerful, persistent pleas for the opportunity of duty." This rhetoric of disinterested morality softened a bold claim to direct political power. Willard suggested as much when she wrote that women's influence must be "condensed in the electric battery of the ballot box, since thus only could it be brought to bear along the tingling wires of law."[18] Willard and her colleagues often spoke of women's gentle natures, but their convictions did not require gentle tactics.

Before a WCTU convention in 1887, Willard dubbed Prohibitionists' approach "the New Politics." There was nothing new about fusing evangelical and political principles, a project dating back to the Whigs. The innovation was the acceptance of women's direct political power. Women's political work was compromised, however, by their lack of voting rights, at least until the new party won elections and could change the laws. Willard acknowledged that "in all [the party's] deliberations we can share, and in its nominations bear our part; but its candidates and voters must be men, except in those states where women are admitted to the partial or complete ballot."[19] Even within the party, much less outside it, Prohibitionist women had to defer to the sensibilities of male voters who might be alienated by women's partisan work. Their constant challenge was to find methods that were both effective and "womanly."

For women shy of public activism, the party offered easy and effective procedures. The WCTU *Union Signal* urged women to "send a list of 1,000 hopeful voters in your county, or 100 members of a church," with funds to cover mailing costs. National party organizers would send the voters ten weeks of Prohibitionist mailings. Collect addresses, the editors urged, and let the words of party leaders "speak to the voters in the quiet of their homes." Union members also distributed handbills, circular letters, and posters at the local level. This work apparently took the major parties by surprise. The *Signal* observed that "our activity in distributing literature seems to arouse their indignation and alarm more than anything else we do."[20]

Frances Willard hoped women would also engage in door-to-door visits and neighborly conversation. The central goal, she wrote, was "*to pledge the individual voter.*" "Thoroughly canvass the community," she instructed, "and secure the largest possible number of pledges to support these candidates. Accompany the work by the circulation of temperance literature and holding prayer meetings." Hinting that she had met internal resistance in the Prohibition Party and the WCTU, Willard added that "no person of intelligence will deny that it is womanly work to strive thus for the protection of the home."[21]

Many midwestern Prohibitionist women agreed, and they carried their New Politics to the polls on election day. WCTU members mobilized for referenda on state prohibition and local option, and some midwestern towns permitted women to vote for or against liquor licensing. A campaign in Keithsburg, Illinois, met all Willard's standards for political action. Weeks of WCTU canvassing concluded with a prayer meeting on election day and a large vote for "no licensing" of saloons. The victors celebrated at Keithsburg Methodist Episcopal Church, serenaded first by the choir and then by the town band. A local WCTU leader reported that townspeople demanded a series of religious revivals in the wake of the campaign.[22]

Women were equally visible in Iowa's state referendum contest of 1884. A number gave stump speeches in different parts of the state. Union leaders in the town of Marion organized a parade of women and children carrying banners that read "Please Vote for the Homes of Marion." Willard reported that in many towns "ladies went the night before and decorated the city hall, engine houses, and other places where the ballot-box was set with pictures, mottoes, evergreens, and flowers. 'Please vote to protect our homes,' 'The father's constituency is his family' . . . were some of these." Other Union women offered hot lunches and coffee near the polls, or distributed bouquets of flowers along with ballots.[23]

Because Republicans and Democrats in the Midwest already sanctioned certain forms of campaign work by women, WCTU activities won acceptance more easily there than elsewhere. But their appearance at the polls was an innovation. In Illinois, Iowa, Kansas, Nebraska, and Maine, observers claimed that women's presence altered male behavior on election day and reduced the occurrence of open drinking, spitting, and swearing. Willard claimed "there was no fighting; there was no rough behavior" where women appeared. According to other sources, though, some men bitterly contested change. A Republican editor denounced Kansas Prohibitionist women for "soliciting" votes, in language that cast doubt on their sexual virtue. Indiana Democrats displayed half-naked caricatures of Prohibition leader Helen Gougar; she sued (and won) after an opponent spread ugly rumors about her alleged affair with a Prohibitionist candidate who was, like Gougar, married. WCTU leaders in rural New York were hung in effigy, spat upon, and cursed; anonymous personages threw a dead skunk into one Union lunchroom.[24] Women at the polls won no immediate guarantee of tranquillity or respect.

Men in the party also suffered ridicule ranging from the light-hearted to the vicious. One humorist asserted that politics "is a man's game, an' women, childhern, an prohybitionists do well to keep out iv it." Laura Cummings of Vermont reported that a local Republican sneered, "the Prohibition Party is a woman's party." The remark made Cummings feel proud, but similar comments must have stung her male co-workers.[25] By sharing power with women, Prohibitionist men violated old political rules and exposed their honor and manhood to public attack. Though several of the party's candidates were Civil War heroes, Prohibitionist men had a less direct claim than Republicans did to the masculine honor bestowed by Union victory.

At first, the bitterness of opponents offered consolation to third-party advocates: their strategy seemed to be working. After Republicans' 1884 national convention spurned WCTU petitions, former Kansas governor John St. John electrified the temperance movement by announcing his defection from the GOP. St. John promptly won the third-party presidential nomination and received almost 150,000 votes, far more than his predecessor's 10,000.

Prohibitionists concentrated their work in key states, especially New York, that they hoped to take from Republicans. In this they succeeded. With over 10 million votes cast, James G. Blaine received only 25,000 less than Grover Cleveland, and New York's electoral votes provided the crucial margin for Cleveland's victory. Though a number of factors influenced the result, Republicans blamed their loss on Prohibitionists. Dozens of mobs burned effigies of third-party candidates; the Republican legislature in Kansas changed the name of St. John County to Logan County.[26]

The realignment Willard and others had forecast did not, however, take place. Prohibitionists not only failed to reach their "Frémont year"; in presidential contests, they never won as many votes as the Free Soil Party had in 1848 and 1852, even though the electorate had tripled. Apparently most voters did not find the liquor issue compelling enough to override war loyalties or rising economic anxiety. Unlike Republicans, Prohibitionists never broadened their appeal beyond a few states nor offered a potent long-term threat to the major parties. GOP national platforms largely disregarded the anti-liquor issue, calculating that a prohibitionist stance would lose more votes than it would win.[27]

Prohibitionists initially hoped to build a coalition across the North-South divide. Because war issues still drove major-party loyalties, this was an important reason to build a third party. Willard wrote that "we could not act in view of Republican efforts for prohibition in isolated states, as Iowa and Kansas, nor yet in view of Democratic, as in Maryland or Tennessee, but we had to act from a national point of view." Campaign speakers and tracts hammered at this theme. For the 1888 Prohibition convention, women hung a giant banner across the stage declaring, "NO NORTH, NO SOUTH, NO SECTIONALISM IN POLITICS, NO SEX IN CITIZENSHIP." Even Willard did not pretend that northern and southern Prohibitionists agreed on all issues. Speaking of the WCTU, she argued that "the constitution of this organization is sufficiently flexible to allow the woman suffragists of the North and the anti-suffragists of the South to work together, side by side."[28]

Within the WCTU, the greatest obstacle to Prohibitionism was Union members' deep partisan loyalties. Southern WCTU members, who were overwhelmingly white, not only resisted suffrage arguments but remained loyal to the party of the Confederacy and its broadly conservative ideology. With notable exceptions in Arkansas, few southern WCTU members served as Prohibition Party delegates, canvassed neighborhoods, or appeared at the polls. In campaign work they relied on the old tactic of petitioning rather than speaking publicly for the cause. An 1888 petition to the national Democratic convention reaffirmed southern women's party loyalty, which they tried to leverage into an anti-liquor plank:

> The Christian Temperance Women of the Southern states demand . . . that your body shall throw the shield of your protection over our homes [for the] protection of the helpless women charged with being "keepers of the home," and in favor of the children whom these women are expected to raise and train to be good citizens, and if they be males, to be Democratic voters. . . . Through the saloon as a corrupting influence, the old Republican carpet-bag and scallawag bosses can control the ignorant negro vote, and endanger both our home and Democratic supremacy.[29]

Appealing to the "sense of chivalry and honor" claimed by "*true*" men," the women signed themselves "wives, mothers, sisters, and daughters of Southern Democrats." The convention ignored their appeal.

Many northern WCTU members expressed equally ardent Republicanism. They shared Willard's political roots and proudly backed the party that had preserved the Union and ended slavery. Distressed by Willard's third-party proposal, they argued that a separate anti-liquor party would attract mostly Republican voters and help Democrats win. Willard replied that this was a short-term result; after losing a few elections, the chastened GOP would heed the message. It took her several years to convince the majority of Union members to support this position. Even in its 1884 endorsement of Prohibitionism, the WCTU national convention did not name their party of choice. "We will continue to lend our influence," the delegates stated cautiously, "to the national political organization which declares in its platform for National Prohibition and Home Protection." This wording gave either Republicans or Democrats (though the latter prospect seemed remote) an opportunity to win future WCTU support.[30]

Even in the North, only a few state Unions and Prohibition structures fulfilled Frances Willard's vision. Midwesterners were most willing to accept the strategy for "home protection." The Illinois party was particularly receptive to women, and Willard held them up as an example to others. In 1888 she noted that Illinois sent eleven women delegates to the national Prohibition convention, whereas many states chose only one. After the state convention she reported that "these men of the prairies stood squarely by [the suffrage plank] without an opposing word. . . . To their caucus women were invited; they were placed upon committees, counseled with from first to last, and never was the intimation made that their presence had 'kept just so many men out,' or was 'weakening' in its effect.[31] Willard's pride in the men of her home state, along with her list of men's objections to women's participation, suggests the resistance she met elsewhere.

Unfortunately for the Prohibition cause, the states where WCTU women were most active in campaigns, and where this activity met the greatest level of approval, were also states where many women had fierce Republican loyalties. Since Whig days the Midwest had been a crucible of both intense party conflict and women's campaign work. Settlers in southern Ohio, Illinois, and Indiana had moved from slave states, while Yankee evangelicals had colonized the northern counties. Conflicts between these groups had intensified before and during the Civil War: northern Ohio and Illinois had been Free Soil strongholds, while southern counties had sheltered Confederate sympathizers. The postwar years witnessed continued struggles between these groups, with the addition of new issues like prohibition and state support of Catholic schools. Throughout the Gilded Age, the Midwest was a crucible of symbols and issues dear to each party.[32]

Extremely high voter turnouts in the region were a result of these issues' immediacy and the narrow margins of many contests. Party leaders could predict results in Vermont or Georgia, but not in Illinois. Both major parties accused the other, often with justification, of purchasing votes and destroying ballot boxes. Large sums of money entered the Midwest before elections. In this intensely competitive climate, women had mobilized for many years on behalf of the major parties, especially on the Republican side. Well before the appearance of Prohibitionism they were marching in parades, organizing campaign glee clubs, and working together to influence voters. In 1880, the women of Cincinnati's Ladies' Garfield and Arthur Club asked every woman "to urge with her influence the success of the party of right and justice—the Republican Party." In the same year, Adele Hazlett of Michigan gave stump speeches around the Midwest. A Chicago newspaper commented on her "thorough Republican convictions" and her "logical, earnest, eloquent, and convincing speeches."[33]

This background was at first a help to Prohibitionists. Midwesterners were accustomed to women's campaign work, and compared to men and women elsewhere they were readier to accept arguments for woman suffrage. But midwestern women's partisan experience quickly proved to be as much an obstacle as an aid. A number of WCTU members from the region not only refused to undertake Prohibition work; some split from Willard's organization to found a separate "nonpartisan" temperance union. Almost all the defectors were staunch Republicans from Ohio and Iowa, with a sprinkling from Illinois, Indiana, Pennsylvania, and New York. All except Iowa—the only state where Republicans could take full credit for banning liquor—were swing states where Prohibition votes would dearly cost the GOP.[34]

The leading internal opponent of the Union's alliance with Prohibitionism was Judith Ellen Foster. Born in New England in 1840, Foster moved to western New York and then to Illinois; after an unhappy five-year marriage, apparently to an alcoholic husband, she divorced, married again, and moved to Iowa. With the support of her new husband, who was both a lawyer and a temperance advocate, Ellen Foster passed the Iowa bar and volunteered as a WCTU organizer. She become a close friend of Frances Willard and by the 1880s won national recognition for her talents. Together, Foster and Willard were "the wheel-horses of the WCTU wagon."[35]

Foster had reason to be a strong Republican as well as a prohibitionist. Her father had expressed antislavery sentiments from an early date; her brother, a minister who moved to the South during Reconstruction, had been killed in 1866 during an anti-Radical riot in New Orleans. Foster also came from Iowa, the only state in the country where Republicans presented a prohibition referendum to voters, endorsed it, and secured its passage. A keen strategist, Foster cooperated with Republican leaders during the referendum campaign of 1882, organizing a systematic canvass of voters carried out largely by the state WCTU. During the campaign she developed a friendship with James Clarkson, who in 1888 became campaign manager for Republican presidential candidate Benjamin Harrison.[36]

Between 1884 and 1889, Willard and Foster traded public accusations in a bitter fight over the WCTU's new third-party strategy. Foster was particularly upset when James Blaine, whom she supported, lost the White House to Grover Cleveland. At Union conventions she submitted repeated motions to repeal party endorsement, but majorities voted her down. Willard accused Foster of succumbing to Republicans' "glittering generalities"; Foster protested "partisan malice" in WCTU ranks. She argued that involvement in the new party would remove temperance from the "moral plane" and lead women to positions on other issues. Prophetically for both sides, she predicted that mixing liquor with an issue like the tariff "would mean the subjection of one and perhaps, in the end, the ruin of both." A close friend of Willard reported that the 1888 WCTU convention was the most exhausting she had experienced, with the issue of party loyalty opened on the floor for delegates to "discuss and cuss." In the following year Foster withdrew from the WCTU with a small band of followers.[37]

The new group styled itself the Non-Partisan Woman's Christian Temperance Union. Its first secretary announced that "we have no more ceased to be republicans, democrats, or prohibition party women since we have met together here than we have ceased to be Methodists, Presbyterians, or Baptists." Few observers, however, believed these protestations. Before the new organization had even held its first convention Ellen Foster was on Republicans' national payroll as a speaker and organizer, and almost all her followers were Republican loyalists. A Mississippi delegate derided Foster's group for mailing "nonpartisan" letters asking others to leave the WCTU. She observed acidly that "if Mrs. Foster would print upon the papers she is circulating throughout the South among our WCTU's, 'I am a Republican,' she need not send any more to the Southern women."[38]

Partisanship was, then, at best a mixed blessing for Prohibitionist women. Some left the WCTU; a much larger number stayed in the Union but refused to undertake Prohibition campaign work. Struggles in the 1880s left a legacy of division within the Union, between those who endorsed partisan Prohibitionism and those who resented Willard's efforts to prod them along. For many if not most of these women, the problem was not their commitment to nonpartisanship but the new party's interference with loyalties they already held. Southern white women considered themselves Democrats; northerners remained loyal to the party of Union and Emancipation. In this politicized context, women like Foster often styled themselves "nonpartisan" to protest someone else's unfriendly allegiance.[39]

Prohibitionism provided an unprecedented model for women's work within a campaign structure. With its evangelical and abolitionist heritage, the third party extended Radical Republicans' impulse toward accepting woman's political influence. Midwestern Prohibitionists now tried to legitimize direct power for women, based on the need to "protect the home." Willard's personal magnetism played a role in this: through strategic skill and persuasive force, she managed both to secure the approval of many Prohibitionist men for women's campaign work and to convince many women that they needed to undertake it. In a pattern that would be repeated, though, women exercised direct power inside a party that did not achieve its goals at the national level. Wartime loyalties still held sway; even within the narrow ranks of anti-liquor advocates, sectionalism and major-party loyalties refused to fade.

Suffrage and Party Loyalty

The woman suffrage movement did not found a political party in the Gilded Age, but it suffered its own internal partisan divisions. Almost all prominent suffragists of the era had started their public careers as abolitionists. If all did not become Republicans during the Frémont and Lincoln campaigns, they did so after Emancipation. As some of the nation's most radical activists, however, they were bound to clash with a party that could remain in power only by attracting at least half the votes of American men. This was especially true after Reconstruction. As Democrats rebuilt their national coalition in the late 1870s and 1880s, GOP leaders became more and more conservative, and prospects for a federal woman suffrage amendment dwindled. Despite constant debates over how best to exert political leverage, Gilded Age suffragists did not find a solution.

Their first partisan rift accompanied the emergence of the suffrage movement itself. During the fight to ratify the Fifteenth Amendment, when Republicans enfranchised black men and ignored women, Elizabeth Cady Stanton and Susan B. Anthony temporarily broke with the GOP and founded a new organization, the National Woman Suffrage Association (NWSA). Lucy Stone, Henry Blackwell, and other staunch Republicans created the American Woman Suffrage Association (AWSA). Its newspaper, the *Woman's Journal*, argued that the nation was not yet ready for female voters but that if women were patient, the GOP would one day enfranchise them. In an 1867 Kansas campaign to win passage of a state referendum, Anthony and Stanton cooperated with a few Democrats who were willing to support woman suffrage. Republican women accused NWSA leaders of indulging in "a weakly sort of partisan coquetry." Anthony responded that Republican leaders intended merely "to delude us into silence" through vague promises of future action. She claimed the GOP was a sinking ship and "female rats ought to know enough to leave."[40]

The ship did not sink, and Anthony and Stanton soon returned to the Republican deck. Around the country both AWSA and NWSA leaders worked for Ulysses Grant's reelection in 1872. Grant's running mate, Henry Wilson of Massachusetts, was a known advocate of woman suffrage; Grant's delegates appeared sympathetic, and the national platform contained for the first time a plank on women's rights. "The Republican Party," it stated, "is mindful of its obligations to the loyal women of America for their noble devotion to the cause of freedom; . . . the honest demand of any class of citizens for additional rights should be treated with respectful consideration." GOP leaders offered funds for Anthony, Stanton, and other suffragists to tour on the party's behalf, and they reprinted thousands of copies of Lucy Stone's appeal for women to "throw the whole weight of their influence on the side of the Republican Party."[41]

Grant won by a large margin and then did nothing toward enfranchising women. Both AWSA and NWSA members watched in outrage. By the late 1870s, not only had Republican leaders failed to introduce a Sixteenth Amendment for women's votes; even the party's Massachusetts leaders had not delivered on suffrage promises, though they endorsed the measure in a series of state platforms. Of these planks, a NWSA leader later wrote that they "seemed to mean something until after 1875, when they became only 'glittering generalities,' . . . as devoid of real meaning or intention as any that were ever passed by the old Whig party on the subject of abolition." She observed that fading Radicalism and increasing Democratic competition made future prospects dim. "From 1870 to 1874 the [Massachusetts] Republican Party had the power to fulfill its promises on this question. Since then, it has been too busy trying to keep breath in its body to lend a helping hand to any struggling reform."[42]

By the 1880s, both AWSA and NWSA members expressed anger at Republican intransigence and often urged women to renounce party loyalties. "Why should we use our talents," asked one suffragist, "for the success of our enemies, as all parties are at present? . . . Certainly we do not propose to voluntarily ascend the auction block as merchandise, to be knocked down by the highest bidder." "Of what good would the ballot be to women," asked Abigail Scott Duniway, "if [a man] could have control of barbed hooks fastened in their jaws, with strings attached and himself clothed with arbitrary power to yank every string?"[43]

A nonpartisan strategy was, however, easy to recommend and hard to practice. Suffrage was a legislative measure: unlike moral reformers, suffragists could not achieve their goal partially or indirectly by founding benevolent associations or inspiring individuals to change their ways. Ballots could come only through the electoral machinery, and as Prohibitionists had noted, "the party in power runs the machine."[44] Despite their exasperation with Republicans and Democrats, Gilded Age suffragists kept returning to the same conclusion.

Both AWSA and NWSA leaders thus alternated between denunciations of the parties and endorsements of partisan action. At times they claimed campaign work distracted women from true advancement. "We who hold woman suffrage to be the paramount political issue must hold parties secondary," declared the *Woman's Journal* in 1880, denouncing "the blindness of party prejudice." Yet one week earlier the same newspaper had encouraged women to take sides in the upcoming campaign. "Let women who have well-defined political opinions and preferences express these with earnestness and vigor, either by voice or pen," editor Lucy Stone had written. "They will thus accustom the public to recognize women as political powers to be enlisted and conciliated, and will strengthen the hand of the advocates of their enfranchisement."[45]

The *Woman's Journal* regularly endorsed Republican candidates, and some of their statements rivaled the party press in enthusiasm. Stone, Blackwell, and other AWSA leaders (with the exception of Thomas Higginson, who supported Cleveland in 1884) argued that Republicans were broadly committed to expanding the franchise. "If I myself had a vote," wrote Stone, "I should undoubtedly give it, under present circumstances, to the Republican Party, [which] freed the slaves and enfranchised the freedmen." Henry Blackwell wrote in 1880:

> For myself, while I freely admit that Woman Suffrage is not directly an issue in this campaign and that General Garfield is not a Suffragist, I still think it is greatly for the interest of Woman Suffrage that the Republican Party should retain control of the government. . . . When I consider the elements that control each party, the classes of men that compose them, the spirit which animates them, the history which lies behind them, and the policy to which they are committed, I see and feel a difference on the principle of Equal Rights.[46]

Blackwell went on to denounce Democratic violence in the South.

Despite their prior disputes with the party, NWSA leaders were also steadfast Republicans in the early 1880s. When Anthony cast a ballot to initiate a lawsuit, she recorded in her diary that she marked the "straight Republican ticket." In 1880 she spoke positively of James Garfield's voting record. Early in the 1884 campaign, Anthony and Stanton issued a call for suffragists to "stand by the Republican Party." They wrote:

> Though [Cleveland] were possessed of all the cardinal virtues claimed, and in addition thereto, the crowning excellence of adhesion to the great principle of political freedom for woman, he could do nothing for any reform with a Congress and a constituency nine-tenths of whom are blind and bitter opponents of all liberal measures. Suppose, on the other hand, the Republican nominee, James G. Blaine, were wanting in all the public and private virtues, with a Congress and a constituency three-fourths of whom are our friends. . . . But he is friendly. . . . Our hope of securing the initiative step to make suffrage for woman the supreme law of the land lies in the triumphant success of the Republican Party.[47]

Anthony and Stanton could hardly have made a stronger argument for partisanship. They were offering to stand by their candidate even if Cleveland made a public pro-suffrage statement and Blaine did not.

NWSA and AWSA leaders differed less in their declarations of party loyalty than in their attitudes toward the few active suffragists who were Democrats. This group included almost all white southern suffragists, a contingent in Utah Territory, key leaders of the New York Woman Suffrage Association, and a sprinkling elsewhere. Anthony and Stanton, aware of New York's strategic importance in elections, were more willing to cooperate with Democrats than were AWSA leaders like Stone and Blackwell. In 1880 New York suffragists Lillie Devereux Blake, Susan King, and Clemence Lozier met with Democratic presidential candidate Winfield Scott Hancock and decided to support him. Anthony urged them to remain silent, but they refused; they made not only a public endorsement but a series of Democratic stump speeches. AWSA leaders ridiculed Blake for claiming that the Democratic platform ("a free ballot . . . must and shall be maintained") applied to women. After printing reports of Democratic assaults on Alabama Republicans, the *Woman's Journal* editors added sarcastically, "we commend the above to Mrs. Blake." They accused

Democratic heiress Susan King of buying votes in urban wards. Anthony, trying to keep peace, defended King and accused Stone and Blackwell of printing
editorials that were "weak, if not wicked." In return, Stone and Blackwell
claimed that Anthony's defense of Democrats would "hinder . . . the cause of
Woman Suffrage."[48]

Party loyalty among many grassroots suffragists paralleled or exceeded that
of AWSA and NWSA leaders, especially in the Midwest. While engaging in
partisan work, some tried to raise the issue of women's rights. Cincinnati
Ladies' Garfield and Arthur Club Number One expressed hope in 1880 that
their campaigning would "present to the men of the nation another and strong
argument for the enfranchisement of women." An Illinois Democrat reminded
her male audience that, unfortunately, loyal women could not assist the party
by voting. Michigan Republican Adele Hazlett used her platform for indirect
suffrage appeals sweetened with humor. "Mrs. Hazlett began by stating that
women were interested in politics," reported one newspaper. "She said: 'You
men will not let us vote, but you permit us to talk, for the simple reason that
experience has demonstrated that you can't prevent it.'"[49]

If forced to choose between suffrage and Republicanism, many women expressed stronger allegiance to the latter. "For my part," wrote Emma Garrett of
Indiana, "even if such an unheard of thing should occur, as the inserting of a
Woman Suffrage plank in the Democratic platform, it would never alter my allegiance to the Republican Party, whose principles I believe to be just and
right, and whose existence is essential to the safety of the nation." Anna
Quinby, founder of Cincinnati's Garfield Club, told a local newspaper that "she
had seen her two brothers brutally assassinated by rebels in Missouri, and their
children thrown upon the mercies of a cold world. Could any one ask her to
favor the election of the Democratic ticket? . . . Never! She was a Republican
to the core, Suffrage or no Suffrage."[50]

This emphatic ordering of priorities posed a knotty problem for movement
leaders. Notwithstanding her own Republicanism, Anthony saw that a wing of
Republican suffragists—centered, not surprisingly, in the Midwest—viewed
suffrage as a secondary goal. In private letters Anthony criticized them bitterly
as "semi-Republican managers" who followed with "sickening sycophancy" the
"gospel of St. Republican."[51] The midwestern GOP loyalties that hindered
Frances Willard presented an obstacle for Anthony as well. In the region where
women were most politically mobilized, Republicans, Prohibitionists, and suffragists appealed to the same group of middle-class evangelical women. In the
competition for these women's attention and talents, the suffrage movement
often finished last.

In the 1880s, rapid growth of the WCTU strengthened the suffrage movement in one way but weakened it in another. The Union's pro-suffrage stance
increased national visibility and backing for the cause of women's voting rights;
at the same time, the WCTU's third-party strategy created new divisions in
suffragist ranks. Many grassroots suffragists, observing that Prohibition platforms offered a concrete promise of votes for women, became disillusioned with

the Republican loyalty of NWSA and AWSA leaders. This was especially clear in 1884, when Prohibitionists were gaining momentum. Stanton and Anthony's call to "back the Republican Party" elicited a storm of protest. Emma Harriman of Minnesota asked, "What have the Republicans done for us women? I know what they have done in this State. They have insulted the women who dared present a petition to their Legislature—openly insulted them." "We should like to ask," demanded another Prohibitionist, "just what the Republican Party has done for the suffrage cause, or for women, to merit their undying gratitude and clinging devotion. For twenty-five years this party has held absolute power, and the political status of woman remains unchanged." Referring to the wool tariff, the writer declared that "the only live issue in the Republican platform is the sheep."[52]

By 1888 Stanton heeded these arguments and split publicly with Anthony, who continued to back Republicans as late as 1892. Stanton wrote to the WCTU's *Union Signal* and declared her support for the third party, which would rise, she said, "as the Republican Party rose from the ashes of the Whigs." She predicted that Prohibitionists would "hold the balance of power in the coming Presidential campaign" and go on to "organize the new Liberty Party for the next generation." She then launched an extended attack on Anthony's position. "No woman with a proper self-respect can longer kneel at the feet of the Republican Party," she wrote. "Susan B. Anthony was arrested by Republican officials, . . . tried by Republican judges, and condemned and fined for voting a clean Republican ticket. . . . Yet she preserves a childlike faith in the final justice of that party towards woman." To Anthony's argument that "we have twenty Republican votes in the United States Senate," Stanton responded that it made no difference as long as GOP conventions refused to act. Stanton's letter delighted the *Union Signal* editors but must have sorely pained Anthony and other Republican suffragists. Quarrels over strategy among movement leaders now mirrored those at the grassroots.[53]

In some parts of the country, resulting rifts lasted for years. Prohibitionist and Republican suffragists in the Pacific Northwest split into opposing factions. Similar divisions became apparent in the Kansas Equal Suffrage Association by the 1890s. Perhaps the worst case was Indiana, where suffragists could not take advantage of leading politicians' support because the state association was practically moribund from 1887 to 1900. Association president Helen Gougar was a Prohibitionist (and later a Populist) who after a series of disputes led only a rump faction. She refused to inform Republican women of meeting dates; from New York, Anthony corresponded with Republican suffragists in Indiana and informed them of the actions of their own state conventions. These women boycotted Gougar's meetings anyway. After 1900, younger women had to rebuild the state movement from scratch.[54]

Faced with Republican indifference and bitter internecine fights, suffragists often wished for a new equal rights party. "The great need of the age," wrote Lucy Stone, "is a new political party, whose watchword shall be, 'Justice for Women.'" "I was a Republican," wrote Margaret Campbell of Iowa, "but that day has passed. . . . Our party is not yet in the field." "Our only hope," remarked a Massachusetts suffragist, "seems to be in the formation of a third party, which shall advocate our own with other leading reforms." Like Prohibitionists, these women looked back to the upheaval of the 1850s as a model for political change. One argued in the *Woman's Journal:*

> When anti-slavery was growing inside the Whig and Democratic parties, the managers did not yield an inch; they could not, because half their party were slaveholders profiting by a peculiar traffic; so there was formed a new party with new managers and a new name, while the old managers, or a great many of them, joined the Democratic. Just so at present with the Republican Party; as soon as it is defeated . . . we shall discover all at once that our noblest statesmen, our best orators, two-thirds of our rank and file, a goodly proportion of Democrats, and the daily press with hardly an exception will enter the new party of Prohibition and Woman Suffrage.

The editor of the Nebraska *Woman's Tribune* offered a similar analysis. "The Democratic Party," she observed, "has always been a strict constructionist party, [while] the Republican is a loose constructionist party. . . . Some party is going to come to the front and insist that according to the constitution, woman suffrage is an issue. When that party arises, it will inevitably be opposed by the Democratic Party, because of the fact that it is a strict construction party." When Americans face "some national crisis or needed reform," they "say to the party of inertia: 'We must put a more liberal construction on this point' and a new party grows and succeeds. . . . Then the party disintegrates and becomes the nucleus of other progressive ideas."[55]

Despite this expressed desire, however, no national suffrage leader supported Belva Lockwood's two presidential campaigns on the Equal Rights ticket. Lockwood ran in 1884 and 1888, arguing that existing parties forced her to do so by refusing to represent women. Her campaign seemed to fit Lucy Stone's prediction that a new equal rights party would arise, and that this was "the party which all Suffragists, men and women, should strive to have inaugurated." Yet Stone, Anthony, and Stanton all urged Lockwood to renounce her candidacy.[56] They did so because they discounted her as an outsider whose party was completely unable to compel a realignment. The Prohibitionist situation was more difficult to assess; Stanton and many rank-and-file suffragists contested Republicans' assertion that the new party could never hold power.

These disputes were often heated. Like temperance advocates, suffragists tended to describe themselves as nonpartisan and criticize internal opponents for "lacking self respect" and "allowing themselves to be used" by partisan men. Suffragists of different persuasions were all capable of arguing that women "should never be partisan in their feelings" and then promptly making party endorsements. One Prohibitionist compared Anthony and Stanton's letter to "the firing on Fort Sumter"—an act of treason against the cause of woman's rights. Another said it shocked her sense of justice. Democrats, Republicans, and Prohibitionists described each other's party loyalties as "wicked" and "iniquitous."[57]

In part, disagreements within the movement were acrimonious because women held passionate beliefs about issues beyond the cause of suffrage itself. Few, if any, women wanted to cast a ballot simply to exercise an abstract right; they wanted to vote *for* specific policies, though some of these were better represented than others by parties in the field. Humiliated by her lack of voting rights, an Indiana woman wrote to a friend that she was "disgusted and sick. One thing I always said I would not do was to live with a Democrat. Certainly I never would have married one. When you marry a Republican, and he turns to a Democrat, what can you do? I am so mortified and ashamed and hurt that I know not how to live through this campaign." Stuck in this situation, should a woman work for suffrage or Republican victory? The Prohibition Party complicated options even more. An Illinois woman pointed out in the *Woman's Journal* that the new party endorsed suffrage, but in practical terms it was helping Democrats win. "What then," she asked plaintively, "is the duty for a Republican Woman Suffrage prohibitionist?"[58] Neither she nor the editors had an effective answer.

Suffragists not only disagreed with each other's partisan choices; they saw that the strategies adopted by other suffragists canceled out their own, by demonstrating to politicians that women would not vote as a bloc. One suffragist observed that if either Democrats or Republicans "could have had assurance of receiving the majority of the woman's vote, it would have been obtained for her long ago without effort on her part, just as the workingman's and the colored man's were secured for them." In other words, Democrats enfranchised working-class men in the Jacksonian era because they hoped to benefit from their loyalty; Republicans enfranchised black men because these new voters would surely support the party of Emancipation. For women, the suffragist noted, "this has been impossible."[59] Women did not constitute a single class, race, or regional interest; the more they joined party politics, the more obvious their disagreements became.

Yet in the competitive atmosphere of the 1880s and 1890s, it was virtually impossible to make a nonpartisan argument for women's enfranchisement. The first question politicians asked was, how would women vote? If, as it appeared, they would divide along the same lines as men, candidates and legislators in the major parties saw no benefit in changing the law. To the extent women might support new parties favoring moral reforms, they were a potential threat. The Prohibition Party raised an issue dangerous to Republicans; it threatened to take away GOP votes and help Democrats win. Thus Republican suffragists were rightly upset about the third-party strategy, and Prohibitionists were right to point out that Republicans were doing nothing to advance the suffrage cause.

Whether they liked it or not, even the most ardent suffragists were stuck with the parties. Other activists could work through churches, organize charitable associations, or find private channels for implementing moral and social reforms. Suffragists could only achieve their goal by convincing state or national legislators to pass constitutional amendments. This was nearly impossible to achieve without the very votes women sought and, in the Gilded Age, without a compelling argument that suffrage would benefit the party in power. Stanton and Anthony's argument that "woman must lead the way to her own enfranchisement" and "not put her trust in man" was an inspirational thought but a practical impossibility.[60] Men—and partisan men—controlled the electoral machine.

3

Democrats and
Domestic Economics

Despite the efforts of Prohibitionists and other reformers, Civil War issues did not fade quickly from politics. In the late 1870s and early 1880s, the erosion of Republican power disquieted many northerners and southern blacks without assuaging the immense bitterness of ex-Confederates. The contested presidential election of 1876, between Samuel Tilden and Rutherford Hayes, went unresolved for three tense months and aroused widespread fear of renewed war. The election hinged on contested returns from several southern states; in exchange for conceding the election, Democrats won a secret promise from Republican leaders that the last Union troops would withdraw from the South. With these developments, the GOP's national prospects looked shakier than at any time since the war.[1]

Close presidential races in 1880 and 1884 reawakened popular worries. "I dread to see the election drawing near," a young Illinois woman wrote to her fiancé in 1880. "The Republicans will be apt to struggle pretty hard before giving up the power. . . . And if there should be a civil war!" In November 1884, thirty-four-year-old Violet Blair Janin wrote in her diary: "Cleveland is elected beyond dispute & I am happy beyond words—but oh the agony of the doubts & hopes & fears of the days following the election—I am so thankful it is all over—Nothing can be worse than a disputed election with a possibility of civil war."[2]

Grover Cleveland's victory, the first by a Democrat in almost thirty years, created consternation in many parts of the North. Caroline Dall reported to the president-elect from Washington, D.C., that "Dixie was openly sung for the first time in twenty years—Women [civil servants] whose brothers and fathers died in the last war were so apprehensive that they were made useless by grief, and were sent home by the Departments." Dall expressed amazement at the number of blacks who "believe it is in your power to return them to slavery." She wrote that her neighbors were ex-Confederates, and that during a Democratic victory parade "a child of seven standing on the steps said 'Hurrah for Cleveland!'" A black woman who worked for the family "darted forward, seized the child & shook him at arms' length . . . and this directly in sight of the child's mother!" For Americans who feared war or slavery, the election of a Democratic president was a matter of immense personal consequence.[3]

Cleveland's presence strengthened the hand of southern Democrats who had feared federal intervention in their elections, but in the North the new president's appeal was as a reformer. Ex-Confederates' party loyalty was secure; elsewhere Democrats needed to divert attention from the issues of war and Reconstruction. The Republican Party remained the most powerful national institution dedicated to remembering the war, while Democrats tried to dismiss it as history, arguing that the nation should move on to new concerns. By the 1880s, cartoonists had begun to represent the GOP as an elephant with a long memory and the Democracy as a rebellious donkey.[4]

Cleveland and his followers focused on economics, criticizing the high import tariffs levied by the federal government. Republicans had raised tariffs sharply when the South left the Union and had kept them high since the war. Democrats argued that this hurt American consumers—especially the working class—by shielding U.S. manufacturers from overseas competition. Updating old appeals, Democrats depicted the tariff as an invasive federal measure that centralized power and wealth in the hands of a few industrialists and politicians. Republicans could not deny that tariffs created a revenue surplus: $140 million lay unspent in the federal Treasury by 1888. In that year, Democrats' national platform claimed the ruling party was "debauched by this immense temptation," leading to bribery, fraudulent pension claims, and other sorts of corruption.[5]

Democrats' arguments seem to have been most effective in the Midwest, where economic woes were beginning to surface. They also attracted support among a young generation of Americans who were tired of hearing about their elders' war exploits and more interested in solutions to the nation's current ills. By emphasizing the tariff, Democrats challenged Republicans' coalition outside the South, exposing divisions between young and old, West and East. Campaigns of the late 1880s also reflected emerging rifts between classes. Democrats focused their appeals, and Republicans their responses, on rural and working-class families who were being left behind by the growing prosperity of the urban middle class. Tariff debates of the 1880s initiated what would become, in the 1890s, a national controversy over the diverging experiences of affluent and poor.[6]

When a party has sustained broad popular support for many years, opponents often try to appropriate parts of its image while maintaining distinct political goals. Thus Democrats, while attacking Republican tariffs, began to make concessions to Republican domesticity. Rather than emphasizing Christian morality, Democrats modernized their view of women's economic roles. Past Democrats had celebrated women's productive household labor, notably in the secession crisis when southern women had dusted off their spinning wheels to boycott northern cloth. With postwar industrialization and the diffusion of cheap consumer goods, appeals to the spinning wheel became untenable. Democrats now addressed women as consumers, recognizing that in an increasing number of families, women were more familiar with prices than were men.

The translation of women's consumer power into politics became apparent by 1890, when leaders of both parties argued that "shopping women," shocked by price increases that were allegedly caused by a new Republican tariff, persuaded their husbands to vote Democratic in huge numbers. The truth of this claim was dubious, but it represented an important new idea. Republican and Prohibitionist women had previously justified their entry into politics based on their superior Christian virtue. In the new Democratic argument, women made political decisions not because they were morally purer than men but because, like men, they understood their economic interests. Women's identities not only as exemplars of morality but as consumers, household managers, and wage workers moved to the heart of partisan debate.

Democratic Domesticity

In 1876, while he was governor of New York, Democrat Samuel Tilden created a sensation when he filled a seat on the State Board of Charities. Tilden chose reformer Josephine Shaw Lowell, the first woman in the nation to hold such a post. "I woke up next morning and found myself famous," the governor remarked. Lowell might have said the same. She had worked for a decade in the movement for prison and asylum reform, but her new position greatly enhanced her authority and public recognition. She served until 1889 as one of the board's most effective members.[7]

Lowell's appointment was a product not only of her reform work but of a new strategy adopted by northern "reform Democrats" like Tilden. Lowell came from a famously Republican faction of the Boston elite. Her brother Robert Gould Shaw had commanded black Union troops until his death in a celebrated assault on Fort Wagner, South Carolina. Lowell's Republican husband had also died on a southern battlefield, and she herself promoted economic aid and education for blacks as a leader of the New York Freedmen's Relief Association. For many years after the war Lowell wore mourning colors in memory of her husband.[8] Her appointment by a Democrat was a superb strategy for canceling Republicans' claim to be *the* party of Union victory.

Though Tilden conceded the 1876 presidential election to Rutherford Hayes, another New York governor continued Tilden's legacy of Democratic reform. Grover Cleveland won a reputation for honesty and fiscal conservatism; enthusiastic followers made a campaign slogan of his statement, "a public office is a public trust." New York, like Ohio, Illinois, and Indiana, was a crucial state whose electoral votes swung on extremely narrow margins. Cleveland's clean image contrasted with that of federal Republican appointees at the notorious New York Customs House, which collected tariff duties for the nation's largest port. In short, Cleveland was an excellent presidential choice for Democrats in 1884.[9]

With their own candidate, James Blaine, widely viewed as corrupt, and with Prohibitionists taking the evangelical high ground, Republicans found themselves in a tight spot. They relied on an old strategy, attacking their opponent as a specimen of typical Democratic manhood. Within a month of Cleveland's nomination, allegations surfaced that he had fathered an illegitimate son while living in Buffalo. For years he had paid support to the mother, Maria Halpin, who had suffered mental breakdowns before and after her child was sent to an orphanage. Cleveland did not deny the charge.[10]

Republican editors took up this issue with glee. The *New York Tribune* called the nominee "gross and licentious" and a "moral leper." Boston editor Charles Dana stated his disbelief "that the American people will knowingly elect to the presidency a coarse debauchée who would bring his harlots with him to Washington." Some of the most outrageous charges were made by the Reverend George H. Ball of Buffalo, who claimed to have gathered local evidence. Republicans around the nation reprinted his report that Cleveland had housed a harem in his bachelor quarters. The young lawyer had "foraged outside in the city and surrounding villages, a champion libertine, an artful seducer, a foe to virtue, an enemy of the family." With an implied comparison to Republicans' respect for women, Ball declared that Cleveland was "hostile to true womanhood." "Some disgraced and broken-hearted victims of his lust now slumber in the grave," he reported. "The issue is evidently . . . between the brothel and the family; between indecency and decency; between lust and law."[11]

Republican-leaning women expressed shock at Cleveland's history. The *Woman's Journal* received a huge volume of letters, few of them defending the Democratic candidate. "When a great political party," argued Mary Livermore, "nominates a man for the Chief Magistracy of the nation who is charged with the gravest and most heinous sins against women, they should not be dumb witnesses of this insulting and demoralizing act." Such declarations presented an ironic problem for Republican strategists: Cleveland had provided them with an issue ideally suited to constituents they had not enfranchised. Party leaders settled for women's meetings at which they praised "Republican ladies" and urged them to use their "influence." Ohio Senator John Sherman stated for the first time, no doubt sincerely, that he wished women could vote.[12]

Democratic women defended their candidate with arguments similar to those used by men. Republican nominee James Blaine was implicated in several scandals; opponents painted him as corrupt and greedy, arguing that his public transgressions were worse than Cleveland's private ones. Democratic women in Muncie, Indiana, held a mass rally to show support. In Buffalo, prominent society ladies invited the Democratic candidate into their homes, an act useful to defenders of Cleveland's character. Party newspapers stressed that women were "as enthusiastic for Cleveland, Hendricks, and reform as the men." A group of suffragists in New York worked quietly on Cleveland's behalf, circulating an appeal to prominent friends. British observer James Bryce wrote that American women hosted a striking number of receptions and wrote copious letters to newspapers in support of both candidates, as well as Prohibitionist John St. John.[13]

The charges against Cleveland had little impact on women's long-term party loyalties. He seems, however, to have judged his tarnished reputation to be a political liability. After winning by a hairsbreadth, the new president not only showed his reform credentials by vetoing pension bills passed by congressional Republicans. Cleveland also countered Republican allegations about his sexual conduct. First he brought his sister to the White House to set a decorous social standard.[14] Then he found a fiancée.

Though marriage was not simply a strategy for reelection, a man as shrewd as Cleveland surely calculated its impact on his next campaign. The timing of his courtship suggests political as well as personal concerns. The president-elect, a bachelor of forty-nine years, began to show romantic interest in his young ward Frances Folsom soon after the 1884 campaign. He proposed to her within a year and she accepted. Cleveland's aides kept the secret until Folsom returned from a tour of Europe, after which they announced the news. A small wedding took place at the White House in June 1886.[15]

Frances Folsom Cleveland became an instant celebrity. Only twenty-two on her wedding day, she was attractive and outgoing; she had recently graduated from Wells College and reporters emphasized her education. In keeping with this modern image, the new first lady answered to the boyish nicknames of Frank or Frankie. Yet she allayed Americans' anxieties about the intentions of educated young women. Instead of a career in public reform work, she chose domestic life with a portly older husband. Newspapers of both parties hailed Folsom as "a lovely and perfect type of the flower of womankind—an American girl," who was "sensible, affectionate, talented, and refined."[16]

The wedding was the most popular act of Cleveland's first administration. Huge crowds gathered to glimpse the couple after their vows, and public demand for wedding news was insatiable. On their brief honeymoon the Clevelands had trouble avoiding the press, and the groom expressed indignation over their lack of privacy. Within ten weeks a small volume titled *The Bride of the White House* offered details of Folsom's life and character. Even the *New York Tribune*, a bitter Cleveland opponent, grudgingly observed that "no American wedding has attracted such general and such amiable attention." Staunchly Republican *Judge* hinted that Frankie would make a better president than Grover.[17]

Because the previous president, Chester Arthur, was a widower, the nation had had no first lady since James Garfield's assassination in 1881, a circumstance that must have contributed to Folsom's appeal. The wedding also relieved national anxiety over Cleveland's transgressions as a bachelor. By accepting his proposal, Folsom largely erased his past and transformed him into a respectable family man. During the 1888 campaign a few scattered Republicans complained about the president's alleged sexual misdeeds, but for the most part the issue disappeared.[18]

Democrats quickly turned Frances Cleveland's popularity to partisan use. The text of *Bride of the White House* reappeared word for word in their 1888 campaign literature. New editions of campaign biographies featured accounts of the wedding and portraits of the bride. Frances Cleveland's picture appeared on everything from badges and banners to handkerchiefs and milk pitchers. Just in time for the 1888 campaign, Lydia Gordon produced a new history of first ladies that differed conspicuously from the earlier work by Republican Laura Holloway. Gordon depicted Julia Grant and Lucy Hayes as ambitious, demanding women who had wielded excessive influence over their husbands. Frances Cleveland, on the other hand, was a model of modesty. "Her popularity," Gordon declared, "makes her the most potent factor in the administration which the Republicans have to face and fight against." Belva Lockwood, running her second campaign on the Equal Rights ticket, agreed. When asked what woman other than herself could most easily win the presidency, Lockwood answered, "Frances Folsom Cleveland."[19]

The Clevelands' admirers echoed longstanding Republican sentiments: marriage was necessary for true Christian happiness; domestic bliss in the White House set a moral example for the nation. Democratic spokesmen, who had previously described their presidential candidates as aggressive men free of feminine ties, now endorsed a semi-Republican ideal. Their praise of wholesome family life was an important element in the remaking of their national image as they promoted political reform. Democrats did so, though, on their own limited terms, fighting a rearguard action against charges of "debauchery" and contrasting their heroine with shrewish Republicans like Lucy Hayes, who allegedly meddled in public affairs.

The Clevelands' wedding launched a decade-long bipartisan celebration of White House domesticity. When Republican Benjamin Harrison took office in 1889, his grandchildren moved to the White House as part of his extended family. They received so much public attention that Harrison's wife Caroline protested the "circus aspect" of their lives. Reporters focused especially on "Baby McKee," his grandfather's favorite. Harrison's exasperated secretary finally asked the press to quit writing about Baby McKee lest the nation "believe the tales about this child's having more influence than the members of the Cabinet." The boy and his sister Mary had a Democratic rival after 1891, with the birth of Grover and Frances Cleveland's first child. Baby Ruth inspired gushing adoration as well as the name of a new candy bar. Grover Cleveland suffered indignity at the hands of his own followers in 1892, when his portrait appeared on a sketch of a diaper with the message, "Vote for Papa. —Baby Ruth."[20]

The public mania for White House weddings and babies marked an apex of sentimentalism in American culture, and it also signified a political shift. Democrats had joined Republicans in idealizing domesticity, at least on a superficial level. The limits of their transformation remained to be explored over the next decade. Women were no longer invisible in Democrats' campaign literature and they even won a few appointments from men like Tilden. Cleveland and his followers, though, still assailed state "paternalism" and called for a smaller, less intrusive government, most notably through reduction of tariffs and pensions. Vetoing a pension bill, Cleveland argued that it would trespass on private life; in determining which veterans were worthy, he demanded, "is the Government to enter the homes of claimants?"[21] The fundamental tenets of party ideology, including defense of men's household prerogatives against an intrusive state, had changed little.

At the national level, limits on Democratic women's campaign activities still contrasted with broader opportunities among Republicans and Prohibitionists. This became clear in the presidential elections of 1888 and 1892, both of which pitted Cleveland against Benjamin Harrison. In the fiercely contested Midwest these campaigns witnessed a continued increase in women's activities for all parties. Women riding wagons, floats, or even on horseback participated in most midwestern parades. Female glee clubs and flag presentations were common around the region. Some Illinois and Michigan rallies featured military-style drills by young ladies' clubs, and at least two women's drum corps performed in Illinois and Indiana. Drawing on the broom as a traditional symbol of cleaning out the opposition, Republican ladies' broom brigades organized to "sweep" Cleveland out of office.[22]

The increasing visibility of young Democratic women was noteworthy in the Midwest. Using the first lady's popularity to justify their political role, young women organized Frances Cleveland Clubs to march in parades and pressure men—especially first-time voters—to support the Democrats. As vice-presidential candidate Allen Thurman crisscrossed the Midwest making stump speeches, clubs of uniformed women met him at almost every stop. Thurman's son reported from Indiana that "men, women, and children, boys and girls, have all gone crazy on the subject of politics. We saw not less than 20 'Frankie Cleveland Clubs,' all dressed in red bandannas. These girls marched in the procession through the mud and rain at Shelbyville and Peru like the boys. At Brazil there was a company of about a hundred on horseback. . . . They rode splendidly and presented one of the prettiest sights I have ever seen."[23]

In the Midwest and West, Democrats' strategy also extended to the employment of female orators. California lawyer Clara Foltz, formerly a Republican, switched parties and gave stump speeches calling for lower tariffs; the new Democratic governor subsequently rewarded her service with an appointment to the State Board of Charities. Laura DeForce Gordon, another Californian, traveled as far as Wyoming to denounce high tariffs. In Indiana, young Louie Hiatt Brown studied tariff laws and went on the stump to advocate reform.[24] These Democratic women worked, however, with little recognition or support from the national party. As the *Woman's Journal* observed, Democrats were "slow to recognize the new order of things" when it came to organizing women's political clubs. Outside the Midwest, the party's old reluctance to acknowledge public roles for women persisted despite their rhetoric of reform.

This was amply illustrated in 1892, when Democratic women tried to organize a national association. Mary Frost Ormsby of New York announced that the league's mission would be to "secure the election of the Democratic ticket" and "defend the homes of the land against unjust taxation"—that is, to support male Democrats in their pledge to lower the tariff.[25] Ormsby wanted to call her association the Frances Cleveland Influence Clubs, but Grover Cleveland objected. He had accepted the placement of Frankie's picture on bandannas, flags, pins, and buttons, and he tolerated midwestern clubs bearing his wife's name, but he drew the line at a national organization. Other Democratic leaders were equally unhelpful. Despite changing her group's name to the National Democratic Influence Clubs, Ormsby got no further with the project and her clubs won little public recognition in the campaign.[26]

In the Northeast, Democratic campaign reform focused on changing the culture of men's politics, not on women's inclusion. Young men began to promote a more domestic campaign style based less on drinking, street parades, and pole raisings, and more on refined debate. These young men had grown up during a quarter-century of Republican rule. Some admired men like George Curtis and Carl Schurz, who presented themselves as nonpartisan reformers and had led a revolt from the Republican Party in 1884 to support Grover Cleveland. These men and their young supporters gradually transformed Republicans' old ideal of manhood—based on self-control and male domesticity—into a bipartisan standard among the middle class. This was a shift for both sides, but a particularly marked departure for Democrats.[27]

In 1888 both Republicans and Democrats of the new generation established leagues of young men's permanent political clubs. Each league held a national convention accompanied by fanfare and front-page press reports. They focused on the tariff and to a lesser extent civil service reform, though Republicans could not resist occasional remarks on the courage of Union soldiers and the perfidy of rebels. Each league announced a "reform" agenda and planned a "campaign of education." Badges worn by one New Jersey club expressed the goal of both groups: "Why not carry into politics the methods of honest men and the courtesies of gentlemen?"[28]

The league conferences gave national recognition to practices that had already been adopted by a number of local clubs. These were primarily northeastern, the first having been founded in Philadelphia and New York. While both leagues claimed to be national, most delegates to their conventions were from the Northeast, along with a few large midwestern cities like Chicago and Cleveland. Men and women outside the Northeast remained faithful to older styles in 1888, demanding parades, glee clubs, and fireworks. Most clubs in the West and South formed only for the duration of the campaign. In the Midwest, this was apparently true of both women's and men's partisan organizations.[29]

In the Northeast, the new young men's permanent clubs brought politics off the street and indoors, even to the home. These young men promoted reading and calm discussion rather than boisterous parades. They distributed pamphlets and statistics; they held debates and met in private clubrooms or houses. The *Boston Globe* praised the quiet atmosphere of politics in 1888, claiming that "there is not a black eye in the whole campaign." Some northeastern clubs publicly flaunted their pledges of temperance, an innovation that alarmed men elsewhere. Upon hearing that a Philadelphia Republican club had eliminated its bar, an Indiana editor expressed shock. Could a party club survive, he wondered, "without liquid enthusiasm being added?"[30]

The new campaign style reflected young men's discomfort with, even hostility toward, war issues. Memories of the war were fading, a trend which worked to Democrats' advantage outside the South. The census made the reason apparent: high birth rates, short life spans, and an influx of young immigrants created a U.S. population exceptionally young by twentieth-century standards. Among men of voting age in 1890, only half were over thirty-five years old. Veterans of the Civil War generation were finding themselves rapidly outnumbered at the polls by millions of younger men. Leaders of both parties faced the immense problem of maintaining broad national coalitions by assimilating new voters who were less responsive to old appeals. One young Kansas Republican mocked the old issues of secession and Union as "shopworn ordnance" that kicked and injured those who used it. Local party elders protested, denouncing young men's "scheme of getting on in the world by belittling, organizing against, and crowding out older men."[31]

In both North and South, black men became increasingly independent of the GOP. Those born since slavery argued, with justification, that Republicans were doing little more for blacks than were Democrats. F. J. Loudin, a friend of former Congressman John Patterson Green of Ohio, summed up the sentiment of many: "I don't like the idea of the white man being able to tell the complection of our politics by our color. . . . I confess I can't be a Democrat but am glad when I see a Negro with stomach large enough and digestive organs strong enough to swallow them." In the North, sons of Union veterans were more receptive than their fathers to Democratic criticisms of Republican corruption. Young men of both parties were more interested than their elders in moral reform and social purification. In state legislatures, for example, a decade of debate over age-of-consent laws ran largely on generational lines. Younger men favored protecting girls by raising the age of consent and strengthening penalties for statutory rape; older men tended to oppose these reforms.[32] With Republicans' increasing conservatism and Democrats' new claim as reformers, old party lines sometimes broke down, revealing generational and regional divides.

Vicariously, at least, uniformed marchers in campaign parades identified themselves with the heroes of Gettysburg and a hundred other battles. In an era of peace young men could not possibly duplicate the achievements of their soldier fathers, not to mention such exemplars of manhood as General Garfield. Members of the new permanent clubs preferred to present themselves as gentlemen rather than pseudo-soldiers. Military symbols were constant reminders of an older generation's accomplishments, but the new clubs hailed achievements in the realms of business, education, and culture, where young men could make their own mark. The members of a Young Business Men's Republican Club, or a Democratic club that debated the tariff in a gentlemanly way, could feel proud of their independence. They stood less in the shadow of older heroes.

The transformation was gradual and incomplete. Neither parades nor stump speeches immediately disappeared, even in the urban Northeast, but leaders of the new leagues proclaimed a trend. Chauncey Black, chair of the Association of Democratic Clubs, praised his followers for abandoning fireworks and drills and making a "straight, constant, and manly appeal to the intelligence of the voter." James Clarkson, president of the League of Republican Clubs, stated in 1892 that "there is left to be made by each party a campaign of education."[33]

Meanwhile, the Northeastern press began to ridicule old-fashioned political rallies and to present uniformed marchers as ethnic caricatures. Republican journalists described opponents' parades as festivals for drunk Irishmen, while Democrats claimed that the purpose of GOP parades was to excite ignorant blacks, who supposedly loved ostentatious display. This was a clear sign that white middle-class men were distancing themselves from the whole project of mass-based campaigns. In a reversal of gender ideals, the press began to suggest that getting drunk and cheering in the streets were unmanly enterprises. *Puck* offered readers the tale of Balthazar Blivens of Brooklyn, who preened before the mirror in his campaign costume. As a result of drinking Blivens got separated from his parade unit, had his pocket picked, and was beaten up by a streetwise member of New York's labor faction. His pretensions deflated, Blivens voted for Equal Rights candidate Belva Lockwood. Loyal to the old political culture, he ended up a feminized figure.[34]

In the context of changes in the Northeast, midwestern women's participation in such male traditions as pole raising may have been a sign that rituals were beginning to lose their power. Party editors began to refer to parades and barbecues as "old-fashioned" events, and midwestern politics echoed a few of the tendencies emerging in the Northeast. Growing numbers of midwesterners sponsored pole raisings in private yards rather than public squares. Families showed their loyalties by placing candidates' pictures in their parlor windows; both parties reported on the numbers of such portraits. Democrats in Monticello, Indiana, issued what sounded like a ladies' social invitation. They announced that they had opened headquarters in rooms above the local drugstore and that "all who favor tariff reform are requested to call and make themselves at home."[35]

Women and Tariff Reform

Americans took up new issues along with new tactics, as Democrats pushed the tariff to the forefront of campaigns. In the late 1880s the Midwest suffered from deteriorating labor conditions and bitter strikes. In a competitive atmosphere, both parties recognized that they might win or lose national contests in Illinois, Indiana, and Ohio; pressure for lower tariffs was strong in these states, especially among laborers and farmers, and some Republicans took a tariff-reform stance. In response to economic distress, midwestern Democrats and Republicans shifted away from racial and Civil War themes. Jobs, wages, and prosperity came to the fore, and Democrats focused on these issues through the lens of "tariff reform."[36]

Democrats found that tariff reform had both economic and moral appeal, especially among younger Americans. Import duties flooded the Treasury with millions of dollars that many saw as a source of corruption. Some Americans considered tariff reform or "free trade" analogous to civil service reform, temperance, and other efforts to purify civic life. Young M. Carey Thomas, later president of Bryn Mawr College, listed in a letter her political priorities for the 1880s: "First: Hard money. Second: Free trade. Third: Civil service reform. . . . Fourth: Universal Suffrage for Woman." Suffrage leader Harriet Hanson Robinson declared in 1888 that "young men of to-day, or many of them, are interested in something besides discussing what the 'GOP' has done, or what the wicked democrats did before the last war. They are thinking of temperance, labor reform, free trade, and the woman question."[37]

A faltering economy played into Democrats' hands over the next few years, and the tariff became the absorbing political question of 1888, 1890, and 1892. In the first of these elections, Democrats' bid failed: Republicans recaptured the presidency and a large majority in Congress. But Cleveland and his allies had forced their opponents into a difficult spot, and GOP leaders decided to open debate on the tariff. In 1890 Congress undertook exhausting rate revisions under the leadership of William McKinley, a rising Republican star from Ohio. The new McKinley tariff proved politically disastrous. It was extraordinarily complex; the drafting process showed Republicans in their worst light, as a parade of rich industrialists visited Washington to hobnob with congressional friends. Most of all, the tariff seemed to prompt a sharp rise in consumer prices without demonstrating immediate benefits. In the 1890 midterm elections, Republicans lost 93 of their 179 House seats. Democrats completed their triumph in 1892 by winning majority status in the Senate and retaking the White House. While other issues played a role in this dramatic shift, commentators on both sides argued that tariffs were key.[38]

In keeping with their reform stance, Democrats in these years developed dramatic appeals to American consumers. Tariffs, the party argued, were a tax paid by ordinary Americans on goods they purchased. The tax created domestic monopolies and enriched manufacturers, giving them arbitrary power over markets and workers. One Indiana newspaper claimed, "This is a fight between monopolists, trusts and high taxes on one side and labor, low taxes and cheap necessaries of life for wives and children on the other."[39]

To illustrate their argument Democrats published lists of everyday goods and the estimated tariff on each item. The *Boston Globe* offered a room-by-room survey of an American home, listing "Taxes on the Parlor" and "Taxes on the Kitchen." One widely circulated cartoon depicted over thirty items, including clothes, linens, sewing materials, and kitchen goods. The sketch looked like an advertisement for a dry-goods merchant; instead of prices, it listed various amounts of tariff "plunder." In the House, Texas Congressman Roger Q. Mills held up a suit of clothes that cost $20; he claimed that without the Republican tariff, it would cost only half as much.[40]

Democrats' objective was to convince voters, but they recognized that not all consumers and price watchers were men. Consumption patterns were undergoing rapid changes as the United States became more urban and prosperous. Some farmers still purchased family supplies when they went into town, but in many areas shopping had become a female responsibility. This was especially true for women in middle-class households who did not work for wages. They could devote substantial time to shopping and found a variety of stores—even whole districts—where they could do so. Urban newspapers were beginning to joke about wives' penchant for spending their husbands' paychecks, and about the bewilderment of men who entered department stores.[41]

Middle-class women were not the only women who shopped. Increasing numbers of young women worked for their own wages; many contributed to family incomes, but thousands supported themselves. Among single women in 1880, 73 percent of blacks and 24 percent of whites reported paid jobs, and the percentage for white women grew steadily over the next two decades. Democrats included both working-class and middle-class women in their appeals. In the 1888 campaign, one "old soldier" pointed to the plight of "the poor girls of Chicago and New York, many of whom are the destitute children of our comrades." He claimed the poverty of these seamstresses was a result of Republican tariffs, which raised the cost of necessities. An Indiana newspaper argued that "if a young woman pays $9 for a shawl she gets $6 worth of shawl only; the other $3 she presents to the manufacturer to 'protect him.'" New York men's Democratic clubs designed campaign materials with slogans appealing to female consumers. After passage of the McKinley Act, which raised the duty on tin, midwestern Democrats paid door-to-door peddlers to sell pie tins at grossly inflated prices. When housewives expressed horror, the salesmen blamed the new tariff.[42]

Along with this approach, midwestern Democrats moderated their old stance of masculine independence just as Grover Cleveland had abandoned bachelorhood. A measure of the shift was their attempt to co-opt the temperance issue. Instead of railing against intrusive do-gooders, midwestern Democrats began to seek moral high ground, arguing that Republican tariffs inflated the cost of necessities while leaving liquor and tobacco on the "free list." Depictions of the GOP as the "free whiskey and free tobacco party" included a domestic illustration published by the *Indianapolis Sentinel*. In it, a mother warms her hands over a giant pipe while her hungry children drink whiskey. The family's flour barrel stands empty in a corner.[43]

Democratic arguments also had a moral edge in their calls for greater economic justice. The *St. Louis Post-Dispatch* condemned tariffs as "class legislation." An Indiana paper argued that tariffs were lowest on "articles of luxury and personal adornment, consumed almost exclusively by the rich, such as diamonds, precious stones, fine jewelry and costly fabrics for dress and opulent display." Another Democrat listed goods even more specifically: on the free list were "Velvet, Black Silk, Silk Laces, Diamonds," while "the Poorer Classes" paid inflated prices for "Woolens, Flannel Shirts, Cotton Laces, Black Alpaca, Cotton, [and] Corduroy."[44]

With their lists of luxury goods, Democrats continued to associate the upper class with femininity, suggesting party spokesmen's ambivalence toward the new, more domestic model of manhood the party was beginning to adopt. Criticism of "free" silk and velvet was, in one sense, a new version of Democrats' traditional attacks on genteel, effeminate men. Women also served as symbols of aristocracy. When Anna Dickinson, a Republican stump speaker of the Civil War era, returned to Indiana in 1888 for a campaign tour, Democrats included her in their class-based attacks. The *Illinois State Register* alleged that "Anna Dickinson's campaign toilet in Indiana is a garnet plush suit, cut princess style and profusely trimmed with lace. Diamonds sparkle from her ears and throat. How her eloquent periods must thrill the Hoosier workingman in his blue jeans." A Virginia editor reported that Dickinson demanded lavish accommodations and ran up "dressmaking bills amounting to $800." The *Louisville Courier-Journal* of Kentucky reported the tour under the headline "Miss Anna Dickinson, Diamond and Silk-Bedecked, On Indiana's Raging Stump." The paper insinuated that Dickinson spoke only for profit: in effect, that she was a high-class prostitute for Republican bosses.[45]

In contrast to Dickinson, a few Democrats celebrated heroines in their own party, especially women of the working class. A newspaper in Greenfield, Indiana, published this tale of Republican bribery and female virtue:

> A poor man in the northwest part of town, with a plucky wife and a number of small children, was repeatedly visited by . . . Republican workers and inducements held out to him to vote the Republican ticket. The wife soon tired of these visits and spoke to them about as follows: "My husband is a Democrat and so am I. He is going to vote the Democratic ticket if we all have to go to the poor house. I want you to leave my house and return no more." They departed, and to end the matter she, with her children, escorted her husband to the voting place where he deposited a Democratic ballot without a scratch. The Democrats, hearing of her action and approving of it, made up a small sum of money and presented it to her as a token of their respect.

The happy ending suggested that those who withstood Republican bribery could win financial reward as well as public praise. As in older Democratic appeals, women did not pressure for legislative action. Instead, the ideal Democratic woman helped protect her home from external corruption, represented in this case by Republican bribes. No wonder the same newspaper urged Democrats to bring "wives and sweethearts" to a rally in order to "strike terror to the corrupt [Republican] ring."[46]

Consumer appeals revealed the same assumptions. Democratic women who tried to organize the national Frances Cleveland Influence Clubs stated that their purpose was to "defend the homes of the land against unjust taxation."[47] Democrats had not changed their underlying conservatism on the issue of state power. They argued that tariffs were an intrusive tax that robbed working families of their rightful income. Virtuous Democratic women were those who managed modest households and fed and clothed their husbands and children—unlike Anna Dickinson, a wealthy single woman who wasted Republican money on extravagant display. Democratic women could also help protect the patriarchal family against government intrusion, a position that ultimately reinforced their subordination.

For both men and women, Democrats continued to articulate a defensive position. Democratic men now sheltered their dependents with paychecks, rather than as soldiers or defenders of white women's sexual purity. The new male virtues were labor and devotion to family, not readiness to commit violence. As one Democrat said of the 1888 campaign, the issues were "our firesides, our homes, fair play and a chance to live."[48] Though such rhetoric echoed Republican and Prohibitionist appeals for "protection of the home," it was used for opposite ends. Democratic men and women did not use domesticity to justify state action. Rather, they continued to seek limitations on state power, protecting the home not *through* government, but against it.

Democratic appeals to female consumers generated a debate in 1890 over women's political influence. It is impossible to prove the extent to which anti-tariff arguments contributed to Democrats' sweeping victories; journalists and politicians in both parties, however, believed tariff arguments had been the key factor, and their attention turned to women. After the campaign Dr. Francis Peabody of Harvard, a tariff reformer, asserted that "women defeated the Republican Party in the last election on the tariff issue." Other Democrats seconded his arguments, as did protectionist newspapers and Republican leaders. Most notably, House Speaker Thomas B. Reed said he was "inclined to think that the most important factor in the result of the election is the women of the country. In their shopping excursions they found the rise of prices explained as due to the McKinley bill, then they went home and told their husbands, and this had a tremendous effect at the ballot box." Women's rights advocates welcomed this analysis. "'The women were at the bottom of it' seems to be the verdict of leading Republicans in accounting for the recent defeat," remarked the *Woman's Tribune*. "It is delightful to know that political parties are beginning to take note of what will be women's wish."[49]

Democratic men were more ambivalent. In a letter to the *New York Times*, Democrat J. S. Moore wrote that "it is really amusing to notice the shrieks [of] high protectionist newspapers and protection leaders" trying to "lay the result of the last election at the door of the women." He stressed that male Democrats had made the real decision at the polls. Moore, however, happily anticipated female influence in the future. A winning party, he declared, had to have "the women of the country on their side. And it goes without saying that, if the women of this country once understood the outrageous tariff robbery, the end would soon come." This projection of women's influence into the future offered an ironic counterpoint to the rhetoric of Republican men, who were busily praising the past moral leadership of female abolitionists. Both parties acknowledged women's political influence but tried to distance it in time: power exercised in the present was reserved for men. Nonetheless, the influence of "shopping women" became a staple of political analysis. Looking back from the vantage point of 1898, the *New York World* credited women not only with the defeat of Republican congressmen but also with Grover Cleveland's second victory.[50]

The alleged political influence of women as consumers was an extension of trends in the larger society. For a decade, urban newspapers had identified female shopping as a source of anxiety. Men were still supposed to work and earn money; women were now supposed to shop and spend money. In this sense, middle-class women entered a new era of consumption and material fulfillment before men did, since men upheld older values of hard work and self-sacrifice. The shift was disturbing to contemporary Americans for several reasons. Throughout the nineteenth century, both among those who embraced domestic ideology and those who did not, American women had been viewed as guardians of tradition, conservators of family and home. Now women seemed to participate in economic changes before men did, in public spaces created just for them. Department stores and even whole shopping districts, such as New York's "ladies' mile," offered women a promise of freedom through products and the act of buying them. It was no accident that women's rights advocates hailed the liberating effects of mass consumption as well as its influence on politics.[51]

Commentators who described the influence of "shopping women" detected a larger change in society and economics. The importance of Americans' identities as consumers was growing in relation to their identities as workers. The change was gradual, extending from before the Civil War until well into the twentieth century. But it made a sudden impact on politics between 1888 and 1892. Democrats hoped the shift would help them reach voters; Republicans worried that American families were abandoning them to follow Democrats' seductive promise of prosperity through lower prices. Though both groups needed male votes, both saw the rise of consumerism as a shift from male to female power and identified "shopping women" as agents of the new ideology.

This political recognition of woman's position as "family treasurer and disbursing officer," as one editor put it, was a new step in the evolution of women's partisan role.[52] Republicans had recognized women's moral judgment on such issues as slavery and preservation of the Union; Prohibitionists endorsed women's political activity based on their roles as Christian mothers and wives. In both cases, justification of women's partisanship stemmed from the connected forces of evangelicalism and domestic ideology. As described by political leaders, the consumers of 1890 did not exercise such moral judgment. Rather, party leaders saw "shopping women" as constituents who made political choices based on day-to-day concerns.

Democrats still rejected the maternal family model that lay at the heart of Republican domesticity. If Democratic women influenced their male relatives, it was by appealing to the family's common economic interest. The new Democratic arguments did not give women leverage as pure beings who could exert political pressure on men by virtue of superior morality. Nor did Democratic arguments provide, for either men or women, justification for expanding government powers based on any belief in the benevolence of state authority. Instead, Democrats argued the opposite. Lower tariffs meant less government, less centralized power, and less corruption. Both parties, however, were now worrying over women's influence at the polls.

That this recognition took place at the locus of consumption was a signal for the future. Democrats and Republicans had begun to recognize new political interests among women. Men, too, appeared to be making electoral decisions in new ways. Looking back on the 1880s, Republican manager James Clarkson wrote: "That was the beginning of the change of political discussion from the open field, as in Lincoln's day, to the private home where each family began to examine and discuss for itself the policy of the parties, to find which party promised the most for the elevation and comfort of that special home. It was an evolutionary result, arising from the demand of changing conditions from sentimental to economic issues."[53] Clarkson's dismissal of Civil War issues as "sentimental" was itself a sign of changing times. Democrats had made limited but visible concessions to Republicans' domestic ideal; young men in the Northeast were stressing reasoned debate rather than emotional rallies. Now, party leaders were beginning to realize the impact of family economics. It was the first glimmer that politicians were recognizing public opinion in the modern sense. With economics at the forefront, and with women working publicly to sway men's loyalties, electoral victory might increasingly depend on conceiving public opinion in broad and secular terms.

A new political identity as consumers would, over the next two decades, prove extremely useful to women in politics. Providing an alternative to the model of Christian virtue, it particularly appealed to those who believed that economic problems were more pressing than such evangelical concerns as prohibition of liquor. By the early 1900s, middle-class women in organizations like the Consumers' League would use their economic clout to support the demands of wage-earning women for fair labor practices and decent pay. These innovations stemmed, in part, from the tariff debates of the 1880s. Democrats had already used consumer-based arguments on behalf of the working class and had established women's place in this national debate. It remained to be seen how Republicans would respond.

4

The Gospel of
St. Republican

Is it wrong for women to take part in politics? That depends,
it seems, entirely on which party they support.
—Woman's Journal, *8 November 1884*

In September 1888, Republican newspapers printed a statement from
J. Ellen Foster, president of the new National Women's Republican Association. "I am a Republican by hereditary influence, past environments and
present conviction," Foster declared.

> Because—First—The Republican Party in the past has stood for all that is
> liberal and progressive in legislation. Second—The Republican Party freed
> the slave. Third—The pronounced and emphatic legislation on moral ques-
> tions has come most largely from republican legislators. Fourth—The Repub-
> lican Party has always been the champion of protection—protection of the
> citizen, protection of the negro, protection of the ballot-box, protection to the
> wage earner, protection to the wage payer, and now, right in the line with its
> past professions and performances, it declares protection to the home.[1]

Foster's statement and her new organization were part of a broad Republican
defense mounted in the late 1880s as the party faced Prohibitionist defections
and a challenge from reform Democrats. Foster's appeal for "protection to the
home" had a double meaning. She defended high tariffs, which allegedly provided working-class men with a family wage; "home protection" was also a slogan of Prohibitionists, who had earlier borrowed the term from pro-tariff Republicans.[2] Because Foster was a former WCTU leader, one of her chief tasks
was to persuade potential Prohibitionists that Republicans were a better choice.

In adjusting to new economic debates, Republicans drew on old themes of
domesticity. Under the tariff, one Republican argued, workingmen could keep
"their wives at home and their children at school." GOP speakers painted a

lurid picture of family life in Europe, where free trade supposedly drove women to humiliating forms of manual labor and even prostitution. Appealing to working-class men, Republicans warned them to "ask their wives" before voting Democratic: women knew that Republicans would "protect" them. On the tariff and other issues of the late 1880s, the GOP upped the ante on domesticity. They referred to themselves with increasing frequency and vehemence as "the party of the home."

By challenging Republicans on economic issues, however, Democrats diverted their opponents from the evangelical sources of domestic ideology. To be sure, a tariff that prevented prostitution was a force for moral good, preserving the family as the foundation of "American civilization." Campaign debates, however, were increasingly couched in terms of women's economic roles rather than their virtues as Christian mothers and wives. Disciples of "the gospel of St. Republican," as Susan B. Anthony had angrily called them, began to use more secular arguments to defend their party. In the years between 1886 and 1893, as the economy gradually sank into a depression, both parties focused their campaigns and platforms on men's and women's work, the prices of consumer goods, and Americans' standard of living. For Republicans the new arguments were clearly not as salient as Civil War issues had once been. Their old Union coalition was fragmenting, and until 1894 it appeared that Democrats were winning the new debates.

The Party of the Home

Republicans' first reaction to the Democratic onslaught was to intensify their appeals to old war loyalties. Historians have seen this as a cynical strategy of "waving the bloody shirt," which in part it was. But exhortations to remember the war surely resonated with thousands of Unionists who lived among disabled veterans and had lost neighbors and loved ones in the conflict. The party of Lincoln exerted a powerful pull on black Americans who remembered slavery. Furthermore, Republicans' defense of their war record centered on the home. They were trying to sustain their old claim as the party of domesticity.

Abolitionist women, ignored by party leaders in the 1850s, were now hailed as the moral vanguard who had urged men to take up a noble cause. Republican spokesmen extolled Harriet Beecher Stowe, author of *Uncle Tom's Cabin*, as a paragon of female political influence. Young Lincoln voters of 1860 were said to have listened as their mothers read aloud from the book. By the 1890s, historians wrote that "the mother's opinion was a potent educator in politics between 1852 and 1860. . . . The Republican Party attracted the great majority of the schoolboys." A suffragist attending a New York GOP rally reported that the speaker "recounted the debt of gratitude" that the party owed to abolitionist women. She observed that it was "not easy to give ear" when the same party had withheld woman suffrage.[3]

Women who had sacrificed sons and husbands for the Union received even more lavish praise. After watching a uniformed parade, a Republican editor in

New Hampshire recalled "those first regiments of '61 filing down Broadway, called out by the tocsin of a war into which we were betrayed by a Democratic administration. . . . I stood with mothers and wives and lovers who watched through proud tears to see their darlings go. What heart's life went out with those waving handkerchiefs, those wafted kisses, those upbreathings of silent prayer!" Ohio's "Fire Alarm" Joe Foraker, a Republican known for his heated rhetoric, paid tribute in a campaign speech to "the lonely wife with her hapless babe" who in wartime had "struggled to eke out subsistence." Foraker excoriated Grover Cleveland for fishing on Memorial Day, when the nation's women were placing flowers on the graves of Union dead.[4]

Such appeals peaked in disputes over Union pensions. In the 1880s a Republican-dominated Congress passed thousands of bills for individual pensions, most of which President Cleveland vetoed. GOP leaders took their case to the stump, describing distraught widows whom Republicans sought to rescue from the poorhouse, but whom the president had cast back into poverty. At a rally in Connecticut, Foraker told of a woman who had lost two sons on the battlefield and two more from war-related injuries. When he described Cleveland's veto of her $12-a-month pension, the audience cried "Shame, Shame!," and according to a Republican account, "many of the ladies present were moved to tears." Democrats ridiculed these "harrowing tales of the cruel veto" as mere fictions, invented by corrupt women who were angling for a handout. Foraker and his colleagues were indignant. An Indiana Republican retorted that "Grover Cleveland, a man who has ruined a score of women, is a nice man to question a woman's moral character."[5]

Benjamin Harrison, Republicans' presidential nominee in 1888, placed special emphasis on domestic rhetoric. Following the example set by James Garfield he ran a front-porch campaign from his Indiana home. Delegations included dozens of young women's campaign clubs from around the Midwest. No doubt concerned about the popularity of Frances Folsom Cleveland, Republican journalists stopped by to interview Carrie Harrison, who stood beside her husband and shook hands with thousands of visitors. "It is my pride," the candidate announced, "that the Republican Party has always been a promoter and protector of the home. By the Homestead Act it created half a million homes, and by the Emancipation it turned one half a million cattle pens into homes." In case readers missed the point, the *New York Press* carried news of this speech under the front-page headline, "Happy Homes of America."[6]

By the late 1880s, the most important application of Republican domesticity was on the tariff issue. The party's war accomplishments were beginning to fade, despite strenuous reminders from men like "Fire Alarm" Joe. Criticisms from Cleveland and congressional Democrats, who submitted a series of lower tariff bills, forced the GOP to shift ground and defend its economic policies. Republicans rejected Democrats' appeal for lower consumer prices, emphasizing instead the need for jobs. A five-cent reduction in the cost of salt had little value, they argued, to someone who was unemployed. It was better for everyone to pay a bit extra as consumers so all Americans could earn a decent wage.[7]

Republicans supported this proposition with folksy analogies to family life. "I am like the boy who hired his sister to make his shirts," wrote one tariff advocate. "Someone said: 'You could have taken those shirts to the factory and had them made and saved $2.' 'Yes,' said the boy protectionist, 'Sister Sally got a pretty good price. She always pays me well for what I do for her. That $2 bill is still under the same roof with me, and if sickness or trouble or hard luck comes to any of our family that money is there in the house.'" In the widely distributed *American Protectionist's Manual,* Giles Stebbins argued that "the nation is a great family." "Protection," he added, "cares for those of our own household."[8] The party of the Union was trying to maintain old links between national unity, security, and the home.

Like Democrats who directed their arguments at consumers, Republicans quickly translated their appeal to the real homes of working-class voters. "A strong force in this campaign is the wife of the workingman," declared a Republican editor in Indiana. "She goes to meetings and there hears discussions, and the first topic in her mind is, what effect would these proposed changes have on wages. . . . She has no vote but she has her influence. Consequently the Republicans are always glad to see ladies at their meetings."[9] In such appeals, Republicans recognized the new consumer interests identified by Democrats: women understood prices. The GOP, however, directed women's attention to wages, warning that free trade would lead to widespread unemployment among the industrial working class.

By referring to workingmen's wives as "ladies," editors indirectly suggested the benefits of the tariff for American women. Republican tariff appeals spoke broadly to fears about the consequences of industrial poverty. Following tradition, Republicans focused on upholding proper ideals of manhood and womanhood, but they now emphasized the dangers of poverty and prostitution. The *New York Press,* a leading high-tariff paper, argued that free trade would "deprive defenceless women of the means of honorable subsistence, and increase temptations that undermine the nation's moral welfare." Many Republicans predicted that low tariffs would lead to "women's degradation" and "fill the brothel." One argued that, under free trade, female operatives at a New Jersey sewing machine factory would find their jobs removed to Scotland; the headline read "Singer Women in Danger." For working-class women, economic danger was also moral danger. They, rather than men, served as the best gauge of the moral "protection" provided by tariffs. This is doubtless what one Republican intended to convey when he denounced tariff-reform doctrine as "the harlot of free trade."[10]

Republicans recognized that many wage-earning women had entered the paid labor force since the Civil War. More often, though, party leaders tied high tariffs to the place of American wives and mothers in the home. They argued, in effect, that the tariff allowed men to earn a family wage, though the term was not yet in use. On this basis, under the heading "Woman's Elevation," Stebbins appealed directly to women in *The American Protectionist's Manual.* "Every woman should be a protectionist," he wrote, "for free trade degrades her even more than it does man. . . . The larger pay of our factory workmen enables the mother to be in her home, where her children need her in their tender years. For girls, or married women who choose factory work, the pay is better, and a more self-respecting and womanly life possible." Stebbins described the benefits of tariffs as "the elevation of labor," "education," and the means for "comfort and taste" in working-class homes.[11]

Benjamin Harrison made similar points in a speech to recent Irish immigrants:

> Who, if not Irish-Americans, versed in the sad story of the commercial ruin of the island they love, should be instructed in the beneficent influence of a protective tariff . . . upon their individual and upon their home lives? [Applause.] Which of you has not realized that not the lot of man only, but the lot of woman has been made softer and easier under its influence? [Applause, and 'Hear, Hear,' and 'That's what's the matter.'] Contrast the American mother and wife, burdened only with the cares of motherhood and of the household, with the condition of women in many of the countries of the old world where she is loaded also with the drudgery of toil in the field. [Applause.] I know that none more than Irishmen, who are so characterized by their deference for women, and whose women have so finely illustrated that which is pure in female character—will value this illustration of the good effects of our American system upon the home life.[12]

The potential force of this argument was that it evoked domestic ideology in such a way that people of many classes and ethnic groups could embrace it. Harrison's listeners were recent immigrants and laborers. Many women in the audience probably worked for wages outside the home or took in boarders or laundry to make ends meet. They could subscribe, nonetheless, to the ideal of the maternal family: later in life or in the next generation, these women or their daughters could quit wage work and devote themselves wholly to their families.

Republican arguments may have held special attraction for recent immigrants because they drew direct comparisons with Europe. At root, GOP appeals were based on fear. They offered shocking descriptions of labor conditions in "free trade" countries, where women worked long hours for wages and did heavy farm labor. Tariff reduction, Republicans declared, "means that our wives and children shall go into the shop, the factory and the field and work with the men from early morn till late at night, as they do in every country of Europe." The *San Francisco Chronicle* published two illustrations: "the American workingman" and "the kind of unprotected labor the free trader wishes him to compete with." The latter was a peasant woman who had roped herself to a plow.[13]

In 1888 and 1892, Republicans issued reports on conditions in the industrial regions of "free trade England" as witnessed by American travelers. Most frequently reprinted was an account by Nathaniel McKay, billed as an "expert" industrial researcher. McKay expressed pity for the workers he met, "especially the women, the sound of whose hammering on the anvil, the clank of the chains at which they work, and the noise of the pit upon which they shovel and wheel coal, were still all too horrible to the ear of one accustomed to seeing the mothers, wives and sweethearts of his fellow-workmen comfortably housed and spared the terrible burdens which these unfortunates have to bear. . . . Where in our land of the free," McKay asked, "can we find mother and daughter—aye, and often granddaughter—toiling day after day for a lifetime, side by side, at the forge or on the coal pit?"[14]

McKay's illustrated reports focused almost entirely on women. He described a colliery worker in Wigan, England, "whose face was wrinkled and the features hardened. Her muscles stood out like an animal's. She stated that her name was Eliza Rider, 55 years old, and she has been wheeling coal for 40 years. . . . Asked about her clothing, she remarked that she wore trousers that were cast off by the men." Elsewhere McKay found a fourteen-year-old female chainmaker, "a young woman, an expert, at a man's trade, standing over an anvil wielding a hammer all day for $1.65 a week." She was among "scores of women and girls, who were engaged in chainmaking, a trade that belongs to men." One young woman, McKay reported, "blows the bellows herself and handles the tongs as a man would a piece of meat on a fork." In another pamphlet McKay described "women blacksmiths! Husband and wife stripped to the waist at the same forge."

Women's work in heavy industry implied not only usurpation of men's rightful place as breadwinners, including literally wearing the trousers, but also promiscuity and irregular family life. One English smithy "was only 21, but a mother, and had her forge in the same building in which she lived. In the same room were five other women working at forges." Some had six or eight children and now, pregnant again, were working fifteen-hour shifts. One mother spent "nearly all her time in the shop for 2s and 10½d a week, with the evident result that, at least, all she may earn is lost by defective housewifery and neglect of family." Lest readers miss McKay's message, editors supplemented his account with pointed questions. "Do we want to try any experiments by adopting England's free trade ideas?" warned one. "Let good enough alone." "DO WE WANT THIS IN AMERICA?" demanded the *Los Angeles Times*.

The causes of European industrial poverty were obviously more complex than Republicans admitted, just as lower tariffs were not the panacea Democrats claimed. Forced to cope with an increasingly complex economy—whose condition was deteriorating fast—both parties found it difficult to invent solutions to the problems of urban industrialization. Over the next decade their ideas would look increasingly simplistic; some reformers, already impatient with the GOP, had moved to a free trade stance and in time would become disillusioned with even this proposed reform. Philadelphia's most famous pro-tariff legislator, William D. "Pig Iron" Kelley, admitted privately by the 1880s that Republican tariffs were not preventing the rise of industrial poverty in the United States.[15]

Republican tariff arguments were significant, not as an answer to the nation's industrial ills, but as the strategic response of a once-dominant party struggling to regain control. Though Union victory had carried religious force, the evangelical agenda of the 1880s was not as broadly popular. Anti-liquor

and anti-Catholic sentiment ran strong among some Protestants, but these issues could not help Republicans build a broad coalition. Thus while evangelicals remained a core constituency of the GOP, their presence was a mixed blessing. In tight elections, Republicans had to win votes from men who were
suspicious of evangelical goals. At the same time they faced a Prohibitionist
threat and had to reassure potential defectors that the GOP would do something about the liquor traffic. Promises had to be vague, though, or other voters
would choose the Democrats.[16]

The result in 1888 was a national Republican plank stating that "the concern of all good government is the virtue and sobriety of the people and the purity of the home. The Republican Party cordially sympathizes with all wise and
well-directed efforts for the production of temperance."[17] This was hardly satis-
fying in light of Prohibitionists' forthright call for anti-liquor legislation. In
addition, Republicans focused vastly more time and attention on the tariff than
they did on liquor. In a two-party system, Republicans chose to build the
broadest possible coalition. In doing so, they moved away from the evangelical
origins of their ideology to focus on economic questions. The defense of high
tariffs was a hybrid result: an economic policy defended in moral terms, on the
basis of old Republican appeals to the sanctity of the home.

Democrats, by forcing Republicans to adapt their domestic arguments to
new issues, had forced a shift in the foundations of that ideology. Economics
was now key; if female morality was at stake, it was due to international market
conditions rather than domestic sin. Republicans still advocated a stronger centralized government than did their opponents. Uncontrolled Democratic manhood was, however, no longer the chief threat to proper family relations. Republicans were relying on industrial experts to make their moral case. Tariff
debates were gradually altering campaign rhetoric, replacing the language of
evangelicalism with that of economics.

Democrats had taken the lead in this transition; Republicans' arguments
were a defensive response, in which they tried to sustain old domestic themes.
If the GOP could not occupy moral high ground it was going to be seriously at
a loss, because the party had always based its program on a vision of evangelical
domesticity, supported and enforced by benevolent extensions of government
power. This perhaps explains the increasing stridency of Republican warnings
about the danger Democrats posed to the home. Denouncing the "harlot of free
trade," Republicans were desperately trying to affirm their moral superiority.

Women in Defense of the GOP

Despite widely publicized claims that wives were influencing their husbands to
vote Democratic, many American women agreed with Republican leaders that
the tariff protected women. In Nebraska, members of a young women's Republican glee club wore "protection caps." In New York City, wealthy suffragist
Emma Beckwith announced that she was seeking a man to vote as her substitute. She would pay him well, but "he must not be a Democrat or Prohibi-

tionist, because she believes in protection." At Vassar College, a Republican student placed signs in her window promoting "American Wages for the American Laborer" and "Protection." A Democratic student responded with the slogans "For Baby Ruth" and "Democratic Tariff—Taxation for PUBLIC Purposes ONLY." Even Belva Lockwood, presidential candidate on the Equal Rights ticket, weighed in. Her platform called not only for women's rights but for "a moderate tariff." In a classic compromise, she explained that her policy would be less onerous to consumers than Republicans' expensive duties, but safer than Democratic "free trade."[18]

In keeping with tradition—and with Democrats' push to capture the region's loyalty—midwestern Republican women were most vocal in demonstrating their tariff views. In Indiana, one women's Harrison and Morton Club rode in a parade with a sign reading, "Father, protect your daughters by your vote." The wagon behind them carried "about 15 children with a banner, 'Protection to American labor is protection to our children.'" The Indianapolis Young Ladies' Harrison Club presented Irish-American workers with a green banner that sported a gold shamrock and "the American word, Protection!" Young Michigan women displayed a similar banner: "We work in mills and factories. The owners are protected. Protect us." Women in a Chicago Republican parade dressed one wagon with "turkeys, chickens, crackers, bread, oysters," and other foods, labeled "Protection Meal." A second wagon carried only "a bean pot and a tough looking piece of hide," designated "A Free Trade Dinner."[19]

Appearing as far west as the Great Plains, where families from the Midwest had settled over the previous two decades, Republican women's campaign clubs joined the old mass-based rituals. One Nebraska rally featured "the shooting of Roman candles by the Humboldt Ladies' Harrison Club." In Chicago, a contingent of black women marched in the GOP's largest parade. Competition was fiercest in Indiana; by a conservative estimate, at least 20,000 women joined partisan clubs there during 1888. Several Indiana towns featured pole raisings by women's Republican clubs. One woman hosted a pole raising in her yard for friends and party supporters. Elsewhere, a local editor proudly noted that Republican ladies had raised a fifty-three-foot pole "without the aid of any men."[20]

Watching the success of Democrats' Frankie Cleveland groups, young Republican women countered by forming Carrie Harrison clubs. They participated in old traditions but also adopted more domestic, educational tactics; like young men in the Northeast, they slowly began to stress reasoned debate over parades and fireworks. Carrie Harrison clubs in Indiana declared their intention to "distribute Republican campaign literature, influence voters, and study Republican principles." They promised to discuss the campaign with "lovers, brothers, and acquaintances." Mary Knout, reporting from Indiana, described the Carrie Harrison clubs as "efficient" and added that "those who have been about the State tell me that the influence of these women cannot be overestimated."[21]

Knout cited temperance activities during the early 1880s as the source of Republican women's increasing public confidence. She thought it natural that women would use their new skills in the service of Republicans, who argued that the tariff took precedence over Prohibition. On the other hand, some Prohibitionist women were former abolitionists who had appeared in Republican campaigns before the Civil War. In the 1880s, a large percentage of Republican women probably embraced both senses of the term "protection" and were broadly sympathetic to the temperance cause. Many, however, saw their first duty as helping to defeat Democrats, the party of former rebels and "free trade."

Unwilling to grant suffrage, Republican leaders nonetheless capitalized on women's loyalty. Benjamin Harrison's campaign manager, James S. Clarkson, was a careful observer of political trends. Years later he recalled his surprise in the 1880s "when the brass band, the red light, and the mass meeting seemed suddenly to have lost their power." Clarkson announced in 1892 that "the woman has appeared in American politics and the home has become the unit of American politics. Conservative people may scoff at it, old-fashioned men may deride it, but the power of the home is going to be more and more potential in American affairs." Clarkson hoped his party could turn women's political work to their own advantage.[22]

A native of Iowa, Clarkson had watched the WCTU mobilize successfully for a statewide anti-liquor referendum. Iowa was one state where the Republican Party took an unequivocal prohibition stance; thus WCTU leaders like J. Ellen Foster remained loyal and refused to join Willard in endorsing third-party action. Clarkson was aware of Foster's formidable talents. He followed disputes within the WCTU and apparently advised Foster during the years when she split with Willard and formed the Non-Partisan WCTU. On all sides, the press regarded Foster as a representative of "Republican campaign leaders." Clarkson may have been responsible for securing Foster's husband a post as assistant secretary of the National Tariff League. As a hostile editor observed, Ellen Foster's record as a nonpartisan was "peculiar."[23]

Clarkson apparently paid for his female ally to travel abroad and observe women's partisan organizations. After her bitter break with Willard, Foster toured Britain and Ireland to observe the Conservative Party's Primrose League. As an Irish American she was ambivalent toward Conservative aims, and she sent reports to the *Boston Journal* in which she condemned British oppression of Ireland. She must have been impressed, however, with the Primrose League's organizing skills and sponsorship of mass rallies and entertainment. Only four years old, the League claimed 1,700 local chapters and over 560,000 members by the time Foster visited.[24] She came home ready to begin some partisan work of her own.

In 1888 Foster and Clarkson announced formation of the National Women's Republican Association, led by Foster with Clarkson securing funds. Though accounts have not survived, it appears the Republican National Committee offered generous support. John D. Rockefeller, a wealthy industrialist and leading pro-temperance Republican, was already providing the Non-Partisan WCTU with almost half its operating expenses. Now the GOP provided much more substantial aid for the women's association. By 1892, the NWRA's paid staff included Foster, a secretary, a publicity director, and 300 field workers. Republican leaders apparently covered all expenses, including travel funds and elegant headquarters in New York.[25]

Foster declared her new purpose was "to lead women to think and act sanely on political issues with the unanimity and enthusiasm that they had shown for party prohibition." Her main argument against the Prohibition Party was the same used by Republican suffragists like Susan B. Anthony: it could never win national power. Foster claimed that male Prohibitionists wasted women's time, placing them "on meaningless committees and tickets impossible of success." "There is no grace in defeat," she observed. "The result of an election is an aggregate result. . . . Politics deal with the masses, reforms deal with the individuals. As a reformer I am a Prohibitionist; but as a Republican I am the best I can get."[26]

Foster was not blind to the GOP's weaknesses, but she believed they were the inevitable result of broad coalition building. Like former abolitionists, she looked back to Republicans' hesitant statements on slavery in the late 1850s and Emancipation only a few years later; she hoped for similar progress toward the prohibitionist goal. "Abraham Lincoln," she observed astutely, "was no more heroic on the slavery question than Harrison is on the temperance question. . . . Some people," she added, "say we shouldn't train with the Republicans, because some of them drink or sell liquor, or break the law, but they are going to gain the points that we want, and hence we go with them. All the men in the war were not saints, and the sinners shot just as well as the saints." On another occasion, Foster estimated that "of those male voters who favor prohibition, no more than five percent are in the 'third party' and ninety-five percent are in the Republican Party and the better element of the Democrat[s]."[27]

Foster charted a tricky course in 1888. As president of the NWRA, she announced that "we are straight out-and-out Republicans and stand on the Republican platform." She advertised that she had attended the GOP national convention and had helped write the plank expressing sympathy for the temperance cause. At the same time she issued "nonpartisan" press releases as leader of the Non-Partisan WCTU. Of Willard's WCTU she wrote, "they have deliberately chosen to become a wing of one political party," as if she herself had not done the same. Opponents were not fooled. The *Lynchburg Virginian* howled in protest when Foster issued a statement on tariff protection. "It is very evident that she isn't promoting the cause of temperance," wrote the editor. In taking a "partisan attitude" she was, "to use plain English, meddling with a matter with which she had no business."[28]

Putting the best face on the controversy, Frances Willard cheerfully appraised the NWRA as another example of third-party effectiveness, noting it was "the first time that women had ever been recognized as helpers by either of the great parties." She attributed this to "the attitude of the Prohibition Party, which had from the first recognized women as integral forces in its organization."[29] Willard was almost certainly right about her party's influence on the GOP. The national campaign of 1884 had been a disaster for Republicans, partly because of Prohibition votes. They needed a way to win back these voters without adopting a full anti-liquor plank that would alienate other voters and result in a net loss. Women's leadership and grassroots work in Prohibition ranks were evident to Clarkson and other Republican men. Delegates' enthusiastic ovation to Foster at the GOP convention, and the funds allotted by the party for her work, were a result of these political considerations.

If Foster's intent was to capture the GOP for the anti-liquor cause, she was quickly diverted. Her early statements stressed the futility of voting the Prohibition ticket, and she published supportive letters from members of the WCTU. By October 1888, a speech she delivered in Rhode Island gave insights into the conflicting pressures she faced. She emphasized the importance of the tariff, perhaps addressing her own inner doubts: "third party people have a way of sneering at the tariff question, and it is unworthy of the dignity of an American citizen to talk that way." She then tacked in a wholly different direction: "men should vote for prohibition first, last and always. . . . Because I believe this, I want you to vote the Republican ticket."[30] Like Republican suffragists, Foster preferred to cast her lot with the most palatable party in power and wait for it to take up the issue closest to her heart.

This waiting strategy was perilous because prohibition could and would get shunted aside, year after year. In the meantime, the exigencies of campaigns forced Foster to address another issue. The Prohibition Party was beginning to fade; at the national level, Republicans faced a far greater threat from Democrats, and thus Foster's leverage on the liquor question grew weaker every year. If prohibition remained her private priority, she did not achieve it through the GOP. Within a few months of becoming NWRA president she began to devote most of her time and energy to the tariff issue. Meanwhile, in her capacity as leader of the Non-Partisan WCTU, she rejected calls for woman suffrage agitation, predicting that "calamity . . . will overtake our temperance motor in loading it down with other reforms."[31] Within the much larger engine of the Republican Party, Foster's temperance motor ground to a halt.

The alternatives must have looked worse: she could join a third party that would never hold a congressional majority, or she could try to win votes from deeply partisan legislators while maintaining an aloof, nonpartisan stance. Willard's strategy was failing, and Foster's experience must have persuaded her that nonpartisanship was virtually impossible. In the late 1880s and early 1890s, Susan B. Anthony's suffrage strategy paralleled Foster's for prohibition. Around the time of the NWRA's formation, Anthony issued yet another call for women to back the Republicans. Foster, who declined to work for suffrage herself, proudly advertised this advice.[32]

Rather than promoting parades and fireworks, the National Women's Republican Association copied the educational campaign style pioneered by young men in the Northeast. From New York City, Foster and her staff directed

women to form local clubs that would "study, discuss, and circulate party literature." They distributed a series of pamphlets called "The Home and the
Flag," addressing campaign issues from a Republican perspective. These were
cleverly tied to a previously published, nonpartisan series on government and
history called "The Home and the Flag Reading Course," which the association
recommended. Endorsing civic education, Foster offered prizes for "the best essays written by women on government topics." Criticizing Prohibitionists indirectly, one association leader instructed women, "I don't want you to stand
near the polls and peddle votes, but I want you to think, read, and influence the
husband, brother, or sweetheart." In a measure of Republican desperation, she
added: "if there isn't a sweetheart, get one until after the election."[33]

NWRA leaders built arguments similar to those of Republican men, with
perhaps even greater emphasis on domesticity. They appealed to war loyalties,
reminding voters which party had ended slavery and preserved the Union. Denouncing Grover Cleveland's pension vetoes, association publicist Edith Ses-
sions Tupper issued this appeal to Union mothers and wives:

> All over this vast country . . . there are homes in which the most sacred
> memories cluster around a faded red sash twisted over a picture, a battered
> sword, or perhaps an old blue coat laid away in the drawer in the spareroom. I
> know how you steal away by yourself and take out that coat and moisten it
> with your tears. I know how you reverently handle the faded sash and remem-
> ber how bright and brave he looked when he came home on his last furlough.
> Never forget the action of the man who refused to sanction the poor little
> pension. . . . Perhaps there is a son or brother left. Plead with him not to
> vote for the man who danced on the Union grave of your loved dead.[34]

Tupper's invocation of the bloody coat, addressed intimately to women's grief,
surely moved her audience as effectively as any speech by "Fire Alarm" Joe.

On the tariff issue, the Women's Republican Association also appealed to
women's special interests. Foster said that Republicans viewed the nation itself
as "one large family," and she repeated Nathaniel McKay's arguments almost
verbatim. "Because labor is degraded in foreign countries the women are degraded," she declared before a mixed audience. "God forbid that the women of
our country should be forced down as they are in foreign countries." Republican newspapers reprinted a letter from Mary Treadwell, an NWRA member in
New York, making the same point. "When our country introduces free trade,
women, too, must come down on a level with the women of Europe, and their
state is truly deplorable." Treadwell argued that she was a strong prohibitionist, but that women must not desert the GOP in "this hour of peril." She compared the tariff issue to Fort Sumter, and expressed hope that the party would
find a new Lincoln to lead the way.[35]

In September 1888, Foster organized a delegation of working women who
attended U.S. Senate hearings and requested maintenance of high tariffs to protect American jobs. Presenting these women to the Senate Finance Committee,
Foster noted that "although one-third of the wage-earners in America are
women, they have not been considered in the current discussion of the tariff

problem." Edith Tupper described tariff benefits to working families in the most concrete terms. Republican protection, she argued, was "why your homes can have a Brussels carpet, an organ, and pictures on the wall; why Janie can take music lessons and you can have a fine black silk for Sunday wear. Make John vote this fall."[36]

Foster and her co-workers appealed both to wage-earning women and to women as consumers, apparently copying Democrats' approach. The association published several fictional pieces about Dorothy, a young woman who came to support the tariff through her shopping adventures. Purchasing lace curtains for her apartment and china cups as a wedding gift, Dorothy learned about the china and lace tariffs. At first she complained of the cost of imported goods, but a kindly shopkeeper told her about the conditions of laboring families abroad. Dorothy responded by purchasing products made in the United States, where workingmen and women benefited from Republican protection. "It had never occurred to me that that tariff had anything to do with us girls," said Dorothy, but she decided it would be "a wicked thing if Grover Cleveland should be elected."[37]

Dorothy represented a new type: a young wage-earning woman, possibly a clerk or secretary, who lived in her own apartment and spent her own income. The number of Dorothys in America was growing, along with the consumer clout of wives and daughters who worked in a family economy. Like Democrats who appealed to "shopping women," Republicans clearly worried about the connections between women's economic choices and their political sentiments. The GOP was fighting uphill. They had to persuade women to pay more for consumer goods, by claiming that the extra cost went to working-class families to prevent misery and moral degradation. Democrats objected that tariff revenues went into industrialists' pockets; American workers did not earn more than Europeans, but through the tariff they were enriching manufacturers.

Republicans were, in a limited way, trying to bridge class and regional gaps that were undermining their coalition. As part of this strategy, the NWRA was an effort by middle-class women to appeal to women across class lines. Foster and her colleagues could point proudly to Republicans' 1888 platform, which for the first time endorsed "equal pay for equal work." The strategy seems to have been effective in the Northeast, especially among women in the textile industry. During the late 1880s, thousands of women in Rhode Island, Massachusetts, and Pennsylvania signed petitions to Congress, urging the continuation of high tariffs. Employers probably arranged for collection of these signatures, but public opinion seems to have concurred: areas with major textile operations stayed firmly in the Republican column. Large numbers of both men and women in the northeastern working class seem to have concluded that they benefited from Republican rule.[38]

The Midwest proved more difficult for Republicans to hold. Here, Foster and Clarkson faced class-based partisan divisions much deeper than in the northeastern textile states, and the class limits of the NWRA were more visible. Foster's organizing model was similar to that of young "gentlemen's" campaign clubs in the Northeast, and drew also upon the legacy of middle-class women's benevolent reform groups. The association urged reading and discussion in the home, not pole raisings or marching in the rain as young midwestern women were doing for both major parties.

Refined, domestic Republican women's clubs paralleled in both substance and timing the growth of nonpartisan women's clubs: both proliferated in the 1890s, and both attracted affluent native-born ladies with leisure time for public service and intellectual pursuits. Both adopted similar approaches to political discussion. The founding dates of a number of nonpartisan Current Events Clubs coincided with the elections of 1892 and 1896. A woman's club in North Dakota reported that "it was the heat of political discussion that first stimulated the women of Langdon to form a class for the study of the tariff, the currency question, and the U.S. Constitution." Meanwhile, Republican clubs were urging women to undertake civic education through the *Home and Flag* reading course. In New York City, the Women's West End Republican Association debated "what is the function of government?" and "what are the essentials in an elementary education?" Toward the turn of the century, Republican and nonpartisan women's clubs both engaged in the "scientific" discussion of public questions.[39]

In the electoral sphere, then, and especially in class terms, Republican women occupied a conservative space in relation to third-party movements. Foster's association reaffirmed the old evangelical model of women's indirect influence on men, with a new recognition of women's roles as consumers and wage-earners. Women should not "peddle votes," they argued, nor demand suffrage or power within the party. Republicans remained more open to women's participation than did Democrats; the restrictions of the Republican model were evident, however, when compared with Prohibitionists. By the early 1890s, Populism would also give women opportunities for party decision making and suffrage advocacy. At the national level, temperance and suffrage leaders like Willard, Anthony, and Stanton were beginning to recognize an emerging irony. They could work for winning parties that offered them no direct power, or they could work for third parties that recognized women as delegates and endorsed temperance or suffrage planks, but could not win.

The class limitations of the NWRA reflected not only its leaders' background but also the fundamental conservatism of Republican policy goals. Despite Foster's declaration that the GOP was "liberal," "progressive," and "moral," the party was no longer taking up new reform issues. Appeals to Union and Emancipation were more than two decades old, and the argument for high tariffs was a defense of the status quo. When Republicans warned of the degraded condition of overseas labor, they implied that no such conditions existed where tariff protection was in place. For GOP publicist Edith Tupper, the main problem for working-class Americans was the cost of Janie's music lessons, or whether the family could replace its Brussels carpet. Republican economic appeals were self-satisfied and optimistic; before 1893, they refused to admit that anything in America was wrong.

"Domestic protection" served several functions for the party. It enabled Republicans to reassert their old ideal of the maternal family, now threatened by economic conditions rather than the sins of Democratic men. As Giles Stebbins argued, the tariff preserved "the nation as a great family," offering a nationalist vision to oppose Democrats' emphasis on states' rights and limited federal power. Most important, Republicans sought to preserve their old wartime coalition outside the South. The party's need to hold working-class voters was especially urgent because the GOP had abandoned its southern black allies and no longer had much chance of regaining power in southern states. Warnings about the degradation of European women and the moral perils of a low tariff aimed to cross class lines. Republicans hoped that their middle-class and working-class supporters shared a commitment to the maternal family and women's place in the home, and that they would support the tariff on these grounds.

Growing industrial unrest exposed the class and regional limitations of this appeal, and suggests why Republicans had difficulty sustaining power between 1884 and 1893. In 1886, 50,000 coal workers in southwestern Pennsylvania clashed with employers in a bitter strike; thousands of railroad workers also struck for better pay. The Knights of Labor and the growing American Federation of Labor led factory walkouts in Milwaukee, Cincinnati, Chicago, and New York, calling for an eight-hour day to reduce unemployment. As the economy spiraled downward, employers began to make drastic wage cuts. Andrew Carnegie responded to protests at his steelworks in Homestead, Pennsylvania, by hiring a small private army; sixteen died in the resulting battle. Agricultural depression struck in the South and West, and thousands of farmers faced foreclosure and starvation.[40] Under such conditions, few families worried about buying a piano. Republicans' self-congratulation over the benefits of the tariff rang hollow to poor women and men.

Some Republicans tacitly recognized that this was the case; while defending the tariff as crucial for American prosperity, party leaders began tentatively to seek additional solutions. In doing so, they continued to stress "protection" as the chief object of government policy, and they focused on women as the workers who faced the greatest moral peril. During the 1888 campaign, the *New York Press* published reports from the Working Women's Protective Union, a nonpartisan women's organization. Florence Ives documented cases of wage-earning women whose employers had cheated them of their pay, and she reported that the Union was recruiting lawyers to take up these cases. The *Press* ran Ives's call for "women's protection" side-by-side with appeals for "tariff protection" to preserve the American home. Meanwhile, the Woman's Industrial League of Washington, D.C., published a campaign issue of their magazine, *Working Woman*, "devoted especially to the interests of protection"—that is, endorsing high tariffs.[41]

Republicans' defense of the tariff, then, was part of an emerging debate over industrial poverty. Faced with the exigencies of the Civil War, Republicans had used federal power to preserve the "family of States" and end slavery, turning "half a million cattle pens into homes." In the postwar era their chief federal accomplishment was the tariff, which Democratic attacks forced them to defend in both economic and moral terms. After 1900, GOP leaders would adapt the same rhetoric, justifying new projects based on "protection" of American women. The tariff, more than any other Gilded Age policy, provided the framework for Progressive Era extensions of federal power.

These extensions did not happen, however, in the fiercely competitive political climate of the 1880s and 1890s. Middle-class women's advocacy on behalf of wage-earning women, as in the Industrial League and Working Women's Protective Union, did not yet translate into limitations on the hours of working women, mothers' pensions for poor widows, or other policies to "protect" women of the working class. Such possibilities were only marginal considerations in electoral battles between Democrats and Republicans on the tariff issue. Before Republicans were willing to move beyond the tariff and advocate new forms of labor protection, they would need to recapture firm control of Congress and the White House. In the meantime, a new third party would make more radical proposals for transforming government, and partisan campaigns would produce a realignment in the ideal political roles of women and men.

5

Populism

It used to be very effective to say, "What is home without a mother?" But now the burning question is, "What is mother without a home?"
—*Colorado Populist Julia Catlin*

Debates over economics revealed deep political fissures among Americans, who began to weigh old Civil War loyalties against pressing bread-and-butter concerns. By 1890 their arguments became more urgent as the economy worsened, especially in rural areas. Regional political structures shaped these intensified debates. In the Northeast and Midwest, a strong two-party system managed to contain the disputes, with Republicans holding their lead in New England and Democrats tending to benefit elsewhere. In the South and the trans-Mississippi West, two-party politics was not so strong. In these regions a coalition of farmers, labor unionists, and advocates of silver currency created a new party, proposing new federal interventions in the economy.

Some aspects of Populist platforms resembled those of reform Democrats. Both blamed poverty on high tariffs, monopolies, and the short-sighted greed of eastern financiers. Populism never gained ground in the Midwest because in a sense it was already there: Democrats in those states, pressured by close party competition, adopted certain hallmark Populist themes several years before the new party appeared. But in states where the old minority party was weak and discredited—as Republicans were in the South, and Democrats were in Kansas and Nebraska—voters sought a third party to make the same transition. Freer from old structures, the People's Party proposed more radical solutions to the nation's industrial ills.[1]

The Populists themselves faced internal regional divisions, revealed with clarity in their debates over the political roles of women and men. In the South, most white Populists were former Democrats. Even those who were not, including black Populists who had once been Republicans, faced a more conservative social and political climate than did Populists farther West. Southern Democrats, who dominated every state government except North Carolina's, still urged voters to defend the patriarchal household from intrusions by federal authority. In keeping with this tradition, southern white women were unaccustomed to organizing partisan clubs, speaking from the stump, or canvassing voters. This was true even of the region's WCTU members, who seldom worked publicly for the Prohibition Party. Southern Populists were innovators for their region, but limited by longstanding conservatism on issues of gender.

Populists in the Plains and Mountain states spoke to voters who were, by large majorities, former Republicans. Much more than their southern allies, western Populists drew on Republican precedents to explain America's economic problems in domestic moral terms. Many identified themselves broadly as reformers. Their newspapers denounced child labor and expressed solidarity with striking workers; they exhorted against the liquor threat; and they raised other questions of social and economic justice. A key measure of western Populists' willingness to innovate was their acceptance of women in positions of power. Populist women served on key committees, joined convention debates, and ran for office. Southern Populists—with the help of some conservative westerners—blocked the national party from endorsing woman suffrage, but when Colorado and Idaho Populists captured their legislatures, women won the vote in those states.

Populists fused an evangelical political impulse, inherited from Republicans and Prohibitionists, with Democrats' traditional concern for the plight of labor. The result was an unprecedented vision of an activist American state. The GOP had abandoned its most ambitious projects with the end of Reconstruction, and Prohibitionists called only for anti-liquor legislation. Populists proposed much more sweeping measures. They weighed farm foreclosures and industrial poverty against capitalists' vast new accumulations of wealth, and they demanded federal action to mitigate these inequalities. Their platforms called for an aggressive monetary policy to benefit the working poor, a national progressive income tax, government aid to farmers, and public ownership of telegraphs and railroads.

The People's Party never closed the gap between farmers and urban laborers, and it never won the latter's support at the polls. Nor could former Democrats and Republicans, southerners and westerners agree fully on what needed to be done. The diverging experiences of rural and urban, middle- and working-class Americans had weakened the major parties, giving Populists their chance to organize; the same divisions prevented their success. Central to their dilemma was the old issue of domesticity. How should government protect the home, and what part should women play in campaigns to win that protection?

Populist Domesticity

Decades before Populism, agricultural societies like the Grange had built a tradition of civic cooperation among rural men and women that later extended to partisan politics. The Grange, formally known as the Patrons of Husbandry, reached peak popularity in the 1870s. Some local Granges founded cooperative stores; most organized social events for farm families. Picnics, basket dinners, and Fourth of July celebrations brought rural people together for companionship and fun. Local Granges also appointed lecturers after the style of town lyceums. These men and women organized educational readings, literary debates, and talks on "home questions."[2]

Grange membership faded after 1880, but in parts of the country the order gave way to the new and energetic Farmers' Alliance. From its unassuming start in Lampasas County, Texas, the Alliance spread across the South and Plains, incorporating the Agricultural Wheel of Arkansas and other local associations. The Farmers' Alliance cooperated with a segregated black Alliance in the South, but otherwise its membership mirrored that of the Grange: white Protestant farmers, some of them landowners, many renters and sharecroppers. Despite political grievances, leaders of the order chose at first not to form a third party, but instead pressured Democrats and Republicans on farm issues. The Alliance's first concern was economic self-help.[3]

A massive depression pushed the Alliance into partisan action. Though industry did not feel the full impact of depression until 1893, the shock to agriculture came several years earlier. In 1888 a major drought hit the Plains. Encouraged by Republicans' generous Homestead Act and five years of plentiful rain, farmers had settled marginal areas; now crops failed. The bust precipitated migrations back east and improverished those who stayed behind. A comparable crisis hit the South. In 1890, cotton prices reached their lowest level in thirty years; thousands of indebted farmers faced bankruptcy or hopeless debt. Alliance members in Kansas and Nebraska turned to third-party politics more quickly than southerners did, but by 1892 all joined forces in the People's Party.[4]

The new party included not only farmers but also labor unionists, and its leaders tried to construct a broad-based coalition of urban workers, miners, and other "producers." In 1889 the Alliance merged officially with the Knights of Labor, incorporating leaders of local Workingmen's parties. Many former Greenbackers also joined the movement. Like Grange and Alliance members, trade unionists who became Populists included female members and organizers. The Knights, for example, hired women as paid lecturers and organized domestic workers and housewives into union locals. Women voted at Knights meetings, and leaders of the movement encouraged temperance and domesticity for men.[5]

Populists added to their coalition an assortment of middle-class reformers concerned about the plight of labor. The tiny Socialist Party was led by recent immigrants from Germany, who in most places ignored or denounced the People's Party, but reformers who identified themselves more loosely as "Christian Socialists" became interested in the Populist cause. They included many members of Nationalist clubs, based on Edward Bellamy's influential 1888 novel *Looking Backward*, which described a government-supervised utopia. Western reformers and a handful of northeasterners hoped Populism would be the new party they had sought since Reconstruction. Third-party agitation would force a realignment and lead to new federal initiatives for economic justice, prohibition of liquor, and women's rights.[6]

Notwithstanding the Republican backgrounds of most western Populists, several of the party's most prominent authors were influenced by midwestern Democrats' arguments for lower tariffs. In *The Protective Tariff Delusion* (1886), former Democrat and Greenbacker Marion Todd of Michigan denounced high tariffs as detrimental to consumers. For Populists, however, the tariff was a secondary issue. Todd herself discarded it after 1890, when she joined the new party and began to focus on problems of currency and corporate monopoly. Sarah Van De Vort Emery, also from Michigan, ignored the tariff question from the start. Her politics drew less on Democratic ideas than on those of the Greenbackers, whom she supported in 1887 when she first published her famous tract, *Seven Financial Conspiracies Which Have Enslaved the American People*.[7]

Like Greenbackers, Populists believed that Republicans' printing of paper money to finance the war, followed by return to the gold standard, had contracted America's currency and caused widespread poverty and unemployment. Republicans argued that currency should find its "natural" level by the laws of the market, but Populists saw nothing natural about tying the number of greenbacks to the gold supply. Authors like Todd and Emery recommended not only currency expansion but also other remedies far more innovative than tariff reduction, including direct aid to farmers and government ownership of transportation networks. Unlike Democrats, who wanted less taxation, Populists called for replacing tariff revenues with new funds "derived from a graduated income tax." Their fiscal policies would require the rich to help the poor.[8]

Like Republicans and Prohibitionists before them, western Populists described their cause as God's work, announcing, "we vote as we pray." Christian imagery pervaded party rhetoric. In the Kansas campaign of 1890, which observers described as a "revival," one speaker announced that "Christ himself was the author and President of the first Farmers' Alliance." Southern Populists also used Christian imagery, but they had fewer precedents for using evangelicalism to justify expansions of federal power. Instead, they tended to rely more on Democrats' old language of centralized sexual corruption. One South Carolina Populist charged that Grover Cleveland's party was but "a prostitution of the principles of the Democracy." A Texan denounced his state's Democrats by comparing their "debauchery of the ballot" to other "social crimes" that destroyed "purity."[9] The result of Populists' multiple antecedents was a blending of moral vocabularies—sometimes powerful, often contradictory. Depending on the region and context, Populists drew upon both Republican domestic ideology and Democratic warnings about the sexual corruption of those who held power.

Western Populists used abolitionism as a precedent for their own cause. Sarah Emery analyzed what she called the "chattel mortgage system"; pamphleteer Mary Hobart called for "emancipation" from the "bondage of class legislation." Reverend S. J. Brownson, editor of a Populist newspaper, argued at a rally that "we are now in the dark night of slavery. . . . Sixty millions are in absolute slavery today, but the Alliance will emancipate them." Party newspapers printed cartoons of laboring men bound in chain gangs, led and owned by eastern financiers. Populists also linked the sufferings of "wage slaves" with the martyrdom of Christ. When presidential candidate William Jennings Bryan declared in 1896, "you shall not press down upon the brow of labor this crown of thorns, you shall not crucify mankind upon a cross of gold," he echoed a longstanding Populist theme of male victimization.[10]

Even more than the predicament of farming and wage-earning men, Populists emphasized the moral perils faced by poor women. Every major Populist writer and speaker touched on the issue of prostitution. They returned to it frequently as the fundamental moral consequence of bad policy—as did pro-tariff Republicans, who claimed it was a European problem, not an American one. Describing the rapacity of rich employers, Populists drew on Democrats' old denunciations of centralized wealth as a cause of sexual corruption. At the same time, they evoked Republican domesticity to argue for federal aid. One of the Populists' most famous orators, Mary Lease of Kansas, deplored the state of affairs when "over 100,000 shop-girls in New York are forced to sell their virtue for the bread their niggardly wages deny them." Marion Todd recounted the plight of "the victimized Rachels of a debauched government." A Populist editor in Georgia offered this picture to readers: "A cold winter day. A millionaire by his fireside surrounded with all the comforts of home. . . . Then a thousand poor laborers shivering in the cold. . . . Their older daughters selling their virtue for bread."[11]

The implications of this argument led in several directions, reflecting Populism's internal tensions. Attacks on the sexual corruption of wealthy "plutocrats" could have the racial overtones of Democratic calls for white women's protection. In Ignatius Donnelly's futuristic novel *Caesar's Column*, promoted in party newspapers, an evil dark-skinned plutocrat buys a young woman for $5,000; the heroine and the hero who preserves her virtue are both overtly Germanic. For Donnelly, a former Greenbacker who drafted portions of Populists' 1892 platform, the threat of white women's degradation was racial as well as sexual. Other Populists stressed poverty as the source of sexual corruption without reference to race. In *Seven Financial Conspiracies*, Sarah Emery argued that the "bread and butter question" was "the shackle that binds innocence to guilt and drags virtue from its highest pedestal to wallow in the slums of vice. . . . The poor girl does not need pity. She needs money." Marion Todd asked, "How many women fall, do you think, dear reader, because of starvation wages?" She argued that when the price of wheat rises, "down goes virtue."[12]

At its most innovative, this argument led Populists to express solidarity with prostitutes. Republicans had described women's degradation as a foreign evil prevented in America by the tariff; Populists, who saw an immediate crisis, described ordinary neighbors who faced a choice of prostitution or starvation. "Would it not be well to ponder [the] pathetic story of fallen women?" asked an editorial in the Kansas journal *The Farmer's Wife*. "Does it ever occur to you that in the fate of the thousands of women wage-earners of to-day, might possibly be mirrored the lives of your darling girls?" "Grandma B" admonished women in the *Nonconformist*, "don't be afraid of your sisters, no matter where they live, or what they do; . . . many a noble heart beats beneath a ragged dress. And don't be afraid of the fallen sisterhood either. For there is many an ugly, bald-headed old moneybags who would soon be on his way to the great conflagration, if the votes of his *qua* wives could send him there." Another Populist remarked that prodigal sons had an unjust advantage. "How about the prodigal daughter?" she asked. "There is only a step, as it were, from honor to dishonor, and they who turn with scorn from a misguided woman may at that moment be standing on the brink of a yawning chasm."[13]

Some Populists drew from these concerns a strong link between class and sexual oppression. Western Populist editors advertised a number of novels advocating women's rights, including favorites from as far back as 1870. *Helen Harlow's Vow*, by Lois Waisbrooker, told the story of a young woman's seduction and ostracism; the author offered repeated lectures on the injustices of the double standard. In *The Strike of a Sex,* George Noyes Miller described the mythical town of Hustleburg, where all the women went on strike. They asked not only for equal wages and political rights but for every woman to have "perfect ownership of her own person" in matters of sexuality. After agonized debate, the men of Hustleburg granted these rights and harmony was restored. Miller explained that the strike was inspired by the labor movement; once labor united against capital and won, women easily applied the lesson. The key to their victory came when they discarded "the idea that the courtesan [is] a special sinner to be approached with a moral tract and a condescending kind of forgiveness." Instead, middle-class ladies accepted prostitutes "as sisters" and made abolition of the sex trade one of their key demands.[14]

Populist men and women blended the vocabulary of Christian morality with that of economics. As suggested by Mary Hobart's title *A Scientific Exposure of the Errors in Our Monetary System*, tract writers and stump speakers used legislative reports, statistics, census data, and the work of noted economists to build a "scientific" case. Emery referred to politics as "the science of government," a "research into the best methods" for obtaining peace and prosperity. Todd analyzed the wool and iron industries and addressed such issues as "Raw Material and the Cost of Production" and "The Balance of Trade and Ship Restrictions." These women's rhetorical style paralleled that of male Populists, in works like Donnelly's *The American People's Money* and W. H. Harvey's popular *Coin's Financial School*.[15]

Economic arguments served, however, Christian moral ends. Continuing the old evangelical impulse to reform society through politics, Kansas stump speaker Annie Diggs predicted that Populists would usher in "the Millennium." They would give women the vote, and men and women together would ban liquor and end poverty, thus elevating both work and home. Colorado Populists' ballot emblem was the Cottage Home, a symbol with combined domestic and religious meaning. Poets rhapsodized on it: "O, cottage home! beloved shrine! / Where love's benignant labors shine." Newspapers sketched it on election day. Speaking to Colorado women after they won the vote, a Populist speaker cleverly urged them to use their ballots to "place a cross opposite the cottage home."[16]

Populists' arguments for "protection to the home" drew on both Republican and Prohibitionist precedents. In most places women could not cast a ballot, and Populists argued that men must protect their families on election day. They urged men to "vote for Sallie and the babies," probably borrowing the phrase from the anti-liquor party. The slogan appeared frequently in editorials, poems, and speeches, rendered as Katie and the babies, Betsy and the babies, or Mollie and the babies. It always meant the same thing: a vote for the major parties was a vote for corruption. Populism stood for the homes and families of plain folks. An orator in Colorado exhorted his listeners, somewhat contradictorily, to "be men, be women. Be true to your wife and child and your own home, and vote the straight Populist ticket."[17]

Like major party slogans, this phrase appropriated women as symbols of virtue. Men who voted for Sallie and the babies fulfilled their traditional role as protectors of the home. Populists borrowed the phrase, however, from a party that endorsed woman suffrage, and wherever women voted in Alliance meetings or served as convention delegates that background also lay behind Populist rhetoric. "Voting for Sallie and the babies" indicated women's inclusion in politics despite their lack of power at the ballot box. Populists reminded their audiences that farm families were in the struggle together. "The old parties are taking the bread and butter from wife and children and will eventually take the home," wrote one Kansas woman. "Which will you do, be non-partisan and insure the welfare of family and home, or stick to the parties?"[18] Nonpartisanship meant, of course, a ballot for Populism.

Western Populists adapted for their own uses the old attacks on sinful Democratic manhood. Like Prohibitionists, they turned it against men in both major parties, especially Republicans in league with monopoly capitalists. In *Pizarro and John Sherman*, Marion Todd launched an extended comparison of the cruel Spanish conquistador and the Ohio Republican, concluding that the latter, whom she accused of gross corruption, was "the greater brigand." A year later, Populist presidential candidate James B. Weaver may have drawn on Todd's account in producing his manifesto, *A Call to Action*. Weaver described the typical capitalist as a "highwayman." His traits, analogous to those that Republicans attributed to Democrats, were "physical courage, disregard of moral obligations, . . . stolid indifference to human suffering, and defiant disregard of the law. [He] looks upon Government simply as an organized police force and as his natural enemy. . . . His only restraint is fear, and even this enhances his cruelty."[19] In describing uncontrolled manhood, Republicans had emphasized the tendency to violent rebellion; Prohibitionists, drunkenness and lust. In keeping with their economic platform Populists stressed greed, but they again described political disorder as the result of male sin. Because leaders of both major parties were in league with "pirates," Populism was the only way for good men to reassert political control.

Affinities between Prohibitionists and Populists were strong enough that factions in both camps hoped they would merge. The Farmer's Alliance and Knights of Labor had encouraged voluntary temperance; Kansas Populist Annie Diggs claimed every woman in the party was a temperance advocate, and in some areas the issue was a key attraction. A Georgia Methodist reported to his bishop that church members were flocking to Populism because of its temperance stance. "People are losing their heads," he warned. "Georgia Methodism as the established church of Populism would be a spectacle." Meanwhile, some Prohibition leaders took a sympathetic view of Populists' economic arguments. By 1889 Frances Willard described herself as a Christian Socialist and argued that working-class temperance depended on decent living and working conditions. In her annual address to the WCTU she called for federal relief to the unemployed, legislation to limit work days to eight hours, and public ownership of railroads.[20]

Several WCTU leaders served as delegates to the Populists' founding convention, and Frances Willard diligently worked to unify Populism and Prohibitionism into one reform party. The alliance never materialized. At their 1892 convention Populists omitted temperance from the national platform, arguing that the party should not let side issues distract them. Meanwhile, former Republicans in the Prohibition camp, like Kansan John St. John, resisted Willard's socialist appeals and vehemently refused to join the People's Party. Willard gave up in despair, increasingly disillusioned with the Prohibition Party as a vehicle for reform. Women like Annie Diggs, despite their WCTU membership, stuck with the People's Party.[21]

Deep-seated differences lay at the root of the split. For many Prohibitionists "the drink evil" was "the cause of poverty," as Helen Gougar of Indiana declared after a Populist convention. The Prohibition Party's 1892 platform declared that the liquor traffic was "the citadel of all the forces that corrupt politics, promote poverty and crime, degrade the nation's home life, thwart the will of the people and deliver our country into the hands of rapacious class interests." Even Populists who sympathized with Prohibition goals objected to this analysis. Responding to Gougar's contention that alcohol caused poverty, Annie Diggs wrote that "poverty is the large underlying cause of intemperance." Sarah Emery declared that "the Populist theory is: Better to go home drunk, than to have no home to go to either drunk or sober." Kansas Populist Ben Clover, a longtime temperance advocate, wrote that "excessive wealth on the one hand and extreme poverty on the other lead to intemperance and vice. Abolish both, and the prohibition battle is two-thirds fought." Frances Willard now agreed, but she could not persuade the majority of Prohibitionists to follow her line of thinking.[22]

Divisions within Populism and between Populists and their potential allies were problems of both region and class. Outside the South, middle-class Prohibitionists were largely former Republicans, and most could not stomach association with a coalition of alleged socialists and ex-Confederates. At the same time, southern Democrats who had become Populists resisted alliance with anti-liquor evangelicals who claimed to be the true heirs of abolitionism. Prohibitionists had been unable to fulfill their campaign promise, "no sectionalism in politics, no sex in citizenship." On both counts, Populists encountered the same obstacles to building a party across class and regional lines.

Women and the People's Party

If the liquor issue revealed regional tensions within Populism, women's different roles in the party's southern and western wings reflected those divisions even more clearly. Southern farm women still struggled with patriarchal expectations that domestic ideology had long since altered among northern evangelicals. The Grange and Alliance established limited standards for women's public participation, but they were not always honored in practice. North Carolina leaders constantly had to remind local Alliancemen that women had voting rights. In Georgia and Mississippi, outspoken or dissenting women faced pressure to quiet down. Texas Populist Betty Gay wrote that women should serve in both their families and the Alliance as the subordinate "helpmeet of man." In the meantime, up in Kansas, Mary Lease was proclaiming that Populists would "place the mothers of this nation on an equality with the fathers."[23]

Southern women tended to work through the Alliance more than the People's Party, and they used meetings and letters to advocate greater female autonomy within the household. One southern editor wrote that suballiances gratified female members when they discussed "conveniences for the good and faithful wife." Farm men were admonished that a wife should not be "a slave and a drudge," but should have opportunities to "give her virtue and intelligence full play." Such discussions pushed southern white families toward the ideal of the maternal family, in which wives and mothers held moral authority to which men should defer. One North Carolina man reported that a female lecturer "handles husbands quite roughly, but it is received in the proper spirit."[24]

Rebecca Felton of Georgia, the only southern Populist woman widely known as a speaker, promoted the interests of farm women within the family. In one speech she reproached

> the little two-by-four farmer who nags his wife about her breakfast and her work, . . . when he can and often does take time to go to town and talk politics or sit about the front door and spit tobacco and boss the whole concern from the standpoint of the woman's lord and master. When such little somebodys prate about my farm—my crop—my house—and such like, I do wish I had the power to put them to the cookstove and washpot for a couple of these hot days, because I believe they would get willing, after such an experience, to talk genteelly to the wives and mothers and call the business our crop—our farm—our house—and generally our everything else.

Felton urged men not only to "talk genteelly" but to provide women with independent income. She suggested that families cultivate "a little crop that is known as the wife's crop and which belongs to her. . . . Whatever it brings should be placed in her hands to spend as she desires." Felton anticipated her audience's reaction: "Don't smile—and say 'Pshaw!'—I mean every word of it. It will be the best crop you raise . . . because your wife will entertain serene satisfaction in her heart, that you loved her and wanted her to feel independent." Felton also urged husbands to give their wives vacations from the farm.[25]

These goals did not draw southern women into public campaign work. Their place remained limited to private discussions, talks at Alliance meetings, and letters to Populist newspapers. The region's political culture offered no precedent for women to become stump speakers, march in parades, or work the polls on election day. Most southern Populist women supported their party as other southern women supported Democratic and Republican candidates: by sewing banners and cooking for barbecues and picnics. When a dispute between Populist and Democratic women broke up a Methodist dinner in Hopewell, Georgia, it became a topic of scandal and amusement. Southerners were still unaccustomed to hearing women's public political voices.[26]

Even in the West, many farm women focused their energy on altering women's roles within the home. Poverty and rural labor patterns mitigated the benefits of domestic ideology; in families toiling to meet mortgage payments, women could not afford to leave breadwinning entirely to men. Anger over the drudgery of farm women's work remained a persistent theme among Populists in both West and South. Bina Otis of Kansas described "the cook-stove and washtub" as "a combination that makes a slave of the majority of farmers' wives and sends many of them to a premature grave." Other Populists described farm women as "overworked" and "old and tired" by age thirty. These protests reflected anxiety over where farmers fit in a society with deepening class inequalities. In towns and cities, prosperous women were engaged in a host of social activities; ladies' journals offered shopping advice and suggested pursuits for leisure hours. Farm families saw themselves being left behind.[27]

Middle-class Populist women expressed concern from a different perspective: they viewed poor farm women, like the urban working class, as a rescue project for reformers. Annie Diggs, whose husband was a clerk in Lawrence, Kansas, frequently informed her audiences that the majority of patients in insane asylums were women from farms. She attributed this to isolation, the monotony of rural life, and farm women's inability to "keep pace with the women of the towns and cities [in] the march toward independence and prosperity." Diggs thought farm women might be uplifted "by the reading of something not seen and learned in the daily round of farm life"; she and her co-editors sprinkled the pages of *The Farmer's Wife* with accounts of fashionable summer resorts, European styles, and urban luxuries. This approach, Diggs hoped, would elevate rural homes to a middle-class standard.[28]

Such strategies demonstrated tensions between middle-class Populist reformers and their farm allies, not to mention an experiential gap between both these groups of Populists and urban laborers. Farm poverty encouraged Populists to identify with the industrial working classes and work for a political alliance of producers; at the same time, many farm families saw themselves as part of the middle class. From their point of view, the problem was income. They shared middle-class values; they just could not make enough money to achieve respectable domesticity.

In western farm households, sexual inequality often took a different form than it did in the South: more men approved and even encouraged women's political work, but overburdened farm women still lacked time and energy to attend Alliance meetings. "We wish our sisters would come out more generally," coaxed Mrs. C. E. Lindsley of Kansas. "Let your supper dishes go unwashed once a week, and come out to the Alliance! . . . Let the outside world see that wives, mothers and sisters have an interest in home outside and beyond washing dishes, milking and making butter and the general run of work in the home of a farmer." Luna Kellie, a dedicated member in Nebraska, reported that her "hands were very full"; she wrote letters to Alliance newspapers in "extra time when others were asleep." Kellie's essays were read across Nebraska and her husband attended state meetings, but Kellie herself didn't "feel able to attend" until the Alliance convened in Hastings, less than sixty miles from her home.[29]

Mrs. S. V. P. Johnson of Kansas described the constraints of farm life in a letter to Populist leader Leonidas Polk. Johnson told Polk that her husband and brother "went to Parsons City last Fall to hear you speak & I did want to go so much but I was suffering from the contraction of the currency—you know what kind of a disease that is, it is pretty hard to control." She reported that she was "writing a few essays to read at the Alliance meetings . . . but lack one thing, & that is confidence in myself—I don't know if I have the ability to write anything worth reading." Conscious of their appearance, some women worried about their clothes and hesitated to attend meetings dressed in rags.[30]

Middle-class women like Annie Diggs recognized that they were working on poor women's behalf and they struggled, often unsuccessfully, to represent them. When Republicans criticized Diggs for her urban background, she answered sarcastically that "nothing is easier [for farm women] after the washing, baking, scrubbing, mending, house cleaning, churning, and a few other chores are all done, than just to up and run into town and edit a newspaper." Years later, Eva Valesh described the contrasts between her rural tours as a young Populist stump speaker and her life in Minneapolis, under the eye of her middle-class mother. "Steady traveling was hard on clothes," she recalled, "so I dressed quite plainly. The farmers liked that. They said, 'She's one of us. She isn't any better dressed than one of our own daughters.' When I came home, I sought the beauty parlor and dolled myself up, and went to lunch and matinees with my newspaper friends, so my mother was somewhat appeased."[31] By virtue of their leisure and relative prosperity, middle-class Populists like Diggs and Valesh always held disproportionate power in the movement.

Despite their lack of voting rights, many rural women saw partisan action as the most effective available strategy. Eppie Winter reported that suballiances in Cloud County, Kansas, had built a cooperative store and started a newspaper. "But how long will it last?" she asked. "Will it do the next generation any good? Just as soon as our work ceases, just that quick will the benefit stop un-less we make use of politics and partisan politics at that." Populist women often expressed impatience at men's reluctance to join the new party. "You might as well shout 'scat' to a lot of wild cats as to say 'party' to a man," wrote a Kansas woman in disgust. "They would scatter just as quick. . . . We women could come right out and say what party it was that passed laws detrimental to our interests." "Even now there are hosts of men who still cling to these old rotten parties," wrote another farm woman. She advised newspaper readers whose hus-bands did not support Populism to "leave them at home on election day to rock the babies, while the women go to the polls and work for the good of the cause."[32] These Populists challenged voters to support the party or risk being labeled weak and effeminate. If a husband was reluctant to vote for "Katie and the babies," some Katies were willing to use prevailing masculine ideals to exert a little leverage.

Western Populist women drew on political precedents unavailable to their counterparts in the South. By 1896 most state Granges outside the South had endorsed woman suffrage. Among the first to do so were the Granges in Indi-ana, Iowa, and New York, where women played active roles in electoral cam-paigns. New England Granges lagged fifteen years behind, those in the South even further. Before the advent of Populism, northern and western farm women also had more opportunities to serve as elected officers inside the Grange.[33]

The Knights of Labor had encouraged women to join local assemblies and hired women as lecturers and organizers, most successfully outside the South. Almost every prominent Populist woman had worked, in fact, for the Knights. Mary Lease was a Knight who had stumped for that movement's short-lived Union Labor Party. Fannie McCormick, also from the Kansas Knights, edited a Populist newspaper and ran for state superintendent of public schools. In Ore-gon and Illinois, respectively, Knights leaders Sue Ross Keenan and Emma DeVoe became Populist orators. In Minnesota, eighteen-year-old Eva Valesh left her work for the Minneapolis Knights to become a Populist lecturer.[34]

None of these women lived on farms, though a few were farmers' daugh-ters. Lease and McCormick, along with authors Marion Todd and Sarah Emery and Montana Populist Ella Knowles, were former schoolteachers. Todd and Lease had passed the bar. Valesh, a journalist, had studied law with her husband but found no time to finish the degree. De Voe's husband was a merchant, as was the father of young stump speaker Cora Diehl, who toured Oklahoma for the new party. These women's experiences—like those of middle-class reform-ers like Annie Diggs—lay firmly in an urban context.[35] It is ironic that they became famous as leaders of a farmers' protest movement. The most famous Populist women came from the movement's labor wing, and they spent the early 1890s trying to build a labor-farmer coalition.

Unlike farm women, female labor leaders had already come to terms with abuse and disapproval of their public activities, and many were effective speak-ers. The best was Mary Lease, who embarked on exhausting nationwide tours and drew tremendous crowds. Rather than emphasizing her femininity, Lease adopted a masculine style that suited her low voice. Even a bitter opponent described it as "a deep, rich contralto, a singing voice that had hypnotic qualities." Lease won praise around the country. A Colorado newspaper remarked that "those who heard Mrs. Lease, of Kansas, speak in Denver, will not wonder that [Republican Senator] John J. Ingalls would not meet her in joint debate." A resident of Virginia City, Nevada recorded in his diary: "evening attended the Weaver-Lease reception & speaking at Theater—Densely crowded with gents & ladies— . . . Mrs. Lease spoke an hour, giving one of the best if not the best and most eloquent address I ever heard from a woman. Splendid style, voice and elocution." A southern Democrat compared Lease to renowned Georgia orator John Temple Graves, reporting that her speeches had a "remarkable" effect.[36]

Lease and her co-workers drew on the long tradition of women's partisan campaign work in the Midwest and Kansas, which settlers had now carried farther west. Describing the 1890 Kansas campaign, Annie Diggs wrote that farm women "rose earlier and worked later to gain time to cook the picnic dinners, to paint the mottoes on the banners, to practice with the glee clubs, to march in procession." A Nebraska correspondent wrote that Populist mass meetings included "glee clubs, composed generally of pretty country maidens, dressed in the national colors." Western Populists also sponsored parades, barbecues, picnics, and pole raisings. Women took a prominent role in such events in Kansas, Nebraska, Oregon, the Mountain West, and occasionally as far south as Texas. Copying campaign rituals from the old midwestern parties, Populists strove to create a regular organization and force rivals to take them seriously.[37]

Unlike Republicans—who joined separate clubs according to gender— Populist men and women tended to work together. In Colorado, for example, observers noted that Populist women "concentrated their efforts with the men in the committees and club organizations of the party." A Republican remarked that "the People's Party, in all its lines of activity, makes no distinction of sex. Its women have shown no disposition to separate their work and have been battling side by side with the men."[38] In this sense, Populists broke with major-party tradition. They saw no need for separate women's clubs because, within the party structures, men and women shared power.

At the local level, western Populist women's freedom to join debates and vote at party meetings far exceeded that of their Republican counterparts. Populist women's role was much closer to that of female Prohibitionists: many served as elected delegates to county and state political meetings. Mountain states produced more female delegates than other regions, but the custom was widespread. Delegates to the 1892 national convention included women from Kansas, Iowa, South Dakota, Missouri, California, and even Arkansas. At critical points in debate over the presidential nomination, Mary Lease spoke from the floor and the convention heeded her advice. Lease then seconded James Weaver's nomination. In many ways, Lease's role in Populism paralleled Frances Willard's in the Prohibition Party. Both gave major addresses at conventions, toured with presidential nominees, and sat in their parties' inner councils.[39]

This power extended to nominations for office in many parts of the West. Though women had voted in Wyoming since 1869, the first female legislative candidate was Populist Winona Taylor in 1894. Ella Knowles won the Populist nomination for attorney general of Montana. Populists chose the first female state superintendent of schools in North Dakota; in the next election, Republicans nominated a woman to run against her. After Colorado women won the vote, Evangeline Heartz took a seat in the state legislature, the first and only Populist woman to do so. Orator Nellie Matteson appealed to Colorado women by declaring that "the desire of the People's Party is for new and better conditions. And it is their chief desire that women should be received in their councils. Is this the dominating desire," she asked, "in the ranks of the Republicans?"[40]

Though Populist women exercised far more power in their party than did members of the National Women's Republican Association, both viewed their parties' goals as more important than women's rights. The ironies of earlier debates between Republican and Prohibitionist suffragists were replicated in the 1890s: some women held power in a party that did not win national campaigns, and others worked for a winning party that did not give them power. J. Ellen Foster and her colleagues won patronage jobs, but Republican women worked separately from men and almost never voted in party councils or conventions. Their role was not to press for specific planks or candidates, but to accept men's decisions on these matters and work for victory. Populist women had scant financial backing, but they served as delegates and decision makers. In Kansas, one of them expressed pity for the poor Republican women who were "under the despotic rule of their lords and masters." She contrasted their "puny" efforts with those of "the *real* women of Kansas."[41]

The majority of western Populists, both women and men, endorsed woman suffrage. Even the Republican-leaning *Woman's Journal* acknowledged in 1894 that suffrage was in the Populist platform of "nearly every northern State." Populist legislators in a number of western states submitted bills to enfranchise women. Approval was strongest in the Rocky Mountains, where the party had a solid base of union members; the same labor wing that furnished so many female orators also offered consistent suffrage support. Kansas Populists were more divided, and the suffrage cause languished after legislators from the new party cast their lot with anti-suffrage Democrats. Other Kansans were infuriated at this alliance, which they saw as a betrayal of third-party principles. "A political party is either right or wrong," one Populist editor wrote. He recalled "the inquiry of the great apostle to the gentiles, 'What consort hath Christ with Balial?'"[42]

At the Populists' 1892 national convention, delegates from the southern wing blocked a full suffrage plank despite eloquent pleas from both western Populists and national suffrage leaders. A committee chaired by Frances Willard approved a suffrage plank written by Annie Diggs, but it failed on the convention floor. One suffragist reported that "the Northern men would have gladly declared for our ballot, but they were afraid of the South." Willard blamed "the liquor wing," including Kansans who were former Democrats, and "the conservatives of our southern brethren." Emma Ghent Curtis of Colorado proposed an alternative plank that passed, so that the platform stated, "we demand that the question of woman suffrage be submitted to the state and territorial legislatures for favorable action."[43]

In Colorado and Idaho, Populist-controlled legislatures followed this advice. They sponsored suffrage referenda, and party leaders' endorsement helped win majority approval in each state. Political conditions in the Rockies militated for passage; voters combined Populist leanings with an overriding interest in the silver currency issue. The mining industry dominated both states' economies, and women voters could help represent this cause in Washington. "If the fight for free silver is to be kept up," argued one Colorado editor, "the silver states will need all the votes they can get. . . . This can be done by putting the cross after 'Equal Suffrage Approved.'" The Colorado suffrage association called anti-suffragists "traitor[s] to the white metal and to the best interest of the state." Newspapers of all parties agreed that "a vote for equal suffrage is a vote for silver." The referendum won overwhelming support in mining areas. Three years later, Idaho Populists swept into power and voters endorsed woman suffrage in the midst of a massive free-silver campaign.[44]

For several years before the advent of suffrage in 1893, Colorado Populist women had been visible and numerous as stump speakers and organizers. State party leaders expected the majority of women to vote Populist, arguing that they were grateful for suffrage and sympathetic to reform. As the 1894 election approached, Populist governor Davis Waite expressed confidence that his party would win most of the new voters. Republicans expressed equal assurance that women would vote as a bloc for their cause. Suffrage prompted a dramatic change in male Republicans' attitude toward women: more than any other party, they singled out female voters for attention and flattery. "The ship of state will never sink if it is in the power of our female fellow-citizens to hold her on her course," one candidate proclaimed. A Georgetown editor wrote that "a woman's intuitions will reach the truth at a bound long before the laborious logic adopted by the masculine mind has arrived at a conclusion." The *Denver Times* gushed over "the grace, ease, and thorough, practical understanding with which the women of the Centennial state have entered upon equal rights." The paper hired a female columnist to report on women's political affairs.[45]

Along with praise, Colorado's male Republicans offered women a sudden share of power. They began to appoint county organizing teams consisting of one man and one woman. After temporary male resistance, several women won seats on the Denver campaign board. Two women joined five men on the state party committee. GOP women also sought nominations to local and state conventions and many were elected, so that in the space of a year women's decision-making power reached roughly equal levels in Republican and Populist camps. Each party nominated a woman for state superintendent of schools and each ran three female candidates for the state legislature. Democrats largely ignored the implications of woman suffrage, though they nominated a woman for state superintendent of schools. One newspaper noted that the Denver Democratic Women's Club showed "less activity than that which is shown by the other parties. . . . Their number is so small that it is useless to try to canvass the state or labor after the fashion of the other women." Leaders of the club spent much of their time fighting the stubborn resistance of male Democrats and refuting Republican accusations that they were Populists.[46]

A massive Republican victory in 1894 embittered Colorado Populists who had supported woman suffrage. A number of Populists blamed women for the election results. One reported that Cripple Creek went Republican because "there is more than 1000 prostitutes and pimps in that town. . . . It is overflowing with the scum of humanity." Another man reported from Amethyst that a local woman had sold her vote for a new dress. "I was never so near hating my own sex as I am tonight," a Durango woman wrote Governor Waite on election night. She added that she considered Waite's support for woman suffrage "the one mistake of your public career." Waite apparently agreed. He told Ignatius Donnelly that "lewd women" and "ignorant hired girls" had carried the Republican vote in Denver. The governor's wife, Celia Waite, told a New York reporter that women had sold their votes "for a package of gum and a carriage ride." During a visit to Minnesota soon after the election, Davis Waite gave an angry speech against woman suffrage. Donnelly reported later that "the statements you have made here have ended woman's suffrage in the People's Party."[47]

While the suffrage issue divided Populists, the Populist issue divided eastern and western suffragists. Within the People's Party suffragists and their male allies expressed willingness to remain loyal. Asked about Populists' failure to pass a national suffrage plank, a female editor from Florida declared that "both my papers shall be run in the interest of the party." Marion Todd told the convention that if they would not adopt woman suffrage and prohibition, "we will wait until you have blossomed a little fuller in the principles of justice and equity." Some Populist women argued that suffrage would hurt the party's chances of national success; almost all seem to have agreed that their party's economic policies were a higher priority than suffrage rights.[48]

Some western suffrage leaders nonetheless saw Populism as the most promising vehicle for change. The *Woman's Tribune* of Nebraska argued that "in a party that allows women delegates, elects women officers, and in fact, gives them equal rights and opportunities from the first rural meeting to the great national convention, the opportunity is before women to use the party and bind it to their interests." Eastern suffragists were much more reluctant to credit or cooperate with the new party. When Lucy Stone and Susan B. Anthony merged their coalitions in 1890 to create the National American Woman Suffrage Association (NAWSA), the group established joint headquarters in Boston and focused its energy in the Northeast. NAWSA leaders viewed the new party suspiciously at best. Editors of the *Woman's Journal* gave scant coverage to Populist women's activities and maintained GOP ties. Anthony stumped for Republicans as late as 1892 in Kansas, at which point she was backing the opposition party against Populists who held state power. Only Elizabeth Cady Stanton, who had endorsed the Prohibition Party in 1888, seemed at all willing to break from Republicanism.[49]

Northeastern suffragists, with their long history of loyalty to the GOP, looked on events in the West through the eyes of middle-class Boston. Most of the eastern press and public viewed Populists as wild-eyed fanatics who advocated communism. Even if Susan B. Anthony and Lucy Stone had sympathized with Populists' economic program—which apparently they did not—suffragists who had rejected Prohibitionism as a doomed minority party must have been even less sanguine about the prospects for Populism in the East. To westerners, however, the new party looked like the future incarnate. In Kansas and Colorado it seemed poised not only to replace Democrats as the second party, but to relegate those states' Republicans to minority status.

Regional and class tensions among eastern and western suffragists were thus enormous. Populists like Eva Valesh and Mary Lease dismissed middle-class club women and suffragists as "Republican sympathizers" or deluded idealists who were "engaged in a futile attempt to believe that women are nonpartisan." They accused Anthony and her New England allies of being ungrateful and unreasonable. At the same time, NAWSA's support for Colorado's Populist-led referendum campaign was so minimal that Populists expressed public anger at the insult. Caroline Churchill, a Colorado Populist, later claimed that Lucy Stone had "never had a good word" for her during fourteen years of suffrage cooperation.[50]

The split was especially deep in Kansas, where a woman suffrage referendum sank in the campaign storm of 1894. Populist legislators and self-described "Young Republican" men placed the referendum on the ballot, and suffragists formed a ten-woman campaign committee to lead the fight for ratification. The committee included some of the state's most prominent women stump speakers, such as Populist Annie Diggs; it elected as its leader Laura Johns, president of the Kansas Women's Republican Association and an associate of Ellen Foster. Committee members were carefully chosen to correspond to the relative strength of state parties: four Republicans, four Populists, one Democrat, and one Prohibitionist. Johns announced that the group was "non-partisan in its work, though ALL PARTISAN in its make-up. . . . Not for one instant will these women be disloyal to their respective political or religious affiliations." Suffragists proved unable to accomplish this in what one called the fiercest partisan battle ever waged in Kansas.[51]

Johns quickly became entangled in a power struggle with Topeka Populists, who mistrusted her leadership and even accused her of diverting suffrage funds to her Republican allies. She fought a second battle inside the Kansas Republican Women's Association. Some members of the group proposed a weak convention resolution claiming suffrage was not a test of party loyalty. Johns and Susan B. Anthony demanded and won a stronger resolution, but trouble was brewing. In the course of debate Ellen Foster, visiting from New York, declared that "I care more for republican principles than woman suffrage." Anthony accused Foster of being a "hired emissary of Republican politicians who have determined to silence the women."[52]

Anthony's Republican loyalty was wearing thin, and when state GOP delegates convened she addressed them coldly. "I know you are not idiots," she said. "You will put every question in your platform that interests you. . . . The same experiment of treachery in the Republican Party has become tiresome." Anthony hardly won an endorsement with this approach, but neither did Johns and Foster, who offered stirring declarations of party loyalty and swore that Kansas women would show everlasting gratitude for suffrage with solid Republican votes. The convention was a disaster. Republican delegates rejected suffrage unanimously and without debate. Suffragists then had to fulfill their public pledge to visit all the party conventions. Populists endorsed the proposed amendment after exhortations from Annie Diggs to "have the courage of your convictions." Democrats declared firm opposition to woman suffrage "as tending to destroy the home and the family." Suffrage was now a Populist plank.

Republican suffragists found themselves facing the same dilemma Populist women had suffered in 1892, after the national Omaha convention. Should they leave the party to work for women's votes, or stick with the party despite its rejection of suffrage? Laura Johns tried to do both. She remained on the suffrage committee but also continued working for Republican victory, a contradictory course at best. Johns told eastern suffrage leaders that defeating Populists' "financial heresies" must be the first priority. Anthony, furious, retorted that without woman suffrage the state would "sink to the depths of hell on moral issues."[53] The nonpartisan, all-partisan suffrage coalition was showing serious strains.

Rejected by Republicans and pressured by Populist delegates, Anthony had vowed to stump for the Kansas People's Party if they endorsed the referendum. She fulfilled her pledge with relish. For the first time in a quarter century, back in the same state where she had campaigned with Democrat George Train in 1867, Anthony abandoned the GOP. Her decision delighted Populists but horrified Republican suffragists in both Kansas and the Northeast. The *Woman's Journal* denied that Anthony had gone over to Populism and told Republican women to stick with their party despite the Kansas debacle. The editors reprinted an interview in which Anthony declared she was not a Populist. "I have been like a drowning woman for a long time," Anthony explained. She said the Populists had "thrown an excellent plank in my direction, and I stepped on it. I didn't step on the whole platform, but just on the woman suffrage plank." She proceeded to give several weeks of speeches from Populist rostrums.[54]

The majority of Populists did little to help the suffrage cause. They saw survival of the People's Party and its economic platform as the paramount issue and their newspapers practically ignored the referendum. One editor expressed sympathy for suffrage but explained that the economic crisis took priority; he had to attend "to the maintenance of what few rights we now have." Republican men denounced suffrage as a Populist measure and vowed to vote against it. Some expressed hope that Populists' endorsement of suffrage would contribute to that party's defeat because "the first great and overshadowing work of the people is to redeem the state from Populism." On a suffrage tour, young Carrie Chapman Catt found that wherever she spoke at the behest of Populists or Republicans, the other side refused to show up. The result on election day was predictable. Voters defeated the suffrage amendment, 139,000 to 95,000.[55]

The only women satisfied with these results were anti-suffrage Republicans, whose party had recaptured control of the state. Populists were miserable, and Populist suffragists were crushed by their double defeat. Republican suffragists were not much happier. One called the election a "bitter, cruel and humiliating disappointment." "I have mourned and mourned and mourned," Laura Johns wrote to a friend. "I don't deny that I am almost heartbroken. . . . Every morning I wake with a sense of a burden of disappointment." At its next convention in 1895, the Kansas Equal Suffrage Association crumbled as partisan factions accused each other of selfishness and treachery. The group sank into obscurity for more than a decade.[56]

For national suffrage leaders, the trauma of this defeat was compounded two years later in California. With another state referendum on the ballot, suffragists again made the rounds of political conventions and asked for party endorsements. Democrats predictably rejected the measure. State Populists strongly supported it; thanking the convention, Anthony joked that they were "the ninety and nine sheep that are saved," and for the lost sheep she would "have to go somewhere else." Republicans, pursuing a different strategy than had the Kansas party two years before, endorsed suffrage at their state convention and then did nothing. Stump speakers ignored the referendum; most Republican papers refused to comment or even opposed suffrage, though it was a plank in their own platform.[57] Suffragists again found themselves fastened, like it or not, to the losing Populist side.

Surveying a familiar scene, Susan B. Anthony finally switched tactics and expressed her conviction that suffragists should eschew all party work. "Oh I have been through the partisan battle," she commented to a relative. "I don't want to see it again." In a letter to a California colleague, Anthony directed that all suffragists be "nonpartisan. . . . The suffrage committee will have nothing to do with any Party women speakers!" Yet Anthony was keenly aware of the parties' power, and she predicted that suffrage would not pass unless all parties gave suffragists a place at their meetings. She was right. Only Populists invited suffrage leaders to speak, and the referendum failed by a substantial margin.[58]

Anthony spent the whole campaign in California, exasperated by women's party loyalties. She wrote, after hearing Mary Hobart give a Populist address, that "the one difficult thing is to hold women back from declaring themselves for one political party or the other—they must be nonpartisan or all partisan." While echoing Laura Johns's words, Anthony must have been keenly aware of this strategy's failure in Kansas. She could hardly forget her own history of Republican endorsements, from the Grant campaign of 1872 to her 1884 call for women to "stand by the Republicans" and her 1892 cooperation with the GOP in Kansas. Her new strategy ran counter to twenty years of practice, and she found her allies slow to change.[59]

Party politics thus frustrated women's rights advocates as well as women who supported losing parties. Even Anthony, for whom suffrage was the paramount goal, was slow to renounce her abolitionist and Republican heritage. In the West during the 1890s, Populists seized the suffrage initiative from Republicans, and it is perhaps no accident that Anthony chose this moment to insist on her movement's strict nonpartisanship. With parties the key vehicles for political action, however, no suffragist could escape the implications of party platforms that favored—or failed to favor—women's political rights.

The irony was that Populism offered a combined vision of greater class and gender equity, not unlike the goals Anthony and her colleagues had worked for in the Labor Reform Party of 1867. Populists had moved beyond the old Whig and Republican model of women's indirect "influence." Like Prohibitionists they treated women as full party members, convention delegates, and voters. In the tradition of the earlier third party and of Radical Republicans, they still used the rhetoric of motherhood and evangelical faith; but in addressing economic questions they also used the "scientific" vocabulary of economics in their bid to protect the home. By the Progressive Era, middle-class reformers would find such arguments effective in their efforts to expand federal power. But as Anthony and other eastern suffragists estimated, the nation would not accept them in the 1890s when they were proposed by a farmer-labor insurgency based in the West and South. The regional and class divisions that led to Populism's rise—as the major parties lost their grip on old wartime coalitions—also led to its fall. By the late 1890s, the destruction of Populism would also prove to be a national defeat for women's rights.

6

Redemption

If I were an angel in heaven, I'd come back to earth and live another life of suffering just for the privilege of voting the full Republican ticket this year.
—*Miss Ada Sweet of Chicago, 1894*

The depression of 1893 was one of the worst economic crises ever to hit the United States. While it did not devastate financial markets as severely as the Great Depression would in 1929, the effect on industry was catastrophic. A quarter of the nation's railroads went bankrupt. Production slumped in almost every manufacturing sector and ensuing layoffs were massive. Outside agriculture, which had its own problems, unemployment reached an estimated 2 million. Thousands of displaced workers sought charity in the cities, wandered the countryside, or starved from want. Some who kept their jobs fared only a little better, as wages in the textile and mining industries dropped more than 25 percent from levels that were already depressed. In real terms, American wages lost a fifth of their value in two years.[1]

The early phase of the depression influenced politics before 1893. The legality of strikes became a key issue as wages declined and workers protested. In response to drought and falling crop prices, southern and western Populists organized by 1891. This first stage of economic distress increased the competitiveness of the party system. Populists presented a challenge in states that had been one-party strongholds, while in the Northeast and Midwest, Democrats won major victories. Explaining these developments, observers pointed to the increasing hardships faced by farmers and the working class.[2]

When the full impact of the depression hit in 1893, political repercussions were even more dramatic. Grover Cleveland sat in the White House and Democrats controlled both houses of Congress. In Colorado, Kansas, and other western states, Populists held a large share of power. A majority of voters blamed these parties, decisively ending their recent gains. Republicans won sweeping victories in the 1894 races and Populists' national prospects began to fade. Two years later, the election of Republican President William McKinley reduced Democrats to a minority party and wiped Populism almost off the electoral map. After 1896, the GOP controlled the presidency and both houses of Congress for sixteen years.[3]

In the Northeast and Midwest, a few middle-class reformers protested these developments. Some in the older generation had been ardent Republicans in the Radical years but had turned from the problems of slavery to those of industrial poverty. They had followed the Greenback revolt, accepted Democratic arguments for free trade, and watched Populism with sympathy. In the 1890s more economic reformers broke from the Republican camp. Shocked by the depression, they contrasted the desperation of farmers and the misery of urban slums with the lavish wealth of industrialists and financiers. Some identified themselves as Christian Socialists and began to seek more radical solutions to the problems of industrialization. Men and women like Frances Willard, Florence Kelley, and Henry Demorest Lloyd advocated new expansions of federal power to cope with a crisis of class. Temporarily ignored, their ideas would become influential after the turn of the century.[4]

A much larger proportion of middle- and upper-class Americans, especially in the Northeast and Midwest, took a sharp conservative turn. They viewed Populists and socialists as dangerous extremists who threatened class warfare. Fearing that strikes and riots were signs of impending anarchy, they supported police and military campaigns to put down worker protests. Nebraska Populist Cecilia O'Neill reported on an eastern trip that she encountered "heartless indifference" to the distress of the unemployed. When she told Pennsylvanians of "the dangers imminent from the unrest of the people, they said 'O, that is only around the mines, the Army and our Militia will keep order there.' No one," O'Neill added, "can make the fortunate and comfortable comprehend that humanity around the mines is of the same nature as his own."[5] The depression split America into anxious haves and dissenting have-nots.

In 1894 and 1896, the haves mobilized in overwhelming numbers for Republicans, who used the depression as evidence of the moral failings of their foes. As in earlier tariff debates, GOP leaders used domesticity as a basis for their arguments, but now economic policy became a secondary concern. Americans not only needed a return to higher tariffs and the gold standard; men also had to defend their homes against the immediate peril of "anarchy and communism." Republicans deployed evangelical language in this class context. They denounced Bryan's platform as "wicked" and "heretical." One New York minister argued that the gold standard represented all that was "good and clean and pure"; another branded silver Democrats' platform "immoral" and declared it against God's law, as set forth in "the Ten Commandments and enforced by the teachings of Jesus Christ." Republican women, as well as ministers, helped advance these religious and moral arguments. Speaking in Colorado, Ellen Foster urged women to play their part in "redeeming the state" from Populists' "unclean hands."[6]

The identification of new enemies brought not only a political realignment but also a shift in Republicans' gendered arguments. Party leaders still denounced the violent tendencies of uncontrolled manhood; the sectional threat from "anarchists and socialists" allowed them, as in the years of southern secession, to assert a claim as protectors of both nation and home. Their new appeals differed, however, from those of the war years. Early Republicans had portrayed southern Democrats as cruel aristocrats and their platforms had claimed to protect laborers, both slave and free. Now the threat was from laborers themselves. In response, eastern and middle-class Republicans styled themselves men of law and order, who would control a threat posed by criminal "riffraff."[7]

The shift reflected not only a chasm between economic classes but also Republicans' growing conservatism in relation to their opponents. Republicans were no longer the party most committed to expansion of government power. By advocating new federal measures to help farmers, the urban poor, and the unemployed, Populists had flanked the GOP; the gendered rhetoric of each party reflected its relative position. Populists used old Republican-style approaches, demanding government intervention to end "wage slavery" and provide economic "protection" to wage-earning women and men. In response, Republican leaders began to echo Democrats' arguments from the days of Reconstruction, warning that Populists would illegitimately enlarge the scope of federal power. Republicans now protected the home as much *against* government as by the use of it. Like Democrats, they described men's duty as the protection of homes against a violent physical threat.

The shift in Republicans' position was especially clear in their depiction of western Populists. Populist men were simultaneously weak and dangerous: they were both anarchists and potential tyrants. At the same time, Republicans launched an attack on Populist women comparable in its emotional intensity to antebellum Democrats' critique of abolitionism. Populist women were aggressive and threatening "harpies" and "shrews" whose power destabilized politics. Because Republicans now located civic order more in the private household than in activist government, they echoed Democrats' old fears that excessive federal power threatened gender order within the home.

Southern Democrats, in the meantime, waged a battle to defeat Populists in their own states. Consistent with party tradition, they used racial arguments to unify white male voters across class lines. Like Republicans in other parts of the country, southern Democrats drew on larger fears created by economic change, in this case the fragmentation of communities and growing fear of black crime. By the late 1890s, white southerners convinced each other and the nation that they were witnessing an epidemic of rape by black men. To avert this threat to white womanhood, southern Democrats openly advocated white supremacy. Their new arguments built on traditional Democratic views: white men appeared as protectors, white women as victims, and black men as a threat to public order, while black women did not appear in party rhetoric at all. Invoking the "black brute . . . lurking in the dark, a monstrous beast, crazed with lust"—as one commentator put it—brought potent political benefits.[8] Democrats solidified their control in the South, and by the turn of the century white supremacists won northern acquiescence in the projects of disfranchisement and segregation.

Both Republicans and southern Democrats, then, argued that the menace of Populism demanded an aggressive political stance in which men protected women physically by voting for the party of law and order. Faced with a massive depression, discontent among the poor, and proposals to expand state and federal power, conservatives in both camps reacted in similar ways. In the South, "protection to the home" meant Democratic white supremacy. Elsewhere it meant Republican economic policies, and control of government by elite men.

Unbalanced Men and Hysterical Women: The Republican Attack on Populism

There was an irony in Republicans' gender-based attacks on Populism. The People's Party never endorsed suffrage in its national platform; Populist women declared economic policies to be their first priority, and the most famous of them, Mary Lease, often proclaimed her indifference to suffrage. Opponents nonetheless ridiculed the party for advocating women's rights because its women held power as decision makers. The *Chicago Tribune* characterized a Populist national convention as "Old Mother Hubbard's cupboard," its delegates "of a family nature, all boys and girls together." Eastern papers took note of Lease's seconding speech for presidential candidate James Weaver, and of women's participation in committee and floor debates.[9] To outsiders, a party that rejected suffrage appeared to favor women's rights because it elected female delegates.

Republicans implied that women's power rendered the new party shrill and irresponsible. One California paper warned that "Populists in Petticoats" occupied seats at a party convention. The *New York Times* denounced "unsexed women of the Western border," suggesting not only Populist women's lack of femininity but their geographic and social marginality. A Chicago paper caricatured Populist delegates as ugly old hags. One Republican cartoon updated Robert Burns's poem "Tam O'Shanter": Tam was the American voter, fleeing from a horde of witches who represented western sectionalism, free silver, and anarchy.[10]

Reporting on Populist activities, eastern newspapers ran wild tales of female aggression. Under the headline "Women in Politics: Disgraceful Scenes at a Populist Convention in Denver," the *Philadelphia Public Ledger* offered this account: "Populists met here yesterday and adjourned after three hours of fighting. Women were in the thick of the melee, and they were in several instances instigators of the attack. . . . On being asked by Mrs. Reed if it was not 'time for him to go out and choke himself to death,' Mr. Akers retorted that Mrs. Reed had not added anything to her reputation by going out as a street singer. . . . Mrs. Reed and Mrs. Holmes administered the punishment themselves, and tore most of Mr. Akers' beard out." The report gave pause to eastern readers who might sympathize with Populism or woman suffrage. Annie Haines Barton of New Jersey mailed the clipping to a friend in Colorado, attaching an anxious query. She wrote that she supported suffrage but, on the other hand, the *Ledger* was a paper of "exceptional reliability."[11]

Western Republicans joined easterners in these attacks. William Allen White of Kansas denounced Populist "harpies" for telling people the state was "raising hell and letting the corn go to weeds." Local critics exaggerated Populist women's power in the party. Kansas Republicans called Annie Diggs "The Boss" and billed Mary Lease as "the woman who beat Senator Ingalls," implying that she controlled thousands of men. Explaining their loss in 1890, state Republicans claimed "it was the farmers' wives that did it," though women had not cast a single vote. These reports circulated back east. By the end of the decade, *Harper's Weekly* assessed women as "a disturbing and uncertain element" in the politics of western states.[12]

The claim was both class- and gender-based. By "unsexing" themselves, Populist women had relinquished the beauty, refinement, and sexual purity of middle-class ladies. One Kansan charged that Mary Lease was selling her voice—"the only thing marketable about the old harpy"—wherever she could get "the highest price." Lease was called, among other insults, a "loud-mouthed virago" and a "petticoated smut-mill" who had a "voice like a cat fight and a face that is rank poison to the naked eye." After converting to Populism, Helen Gougar of Indiana won the nickname "Yellin' Gougar." Though Lease's middle name was Elizabeth, some Republicans reported it as Ellen and made the same rhyme. One critic dismissed Populist stump speakers as a bunch of "short-haired amazons."[13]

In the eastern press, Populist women appeared to lack the proper domestic virtues. Describing the 1892 campaign in western states, *Leslie's Weekly* described them almost as roving bandits: "The People's Party appears to be utilizing women 'for all they are worth' in the promotion of its canvass. In some localities the campaign has been committed almost entirely to the hands of women, who have abandoned their homes, so to speak, and taken to the road. Forming themselves into bands, with a view of covering the utmost possible area of territory, they visit gatherings of men wherever they can find them." *Leslie's* suggested that eastern anti-suffragists should express their disapproval. Populist women then "might be induced to abandon their peculiar style of electioneering, and return to their deserted homes to take up more natural and womanly domestic duties."[14]

Populist farm families often endorsed the ideals of middle-class domesticity, but opponents rejected the claim that Populist women could be ladies. Their class-based attacks drew on longstanding fears of poor women who protested economic inequality. During labor disputes, commentators had often referred to working-class women as "shouting Amazons" who threatened social stability. Employers and editors compared striking women to prostitutes who "walked the streets shamelessly." These images resonated with urban middle-class men and women who feared social conflict. Facing Populism and economic crisis, GOP leaders began using the stereotypes in their electoral campaigns.[15]

At the same time, Republicans praised women like Ellen Foster for eloquently defending the GOP. The contrast was a matter of both partisanship and class: women who assisted one's own party were ladies, while opposing women were deviant and, in this case especially, lacking refinement and self-control. Foster and her colleagues also made no claim to power in Republican councils. Outside Wyoming and Colorado, where women voted, party conventions were exclusively male. Therese Jenkins of Wyoming served as an honorary national delegate in 1892, but upon arrival she stressed in a public statement, "I have no vote in the convention. I am only here by the courtesy of the State." Speaking to the same convention, Foster announced that women sought "no recognition." "In our service of Republicanism we know no personal preferences or factional strife," she declared. "Gentlemen, we have come; we are for service."[16]

In 1894, Colorado GOP leaders asked for help from Foster and her association. She must have been delighted with the request; Colorado governor Davis Waite had become a national symbol of "Populist misrule," and women had just won suffrage under his administration. Republicans were developing a moral line of attack, calling Waite an anarchist and a "corrupter of morals by his profane and violent language" (his propensity to cuss was widely known). A Leadville speaker told local Republicans their party represented "the sanctity of the home." "There is no man in the state with a home," he added, "who will not thank God as he walks to the polls next month with his wife at his side that she too will exercise her protest to Populist misrule." The key principle of the election, an editor wrote, was "the suppression of infamy, lawlessness, and crime"—that is, Populism. One disgusted Populist labeled this set of arguments the "decency racket."[17]

Middle-class women's campaign work complemented Republicans' moral allegations. Foster traveled west months before the election to train speakers and organize women's Republican clubs; she returned to stump all over the state. As she had in the past, Foster framed her party's moral and domestic arguments in woman-to-woman appeals. In Pueblo, she denounced Populists for having laid "unclean hands" on the body of American law. "To women," she proclaimed, "is given this magnificent privilege, not a cross, of redeeming the body of liberty from this pollution." Governor Waite was unfit to hold office: "for the love of your children," Foster pleaded, "I ask you to put this man away. . . . Stand with the party of law and order, decency and good government." Inspired by women's campaign work, the *Denver Times* illustrated the uncleanness of Waite and his colleagues in a cartoon published just before the election. It showed members of the Ladies' Republican League and the Denver Woman's Club engaged in "November housecleaning," sweeping out Populist insects with soap and lye. The insects, as they disappeared into the street, shouted "Down with the rich" and "To hell with capital."[18]

Guided by Foster, Republican women's campaign work expanded rapidly. In Waite's hometown of Aspen, Populists boasted that they would double their

Figure 1. Frances Willard, president of the national Woman's Christian Temperance Union as it rose to prominence in the 1880s. An architect of the Prohibition and Home Protection Party, Willard was one of the most famous women of her day. By the 1890s, frustrated by the failure of her third-party strategy, she dismissed parties as empty "tin cans"—structures that promised much and delivered little. This photograph dates from the 1870s, a few years before Willard assumed leadership of the WCTU. Courtesy Illinois State Library.

Figure 2. Judith Ellen Foster, president of the National Women's Republican Association from its foundation in 1888 until her death in 1910. Influential in WCTU councils until the mid-1880s, she left in protest over the union's endorsement of third-party work. In the 1890s Foster focused on the tariff issue. Like other Republicans, she argues that tariffs "protected the American home" by allowing men to earn a family wage. This 1908 portrait was taken in Washington, D.C. Courtesy Library of Congress.

Figure 3. Mary Elizabeth Lease, the Populist orator who rose to fame in the Kansas campaign of 1890 and conducted nationwide tours for the People's Party in 1892, garnering abuse from both Republicans and Democrats. Embittered by her exclusion from Kansas patronage posts, Lease left politics after 1896. This photograph was taken in the mid-1890s. Courtesy Kansas State Historical Society.

Figure 4. "Political Enchantment," 1884. Thomas Nast depicts (from left to right) New Jersey Republican William Walter Phelps (whom he labels "the New Jersey Lily"), GOP presidential candidate James Blaine, and *New York Tribune* editor Whitelaw Reid ("the Tribune Daisy"). Nast adopts the traditional Democratic tactic of labeling his opponents effeminate aristocrats. The larger reference is to witches, traditional symbols of corruption and gender disorder, but the Republicans here are ridiculous rather than frightening. In the caption, Phelps says the brew is "too, too utter!" *Harper's Weekly*, 10 Oct. 1884.

Copyrighted 1893 by F. Miller.

President and Mrs Cleveland

Figure 5. President Grover Cleveland and Frances Folsom Cleveland, soon after the former's reelection in 1892. Portraits like this circulated widely in the 1888 and 1892 campaigns, printed on posters, cards, banners, bandannas, and even china. Celebrating the Cleveland's wedding, Democrats invoked a sentimental domesticity that had previously been a Republican theme. Courtesy Library of Congress.

Figures 6 and 7. "English Free Trade Illustrated." Pictures of coal workers in England accompanied Republican warnings of the perils of lowering import tariffs. These women, manual laborers, would have appeared to Americans as "unsexed" and degraded. Left image printed in New York as a postcard; courtesy Division of Political History, Museum of American History, Smithsonian Institution. Republican "industrial researcher" Nathaniel McKay reported that Eliza Ryder, with the wheelbarrow, told him she had been "forty years wheeling coal" and wore "trousers cast off by the men." Both images appeared in the *Minneapolis Tribune*, 5 Oct. 1892, *Los Angeles Times*, 11 Oct. 1892, and many other newspapers.

Figure 8. "The Tariff and the Workingman." Democrats charged that high tariffs, far from helping working families, drove up the cost of living. This image, similar to a dry-goods advertisement, lists the tariff "cost" on various goods. Starting in the upper left, it also tells two stories. Clockwise, "the laborer rises in the morning and puts on his flannel shirt (taxed 88%), his trousers (taxed 57%) . . . "; counterclockwise, "his wife wears a woolen dress (taxed 60%) . . . [and] uses thread (taxed 53%)," continuing with a sewing machine, scissors, and other items. Produced by the New York Tariff Reform Club for campaign use and printed in the *New York Post*, 25 Oct. 1888. Widely circulated; see for example *Lynchburg Virginian*, 29 Oct. 1888.

Figure 9. "The Two Counters. It is the shopping women who have done this.—Ex-Speaker [Thomas] Reed, referring to the great Democratic victories of 1890." This Democratic cartoon shows women contemplating the alleged impact of the new Republican tariff, shepherded through Congress by William McKinley. Note Democrats' class-based appeal to the working woman on the right, rather than the sumptuously dressed lady. *Philadelphia Record* reprinted in *New York World*, 31 Oct. 1892.

THE CAMPAIGN OF EDUCATION!

Figure 10. "The Campaign of Education!" A Populist view of political mobilization. The caption read, "Political Ignorance is the Politician's Pride. The above is the kind of work which 'Carried Kansas' and is the only hope of the Nation." A woman serves as librarian and educator for a diverse group of male voters, including businessmen, working-men, and farmers. Books by women are prominent in the library. *American Nonconformist*, 9 July 1891.

Figure 11. Caricatures of a Populist woman and suffragist, at the 1896 Chicago Populist convention. The lefthand sketch may be Susan B. Anthony. "Sweet 16 to 1" is a reference to the Populist plank of silver coinage at a 16:1 ratio with gold, and also contrasts the proper behavior of "sweet" young women and the political roles asserted by Populists and suffragists. Clipping from unknown newspaper (probably Chicago), Herman E. Taubeneck papers, American Heritage Center, University of Wyoming.

THE GODDESS OF DEMOCRASY.

Figure 12. "The Goddess of Democrasy [sic]." A cartoon appearing during the North Carolina white supremacy campaign of 1898, in which Democrats swept a Populist/Republican coalition out of power amid widespread violence and intimidation by white supremacists. The goddess carries a cornucopia marked "Prosperity and Peace" and holds out a wreath labeled "Protection to White Women." Democratic women appeared at white supremacist rallies, often dressed in white. *Raleigh News and Observer*, 28 Sept. 1898.

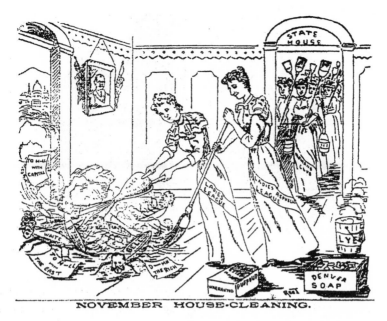

NOVEMBER HOUSE-CLEANING.

Figure 13. "November Housecleaning." A Republican cartoonist shows members of the Ladies Republican League and Denver Woman's Club entering the State House to remove the occupants. Governor Davis Waite and other Populists appear as insects who are swept out the door as the women clean with soap and lye. Middle-class and elite Republican women were highly visible in the campaign, the first in which Colorado women exercised full suffrage. *Denver Times*, 27 Oct. 1894.

Figure 14. "You Can Always Find Them. While the wife is at home taking in the washing to support them, the free-silver 'statesmen' are hanging around the corners formulating financial plans for saving the government." In this Republican cartoon, Populist men let their wives support them, and women are unsexed by hard physical labor (note the neglected infant on the floor). The shabby clothes suggest the class bias of Republican attacks. *Los Angeles Times*, 23 Oct. 1896.

Figure 15. "Warning of the Ghost of Kansas: 'Beware, Little Girl—He Ruined Me.'" A Populist suitor tries to seduce the state of Washington, while Kansas (which voted Populist in 1890) issues a warning from beyond the grave. The GOP cartoonist conflates women's sexual corruption (ending in death) with economic depression. Numerous cartoons of the 1890s used "courting" as a metaphor for partisan appeals to voters. Almost all set the scene on park benches, a recognizable location for romance—or seduction. *Seattle Post-Intelligencer*, 27 Sept. 1896.

Figure 16. Theodore Roosevelt as a cowboy, in one of thousands of cartoons that portrayed him on horseback, hunting, or fighting. Roosevelt fashioned an aggressive public image, starting with carefully shaped reports of his military feats in the Spanish-American War. In the Progressive Era he represented, more than any other man, a reassertion of traditional masculine virtues.

This cartoon, from 1904, shows him rounding up states in the presidential election. Alabama, a Democratic maverick, is stuck in the herd. Courtesy Library of Congress.

previous majorities because of "the great interest displayed by the women of Aspen," but privately they were not so sure, and the local Populist committee wrote to the governor's wife for assistance. "Our opponents are making a special effort here to secure the women," he reported. "I understand that you are sending out Phoebe Couzins to stump the state. Could she take in Aspen? . . . We would of course give her a good reception." A Denver Republican confidently predicted that his party would win the votes of two-thirds of registered women.[19]

On election day, his estimate proved accurate. Women's overwhelming Republican majorities reflected general sentiment in 1894: depression had devastated the state and Coloradans reacted by voting out the ruling party. In addition, Populist strongholds were in mining districts where the ratio of women to men was low. A doubtful Populist editor had noted in October that almost two-thirds of Colorado women lived in districts with previous Republican majorities. These included eastern farmlands and cities, especially Denver. Female voters probably did not swing the election, but Populists who expected women to vote for them as a bloc found they had miscalculated. Local Republicans were delighted. "Women were a prominent factor in cleaning up our politics," boasted a Georgetown editor. The *Greeley Sun* declared that Colorado owed "a debt of gratitude to Mrs. J. Ellen Foster."[20]

Political housekeeping thus emerged in post-suffrage Colorado as an overtly Republican enterprise. To "elevate and purify politics," as one stump speaker described it, was to throw Populists out of office. Allegedly nonpartisan women's groups like the Denver Women's Club took part in the campaign and received Republican praise for being "good housekeepers," using their brooms to sweep away political dirt. The new goals of Republican women reflected both class and partisan concerns. After the election, Denver women's clubs pressured state legislators to raise the age of consent from sixteen to eighteen and to grant divorced mothers equal rights to their children. At the same time, Republican women's clubs undertook campaigns for public hygiene and the installation of park benches. While some of these initiatives protected women, none addressed labor issues or specifically aided the working class.[21]

Middle-class women in New York City undertook similar work in 1894, "purifying politics" by electing Republican men but directing their animus against Democrats rather than Populists. Since 1890, a group of Episcopalian ministers had tried to organize middle-class citizens against Tammany Hall Democrats, who held a firm grip on city offices. The Republican reformers made little headway until their leader, Reverend Charles Parkhurst, took note of women's involvement in Charles Schieren's 1893 campaign for mayor of Brooklyn. The Brooklyn Woman's Protective Health Association, impatient with official apathy, had successfully recruited a number of women's groups to promote Schieren's election. Parkhurst concluded that women could lend moral weight, celebrity, and a great deal of volunteer labor to his New York City campaign.[22]

Leaders of the anti-Tammany movement insisted that women would play a nonpartisan role. Parkhurst claimed "there is no politics in the matter. It is a question of right against wrong." Calling his group the Women's Municipal League, he declared, "if the mother loves her child, I can conceive of no object for which she can use her power to greater advantage than to help in the formation of a government in which that child shall be proud to live." Few observers seem to have taken these statements seriously. Author William Dean Howells endorsed the movement but added, "I do not see how it can be anything but politics." Elizabeth Cady Stanton dispensed the same opinion in her letter of allegiance: "if regulating affairs of state is not politics, I do not know what it is." Mrs. E. B. Grannis, Parkhurst's first choice to head the Women's Municipal League, declined because she was disillusioned with the Republican Party. "I have been a Republican twenty-five years," she declared, but she pointed out that the GOP had not passed temperance or woman suffrage; why should she do anything on their behalf? Grannis obviously did not believe the anti-Tammany campaign would be nonpartisan.[23]

The extent to which Republicans financed "nonpartisan" anti-Tammany groups is a matter of speculation, but they clearly offered encouragement. The *New York Times* explained that Lincoln Hall, a Republican building, had been "kindly loaned to the nonpartisan movement for good government" by someone at GOP headquarters. And while not all leaders of the Women's Municipal League were Republicans, in 1894 many used arguments with a distinctly Republican cast. They were quick to cite not only municipal corruption but the depression, connecting the two problems and blaming Democrats for both. Speaking to German-American women a League member advised, "You in common with the rest of the people throughout this great city must have felt the hard times. You must have known how hard it has been for your husbands and your brothers to get work. . . . Tell your husband or your brother, or the voter in your family that the time has come for a change." Addressing another group of immigrants, a League speaker urged each one to say to her husband ("when he is in good humor"), "we've had Tammany Hall a long time, and now times are hard. Suppose this year you give the other side a chance." Repetition of this theme suggests that the "moral" campaign was in large part a referendum on the economy.[24]

Despite its nonpartisan claims, the strategy of the Women's Municipal League paralleled that of the New York Women's Republican Association. Both arranged rallies and founded clubs across the city, concentrating on Harlem and the Lower East Side. Both groups printed and distributed campaign leaflets in many languages and addressed audiences recently arrived from Bohemia, Russia, and Poland. Their goals were the same: in the words of one reporter, they sought to "honeycomb" Tammany Hall's "formerly solid hold upon the tenement-house districts." Mrs. Alexander Bremer, a former factory inspector and member of the Municipal League, visited German and Russian immigrants in East Side tenements. An admiring reporter who hailed this reform work remarked in passing that Bremer's husband was an anti-Tammany candidate and that she "did not wholly neglect her husband's interest." In other words, a candidate's wife could stump for her husband and still win praise as a nonpartisan reformer.[25]

Both Republican women and the Women's Municipal League conducted energetic campaigns, but their effect on the vote is questionable. Tammany gave up substantial power on election day, but its losses were smaller than those of Democrats in other parts of the state and nation, and of Populists in the West. Journalists hailed "the defeat of Tammany," but the machine, after taking steps to clean up its image, endured for decades longer. City Democrat George Washington Plunkitt remarked in 1905 that "it's no use to go through the list of reformers who said they sounded in the death knell of Tammany in 1894. They're gone for good, and Tammany's pretty well, thank you." Not until the 1930s did Tammany lose its grip on city politics.[26]

Nonetheless, the anti-Tammany campaign won widespread attention. New York City was still the nation's political headquarters; Tammany was a famous symbol of corruption, and efforts to beat the Democrats in their solid tenement wards elicited widespread comment. When women joined the effort it was a sensation. Observers proclaimed the "regeneration of New York City" and reiterated the nonpartisan nature of the victory. Even some Democrats agreed. Watching from Philadelphia, wealthy matron Katherine Johnstone Wharton wrote that "election day here was very quiet but in N.Y. the excitement has been intense & to have defeated Hill & Tammany is a great triumph, though as a Democrat and free-trader I must regret many things." Beside this entry she glued a news clipping stating that "the victory in Pennsylvania is purely political; in New York it is a moral one."[27]

Such ambivalence among elite eastern Democrats presaged a split in party loyalties that the 1896 election revealed more clearly. In the presidential campaign, Republicans combined their anti-Populist and anti-Democratic arguments into a unified moral and economic warning. Democrats' regional coalition fragmented as young William Jennings Bryan, a Nebraska Democrat, captured the party's nomination on a platform advocating silver coinage. Most Populists endorsed the ticket; though it included only a few of their demands, they hoped it would address their most urgent grievances by expanding the money supply. Fusion with Silver Democrats offered Populists a chance for greater national recognition and influence, perhaps even in the White House. Georgia Populist Tom Watson, though, expressed well-founded fears that endorsing Democrats meant his party would "play Jonah while they play whale."[28]

President Grover Cleveland, still the Democrats' nominal leader, was appalled by Bryan's nomination. Large numbers of eastern Democrats refused to accept free silver or cooperate with "Popocrats." Some voted reluctantly for GOP candidate William McKinley; others ran a splinter Gold Democratic ticket with no chance of success. In the old party tradition, these men denounced proposals to enlarge federal power, especially through silver coinage. Gold Democrats attacked the "compulsory purchase of silver bullion" as a form of "paternalism." One called it "an attempt to paralyze industry by using all the powers of government to take property from the hands of those who created it and place it in the hands of those who covet it." "Toilers of America," this speaker asked, "Guardians of your own homes, . . . will you submit to this conspiracy?"[29]

Republicans joined Gold Democrats in viewing silver coinage as an illegitimate expansion of government power. *Harper's Weekly* explained that the policy was proposed by people "who have little money" and who believed "Government ought to help them to more." GOP leader Chauncey Depew argued that Silver Democrats planned "to enter upon a vague and vast system of paternal government, and to destroy those elements of American liberty by which the Government governs least." The *Philadelphia Record* denounced Bryan's platform for its "doctrines of paternal government and state socialism." GOP speakers and editors referred to silver currency as "fiat" money, whose value would be set by government decree. One speaker told a rally that "a law compelling the people of this country" to accept dollars created "by fiat of Congress" would set up a "Commune in the United States."[30]

The tendency to view Silver Democrats' platform as socialistic was reinforced by its call for a federal income tax. Denouncing Republican tariffs, Silver Democrats argued that if the poor could be taxed to benefit the rich, the reverse must also be constitutional. Their position was a radical departure from earlier Democratic conventions, which had declared themselves "opposed to all propositions which, upon any pretext, would convert the General Government into a machine for collecting taxes." Accepting his nomination in a speech at Madison Square Garden, Bryan declared, "I shall offer no apology for the income-tax plank." He called it "not unjust, considered in connection with other methods of taxation in force" and added that it is "not new, nor is it based on hostility to the rich. The system is employed in several of the most important nations of Europe."[31] The plank offered a stark contrast to the GOP's conservative recommendations for coping with depression, which were to raise tariffs and back all paper currency in gold. Neither was an innovation; they were a restatement of Republican policies from the more prosperous 1880s.

While pronouncing the silver platform socialistic, Republicans also called it anarchic. Silver Democrats like Illinois governor John Altgeld, sympathetic to the cause of labor, had been angered by President Cleveland's use of federal troops to put down strikes; their platform denounced such interventions in a statement opponents dubbed "the anarchy plank." Republican depictions of "anarchists" and "barbarians" drew on older GOP fears about uncontrolled working-class manhood. Party leaders consistently, though, described Silver Democrats as a physical threat to the home, whether by their desire to use federal force or by their permissive attitude toward strikers. In his letter of acceptance, Republican vice presidential nominee Garrett Hobart declared the silver cause a "war upon American homemakers [and] an invasion of the homes of the provident." A Vermont senator called on men to vote Republican and "shield the peaceful citizens of this country, their wives, their children and their homes, from the violence and wickedness of the mob."[32]

Thus construed, Republican arguments echoed the old rhetoric of gender disorder and sexualized corruption once used by Reconstruction-era Democrats. Kansas Senator John Ingalls assailed "the Populism of lust, of boodleism, of corruption, of prostitution, of brutality." A Chicago paper claimed Democratic men were "trained in the school of camp-followers." In Ohio, John Hay called them the party of "fury and passion, madness and crime," while House Speaker Thomas B. Reed warned that "free silver is a seduction and an allurement."[33] These appeals, like those of Democrats in the Radical years, linked expanded federal power to family disintegration and gender disorder, represented by aggressive women and corrupt men.

As in their warnings of impending socialism and anarchy, Republicans conflated aggression and weakness in their opponents. Populist leaders were "a dangerous menace" but also "impotent," their platform "silly" and "nonsensical." As in attacks on Populist women, the latter charges suggested an inversion of men's and women's roles. One Republican politician mailed out hundreds of postcards ridiculing Silver Democrats as the party of "Auntie-Trust." Another suggested that Populist men were "the slack and indolent farmers, those who let the women and gals milk the cows, cut the wood and carry the water." The *Los Angeles Times* ran a cartoon of a Populist man jawing on a street corner while his wife slaved over a laundry tub.[34] The obvious contrast was to Republican men, whose tariff and currency policies offered women protection from wage work and the chance for refinement and leisure.

No one suffered this denigration more often than Bryan himself. The *New York Times* labeled him "the Emotional Candidate." Other papers called him shallow, weak, and wishy-washy, and some claimed he was mentally unstable. Campaigning in Chicago, New York Governor Theodore Roosevelt remarked that "it is not merely school girls that have hysterics; mob leaders sometimes have them, and so do well-meaning demagogues." *Leslie's Weekly* wrote that Bryan "is dominated by emotionalism and is therefore incapable of logical performance."[35]

The source of the stereotype was not Bryan himself. He was an imposing man, over six feet tall, young and handsome, with a powerful voice and legendary campaign stamina. No one could have been less like a schoolgirl, but opponents who described him as feminine conjured images of gender confusion among his supporters. Republican Andrew White dismissed Bryan's followers as "unbalanced men and hysterical women." The *Philadelphia Times* argued that Populist women's political activities were "likely to give level-headed women pause." Woman suffrage, the paper suggested, might "swell the ignorant and cranky vote" more than it would increase the "intelligent" electorate.[36]

In 1896, Republicans successfully tagged their opponents as instigators of class warfare, but their own arguments were blatantly class-based. A Nebraskan suggested that Populists were disgustingly low-bred; he compared them to "what a herd of hogs would be in the parlor of a careful housekeeper" and complained about "the filth they have scattered." A California Republican speaker dismissed the new party as human trash. "It is made up," he said, "of the refuse found in the back yards where the tin cans and dead cats of other political organizations are thrown. (Cheers)."[37] Republicans vehemently denied that classes existed in America, insisting that the interests of capital and labor were the same. In the face of massive depression, their platform advanced not a single new idea; the thrust of their argument was to label their opponents hysterical socialists. With strikes devolving into riots and starving tramps roaming the countryside, fearful middle-class Americans seemed ready to accept these arguments. But the GOP platform did not, in the long term, offer solutions to the conflicts that had emerged in an industrialized nation.

The depth of Americans' class and regional fears in 1896 was apparent in their references to the Civil War. One southern Gold Democrat suggested that Bryan's nomination would lead to realignment and a "revolutionary government . . . as when Frémont was chosen by the Republicans." Some campaigners on both sides predicted war between East and West, a theme especially prominent in the GOP camp. Stump speaker Addie Billings told a San Francisco audience to steer clear of "the siren voice chanting . . . to a silvery tune"; she accused Silver Democrats of supporting states' rights and added, "we thought that blood enough was spilled from 1861 to '65 to settle that question forever, but it comes serenely before you today in true traitor style, hiding in the folds of a silver petticoat."[38]

Sectionalism, as well as class-based fears, justified a strong response from Republicans who feared disunion. If anything, the prospect of renewed civil war resonated even more strongly with Americans than did potential conflict between rich and poor. Republicans conflated the two. They urged veterans to "prefer country to party now as you did in the dark days of the civil war, and rally to the support of our gallant comrade, Major McKinley." Reacting to Silver Democrats' allegation that businessmen were forcing employees to vote Republican, one editor wrote that if "coercion" were needed, it was "such 'coercion' as Abraham Lincoln employed," because Bryan's campaign was "the most stupendous peril which has ever menaced the welfare, the honor, the free institutions of America since they were assailed by the armies of treason."[39]

The bloody shirt, which had proved ineffective for the GOP in the late 1880s, thus reappeared in a new form. Working-class and regional challenges to the political order justified a renewed militaristic masculinity. Strikes in industrial cities and mining towns did not yet constitute a war, but they threatened to become one; to Republicans and Gold Democrats, Populists and Silver Democrats represented that peril in political form. The crisis—as conservatives saw it—required men to think as soldiers, putting aside male domesticity and acting as aggressive defenders of their homes. In combination with the attack on Populist "harpies," this suggested that McKinley's victory would introduce a new conservatism in gender as well as class and regional terms. Republican men were abandoning domestic manhood and representing men's votes as acts of physical protection to their families.

Redemption in the South: The Democratic Attack on Populism

By the start of the 1890s, Democrats held state power in most of the South and Republicans despaired of any support from the region in national campaigns.

But few southern Democrats believed their position was secure. First, Senator Henry Cabot Lodge of Massachusetts presented a major elections bill to Congress in 1890. The proposed law, dubbed "the force bill" by its opponents, threatened to resume federal supervision of elections wherever 100 local citizens complained of irregularities. It lost by a narrow margin. In a competitive atmosphere, Democrats expected Republicans to persist in such attempts to reestablish their southern wing. Even where Democrats held power by overwhelming margins, they viewed black voters as a potential threat while Republicans held national power.[40]

Second, the depression intensified such fears by fragmenting the national Democratic Party and making Populism an attractive alternative. Like many other Americans, southern Democrats blamed Grover Cleveland for the depression, and party leaders in the region distanced themselves quickly from the unpopular president. Sympathetic to free silver and resentful of northeastern financiers, southern Democrats overwhelmingly joined the silver coalition. Though Bryan lost elsewhere, he captured the electoral votes of every ex-Confederate state.[41]

These Democrats did not consider themselves Populists, however, and southern Populists in turn repudiated any state-level cooperative partnership with their old enemies. While Silver Democrats and Populists cooperated in the West, their southern counterparts engaged in a bitter struggle for control of state governments in the region. Appearing in a dramatically different social and political context than that of the Plains, southern Populists' class-based challenge carried an implied threat to racial order. Most southern Populist leaders were white; very few believed in social equality between the races. Nevertheless many endorsed black political rights and attempted to build interracial coalitions with white and black Republicans. In a few places they succeeded. Democrats around the region watched in horror as the North Carolina People's Party fused with state Republicans and took control of the state. With Republicans' national power reestablished in 1894 and 1896, the possibility of another "force bill" loomed; within the South, a winning coalition of Republicans and Populists represented Democrats' worst nightmare.[42]

To cope with the threat, southern Democrats appealed directly for "white supremacy." As Georgia Populist Tom Watson observed, Democratic criticisms of Populism often consisted of one word—"nigger."[43] Facing a challenge on economic issues, Democrats changed the terms of debate. They associated Populists with Republicans, telling ever more lurid tales of the horrors of Reconstruction. As they had in the past, southern Democrats connected black men's voting rights with the threat of rape or violation of the white household. Confronted with Populism, Democrats broadcast this argument more frequently and loudly than ever, and they ultimately used it to disfranchise black men.

Like Republicans, whose campaigns appropriated broader stereotypes of anarchic strikers and working-class amazons, Democrats built their political appeal in the context of a larger social debate. The early 1890s witnessed a rising tide of lynching. Racial violence had long been a constant of southern life, but public, ritualized murders of black men were a new phenomenon that elicited widespread efforts at explanation. Almost all southern white commentators argued that the cause of lynching was black men's proclivity to rape white women. This claim, as one northerner observed, "strained the heartcords" of people across the nation. White Americans were increasingly willing to blame black men for racial tension, and insinuations of rape thrived on the polite rule that public discussions of sexuality should be veiled and circumspect. Frederick Douglass wrote angrily that rape was a crime "most easily imputed and most difficult to disprove." A southern minister, challenged to verify his outrageous estimate of the number of rapes by black men, claimed he could "fill a column of *The Independent* for every week of the current year with the recital of facts. [But] most of these facts, as every decent man knows, are of such a nature as ought not to be published . . . in a journal that goes into private families." Modesty permitted another man to claim in the *New York Tribune* that he knew why blacks were prone to rape, but that "this is no place to explain it."[44]

Because lynching was allegedly triggered by the crimes of individual black men rather than by Republican policy, white southerners argued that it was unrelated to past political violence. In 1892, when Douglass denounced lynching in the *North American Review*, W. Cabell Bruce wrote a quick response accusing nonsoutherners of "partisan hostility." Bruce set the pattern for more than a decade of self-justification by defenders of the white South, most of whom were men. Some voiced perfunctory regret over lynching but asserted its necessity on the grounds that rape was becoming more frequent every year. In the early 1890s, such explanations did not meet full acceptance outside the South. Some white journalists joined Frederick Douglass, Ida B. Wells, and other black leaders in condemning lynching. Self-described "white supremacists," however, had seized an early initiative. From 1897 onward, sympathetic national coverage of their views rose to a peak in 1903, the year in which Georgia's John Temple Graves appeared at Chautauqua, New York, to claim that lynch mobs were "the most potential bulwark between the woman of the South and such a carnival of crime as would infuriate the world."[45]

Southern justifications were so successful, and the issue of rape so explosive, that by 1900 many national magazines expressed open sympathy with lynchers. "The *Outlook* believes that lynching is explicable and even necessary," declared its editor. *Harper's Weekly* denounced "the new negro crime, by which, of course, we mean the assault of a white woman," and its editors tentatively endorsed lynching, castration, and "geographical separation" as remedies for rape. Almost no white commentators disputed the notion that rape caused lynching, even as white-on-black violence spread to midwestern and northern cities. This was largely because the claim of rape distinguished lynching from other forms of racial violence that had provoked national outrage. "Public indifference on the subject of lynching is almost universal the country over," one writer observed. "Many perhaps feel that no punishment is too severe for the chief crime."[46]

Caroline Pemberton, daughter of a Confederate general, wrote from New

York that accusations against blacks "with respect to a particular crime" were "inflaming the passions" of northerners. She reported that educated people were developing "the most astonishing theories to account for such a state of affairs—theories that lead intelligent men to distrust the influence of education on the negro, and to believe that his low brutality demanded a separate course of treatment." Frederick Douglass described the devastating impact of the charge of rape against black men: "The Negro may and does feel its malign influence in the very air he breathes. He may read it in the faces of men among whom he moves. It has cooled his friends; it has heated his enemies and arrested at home and abroad, in some measure, the generous efforts that good men were wont to make for his improvement and elevation. It has deceived his friends . . . for nearly all of them, in some measure, have accepted this charge against the Negro as true."[47]

Black journalist Ida B. Wells tried for a decade to rouse northern public opinion, arguing that lynching was a political act unrelated to rape. She publicized compelling statistics on the causes of lynching, showing that explanations ranged from murder to "giving evidence against a white person" and "inflammatory language," and that rape was seldom the cause. White supremacists' response to widespread circulation of this data was to rewrite their argument. Rather than causing all lynchings, they wrote, rape had *originally* caused them. "At first lynching as a rule was reserved as the penalty almost exclusively for one crime, which appealed for special vengeance," wrote Winthrop D. Sheldon, LL.D. "Very soon, however, other forms of criminality came to be included." Clarence Poe of North Carolina explained that after a rape the "furious mob spirit" could "break through the resisting wall of law and order. Once through, it does not stop."[48]

White commentators were correct in noting that lynchings were not political in the narrow sense. Most were local responses to murders, rapes, or arsons—either real or alleged—and only a few took place during electoral campaigns. Lynching opponents were right, however, to point out the links between white justifications of lynching and the historic arguments of southern Democrats. Public discussion of "the new Negro crime" had broader implications than the phenomenon of lynching, because white supremacists described black men's rape of white women as a result of Radical Republicanism. In her popular book *Dixie After the War*, Myrta Lockett Avary declared that "the rapist is a product of the reconstruction period. . . . He came into life in the abnormal atmosphere of a time rife with discussions of social equality theories." Elizabeth Avery Meriwether, a Memphis suffrage advocate, charged Republicans with innumerable crimes against white southerners. "Rapes of young matrons and maidens and little girl children," she claimed, "were not known in the South until after the savage but slumbering instincts of negro nature had been awakened by instructions."[49]

Judge Henderson M. Somerville of Alabama explained the nature of such instructions to a national audience: "The localities where these heinous crimes [rapes] occur are, almost invariably, those in which the negro holds the balance of political power, or where his unsuppressed vote is honestly contested and ardently solicited. . . . As a voter he is coddled, petted and magnified. . . . The negro thus asserts himself, and his sense of his own importance, which was quiescent and pacific so long as he was kept in political and social subordination, becomes often offensively and insolently inflated."

Thomas Nelson Page argued that "the crime of rape had its baleful origin in the teaching of equality and the placing of power in the ignorant negroes' hands." He added that "to the ignorant and brutal young negro, [equality] signifies but one thing: the opportunity to enjoy, equally with white men, the privilege of cohabiting with white women." A Georgia editor made the point more succinctly. "The floater in politics," he wrote, "makes the rapist in fact."[50] To white supremacists, Republicans' past abuse of federal power remained the root cause of black men's alleged sexual violations of white households.

A few Democrats reintroduced this argument before the Populist threat appeared. During an 1888 campaign against Republicans in North Carolina, a Democratic handbook printed this statement:

> Let no white man, especially let no white woman, fail to read the following extracts from the infamous record made by the Radical party. . . . "Go after the women then. Don't hesitate to throw your arms around their necks now and then when their husbands are not around and give them a good ———."
> . . . We ask the young white men and the young white women of North Carolina what sort of a place this home of theirs would be to-day had it not been for the bold, manly, determined fight the Democrats made against the Radicals? . . . Especially let the young women of to-day think of the insults to their mothers twenty years ago.

By the early 1890s, South Carolina Governor Ben Tillman accused his opponents of "seeking Negro votes by encouraging black men to defile white women" and called the editor of a Charleston newspaper "blacker at heart than the rapist."[51]

Such allegations proliferated in the late 1890s, leveled against both Populists and Republicans. A defector from the Alabama People's Party declared that his former allies wanted to "destroy chastity." In 1896, the *Birmingham State Herald* denounced Populists' and Republicans' combined state ticket by asking readers, "which crowd do you prefer to cast your fate and political fortune with, the 142,000 negroes . . . or the honest white men of Alabama? If you are at all in doubt about what to do consult your wife or mother. They can and will tell you promptly." The *Herald* described the horrors of Republican rule after the war, when the South had burned "red with the passion fires of lust and rapine." The editor went on to praise women's loyalty in a piece titled "Woman's Democracy": "The south's noble women were democrats in reconstruction days and their blood would almost boil when they saw the 'kinky-headed' sons of Ham, armed with guns and backed by federal bayonets, marching to the ballot boxes on southern soil. . . . In the county of Chambers nine-tenths of the noble women are opposed to the 'fusion combine—compromise of principle,' and in favor of white supremacy and the Democratic Party."

"Should the fusion crowd get control of the state," warned the *Herald*, "how long would it be before laws against miscegenation would be repealed?"[52]

The rape issue threatened to resurface wherever political parties sought black support. In Georgia's 1896 gubernatorial campaign, Populists appealed to black voters by claiming that Democratic incumbent W. Y. Atkinson had pardoned a white man guilty of murdering a black. Democrats responded by publicizing the case of Adolphus Duncan, a black Georgian accused of raping a white woman. Atkinson had determined that Duncan was innocent and set him free. Populists then began race-baiting: they pounced on the "Duncan Circular," soon known as the "Rape Circular," and claimed Atkinson's leniency was inciting black men to rape. In a series of appeals to white voters, Populists Seaborn Wright and Tom Watson declared that the circular "of itself ought to defeat the state democratic ticket." Atkinson won the election, but he and his Democratic allies spent the last weeks of the campaign defending themselves against the "Rape Circular"—not an enviable task.[53]

North Carolina's 1898 white supremacy campaign, so-called by its leaders, was the most famous and effective invocation of pure womanhood to justify white rule. For a decade beforehand, North Carolina Republicans and Populists had controlled the state government and many local offices. After Republican gains in 1888, North Carolinian Josie Bowen wrote to her sister that her husband "declares his intention of leaving . . . —that he cannot trust the future of his daughters here, nor that there is any future here for respectable white people." Rather than rape, however, most whites seem to have resented interracial contact and "negro insolence." When Republicans appointed a black postmaster in Rocky Mount, a resident complained that "white ladies have to file in a booth built in front of the delivery window, in order to be waited on. The booth is always crowded with negroes." In another county, a black magistrate angered neighbors by issuing "a civil warrant . . . against as respectable a white lady as there is in Lenoir county." A Democrat in Sanford declared that he hoped never to see "a license for the marriage of one of my daughters be issued by a great big burly negro," as if issuing a marriage license were a form of sexual contamination.[54]

In the summer of 1898 such indignities seemed likely to continue because the Populist-Republican coalition was popular. "It soon became apparent to me," wrote one Democrat, "that we did not have a ghost of a chance to win the election." Party leaders were "burning" to reassert "the supremacy of the white race against the domination of the motly crew that had had charge." Throughout the state, Democratic orators began to agitate the race issue, establishing white supremacy clubs to divert attention from Populists' and Republicans' economic programs. Wilmington Democrats hired a black detective "to ascertain and let us know what the purpose of the negroes was and what they were doing, and we ascertained, I believe, that they were doing practically nothing." Nevertheless, district Democrats threatened violence until all local Republican candidates withdrew. After menacing warnings, state-level Republican and Populist nominees declined to speak in Wilmington.[55]

Throughout the campaign, white supremacists emphasized that their cause offered protection to white women. Gubernatorial candidate Charles B. Aycock appealed for disfranchisement of black "fiends" in the name of "the White Womanhood of the State." The *Raleigh News and Observer* ran a cartoon of the Goddess of Democracy inspiring white supremacists by holding out a wreath with the slogan, "protection to white women." Speaking to cotton mill workers, a Democrat appealed to "every iota of manhood and maternal love" to defeat the "monster" of black political domination.[56]

Just as Republicans in the West and Northeast asked for women's aid in "redeeming" the nation from misrule, North Carolina Democrats invited women to join new White Government Unions and assist with the campaign. One woman reported that "in town after town, Aycock was met by huge processions with brass bands, floats of pretty girls dressed in white to symbolize the purity of white women, [and] contingents of mounted Red Shirts. . . . At Roxboro, he appeared on a float surrounded by a bevy of Person County's most beautiful daughters; inscribed in large letters on each side of the float were the words, Protect Us." In Kinston, Miss Rebecca Strowd presented a banner to local Democratic men and called upon white men to vote Democratic "in the names of their wives and daughters." Writing to the *Charlotte Observer*, another white woman appealed for the protection of "honest, faithful Christian men." In a private letter, Rebecca C. Wood of Edenton called the Republican governor "that infamous malignant blot upon the state" and seconded a politician's call "that our old historic river shall be choked with the bodies of our enemies, white and black, but what this state shall be redeemed." "I wish you could see Anna," she added. "She is fairly rampant and blood thirsty. . . . If the white men can stand negro supremacy we neither can nor will."[57]

Meanwhile, Democratic men armed themselves heavily. A Populist in Duplin County reported that "pistols & Brass Knucks &c are drawn" by local Democrats. Another Populist requested aid from party leaders but pleaded, "Dont publish this from Pocosin NC I have some bad enemys of the Democrats and they mite burne me out. I never seen just such a time in my life." A woman in Wilson, North Carolina, wrote to her daughter that white men with Winchesters had patrolled the streets on election day, disarmed all blacks, and threatened Republicans. "It was an awesome sight," she reported, "to drive through town in the dark and see synods of armed men standing at each corner."[58] As in northern attempts to quell labor protests by use of state militia and even the U.S. Army, southern "redemption" was born in an atmosphere verging on civil war.

On election day in Wilmington, a group of white men were incensed that some blacks still dared to vote. Resident Jane Cronly reported that a few hotheads "started down with the Gatlin and Hotchkiss guns to mow [black voters] down at the poles, but Mr. Elliot and some other sharp lawyers scurried down and told them it would be the worse possible policy, that the Republican leaders would plead intimidation at the poles and so have the whole vote thrown out, and we would loose our congressman."[59] Clearly, white political leaders still feared federal intervention in elections and felt compelled to hide their activities. Election day passed off quietly and Democrats swept into power, having done their work thoroughly before the voting began.

The momentum toward violence, however, was already in place and few local Democrats cared to stop it. Party leaders had planned a show of force for months, placing former Confederate officers in charge of strategy and borrowing artillery to bolster their position. Once the election passed, the target of their pent-up anger became the office of the local black newspaper, whose editor had allegedly published an offensive editorial a few months before. "Poor white men are careless in the matter of protecting their women, especially on farms," read the piece as it was reprinted in white newspapers. "They are careless of their conduct toward them, and our experience among poor white people in the country teaches us that the women of that race are not any more particular in the matter of clandestine meetings with colored men than are the white men with colored women." This statement had made great fodder for Democratic papers during the fall campaign; headlines called it "a base slander of the white womanhood of the South," and "a horrid slander, the most infamous that ever appeared in print in this state."[60]

After burning down the press, white men went on a rampage through several neighborhoods, wounding a large number of unarmed blacks. At least twenty and possibly more were killed; much of the black population fled to the woods for several days. Years later, Jane Cronly reflected on the purpose of the violence when she recalled that "two soldiers [of the Home Guard] were seen to have a [black] mail carrier on his knees and one of them was advocating shooting him. The whole thing was with the object of striking terror to the man's heart, so that he would never vote again." The mob also forced city officials, including the black mayor, to resign instantly and make way for newly elected Democrats.[61]

Because white supremacists acted after the votes were counted, outside observers were slow to suggest a political motivation. Wilmington Democrats explained to the nation that they had defended southern womanhood under extreme duress. A former colleague of Wilmington's mayor wrote to him from Chicago, "while I am an uncompromising Republican I like you would stand up for and defend the honor and good name of the white women of N.C., the South, the North, of America." He added, though, that he hoped "the offenders will be brought to justice," apparently unaware of the direct involvement of the new mayor and other leading men.[62]

Events in Wilmington had repercussions around the South as white supremacists took note of the effective campaign. In the Georgia gubernatorial race of 1906, candidate Hoke Smith openly expressed his desire to imitate Wilmington's leaders. He relied on the revised history of Reconstruction, including allegations of widespread rape, to stir the white racism, anger, and fear that carried him into office. Sexual hysteria was even more pronounced than it had been in Wilmington. Along with "the black menace," temperance was a key issue; partisan newspapers warned that Atlanta saloons were displaying pictures of nude white women and inciting a wave of black sexual crime. Smith himself was accused of keeping a statue of a naked woman in the barroom fountain of his Atlanta hotel. Press reports of a "rape epidemic" reached their apex in August 1906, when rioting initiated by whites in Atlanta left one white man and at least twenty-five black men and women dead.[63]

Once again the nation, convinced of the dangerousness of black men, accepted white supremacists' explanation for the violence. The wire report from Atlanta began, "five assaults by negroes on white women resulted in a deadly race riot here tonight." The front page of the *Eau Claire Telegram* in Wisconsin read, "Cause of the race war: Repeated Assaults on White Women by Negroes." "Georgia Women Terrorized" and "Five Assaults on Women Within a Very Few Hours" headlined articles published in other northern states. A paper in Beverly, Massachusetts, mistakenly reported that white women had led the riot. Many papers relied on the analysis of *Atlanta Journal* editor John Temple Graves, who alleged that "it has been a reign of terror for our Georgia women. There is not a white woman in the region of Atlanta who has had a tranquil day or night within this period." Graves advocated colonization of blacks as the best solution; his views were widely reprinted around the country. The role of the political campaign which stirred the riot—including the unsubstantiated claims of rape made by Graves's own newspaper—was completely ignored.[64]

Democratic redemption led quickly to new constitutional conventions that disfranchised black men. In addition to the arguments of Democratic leaders, the campaigns themselves helped persuade ambivalent white southerners to go along. As charges of rape flew back and forth publicly, many whites concluded that the presence of black voters dragged sensational and lurid issues into politics. Projecting the muck of these campaigns onto black bystanders, Democrats created a rationale for disfranchisement that persuaded not only themselves but also many white northerners concerned about political and moral corruption. As George Winston of North Carolina explained, if the nation wished to purify politics and "subdue the animal passions" of black men, the first step was "the withdrawal of the Negro from politics."[65]

Southern white supremacist women also suggested that disfranchisement would stop rape. "We must look for protection to the men who regard with utter loathing and detestation the crime which threatens the very foundations of society," declared Fanny M. Preston. "We rejoice that the South is still 'in the saddle' in its own domains; for while Southern men rule, woman will be respected." "Out of [a] cesspool of vice rises that hideous monster, a possible menace to every home in the South," wrote Mrs. L. H. Harris of Georgia. "To him liberty has always meant license of one sort or another. Is it any wonder North Carolina, Mississippi, and Louisiana have passed laws virtually disfranchising him?"[66]

White supremacists carried this argument into a number of constitutional conventions where, after intensive debate, delegates created new voting structures and regulations that excluded black men. In Virginia, John Daniel advocated these changes in order to protect "the most defenceless portion of our population." Another Virginian stressed whites' need to maintain "absolute social and domestic separation" and prevent racial assimilation. A participant in Alabama's convention argued that the South needed to protect white racial purity, "the inner temple of her social system." Another Alabama delegate claimed that preventing black men from voting would stop their regression into "barbarism and lust."[67] In denouncing miscegenation, none of these men addressed the obvious issues of white men's rape of black women, interracial prostitution, and consensual relationships between black women and white men. Instead, black men appeared as the sole threat to racial purity, and the sexual threat they posed was linked to their possession of the ballot.

In both South and North, redemption influenced politics for decades afterward, and the intense fears generated by the crisis of the 1890s had ramifications beyond the electoral sphere. In a climate of intellectual conservatism, several college campuses tried to purge professors who dissented from the new orthodoxy. At the University of Wisconsin, economist Richard Ely faced pressure to resign because he had written sympathetically about socialism; he recanted his views to keep his job. Emory College in Georgia dismissed Andrew Sledd for arguing that lynching was caused by irrational lower-class whites and not by interracial rape. At other colleges, scholars faced similar pressure to conform to dominant political views.[68]

Electoral campaigns changed even more dramatically. Southern states became Democratic bastions as literacy tests and poll taxes disfranchised blacks and some poor whites. The impact was devastating. State appropriations shrank, and after 1900 the fraction of them allotted to blacks slowed to a trickle. At the national level, southern Democrats secured disproportionate power in Congress, representing millions of men who were not allowed to vote. "Home rule" in the South became a fact of American political life until the civil rights movement of the 1960s, and Republican leaders made no further attempts to pass legislation regulating southern elections.[69]

In return, Democrats accepted Republicans' national ascendancy after 1896. An economic boom, enthusiasm for foreign exploits, and the personal popularity of William McKinley and Teddy Roosevelt all combined to reinforce the result of McKinley's election. The Populist Party disappeared, Prohibitionists drew only a handful of votes, and even with their control of the solid South Democrats became a long-term minority in Congress. Republicans held the presidency for sixteen years, winning by margins of more than a million votes in 1904 and 1908. They controlled both houses of Congress until 1910 and held almost two-thirds of Senate seats. Once in power, they passed campaign laws that consolidated their strength in key states.[70]

The prerequisite for this sectional accommodation was the fading of Prohibitionists, southern Republicans, and especially Populists. Around the nation, redemption was a conservative reaction to innovative proposals for coping with the economic crisis of the 1890s. Both Republicans and southern Democrats rejected Populists' plans for government intervention in the economy. In the midst of crisis, GOP leaders clung to their time-worn economic policies; southern Democrats endorsed silver currency and a progressive income tax, but upon winning power at the state level they proved to be extreme conservatives in fiscal as well as racial matters. Both Republicans and southern Democrats based their arguments on militaristic manhood and sought to protect the home against a corrupt and intrusive government, whether they saw the threat as working-class socialism or "Negro domination," reminiscent of Reconstruction days.

Around the country, women played a visible role in these redemption campaigns. A New York Republican later remarked that his party needed women "to throw the sentiment, the moral element, into the campaign."[71] Redemption contained, though, countervailing tendencies. In the West, where women had made the most gains in both suffrage and partisan campaign work, Republicans attacked Populist women as aggressive harpies. Like Democrats of the Reconstruction era, Republican redeemers accused their opponents of undermining the social order by giving women too much political power. They emphasized women's potential victimization at the hands of alleged anarchists and socialists, while white supremacists stressed white women's vulnerability to sexual violence. Both Republican and southern Democratic men portrayed themselves as protectors of the helpless and weak.

In the victors' view, Populist plans to expand government power were the brainchild of strong women and weak men. The impact of Populist defeat was temporarily to shut off certain policy options, both for federal intervention to mitigate growing economic inequities and for black men's exercise of political rights. Redemption carried, in addition, a further impulse to drive from politics those elements that threatened the social and political order. In the South, disfranchisement of black men quickly followed Democratic victory. At the national level, redemption also reversed many of the advances women had made in political campaigns.

7

New Parameters of Power

*

The Amerikin eagle ain't a hen burd.
—Judge Waxem's Political Proverbs

In defeating the challenge of Populism, men who led the successful campaigns for redemption identified a threat not only from alleged black criminals and anarchists but from politically active women. Though Republicans like Ellen Foster were reassuringly loyal, women's overall encroachment into political affairs disturbed Republican men as well as Democrats. By the 1890s women no longer limited their expressions of partisanship to demure handkerchief waving from the balconies of party rallies. Many spoke from the stump, canvassed wards, sought access to parties' decision-making councils, and even ran for office. Some men who had welcomed women's assistance in campaign work now began to describe the trend as a danger to political order.

They did so even though women's partisan activities had not necessarily translated into demands for direct power. Young suffragist Carrie Chapman Catt expressed frustration with the "woman of the present" who "espouses principles with ardor, composes majorities at political meetings, marches in party processions, and dons political badges" but who "may shrink with genuine repulsion" from the idea of casting a ballot. Gradual expansions of the franchise had nonetheless accompanied the growth of women's campaign work during the 1880s, in a climate of female activism. A number of states had passed partial woman suffrage laws, usually for votes on school-related matters. By 1890 women held some form of voting rights in states and territories containing about one-third of the U.S. population. Six years later women in Colorado, Idaho, and Utah had secured full ballots. Catt was not alone in thinking of these voters as "the women of the future."[1]

In the 1880s and 1890s women also began to win local elected offices, especially as school superintendents. Partial suffrage accelerated this trend, but in many places office holding preceded school ballots by a decade or more. Almost all candidates sought party nominations, and female solidarity was often negotiated within party structures. Around 1885, for example, the five Republicans of Chugwater, Wyoming, chose Fannie Foss as their delegate to a county GOP convention. Foss's Democratic husband wanted her to send a proxy, but her friend Therese Jenkins convinced her to go and went along to offer support. "Everything went off quite easy until it came to county superintendent of schools," Jenkins recalled years later. Foss nominated a woman, and "had a bomb from an aeroplane dropped there could not have been more surprise. A doctor had the job and the doctor wanted the job. So somebody moved recess, and the way the men got out of that courtroom was a caution, and then they discussed and cussed us." The convention renominated the doctor, who resolved to thank the ladies for their presence. The resolution passed but "the women were mad." They headed to the Democratic convention and won a nomination for their candidate. "Every woman in the county, I guess, voted for her, and she was elected," Jenkins remembered. "We have never had a man for county superintendent since."[2]

Foss and Jenkins found a way to challenge women's exclusion, but in a two-party system they could only do so when male leaders in one party agreed to cooperate. The appearance of third parties was crucial wherever both Republicans and Democrats resisted women's claims. Prohibitionists gave the first and most nominations to women, but western Populists also offered a large number. Proliferation of parties in Colorado and Idaho helped women win elected offices as well as suffrage rights: in both states, nominations for state superintendent of schools promptly went to female candidates after the advent of woman suffrage. Martha Bowman became the school superintendent in one Colorado town by appealing skillfully to all factions. She won endorsements from four local parties—Republican, Silver Republican, Democratic, and Populist. An astonished editor wrote that "it is pretty safe to bet [she] will be elected."[3]

Similar negotiations went on elsewhere. An editor in Clear Creek, Colorado, intimated that "the Populist ladies think it is about time they were recognized in some way besides being allowed to help vote the men into office." When county Populists rejected their candidate, the women walked out and arranged a fusion ticket with a Republican faction that agreed to nominate her. Sarah Christie Stevens first sought the Democratic nomination for superintendent of Mankato County, Minnesota, but met rejection. She secured both Prohibitionist and Populist endorsements and won the race against a male Republican. An observer in western New York, where women had suffrage on school matters, argued that third parties were wise to nominate women because female support helped them win.[4]

Women, then, both benefited from and contributed to party fragmentation. By 1896 they had gained a significant foothold. In addition to appointed posts such as those held by Josephine Shaw Lowell in New York and Clara Foltz in California, women held at least a few school offices in almost every state outside the South, regardless of whether they had school suffrage or not. In

Wyoming and Montana, most county school superintendents were women. In a score of other states women held between 5 and 50 percent of such jobs. Their numbers were greatest in states and territories like Kansas, Oklahoma, Minnesota, and the Dakotas, where third parties had challenged the status quo.[5]

While gaining real power at the local level, women had also assumed a visible place in national campaigns. Their interest in major policy questions was undeniable, and politicians were finding—as in the 1890 discussion of female consumers and the McKinley tariff—that women's opinions could be disadvantageous or at best unpredictable. Middle-class husbands found their wives attending current events meetings or joining women's campaign clubs. In 1896, churchmen in North Carolina opened their AME Zion newsletters to find a message from Sarah Dudley Pettey, a black reformer and devout Republican, urging them to vote for McKinley to bring "better times occasioned by good, sound money." During the same campaign William Jennings Bryan addressed women's mass meetings in Chicago, Duluth, and elsewhere in the Midwest, while Republican Thomas Reed spoke to three thousand women in Topeka. Wealthy Bostonian Marion McBride founded an American Women's Sound Money League that claimed members in thirty-one states. Populist women and a few active Democrats responded by organizing a National Women's Silver League based in Chicago.[6]

In the realignment of the 1890s, men on all sides praised women who worked for the right cause but the winners focused far more attention on the various dangers posed by their opponents. Republicans denounced western Populist women as a danger to social and political order; by 1896 that threat became fused with the cause of woman suffrage. As politicians asserted a new aggressive masculinity, women's campaign work became less and less welcome. Claims to direct power were dismissed outright, and the suffrage movement suffered a quiescent decade from 1897 to 1910.

Realignment thus confined women's political possibilities in ways that endured for years, even decades. Not only was the suffrage movement discredited, but women's attempts to wield political "influence" were circumscribed by Democratic rule in the South and Republican dominance elsewhere, as these parties resoundingly defeated and discredited Populist opponents. After redemption a new climate of conservatism on issues of gender reinforced conservatism of race and class, and vice versa. In the South, white supremacy removed blacks and some poor white voters from the political arena and established a new context for the work of reformers, both black and white, women and men. At the national level, Republican economic policies reflected the party's commitment to the status quo. Women and men who sought women's rights, black equality, solutions to poverty, and aid for industrial labor, faced new obstacles created by the Redemption campaigns.

Men and Electoral Politics After Redemption

Male anxiety over women's political activity appeared most clearly in places where women had won the franchise. To politicians the new voters were a bloc to be assessed, assimilated, and controlled. As suffragists had observed, women's party loyalties were more divided than those of either working-class white men or freedmen, who had been the focus of political calculations in previous expansions of the franchise.[7] Even at the local and school level, in the competitive atmosphere of the 1890s, women's votes could be unpredictable. Both men and women argued that gender identity was the key factor in women's decision to vote for morally superior causes—but multiple opposing parties all made this claim, and some of them lost. As Colorado Populists found to their sorrow, a party that enfranchised women might not benefit at the polls.

Partial suffrage provoked a backlash even where the majority of women voted for the same party as the majority of men. After winning school suffrage in Boston, some middle-class women tried to organize nonpartisan "women's tickets" for the city's public offices in education. Reformer Kate Gannett Wells reported that this alienated Republicans. "All the cultured women," she wrote, believed that the "separate women's party . . . put [full] suffrage back twenty years." Yet subsequent displays of ardent Republicanism created other dilemmas. In the late 1880s, GOP loyalty and nativism among elite Boston women prompted thousands of Catholic working-class women to register and defend their own views. When Democrats took over the Boston School Committee, the Republican-led Massachusetts legislature stepped in and dismantled the ward-based voting system. Though a number of Republican and Democratic women had served on the committee during the 1880s and 1890s, only *one* woman held such an office between 1905 and 1950.[8]

Male party leaders in other states also reacted negatively to the partisanship of their female opponents. When women in Clear Creek, Colorado, divided Populist ranks, a Republican newspaper claimed the situation had "resolved itself into a fight for the offices. . . . All principles seem to have been lost sight of in the desire to secure a place at the public crib." In her race to become school superintendent of Los Angeles, California, Kate Galpin won Populist, Democratic, and Prohibitionist endorsements. She attracted the intense ire of Republicans, who labeled her a "practiced wire-puller" who went "galloping around among all the party conventions, trying to secure an 'indorsement.'" One of her critics argued that voters would defeat her because "they believe in women in homes, not in politics." Galpin lost.[9]

When a coalition of Illinois women's groups won the right to vote for state university trustees in 1894, politicians reacted nervously in the next campaign. Each party nominated one woman on a slate of three. Then party leaders realized in horror that the new voters might split their tickets and vote for three women—one Republican, one Democrat, and one Prohibitionist. "There is a general fear," reported the *Chicago Tribune*, "that enough women voters will cast their ballots for the women candidates to elect at least two of them. In Chicago the leaders are trying to provide against this by urging the women speakers to impress upon their listeners the necessity of [adhering to] party lines."[10]

Women seem to have accepted this advice. Black journalist and anti-lynching activist Ida B. Wells praised Republicans and urged women to "be loyal to their party." Meanwhile, Democratic organizer Charlotte C. Holt declared that "I am a democrat and a Jeffersonian democrat." Dr. Julia Holmes Smith, the Democratic candidate for university trustee, announced, "I do not believe in compromises. If the Democratic, Republican, or Prohibition woman thinks her party represents the best idea it is by all means her duty to vote that ticket. I would not want my dearest friends to sacrifice their ideas to vote with me." Women seem to have accepted this advice, since majorities of both female and male voters elected the full Republican slate.[11]

Demonstrated party loyalty did not assuage men's doubts, and politicians and journalists kept a wary eye on states where women had won full suffrage. The *Chicago Times'* western correspondent alerted men that suffrage had caused a "social revolution" in Colorado. He warned that "those in Chicago who are smiling at [women] because they are allowed to vote for Dr. Smith or Mrs. Flower for school trustees, should see and hear the Colorado women, who have jumped the bars completely." At Populist headquarters in Pueblo the reporter found that "men and women were mingling freely and informally, indulging in tête-à-têtes and table discussions with all ideas regarding a difference in sex banished completely. To be sure, none of the women had their feet on the table and none were smoking or spitting, but in all other things they seemed to carry themselves as men ordinarily do in political headquarters." Ex-governor Alva Adams, a Democrat, declared that "he was getting disgusted with Colorado politics, and should retire. 'I was around the headquarters the other night, and it was full of women. I could neither swear nor spit, and had to light out.'" Adams added that "'If that is so in Democratic headquarters, . . . you can imagine how our Republican and Populist friends must suffer.'"[12] The message for other states was clear: when women won voting rights and a place in party councils, they displaced men.

Tempering their past praise for women's political activity, Republican men of the late 1890s increasingly criticized women's campaign work. "Women and Free Silver," a Republican essay run just before the 1896 election, began by hailing woman's role in keeping "our morals and our literature and our speech clean and pure." The author then defined what was acceptable and what was not:

> The women who make public opinion are not the Mary Leases of the land, gallumphing over the frightened face of nature, but the real women, the women to whom we go home when Hesper summons. . . . None of these latter women are on the hustings shrieking for the "free and unlimited coinage of silver and gold at the ratio of 16 to 1." There are in evidence in our politics and in behalf of Bryanism only the females who have all the symptoms of the termagant and shrew. . . . They are not concerned with anything but their own intoxicating publicity.

Condemning Populist women as "deviating females," the author directed his comments elsewhere. "We would hold sweet converse," he wrote, "only with the women who are not so renegade to the sanctity of their sex's duty in the home as to ape the worst reasonings of men." Having taken up half his allotted space with this tirade, he went on to claim that free silver would raise prices for the average woman, ruining "the dollar that makes her shopping a delight."[13] The author's most urgent message, though, lay not in this argument but in his lengthy denunciation of Populist shrews. Female readers should support the gold standard; better yet, they should stay out of campaigns.

"Since Maw Went Into Politics," a short story published in 1900, summed up the new circumstances. In it the fictional Mrs. Buzzy (known to neighbors for her wonderful pickles) became interested in the McKinley-Bryan contest. As a result of political study she failed to put up preserves, sew her daughter's dresses, and pack lunches for her husband. One night she attended a campaign debate in rainy weather and fell sick. Her terrible fever paralleled her obsession with politics: relatives reported that "she don't know nothin', and is talkin' all kinds of rubbish." "Night after night," the author wrote, "she would sink back exhausted, moaning despairingly, 'I can't onderstand one on it—I can't make head ner tail ov what they mean!'" Mrs. Buzzy's patient husband watched by her bed until the fever broke. "Hev I been sick, Thaddeyus?" Mrs. Buzzy asked then. "'Yes, Maw, you've hed quite a brash of sickness.' . . . Mrs. Buzzy closed her eyes with a sense of infinite relief that the Lord had removed a too heavy responsibility from her inadequate shoulders."[14]

Partisan realignment had a direct, negative impact on the woman suffrage movement. An advisor to New York's Charles Parkhurst told the Women's Municipal League that they should be "careful not to bring up the suffrage question" because it might create "antagonism" and "hurt the movement." The *New York Tribune* reported that "it was distinctly understood that no reference whatever should be made to the subject of woman suffrage." When at one meeting a speaker referred to suffrage "she was quickly called to order."[15] The incident illustrated a larger trend: suffrage was becoming associated with discredited forms of radicalism.

One year after McKinley's victory, author Helen Kendrick Johnson published *Woman and the Republic*, a much-praised and widely circulated anti-suffrage tract. While commending women's moral reform work, Johnson linked suffrage to the doctrines defeated in 1896. "The sound judgment and law-abiding element of this country expressed itself in no uncertain terms at the late election," she wrote, in an implied endorsement of Republicanism. She claimed female voters in Colorado had supported "Free Silver and Populism of the most extravagant type." California men, on the other hand, had voted for "sound money against repudiation, for authority against anarchy" and in an 1896 referendum had cast ballots "heavily against woman suffrage." "Which State," asked Johnson, "can claim that its action rings truest to the stroke of honest metal in finance and in defense of national honor?"[16]

Woman and the Republic described Populism and woman suffrage as a combined force threatening national stability. Johnson argued that western Populist women had voted against the better judgment of Republican husbands and that "socialism and anarchy" were at root hysterical female impulses. "Altgeld and Debs, Coxey and Tillman were only men," she wrote, "but Mary Ellen

Lease furnished to the campaign that strain of exalted fanaticism that at once points out woman's glory and woman's danger." Johnson prophesied that Republican men in Colorado "might be called upon by the United States authorities to put down by force, perhaps to kill, those whose lawlessness their wives had instigated and abetted." Because only unsexed female anarchists wanted to vote, suffrage would initiate "class rule with a vengeance."

Johnson was not the only author to connect woman suffrage and Populism. Though Colorado women had voted overwhelmingly Republican in 1894, *Harper's Weekly* ignored this fact and stressed the state's pro-silver vote in 1896, interpreting this as support for socialism. The *Portland Oregonian* argued that woman suffrage in Colorado and Idaho was "but the outgrowth of the temporary socialistic spirit that prevails in those states." At a constitutional convention in Alabama, one delegate told advocates of white women's suffrage they should move to Kansas. Another declared that "when you put [woman] on a common equality with man and tell her to go out in the debasing arena of politics, you lower her, you brush the bloom from the rose and put Alabama alongside with the Populistic states of Wyoming, New Mexico, and Colorado."[17]

Observers closer to the Populist uprising drew similar conclusions about the potential partisan impact of women's votes. A former Republican congressman from Kansas argued that "the secret of the Alliance success" had been that women "were given equal voice with the men." "For my part," he added bitterly, "I don't care how soon women are given the ballot in Kansas." When Idaho men voted overwhelmingly for both Populism and a woman suffrage referendum in 1896, the same year a majority of California men voted Republican and rejected woman suffrage, these events reinforced the link. Watching suffrage leaders cooperate with western Populists, eastern newspapers denounced the "ridiculous antics of Susan B. Anthony and other so-called leaders" in "espousing the Populist cause."[18]

Republican commentators began to assume that on questions of economic justice, women voters would take the wrong side. The *Boston Herald* observed that western women's exercise of voting rights did not "appear to have been productive of the best results," since the majority of these voters had chosen "immoral" Populist and Silver Democratic candidates. During the campaign a sociologist argued that the danger of suffrage lay in women's "wild gusts of unreasoning, uncalculating, hysterical emotion." Female voters were particularly unreliable on issues of "peace and war" and of "distress and poverty that may be mainly due to improvidence and vice."[19]

These comments help explain the suffrage movement's "decade in the doldrums" between 1896 and 1910, when state associations declined and NAWSA won no further victories. Suffragists got caught between the Republican and Populist parties at the national level just as they had in states like Kansas and California. Because suffrage became law in a few distinctive states, Americans in other regions identified the cause with Populist insurgents, even though Colorado was overwhelmingly Republican after 1894 and Wyoming (contrary to the Alabama delegate's assertion) had scant Populist presence.[20]

In the South, white women had never won the political visibility and limited power that women in the North and West had begun to exercise. Though black women had figured in campaigns of the Reconstruction era, their role faded as Republican men asserted their own leadership. By the late 1890s the party as a whole had suffered intimidation and defeat all over the South. Some southern Democrats seemed anxiously aware of women's political activity in the West, but at home their concerns were different. They took redemption as an opportunity to reassert old Democratic values, especially on issues of racial and family order. The key issue in southern politics was not, as elsewhere, unsexed Populist women and anarchic men, but the alleged sexual danger posed by black men who could vote.

The Democrats' white supremacy campaigns and their disfranchisement of black men ushered in an era of unequaled demagoguery. Despite the removal of most blacks from politics, race rhetoric did not fade. Politicians on the stump had to prove their manhood above all else, and defense of white women's virtue had been reestablished as a crucial ingredient of masculinity. Not surprisingly, white men who had previously held moderate racial views often worked hardest to assert themselves in the new order. Some of the most outrageous rhetoric of the early 1900s came from ex-Populists and ardent free-silver advocates like South Carolina's Ben Tillman, James K. Vardaman of Mississippi, and Hoke Smith and Tom Watson of Georgia.[21]

On the floor of Congress, men like Tillman focused on the rape peril. Other demagogues voiced their views in national magazines or northern newspapers. Some continued to blame Republicans for white women's suffering; justifying lynching for rape, Tillman claimed that "all negroes are not bad; a very small percentage of them are bad; but the bad ones are patted on the back by the politicians at the North." These Democrats found a foil in northern Republicans who showed even the slightest sympathy for black southerners. After Theodore Roosevelt invited Booker T. Washington to dinner at the White House, James Vardaman called the president a "coon-flavored miscegenationist." He promised in 1903 that "a vote for Vardaman is a vote for White Supremacy, a vote for the quelling of the arrogant spirit that has been aroused in the blacks by Roosevelt and his henchmen, . . . a vote for the safety of the Home and the protection of our women and children."[22]

Speaking to a Missouri audience in 1900, Arkansas Democrat Jeff Davis also emphasized sexual themes, claiming "I would rather tear, screaming from her mother's arms, my little daughter and bury her alive than to see her arm in arm with the best nigger on earth." He reserved his most extreme comments for Roosevelt's visit to Arkansas in 1904. "Mr. President," he stated, after praising white women, "when the husband or the brother, the father or the sweetheart of one of these angels of earth, comes home in the evening and finds her in the throes of death; when he sees the cruel clutch-mark on her snow white throat, and watches the pulse-beat grow fainter and fainter as the end draws near, there is not a law on the statute books of Arkansas to prevent [him] from avenging that crime." Other southern Democrats matched the outrageousness of Davis's claims. In his inaugural address, North Carolina Governor Charles Aycock justified white violence on grounds that "the screams of women fleeing from pursuing brutes closed the gates to our hearts." Tillman stated in Congress, "I have three daughters but, so help me God, I had rather find either one of them killed by a tiger or a bear and gather up her bones and bury them, conscious that she had died in the purity of her maidenhood, than to have her crawl to me and tell me the horrid story that she had been robbed of the jewel of her womanhood by a black fiend."[23]

Such descriptions reasserted the longstanding Democratic theme of white women's vulnerability and dependence. Commentators depicted a dire fate for women who wandered too far from their protectors. Thomas Nelson Page warned that when black men perpetrated sexual crimes on white women, "the death of the victim of the ravisher was generally the least of the attendant horrors. In Texas, in Mississippi, in Georgia . . . the facts in the case were so unspeakable that they have never been put in print." Even more telling was the alleged fate of women who survived rape by a black man. Southern white spokesmen described victims as "wrecked" and "ruined," their lives "made over into a living hell." A minister hinted at social ostracism when he described the "lady who has been a victim, living year after year as one in a tomb, ever under the shadow of that great horror, shut in, hopeless and helpless."[24]

With such statements, Tillman, Davis, and other white supremacists offered escalating warnings about female autonomy. In the absence of a credible threat from Populists and black Republicans, southern Democrats adapted their arguments to stress the importance of male power within white households. Their new and explicit focus on virginity hinted that some felt increasing lack of control over young women and were trying to reassert authority by drawing grisly portraits of sexual danger. Political speeches in which young women were "trembling prisoners in their homes" or "pure young girl[s] crawling on hands and knees dying by inches" served as admonitions, depicting young women not only as helpless victims but as literally prostrate before male guardians.[25] Davis and Tillman reassured white male Democrats of their continued relevance as *men*, at the ballot box and in the home.

In both North and South, then, campaigns of the 1890s generated new warnings about the dangers of female independence and women's rights. The conservative political climate ushered in by redemption not only militated against women's campaign work and suffrage rights, it also suggested a broader reassertion of the patriarchal family. Though this was clearest in the South, anti-suffragism in the North also implied a reassertion of the traditional family as the fundamental political unit. Northern suffragists during and after Reconstruction had connected patriarchy in the home to southern white men's rebellion, arguing that "the theory of a masculine head to rule the family, the church, or the State is . . . the fruitful source of rebellion." During the 1890s the connection of support for women's rights to expanding federal authority—always a minority view—became increasingly discredited. Anti-suffragist Madeline Dahlgren made the opposite argument in testimony before Congress. "The family," she said, "is the foundation of the State. Each family is represented by its head. [From] individual representation . . . arises diversity or division, and discord in the corner-stone of the State. Gentlemen, we cannot displace the corner-stone without destruction to the edifice itself!"[26] Both Republican and Democratic redeemers agreed. Faced with these politicians in power, women found their roles in the political arena increasingly restricted.

Race, Class, and Region after Redemption

In fights over political redemption women played visible roles on all sides; after the victories of northern Republicans and southern Democrats, women largely disappeared from national campaigns. Many Populist women abandoned party work as their coalition fragmented. Hearing Mary Lease speak in 1896, Leonora O'Reilly wrote that "it is all bitter, bitter stories she has to tell." Lease retired from politics after McKinley's victory. Luna Kellie spoke for many Populist women when she recalled the fate of her Nebraska newspaper in the late 1890s. "Hardly a reform paper remained alive, and the abuse was hard to bear," she wrote. "I was supposed to send in editorials but to save my life I could not say anything that I felt I had not said before and had not done any good." Kellie sold her press for half its value. Twenty-five years later she told her children she had "never written a word for publication to this day. In fact I found myself a physical wreck and it was over ten years before I had regained my health. And I dared not even think of what hopes we had had. It meant sleepless nights and nerves completely unstrung. . . . I never vote," she added, and "did not for years hardly look at a political paper."[27]

In the few places where Populists continued to win seats after 1896, they did so by fusing with Democrats who were hostile to women's participation. Very few women continued to speak on the Populist stump, even in Kansas and Colorado. The plight of Annie Diggs was especially poignant. In the heat of 1894 she had been one of the few Populists who maintained cordial relations with suffragists in the GOP. After a new wave of Republican victories in 1900 she resigned as president of the Kansas Equal Suffrage Association, fearing her notoriety as a Populist was hurting the organization. Turning to her party, she suggested to male leaders that she organize farm women in the spirit of "old Alliance victories." Democrats forced their Populist allies to repudiate her. One Democrat declared that his "great party" would never be "whipped by a small woman."[28]

Southern black Republican women found themselves in an even worse situation, their male allies not only defeated but disfranchised. The impact was devastating. Between 1896 and 1904, black voting dropped 96 percent in Alabama, 93 percent in Louisiana, and almost 100 percent in North Carolina and Virginia. Under these conditions black women found state governments to be largely instruments of segregation and discrimination, rather than support and reform.[29] They undertook nonpartisan reform work with little hope of co-operation from local or state lawmakers.

For most black women the key political issues continued to be those of race. The brutal realities of economic, legal, and social discrimination, disfranchisement, lynching, and other forms of racial violence overshadowed other concerns. On these issues, black reformers won little assistance from Southern white women. "What a mighty foe to mob violence southern white women might be," wrote black leader Mary Church Terrell, "if they would arise in the purity and power of their womanhood to implore their fathers, husbands and sons no longer to stain their hands with the black man's blood!" Yet no white women's anti-lynching group formed in the South until the 1920s, when lynching was in decline.[30]

For southern blacks, the only hope for government intervention lay outside the region as the GOP reasserted federal control. That help did not come. Theodore Roosevelt's attitude toward lynching epitomized the response of many northern Republicans who remained sympathetic to the problems faced by blacks in the South. Considered progressive on race issues, Roosevelt was reviled by white Democrats for appointing a few black office holders. In 1906 he took the unprecedented step of addressing Congress on the issue of lynching, but his speech was notable for its limitations. He declared lynching a terrible deed but took for granted that white men were incited to it by frequent rapes. Blacks' worst enemy, Roosevelt said, was "the negro criminal who commits the dreadful crime of rape." He argued that the government should control lynch mobs but that blacks must simultaneously work to prevent the rape of white women.[31] The president's thorough acceptance of white supremacists' allegations of rape suggests why few white Republicans were willing to address racial issues at all.

In light of their work in previous decades, northern reformers were notably silent on the subjects of lynching, disfranchisement, and segregation. Well-documented reports of black men being mutilated and burned alive should have provoked northern women's sympathies, but though reform work flourished in the Progressive era, criticism of the South was almost nonexistent. Myths about black men's widespread propensity to rape made it awkward for respectable white women to defend them. Ida B. Wells's disputes during the 1890s with Frances Willard exemplified the rift between black and white women on racial issues. Willard sought to build the WCTU in the South by accepting white supremacist arguments. In the *New York Voice*, she told northerners that "the safety of woman, of childhood, of the home, is menaced in a thousand localities. . . . How little we know of all this, seated in comfort and affluence here at the North, descanting upon the rights of every man to cast one vote."[32]

Woman suffrage advocates had already distanced themselves from blacks in debates over passage of the Fifteenth Amendment, and many were openly racist. Ida Wells considered Susan B. Anthony "a good dear friend," but on the matter of lynching Anthony made it clear that "she, too, belonged to Miss Willard's class." Between 1894 and 1903, NAWSA conventions hotly debated the issue of suffrage restrictions based on education, property, and race. Even

Henry Blackwell, for decades a loyal Republican because the GOP had enfranchised black men, retreated in practice from a full-suffrage position. He acknowledged that, in the South, woman suffrage "evidently . . . must be demanded with limitations of education, or property, or both; since for universal suffrage one cannot get even a hearing."[33]

One white northern woman who tried to protest the southern racial order found her life endangered. Lillie Clayton Jewett, a Boston Republican, was horrified by the 1897 assassinations of black South Carolina postmaster Frazer Baker and his young daughter. Jewett helped relocate surviving family members to Boston, a move that generated intense controversy. When Jewett announced plans for a national women's anti-lynching crusade, white southerners reacted vehemently. Upon visiting Richmond, Jewett received death threats and fled the city with the help of a friend. The *Boston Globe* reported that she was hanged in effigy in Monroe Heights, "the most fashionable portion of Richmond":

> The counterfeit human figure was clad in white and black garments, supposed to represent the races. . . . The placard bore the following inscription: "Lillian Clayton Jewett, south-hater and negroes' worst enemy. A false witness shall not be unpunished, and he that speaketh lies shall perish.". . . The object was soon surrounded by a large crowd. Some looked on in silence, while several remarked that it was a great pity it was not Miss Jewett herself instead of only an effigy.[34]

Anyone, white or black, who contemplated anti-lynching activities was surely dissuaded by the treatment Jewett received.

Populist women and black women were clear losers in the political realignment of the 1890s. Those on the winning side—including Democratic women in the South and Republican women elsewhere—found themselves in a more ambiguous situation. Southern Redemption opened new opportunities for white women to claim power in the public arena, from which black men had been forcibly removed. Democratic conservatism militated against women's public work in political campaigns, but in the South that role—even among Populists—was already far more restricted than in other regions. On the other hand, temperance gained more prominence than ever before as civic leaders around the South built alliances with a newly nonpartisan WCTU. White women's clubs flourished, expanding their work from literary discussions to social housekeeping. Finding that a corrupt board had ruined their school system, a women's club in Jacksonville, Florida, raised money to sustain the schools by producing a woman's edition of the local newspaper. Afterward they proposed a slate of male school board candidates who won election in the city's white primaries.[35] It is hard to imagine white women undertaking these activities before state registration laws and poll taxes had banished black men from politics.

Events in North Carolina illustrated both the possibilities and the limitations for white women in the solidly Democratic South. Before 1898, the Republican governor's wife had advocated both temperance and suffrage and invited her WCTU chapter to meet in the executive mansion. When white supremacist Charles B. Aycock was elected his wife participated in no such activities, tending instead to the couple's seven children. But Aycock was an enthusiastic proponent of women's work to improve white public schools. He endorsed the Women's Association for the Betterment of Public School Houses, founded in 1902 by a leader of the Raleigh Women's Club. The association became a model for similar work in other states. Significantly, white Virginia women initiated such activities one year after their state's disfranchising convention; Georgia women joined the movement around the time of Hoke Smith's election in 1906.[36]

As in the North, men accepted and even praised women for their reform work as long as they refrained from demanding direct power. An embryonic woman suffrage movement had appeared in the South during the 1890s, but after 1898 it virtually disappeared for a decade. Southern suffragists' key tactic had been to advocate enfranchisement of white women as a counterweight to black men's votes. After white supremacists secured control, woman suffragists found they had no effective arguments to present to these Democrats. Suffrage rights in some places were even repealed. Women had won school suffrage in Kentucky cities, for example, but male legislators revoked the law in 1902 because "more colored than white women voted in Lexington at the spring election." Southern suffragists' only victory before 1921 was a limited municipal ballot for Louisiana tax-paying women. The justification was typically Progressive: the New Orleans Woman's Drainage and Sewerage League sought a bond referendum to fix the city's abysmal sewers.[37]

Male allies of such reformers—like many of their Northern counterparts— watched to ensure that women did not overstep their bounds. In Georgia, Methodist Bishop and temperance advocate Warren Candler bristled when women raised the suffrage question. "If woman's suffrage were adopted," he wrote to a WCTU leader, "the negro women and bad women not cumbered with the cares of maternity would have every advantage. . . . It would defeat forever prohibition and bring to pass numberless nameless evils in campaigns." Candler threatened to withhold all support unless the WCTU dropped suffrage agitation immediately; the state organization backed down. An Atlanta chapter was subsequently thrown out of their church meeting place for holding a suffrage discussion.[38]

Northern women who sought a place in politics also experienced losses. After 1896, GOP women's campaign work became more restricted. Ellen Foster focused her energies on the four western states where suffrage had enhanced women's role in party politics. Nationwide, the number of clubs apparently did not grow; the National Women's Republican Association lost much of its funding in 1900 and limped along in diminished form. Outside the western suffrage states, female orators and partisan clubs dwindled in visibility and number. Women's ribbons, pins, handkerchiefs, and jewelry disappeared from campaigns; between 1900 and the end of World War I the major parties produced almost no items designed for women. First ladies also faded to the background. In contrast to the 1880s and early 1890s, portraits of candidates' wives no longer appeared on posters or banners.[39]

While gender order and white supremacy were the foremost priorities of southern redeemers, Republicans who dominated national affairs emphasized gender and class. To the extent GOP women remained in northern and western politics they appeared as elite "ladies." The *Chicago Tribune* claimed local Republicans were "the women of wealth and culture." After an anti-Tammany rally, the *New York Times* boasted that "rarely have there been so many prominent, fashionable women seen at political meetings in this city." Colorado Republican women described their leaders as women of "artistic taste" and "literary talent." Opponents agreed, but with a twist: Denver's Populist newspaper described Republicans as "wealthy matrons" who dressed in "costly apparel and flashing diamonds" while others starved in the streets. A Boulder Populist expressed hostility toward poor women who voted Republican and upper-class ladies who escorted them to the polls. He wrote that women "who had never in their lives been shown the slightest courtesy by those who wear the finest kid gloves, were coddled and counted and carried to the voting places."[40]

Describing women's campaign meetings, male Republican journalists often borrowed the conventions of the society page. They noted the presence of "fashionable" women, describing the dress and jewelry of participants. After a meeting of the East Capitol Hill Women's Republican Club, the *Denver Times* referred to the "brilliancy" of the occasion and described at length the arrangements of "fall blossoms" and "trailing vines of clematis" decorating the hall. Such accounts apparently drew more upon male party leaders' needs and assumptions than on women's real practices. The *Chicago Tribune* described one Republican women's rally as "unlike any other political meeting that has been held in that hall. There was no trace of political 'mud,' but instead the speakers wore beautiful gowns. . . . There was music between speeches, and the harshest political advice given was that the women perform their duty in a womanly manner." The *Tribune* went on to report, however, that a speaker at this meeting made a vigorous verbal assault on the Democrats. Mary Knout "scored Cleveland at the start" and accused him of "colossal egotism." She then contrasted sound Republican policies with the odious record of Democrats. Knout's words obviously contradicted the *Tribune* report of ladylike gentility.[41]

Republican women may have entered politics with the goal of expressing their opinions equally with men, but to male GOP leaders women were most useful in a role they had played since Whig days: they lent "society polish" and a "moral element" to Republican campaigns.[42] In the conservative era ushered in by redemption, the class and racial implications of "ladies'" presence were overt. The stress placed on women's wealth and culture was a clear shift from the 1880s, when midwestern Republican women had marched with men in outdoor parades and GOP leaders had pitched their appeals to the wives of workingmen.

It was, perhaps, the need to sway an increasingly prosperous and urban constituency that prompted Republican campaign manager Mark Hanna to try new advertising techniques in 1896. Though Roosevelt complained that Hanna had marketed McKinley "as if he were a patent medicine," Republican women's activities in the campaign suggested their receptivity to Hanna's consumer-based approach. When a school board member from Cleveland spoke at McKinley's home, she declared that "we come to greet you not as politicians, but as women, wives, mothers and sisters. . . . Every woman has a living interest in the money question. If our husbands earn the money, we spend and intend to spend it."[43] Political recognition of women's roles as modern consumers, which had originated in Democratic appeals, now also became a Republican theme.

In terms of federal power, appeals to consumers had a long history of conservatism. From the Revolutionary Daughters of Liberty to homespun parties during the southern secession movement to Democrats' denunciation of high tariffs, Americans had used consumer consciousness to express their opposition to centralized authority. Rejecting the "socialistic" doctrines of their opponents, Republicans of the 1890s also employed consumerism in their campaign to fend off more radical responses to the depression. A remarkable poll taken in 1896 demonstrated links between Republican Redemption and women's consumer roles. C. W. Post, the inventor of Postum breakfast beverage, invited American women to express their preferences in the presidential campaign. Post advertised his new product by placing instructions for "Ladies' Voting" on the label, and newspapers (especially midwestern ones) reported the results as a news item. The company received over 13,000 postcards from women, 78 percent of whom chose McKinley, 15 percent Bryan, and 7 percent Prohibitionist Joshua Levering. In actual election returns, McKinley won only 54 percent. Women's overwhelming Republican "vote" was a vivid illustration of the GOP's new middle- and upper-class base.[44]

In the full suffrage states of Colorado, Utah, Idaho, and Wyoming some women continued to serve on party committees, in legislatures, and in public office. But for several reasons their numbers declined after the turn of the century. First, the party fragmentation that had created opportunities for full suffrage also hampered cooperation among women reformers. Factionalism splintered the Denver Equal Suffrage Association, Non-Partisan League, and Women's Club, all of which lost Republican members. During the first McKinley-Bryan campaign, Denver Republican women suffered an embarrassing public rift over the currency issue. In the wake of these fights, clubs moved away from partisan campaign work.[45]

More important, Republican victors offered women only a few offices and even less respect. Colorado legislator Frances Klock won appointment as the chair of Military and Indian Affairs, but party leaders directed little business to her committee and her male colleagues nicknamed her "Big Squaw of the Arapahoes." Democratic Senator David Boyd treated the new legislators with public courtesy but he told a friend privately that they were "of very small calabre, the mere echoes of the men." Two, he added, "belong to the Denver yellow dog contingent, the proper gender being considered."[46] Those who had hoped women's presence would make a difference in the legislature encountered new problems of tokenism and marginality.

During the first state legislative session after 1894, the *Denver Times* reported the views of one woman who "had been a suffragist with infinite faith in woman's power as a political factor." "The truth is," this woman reported, "the men members meet around at hotels and talk and smoke and fix things up, and the women don't have a thing to do with their scheme. . . . I'd advocate having the legislature half women, or two-thirds women, and I'd have a bill passed making it a grave misdemeanor for men members to talk business outside the upper or lower houses or the committee rooms. . . . Then there would be some fairness about lawmaking." With such a prospect utterly unattainable, the woman pronounced herself "discouraged." "For my part," she said, "I feel as if I should just go home and attend to the cooking for the remainder of my life."[47]

A few women served as effective legislators. In Colorado, Harriet G. R. Wright investigated conditions at the state insane asylum, and two of her colleagues established and supervised a State Industrial School for Girls. Dr. Martha Hughes Cannon of the Utah Senate sponsored an array of important bills. Through her efforts the state established broad services for the disabled and new measures for public health and education. Yet reformers could not fail to note that they achieved similar goals in other states without electing women as representatives or even winning suffrage. Utah Representative Eurithe LeBarthe wrote one piece of legislation during her term of office: it prevented women from wearing large hats at public events. After one term as a Silver Party representative, Martha Conine left Colorado's legislature, disgusted by her exclusion from the circles of power. She started a legislative committee inside the Colorado Federation of Woman's Clubs, apparently concluding that pressure from the outside was a more effective strategy for women than was office holding.[48]

After 1896, then, women's political practices and the extent of their partisan activism grew more similar in North and South, East, Midwest, and West. Northern women were either forced out or strategically retreated from the goals of office holding, voting, and demanding direct power within party structures. By 1900 they turned to nonpartisan strategies that proved effective in the long term. At the same time, disfranchisement offered southern white women new opportunities for public nonpartisan reform work. Sectional accommodation of North and South, reflected in Republicans' national control and their deference to southern Democrats' "home rule," brought white middle-class women's public political activities into their greatest regional congruence since the days of the Whigs, when northern evangelical women had first asserted their place in the partisan arena.

In contrast to the Gilded Age, women's political work after 1896 was less defined by region but more sharply bounded by divisions of class and race. Around the country, middle-class women pursued nonpartisan reform strategies in unprecedented numbers, as did black women in a largely segregated movement for Progressive reform. For southern white women, this impulse was a new departure made possible by white supremacy; for many women elsewhere, it was a redirection of energies they had previously devoted to party campaigns. With Republican men's new militarism and their attacks on women who sought power, partisan women faced a hostile climate. This is not, however, a full explanation of women's departure from party politics outside the South. Even women who could exercise full ballots—as in Colorado—and those who were still ardent Republicans seem to have decided that partisanship was, at best, a restrictive and partial strategy.

Until the early 1890s, various northern reformers had looked back on the Civil War years as their political touchstone. The Republican Party, a dramatic agent of policy change, had seemed both a vehicle and a model for further action. Events of the late 1880s and 1890s had now exposed weaknesses in partisan strategy. Suffragists had lost multiple state referenda—trapped among Republicans, Prohibitionists, and Populists—and some exchanged recriminations in the wake of these disasters. Prohibitionist and Populist women had invested their hope and energy in party structures that dissolved before their eyes. Not surprisingly, both younger women and experienced campaigners began to act on these new precedents. The exhausting, divisive nature of Gilded Age campaigns, combined with women's inability to win further concessions after the 1890s realignment, persuaded many to try nonpartisan paths.

They did so, however, within the conservative parameters of race, gender, and class relations that campaigns of the 1890s had created. In many ways the new conservatism proved enduring. Accommodation of southern Democratic interests lasted well into the twentieth century, giving white supremacists disproportionate power at the national level by installing their solid bloc in Congress. Black disfranchisement and Jim Crow segregation were facts of southern life until the civil rights movement of the 1960s. These developments rested in considerable part on northerners' willingness to believe, in the 1890s, that an epidemic of black rape necessitated white supremacy and drastic measures of social and political control.

In the North, Republicans' hold on power proved much shorter lived. Those who lost the political battles of the 1890s—including woman suffragists, Populists, and others who sought to redress inequalities of gender and class—suffered a temporary setback between 1896 and 1910. But as the twentieth century began, reformers found new paths for achieving these goals despite the intransigence of conservative Republican men. By investing the old parties with new meaning, on the one hand, and pursuing new nonpartisan strategies, on the other, reformers achieved many goals that had been stuck in stalemate during the prior decades of intense party competition. These men and women worked their way around the parameters set by redemption. Within a decade, on key issues of class and gender relations, they began to break down those boundaries.

8

Progressives and Protection, 1897–1912

In the party if we can, out of it if we must.
—*Republican suffragist, Colorado*

In the competitive political atmosphere of the 1880s and 1890s when most Americans endorsed partisan strategies, a slow revolt was also in formation. Those who observed the machinations of party loyalists indicted not only campaign practices but also the larger operations of government-by-party. *Harper's* dismissed "the usual machinery of processions and torch-light parades and floats and songs and girls in white." What the nation needed, the editor argued, was reasoned policy-making rather than electoral hoopla. The fictional Mrs. Buzzy spoke for many Americans when she noted that in the old days "politics wasn't the corrupt machine it is now." *Machine* gradually became an epithet hurled not only at urban organizations like Tammany Hall but also at national party leaders who seemed to rank the public interest behind their own.[1]

Among the most disillusioned Americans were those whose parties had met defeat in the 1890s. Many Prohibitionists, Populists, and Silver Democrats turned from politics in disgust as their enemies seized control. These frustrated citizens included women as well as men. In Chicago, Florence Kelley was thrown out of her factory inspectorship in 1897 by the defeat of Illinois' socialist-leaning governor and replaced by a Republican man who was solicitous of employer interests. Kelley was forced to seek new ways of winning and enforcing labor legislation in the face of GOP dominance at both state and national levels. Exhausted by the failure of her third-party strategy, Frances Willard dismissed partisanship altogether by 1896. "Parties are of no account," she wrote bitterly. "They are of no more value than so many tin cans." Two years later, after Willard's death, the WCTU repealed its support for the Prohibition Party and declared that its members would continue their work by nonpartisan means.[2]

Other women also found themselves among the losers. Around the country, local and state suffrage organizations had been damaged by partisan and class divisions. Referenda in Kansas, California, and elsewhere had gone down to defeat; to make things worse, many Americans now associated suffragism with socialism, making near-term prospects for further victories bleak. In some cities middle-class reformers were equally frustrated by the limited results of their campaigns. Whether in groups like the New York Women's Republican Association or in nonpartisan coalitions like the Women's Municipal League, they had failed to break the power of such notorious urban party organizations as Tammany Hall. To many urban Republicans, the fruits of national victory seemed of limited value in addressing local concerns.[3]

Ironically, Gilded Age party conflict itself contributed to disillusionment with partisan politics. Fierce campaigns seemed exhausting and wasteful: they spent enormous amounts of public energy to put men in office, only to replace them two or four years later with their old foes. More important, party platforms did not keep pace with the electorate's new concerns. Republicans had promised for decades that the tariff would protect Americans from poverty and economic dislocation, but by the 1890s even some stalwarts admitted that tariffs were not enough. Nor did "sound money" or southern white supremacy address the issues raised by the crisis of the 1890s. They seemed, at best, limited and partial responses to the nation's problems. At worst they appeared to be mere distractions, invented by men whose chief goal was to keep themselves in office.[4]

The criticism was not that parties wielded power. Americans had long spoken of the Republican and Democratic organizations as powerful machines without necessarily seeing them in negative terms. Rather, party leaders now seemed to waste the power they held, using it simply to perpetuate themselves in office. The major parties' goals no longer seemed adequate to address the nation's most urgent problems; party machines had become obstacles rather than engines of dynamic change.

By 1900 the major parties found it more difficult to sustain their places as communities of shared faith and to persuade men and women to maintain strong party ties. In the 1890s Republicans continued to use the language of evangelicalism and southern Democrats the rhetoric of race, but their old arguments no longer had quite the same appeal. The urgency of economic distress had shifted the terms of debate. Though both parties reasserted a soldierly masculinity akin to that of the war years, the issues at stake were not the same. Policies advocated by Republicans, especially, did not evoke loyalties nearly as intense as those of the old wartime party, which to its supporters had been manifestly the agent of millennial change in America, preserver of the Union and emancipator of the slaves.

Partisanship, then, came to mean something different by the late 1890s. In the Gilded Age, *partisan politics* and *electoral politics* had been almost identical terms. From presidential campaigns down to school board elections, parties had been the dominant force in campaigns for office, in policy-making, and in

Americans' view of what politics was about. Following the powerful Republican precedent of the 1850s, reformers unhappy with the major parties started parties of their own. By the 1890s, though, "citizens' tickets" and nonpartisan candidates won an increasing role, especially in municipal affairs. They were not disinterested; like other political movements, they represented class, racial, and even major-party goals, as when the New York Women's Republican Association and the Municipal League worked together to defeat Tammany Democrats. Nonetheless, electoral politics began to take on more meanings outside the realm of the party machine.

After 1900, Americans who were disillusioned with the parties developed new political strategies falling along two broad avenues. The first, especially important at the federal level, was to invest the dominant parties with new meanings and push them to address new concerns.[5] Theodore Roosevelt took this path; it won him widespread popularity and the devotion of many admirers who sought new methods of effective action in the public sphere. Roosevelt spearheaded a bipartisan effort to assert Americans' economic and political interests overseas; he also intervened cautiously in domestic struggles between capital and labor. Over a decade he turned his energy toward projects of social and economic welfare, touching many of the issues Populists had raised. His opinions reflected those of a substantial body of reformers—both women and men—who turned again to third-party action in the Progressive campaign of 1912. Roosevelt's defection from the GOP revived party competition and opened opportunities for a host of new federal and state initiatives.

The second path lay outside the parties, and it looked especially promising at the local level and to those who had lost the electoral battles of the 1890s. In the Civil War years both major parties had forged broad coalitions across lines of class and, for the GOP, of race. By the 1890s neither the Republican nor Democratic organizations fulfilled this role as effectively, and reformers sought new ways to bridge social chasms by building communities of shared faith that would supplement or replace the old parties.[6] Settlement houses were among the most influential and enduring of such experiments, but they were not the only ones. Coalition building outside the parties—or in place of the parties— became an increasingly attractive strategy for those who found their goals and interests neglected by those in power.

The legacy of Gilded Age campaigns shaped both partisan and nonpartisan strategies after 1896. At the national level, Republican men's victory went hand-in-hand with a reassertion of traditional gender roles, in which men physically protected their families and the nation's honor while Christian wives and mothers exercised indirect political "influence." If these ideals had been innovative in the party's early years, they were no longer so as a new century dawned. Rather, they represented a rejection of the more egalitarian models that Prohibitionists and Populists had advanced. The old doctrine of protection to the home, not equal rights for women, set the parameters for federal and state initiatives after 1896. Widespread belief in the "new Negro crime" and the GOP's accommodation of southern Democratic interests also nationalized the goal of protection to *white* women. These related precedents had a profound influence on policies of the Progressive Era.

Despite their limits, the partisan engagement of men like Roosevelt and the innovations of nonpartisan reformers proved in the long term to be compatible strategies for expanding government power. The results became clear when party competition revived between 1912 and 1921. The Progressive Party built not only on the impulses of a reform-minded faction of Republicans but also on Populist and Silver Democratic platforms. The Democratic Party, transformed between 1896 and 1912 by Bryan and others with a new view of federal authority, responded. On issues of class and gender, reformers both inside and outside the parties worked to challenge the boundaries that had been set in 1890s campaigns; in doing so they achieved a number of goals that the political experiments of the Gilded Age had left unfulfilled.

The Manly Virtues in Public Policy

Republicans' sweeping victory in 1896 defined financial issues in sharply masculine terms. Maintaining the gold standard, GOP leaders argued, was the only "manly" decision, the course of honor, duty, and strength. Gold advocates were courageous; silver advocates were cowards. Republicans further identified the gold standard with kings and imperial leaders in Europe, especially England and Germany. Nations that adhered to the silver standard were, in racial terms, composed of lesser men: the "weak" and "effeminate" races of Mexico, India, and China.[7]

The gold standard was part of a much larger strategy, slowly evolving, for coping with the massive depression. Though both were vigorous supporters of the gold standard, Grover Cleveland and William McKinley recognized privately that it was not enough. Leading businessmen who believed surplus production was the chief cause of economic stagnation pressured both administrations to secure open markets overseas. Though Cleveland and even earlier administrations had started in this direction, the drive culminated after 1898 with bold new initiatives led by the GOP. McKinley and especially his successor, Theodore Roosevelt, aggressively defended U.S. interests, claiming a dominant position in Latin American trade and competing with European powers for access to Asia. They sought not a European-style empire, but markets for U.S. crops and manufactures.[8]

The new foreign policy brought Americans together in a surge of patriotic enthusiasm. Though the first confrontations were diplomatic, in 1898 McKinley was pressured into a war with Spain that proved wildly popular at home. The president, representing an older generation who remembered the Civil War, was at first reluctant to enter the fight. Support for the war emerged from business ranks and was whipped up by energetic young politicians and a jingoistic press. The war centered on Cuba, where in the context of a struggle for independence Spanish troops were reportedly committing atrocities against native Cubans. U.S. coverage of these events bore a striking resemblance to southern rhetoric about interracial sexual crime. Cruel, dark Spaniards allegedly engaged in the systematic rape of lighter-skinned Cuban women, while Spanish naval officers boarded passenger ships to strip-search female Americans. Justifications of the war also echoed the rhetoric of Republican campaigns against the impending "tyranny" of Silver Democrats and Populists. Inside the United States, war advocates urged American intervention to rescue "little brothers" who were bravely defending their homes against invasion.[9]

If partisan campaigns of the 1890s helped set the tone for war, memories of earlier conflicts also played a role. Thousands of young men sought eagerly to enlist, hoping for a chance to live up to their fathers' and grandfathers' military ideals. Carl Sandburg, who was twenty years old at the time, wrote later that "over all of us in 1898 was the shadow of the Civil War and the men who fought it." Antiwar voices were ignored. Democrats, who again nominated William Jennings Bryan as their presidential candidate in 1900, took anti-imperialism as their key theme and met resounding defeat. Many observers described the election as a "foregone conclusion."[10] In the United States, freedom for Cuba became a new source of national pride.

The contours of this patriotism had been profoundly shaped by campaigns for redemption, especially the new regional accommodation of North and South. The national press lavished praised on white southern heroes in the Spanish-American War, including some ex-Confederate officers. The war evoked a nationwide celebration of regional harmony and reunion. At the same time, some black men hoped their military service in Cuba would, as in the Civil War, provide an example of patriotic sacrifice that would convince white Americans to support racial justice. The strategy failed. Despite praise from leaders like Roosevelt, black men's battlefield courage did not stem the tide of segregation and disfranchisement. The scope of segregation grew, in fact, as a facet of the masculine "protection" for white women that winners in the redemption campaigns had articulated.[11]

In the wake of the war, the United States asserted its authority more broadly in Caribbean, Central American, and Pacific affairs. The McKinley administration supervised the annexation of Hawaii, Puerto Rico, and temporarily the Philippines. A series of Republican administrations moved forward with plans for an American-controlled waterway across the Isthmus of Panama. By 1907, the United States claimed Cuba, Panama, and the Dominican Republic as "American protectorates."[12] The new militarism in domestic political rhetoric thus extended overseas, as the nation asserted a stronger presence on the global stage.

Theodore Roosevelt embodied the effort to reinvent partisan leadership by projecting bold masculinity. Having built his reputation as a Republican reform governor in New York, Roosevelt leaped to action when the Spanish-American War began, resigning his post as Assistant Secretary of the Navy and recruiting a volunteer regiment of Harvard graduates, cowboys, and employees of Buffalo Bill's Wild West show. The "Rough Riders" won fame for their deeds in Cuba. Employing photographers from an early motion-picture company, Roosevelt staged reenactments of skirmishes for home audiences. He returned to the United States in triumph and won the Republican vice-presidential nomination in 1900. In the wake of McKinley's assassination in 1901, many Americans viewed the new president anxiously, believing he was unpredictable and hostile to business. Roosevelt overcame such misgivings to become one of the most popular presidents in American history.[13]

As early as 1894, in his essay "The Manly Virtues and Practical Politics," Roosevelt instructed voters that "we must be vigorous in mind and body . . . able to hold our own in rough conflict with our fellows, able to suffer punishment without flinching and, at need, to repay it in kind with full interest." Growing numbers of young men echoed Roosevelt's views. The new politician was explicitly masculine, endowed, as Roosevelt wrote, with "virile fighting qualities." In its stress on physical aggression this ideal drew on old Democratic themes, but it combined them with overt middle-class respectability. Roosevelt and his admirers argued that "better men" would rescue America from the crisis of the 1890s. As one observed, politics had been left to the "mercies of a distinctly lower class of politicians" whose campaigns featured "cheap whiskey, the sound of profanity, and possible ruffianism." Republicans and some urban middle-class Democrats now shared the same concerns. Both issued appeals for the patriotic involvement of "thoughtful, conservative, and disinterested partisans."[14]

Roosevelt learned his campaign tactics more from William Jennings Bryan than from his own party. In 1900 he went on tour as a counterweight to Bryan's energetic travels and became, himself, a master of the whistlestop campaign. Shaking hands with admirers or waving from the backs of trains, he developed the art of public appearance more fully than any previous president. His managers ran innovative campaign advertisements; he relished appearances on horseback and in hiking gear. By the 1904 campaign, Republican Senator Elihu Root declared the president "conspicuous among the men of his time as a type of noble manhood."[15]

On the respective duties of men and women, Roosevelt had strong views that he shared forcefully with the public. He denounced weaklings and told men their first responsibility was to protect their own and the nation's honor. Through his own example Roosevelt helped popularize football, boxing, and rugged hiking adventures as avenues to virility and health. He solemnly told young men their duty was to "sow their seed" and perpetuate the race. Cartoonists often poked fun at Roosevelt, but they never questioned his masculinity: they drew him as a cowboy, hunter, gladiator, soldier, and scout. Young men's campaign clubs soon called themselves Rough Riders and Knights of the Big Stick, the latter in reference to Roosevelt's dictum that the United States should "walk softly and carry a big stick" in foreign affairs.[16]

Meanwhile, women's special role was motherhood. Distressed by the declining white birthrate, Roosevelt argued that every white woman had a duty to bear four healthy children. "A healthy state can exist only when the men and women who make it up lead clean, vigorous, healthy lives," he told a Chicago audience in 1899. "The man must be glad to do a man's work, to dare and endure and to labor; to keep himself, and to keep those dependent upon him. The woman must be the housewife, the helpmeet." Invoking heroes of the Civil War era, Roosevelt added that "when men fear work or righteous war, when women fear motherhood, they tremble on the brink of doom."[17] Though not returning to the patriarchal family model celebrated by Democrats, Roosevelt and his colleagues reestablished military valor as the basis of citizenship, reversing the trend toward greater acceptance of women's political role.

The new aggressive masculinity was not simply an effect of Roosevelt's personal charisma, though he dominated politics for a decade. Americans began more broadly to hail reform politicians as heroes. In the 1880s and 1890s, commentators had pointed to Andrew Carnegie and other businessmen as exemplars of success; by 1900 their emphasis changed. "The centre of attention has to some degree shifted from commerce to politics," observed *Collier's* in 1904. "The protagonist is now rather President Roosevelt than J. P. Morgan." Men hailed for their honesty, vigor, and willingness to sacrifice for the public good included not only Roosevelt but also reform mayors and governors like Cleveland's Tom Johnson and Missouri's Joe Folk. Young William Allen White, a GOP nominee for governor of Kansas, wrote that "American politics is bristling with rampant, militant, unhampered men." Such candidates won praise for battling urban political machines, greedy old-fashioned congressmen, and corrupt financiers.[18]

The new heroes embodied a widespread desire for stronger government, stemming from the turmoil of the 1890s. During the Homestead violence in 1892, for example, leading newspapers had denounced strikers as "robbers and murderers" and "wild beasts thirsting for blood," but they had also expressed considerable fear over Carnegie's use of a private army of Pinkerton detectives to put down the strike. "When force is used, it ought to be directed by the State," argued the *Portland Oregonian*. "The only persons who should be allowed to shoot anybody in this country," wrote another Republican editor, "are those who represent government itself. And the only persons who should be shot are those who place themselves in the attitude of rebels." If this failed to clarify exactly who should be shot, it seemed clear that government—not employers—should make the decision. The scale of labor conflicts in the 1890s suggested a need for more federal power.[19]

Roosevelt proved willing to carry this into practice. Shocking the business community, he blocked a giant railroad merger in 1902; coopting the arguments of William Jennings Bryan and other Silver Democrats and Populists, the new president began cautiously to identify certain trusts and monopolies as "dangerous to the public interest." When a bitter strike in the anthracite coal industry threatened to replicate the violence of the 1890s, Roosevelt intervened. Forcing corporate leaders to negotiate with workers, the president threatened to send in troops and run the industry as a receivership. Mine operators backed down. Roosevelt's action was widely perceived as an intervention on behalf of labor. More broadly it represented a show of federal authority.

If strikers threatened "anarchy," the problem could be resolved by a stronger state.[20]

Domestic policies of this kind—in which a new, aggressive federal power acted as a mediating force—were responses to the now-obvious gaps between rich and poor, East and West that Populism and labor unrest had exposed. Other Americans went much further in advocating federal measures to protect workers. The American Socialist Party, founded in 1901, grew for a decade and culminated in Eugene Debs's presidential bid in 1912, when he won almost a million votes.[21]

The growing impulse to expand government power also extended in other directions, notably to enforce increasingly detailed racial segregation laws that were, like militarism overseas, a product of redemption. As early as 1894, Frederick Douglass had drawn a direct connection between segregation and the charge of interracial rape. "The charge of assault upon defenceless women," he argued, had sprung upon the country "simultaneously, and in manifest cooperation with a declared purpose . . . to degrade the Negro by judicial decisions, by legislative enactments, by repealing all laws for the protection of the ballot, by drawing the color line in all railroad cars and stations and in all other public places in the South." The primary purpose of Jim Crow laws seems to have been to separate white *women* from black *men*. In all-male preserves such as bars and race tracks, segregation laws were seldom enforced; nor did such laws prevent black women, in their work as domestic servants, from living intimately with white families. But as the *New Orleans Times-Democrat* argued, "a man that would be horrified at the idea of his wife or daughter seated by the side of a burly negro in the parlor of a hotel or at a restaurant cannot see her occupying a crowded seat in a car next to a negro without the same feeling of disgust."[22]

Segregation laws reflected this gendered motivation. An early point of conflict was the "ladies' car," or first-class railroad coach. White men often rode with blacks in the smoking cars in order to smoke or spit, but first-class cars were white women's domain and thus the focus of segregation. In Natchez, Mississippi, codes governing promenades along the river followed similar lines: one bluff was for "the use of whites, for ladies and children," while another was for "bachelors and the colored population." An Alabama law specifically prevented white female nurses from caring for black patients. Advocates of segregation frequently described "social communion and amalgamation" as twin evils, the former causing the latter.[23] The issue of white women's sexual agency remained blurred: segregationists did not explain whether they feared an increase in rape or in white women's consensual relationships with black men.

Segregation accompanied broader efforts to "protect" white women's position in the family. Around the nation a long, slow reaction to family policies of the Radical era reached its peak around the turn of the century. Antimiscegenation laws passed not only in the South but also elsewhere; some western states tried for the first time to bar interracial marriages between whites and American Indians. In a broader movement for both sexual and racial purity, reformers pressured legislators to raise the age of consent for young women and initiated crusades to cleanse America of prostitution and other illegal sexual activity. Trends in divorce law during the Radical era, which in some states had made it easier for women to obtain divorces and custody of their children, were also reversed. *Purity* was the new, conservative watchword in lawmakers' attitudes toward race relations and family life.[24]

Almost all the varied expansions of federal and state power after redemption were, then, patriachal enterprises. The domestic manhood of the 1880s, celebrated in Grover Cleveland's marriage and sedate gentlemen's campaign clubs, did not survive the crisis of the 1890s. At the regional level southern Democrats reasserted white supremacist manhood by using state governments to enact disfranchisement and segregation. Among Republicans, Roosevelt offered a "conspicuous" example of manhood and new assertions of federal authority from Panama to the anthracite coal fields. These policies built in different ways on old GOP ideals of protection to the home and Democratic calls for protection of white women—goals that were no longer fiercely oppositional, as they once had been in Civil War and Reconstruction days. Both Republican and Democratic men could win admiration as reform heroes, and in some cases partisan victory was no longer the central end. Aggressive manhood was a unifying theme among men who sought to reinvent partisan politics.

Women and Electoral Politics

Large numbers of publicly active women did not subscribe to the new conservatism. Though pushed out of party campaigns, instructed in their duties as wives and mothers, and told that soldierly masculinity was the basis of citizenship, women of the Progressive Era found new ways to advance a variety of political goals. For the most part these women avowed themselves "nonpartisans," a self-description also adopted by some men. Nonpartisanship was particularly attractive to reformers whose agendas were ignored or denounced by the parties in power. Black Americans, former Populists, Christian Socialists, and advocates for women's rights were among those most interested in developing political strategies outside the parties. Within these groups, women had a particularly strong reason to focus on new tactics. Except in four western states, women still lacked the full suffrage rights that gave men direct leverage in the electoral sphere.

The new era did not witness female unity any more than campaigns of the Gilded Age had enabled all women to work together, despite claims to the contrary by men and women in every party. There was, for example, no identifiable "women's position" on the Spanish-American War, even if those for and against the war both made this predictable claim. Thousands of women, many of them Bryan supporters, opposed the war and promoted arbitration as an alternative to armed conflict. For Ellen Slayden, wife of a Texas congressman, the war evoked memories of her Virginia childhood. "The people are getting in the notion of war—a fight or a frolic," she wrote in her diary. Hearing about the destruction of the U.S.S. *Maine* in Havana harbor, she wrote, "I have a prenatal terror of war—a child of the sixties—and my knees trembled and I felt sick all day."[25]

Thousands of other women, including many Republicans who had rejoiced at McKinley's victory, expressed strong support for the war. Swept up in the enthusiasm, some volunteered as nurses and many more formed ladies' auxiliaries to support the military effort. Among these were leaders of the National Women's Republican Association, who continued to work on behalf of the party in power. Despite limited funding they pursued a strategy closer to Roosevelt's than to that of women who eschewed party loyalties altogether. J. Ellen Foster assisted the Red Cross in Cuba and toured the Philippines to investigate women's and children's welfare. Helen Varick Boswell, who had headed New York Women's Republican Association during the 1890s, visited Panama in 1907 and 1911 at the request of Roosevelt and William Howard Taft. On behalf of the U.S. government she set up women's clubs and supervised education and health projects in the canal zone.[26]

Republican women took up other issues while maintaining party ties. Marion McBride, former president of the Women's Sound Money League, edited a domestic science newsletter in which she promoted a "Strong Home Life" and "Cooperation of the Housekeeper with Government Officials." Ellen Foster worked for passage of child labor laws and for better prison conditions in Kansas and the District of Columbia. A biographer summed up the connections between her work before and after 1896:

> Mrs. Foster was able late in life to use for moral or humanitarian ends the most powerful of all organizations, the constituted government. . . . [She] carried on reforms that she never thought of in the early stages of her life. And she carried them on by means that the church worker, the lawyer, even the temperance woman could not have imagined. Her point of pride was now that she could get the United States Government to do them for her.

Like men who defined themselves as "reform Republicans," Foster continued her constructive engagement with partisanship, albeit without a vote. She remained an active campaigner in western suffrage states and won praise in 1900 for helping the GOP capture Utah. Wyoming Senator Francis Warren congratulated her for bringing thousands of women into "the safe channel of party fealty."[27]

Republican women's groups abandoned the old hurrah style once exemplified by Carrie Harrison Clubs in the Midwest. GOP women no longer formed broom brigades, joined horseback units, or decorated wagons for local demonstrations. The Ladies' McKinley and Hobart Club of South Bend, Indiana, attracted 150 members in 1896; they declined to join a local parade and announced that "after the election the club will be formed into a social and educational organization for the benefit of the working girls of the city." In New York, fashionable Republican women heard papers on "Civic Virtues" and

"How a Bill Becomes Law."[28] These women saw the boundaries between political, social, and educational work as fluid and adjustable.

In 1910 the National Women's Republican Association maintained a thousand clubs nationwide, but nonpartisan women's clubs captured greater public attention and undertook major political initiatives on issues like suffrage and public health. Outside the South, these groups and the Republican women's movement had overlapping constituencies. All women's club members were certainly not Republicans, but prominent leaders of the national movement were wealthy matrons from manufacturing and business families. In its mock elections, the Women's Political Class of Boston voted repeatedly for McKinley; Bryan supporter Harriet Hanson Robinson was thankful when her side made a decent showing, "considering all prejudices." The women's club of Girard, Nebraska—in Bryan's home state—gave him only five mock votes in 1900, with two for the Prohibition candidate and sixteen for McKinley.[29] The results, like those in C. W. Post's "election" for women in 1896, suggested the class limitations of political projects undertaken by middle- and upper-class women's clubs.

In choosing nonpartisan strategies, reformers took account of effective projects that were already underway. A prime example was temperance education, which a wing of the national WCTU had undertaken with stunning success. Mary Hunt, a lifelong Republican, had dissented from Frances Willard's Prohibition Party strategy in the 1880s but had not joined her friend Ellen Foster in abandoning the WCTU. Instead, Hunt headed a national initiative to promote "scientific temperance instruction" in public schools. Hunt invited Republican WCTU members to refrain from engaging in the bitter debates that absorbed the energies of Willard and Foster; she urged them instead to lobby school boards and state legislatures. Around the country, bipartisan majorities endorsed this "scientific" measure, and temperance instruction was quickly mandated by the legislatures of forty-three states. Meanwhile, neither Foster nor Willard had won national prohibition through their respective parties.[30]

The settlement house movement offered another model for nonpartisan organizing. Inspired by experiments in Great Britain, hundreds of young middle-class and elite women moved into urban slums to undertake education and reform work. At the most famous settlement, Chicago's Hull House, Jane Addams and her colleagues drew on traditions of "municipal housekeeping" once espoused in Republican campaigns. A number of the movement's leaders, including Addams and Florence Kelley, had been deeply influenced by fathers who were Republican politicians. Savvy understanding of backroom dealing contributed to these women's effectiveness, but their policy agenda moved far beyond those of the old GOP. In fact, they engaged in open conflict with conservative Republican leaders as well as intransigent Democrats. Some settlement workers not only advocated municipal reform and public hygiene but also made a broader commitment to socialism. In some places, the new Socialist Party provided an avenue for women to participate in electoral campaigns.[31]

Denied the vote and excluded from councils of power, Progressive women used whatever leverage they could to advance their political ideas. As in the Gilded Age many continued to make use of their female identities, especially as mothers and housekeepers. Drawing on a tradition of female "influence" recognized for years by Republicans, thousands of women accomplished their civic work through a national network of Mothers' Clubs, founded in 1896. Along with nonpartisan women's clubs, WCTU Mothers' Meetings, and other activist groups, Mothers' Clubs appealed for "protection" to women, children, and families, using the rhetoric of women's special parental role to make their claim. Such strategies were not new, but drew on longstanding claims to "domestic protection" made by the parties that had decisively secured power in North and South.[32]

The effectiveness of women's strategies was shaped not only by partisan debates from previous decades but also by the ways in which those struggles had influenced men in power. The nonpartisan Consumers' League, for example, made a strategic choice to seek mandatory shorter working hours only for *women* because a conservative Supreme Court had already rejected "paternalistic" interference with the contractual obligations of working men. In twenty years of tariff debates GOP leaders had identified women wage-earners in Europe as abused and degraded, and they had defended state action—however limited and ineffective tariffs may have been—to prevent these conditions. Kelley herself was in some ways a product of this viewpoint; in debates over minimum wages, she endorsed the "American tradition that men support their families, the wives throughout life and the children at least until the fourteenth birthday."[33]

Other Progressive Era women's groups advocated mothers' pensions on the grounds that poverty-stricken mothers should be enabled to stay home and devote themselves to their children. The idea spread rapidly from state to state between 1911 and 1913, providing benefits to help poor widows with children stay at home. In their Union pension program, Republicans had a long history of endorsing "protection" to able-bodied widows—but not to able-bodied men. Disillusioned by the broad 1890s pension program, in which all aging Union veterans were awarded pensions, politicians were nonetheless willing to build on an earlier model from the war years, in which government served as a surrogate breadwinner for women and children.[34]

Even suffragists began to affirm woman's place in the home, and some argued that women wanted to vote *as women*, to fulfill a special feminine role. Women would purify politics; they would vote, not in greedy self-interest, but in their nurturing capacities as mothers. In 1910 Rheta Childe Dorr made the extraordinary statement that "social legislation alone interests women."[35] This was not true; for decades women had expressed strong opinions on the tariff, monetary policy, and railroad rates. But in a conservative climate, women found that appeals grounded in their social identities as mothers were effective levers on the men in power.

Political battles of earlier eras had generated other public identities that proved useful to women. Since the northern religious awakening of the early nineteenth century, Christianity had been a central part of women's claim to a public role. Transformed into the "social gospel," Christianity continued to offer Progressive women a basis for political action. Drawing on Republicans' traditional impulse to change their neighbors' habits, urban reformers organized sweeping efforts to end prostitution, promiscuity, and vice. They created new civic leagues, but they also worked through churches and religious groups like the Methodist Woman's Home Missionary Society and the Young Men's and Young Women's Christian Associations. Some evangelicals blamed urban social problems on the working class and recent immigrants, especially Eastern Europeans, Catholics, and Jews. In other contexts, though, Christianity served as a counterweight to the values of the marketplace. At its most radical, the social gospel inspired a vision of class relations transformed by an activist faith.[36]

From campaigns of the Gilded Age, women could also draw upon public identities as consumers. Democrats had used consumer arguments to advocate lower tariffs, and thus a reduction of state power that could be described as conservative. In class terms, however, Democrats had invoked the "shopping women" to defend the interests of working-class families who were struggling to make ends meet. In the Progressive Era, labor reformers began to appeal to female consumers on this basis in order to build ties between consumers and workers. Florence Kelley, who had closely followed fights over the tariff, moved far beyond such issues when she founded the National Consumers' League. A socialist, Kelley tried with some success to harness women's power to boycott. In addition to campaigns for minimum wages and shorter hours, middle- and working-class women in the league promoted the purchase of clothes with union labels, pressuring manufacturers to permit their workers to organize.[37]

In economic debates of the 1880s and 1890s, Republicans, Democrats, and Populists had all begun to rely on the rhetoric of scientific expertise. Women like Mary Hunt, Florence Kelley, and Jane Addams also found such language an effective weapon that women could employ. Reflecting a new concern for the "science" of public opinion, reformers conducted investigations, marshaled statistics, and filed expert reports. They did so not only through newly established professional groups like the American Association of Social Workers but also through the WCTU, nonpartisan women's clubs, and the Consumers' League. Suffragists used similar arguments. "Think of the effect," wrote one, "when a woman, being her husband's political equal, will study social science with him and the sons need no longer go to the beer saloon to be initiated into politics."[38] In a complex, secularizing, urban nation, women's claims to expertise and social scientific methods became increasingly valuable.

This new reliance on female professionalism, asserted for the most part by college-educated and elite women, suggested the class limitations of women's gender-based arguments. In some ways the lobbying techniques of the Progressive Era echoed old strategies from the 1850s, when elite women had used family and social connections to exert political pressure. Progressive reformers appealed broadly to public opinion, but those who eschewed electoral campaigns gave up an important avenue of mass mobilization. For women exhausted by the campaigns of prior decades and frustrated by their results, lobbying public officials must have seemed an attractively straightforward strategy. The enormous effort expended in the Prohibitionist and Populist Parties, for example, had yielded few concrete results. Nonetheless, the change in political tactics had its cost. Women who could practice the new strategies of expert research and lobbying often represented the interests of northeastern Protestant elites.

The structure of Progressive reform work also reflected barriers of race, set decisively by campaigns of the 1890s and the new impulse toward segregation and disfranchisement. With black men disfranchised their communities suffered enormous burdens, and black women found themselves facing multiple problems of gender and race discrimination, poverty, and grossly unfair labor practices. Some black churchwomen forged cautious alliances with white women to promote public health, better schools, and temperance. But, excluded from the ideal of pure white womanhood, they were constantly forced to prove their moral worth—a problem that reflected the chilly racial climate. Black women's groups were denied entry into the General Federation of Women's Clubs and other white reform and social organizations. Within black communities in both the North and the South, attempts to "lift up the race" through middle-class Christian respectability proved partially effective, but at the same time divided black women by class.[39]

After 1900, then, women in various political projects made their arguments as mothers and wives, good Christians, urban shoppers, and industrial workers who deserved "protection." Outside the halls of government such reformers alleviated much suffering, promoted public health, and undertook large-scale projects of rescue and charity. What they could accomplish in legislative terms, however, was determined as always by the structures of politics. Women began to achieve their reform goals in the Progressive Era not because their arguments were new; Christianity, motherhood, consumer power, and the plight of degraded women laborers were all legacies from earlier decades of debate. Rather, configurations of power offered new opportunities for leverage.

Between 1897 and 1910, economic and social-welfare reformers and woman suffragists won few policy victories. Though Theodore Roosevelt was a notable innovator, more conservative Republicans in Congress were unwilling to support new measures. After 1910, reformers achieved a number of long-standing goals in a climate of renewed party competition. Ironically, proponents of domestic masculinity in the late 1880s had implemented few reforms; now male leaders who had cultivated aggressive public images proved willing to heed reformers' call and fulfill their manly duty. Roosevelt, reform Democrat Woodrow Wilson, and dozens of congressmen and local leaders proved increasingly willing to use government to protect the weak.

After leaving the presidency in 1908, Roosevelt became bitterly disillusioned with the conservatism of his successor, William Howard Taft. At the same time he paid new attention to the arguments of professional women like Jane Addams, who persuaded the former president that municipal housekeeping and political extensions of motherhood were legitimate women's goals. By 1912, unable to recapture the Republican nomination, Roosevelt chose to break from the party, denouncing its "impotence" and advocating a sweeping agenda that he dubbed "the New Nationalism."[40]

Roosevelt signified his intentions in a speech at Osawatomie, Kansas, on the centennial anniversary of John Brown's birth. The choice of location was fraught with significance: clearly the former president hoped to remind Americans of the legacy of the party that had abolished slavery. He may also have intended a nod toward a subsequent third party with deep Kansas roots. "The essence of any struggle for liberty," he declared, "has always been, and must always be to take from some one man or class of men the right to enjoy power, or wealth, or position, or immunity, which has not been earned." Adding that "labor is the superior of capital, and deserves much the higher consideration," Roosevelt noted that these words were a quotation from Abraham Lincoln.[41]

Roosevelt's third-party bid generated enormous enthusiasm among reformers nationwide; presented with a party that championed their goals, "nonpartisan" women who were interested in labor and women's issues quickly returned to a partisan strategy. In the tradition of other third parties, the Progressive convention included dozens of women delegates—"doctors, lawyers, teachers," one observer reported, "middle-aged leaders of civic movements or rich young girls who had gone in for settlement work." The *New York Times* dismissed the third party as run by women. Jane Addams offered the seconding speech for Roosevelt's presidential nomination. The time had come, she wrote, for women to engage in partisan work; only parties could directly impact the operations of government power. The platform called for a progressive income tax, child labor laws, unemployment insurance, a minimum wage, and national woman suffrage.[42]

The campaign of 1912 reopened a number of issues from earlier decades. In Progressive ranks, many middle-class women were accustomed to single-sex organizing in separate women's clubs. Party leaders urged them to campaign together with men, in the midwestern and Populist tradition, but in many areas this idea met resistance. At the same time, women failed to unite behind the new party, despite claims by Addams and others that it was an ideal vehicle for many reforms. The National Women's Republican Association regrouped, and prominent women mobilized on behalf of Taft and Wilson as well as Roosevelt. NAWSA's newspaper, the *Woman's Journal,* received volumes of letters in support of all three men but refused to publish any of them. The editor observed that NAWSA's three chief officers supported three different parties—one having accepted a Socialist nomination.[43]

Roosevelt did not win; instead, he helped defeat Taft and throw the election to Democrat Woodrow Wilson. State-level Progressive victories and renewed competition created, however, the impetus for a flurry of creative legislation. Wilson's Democratic Party was no longer the stubbornly antigovernment coalition of Gilded Age campaigns. Silver Democrats' 1896 adoption of the income tax plank had marked the modest beginning of a slow but dramatic transformation in party doctrine. Despite continued racial conservatism, Democrats of 1912 were more ready than the GOP to use government to defend the interests of labor, as Wilson's actions during his presidency showed.

Not surprisingly, many of the measures Wilson signed after 1912 were designed to reinforce traditional family structure—an issue on which Progressives and Democrats could agree. Mothers' pensions won rapid adoption at the state level, reflecting an impulse to use government as a substitute breadwinner and strengthen widows' position in the home. A new federal Children's Bureau, founded as a result of Progressive agitation, established a base for welfare initiatives and positions of authority for professional women, while reinforcing the idea that motherhood and child care were women's natural roles. President Wilson signed legislation to protect labor by limiting work hours—but for women and children, not for men.[44]

Under Wilson's administration the nation ratified the Seventeenth Amendment authorizing Congress to collect income taxes, at last fulfilling a goal of Populists and Silver Democrats. Other reforms—including the establishment of the Federal Trade Commission, a national minimum wage, workmen's compensation, and old age insurance—also won passage, often through the cooperation of reform-minded Democrats with Republicans and Progressives from the Midwest and West. Wilson thus renewed the Democrats' commitment as the party of the working class. Though none of the parties gave much consideration to issues of race, legislative accomplishments of the 1910s transcended some of the class limitations established by the Republicans' national victory in 1896.[45]

National prohibition of liquor, established by the Eighteenth Amendment in 1919, followed quickly upon other reforms. Though Willard's third-party strategy had put the prohibition movement on the map, its goal was ultimately won by other means. The Anti-Saloon League worked state by state with the parties in power, mobilizing blocs of voters to support particular nominees. The league worked largely with Democrats in the South and Republicans elsewhere. As such, they took advantage of the new sectional accord ushered in by redemption—but without trying to unify northern and southern prohibitionists in one party.[46]

The question of women's political rights remained an outstanding issue. In 1911 women won suffrage in California and Washington; in the following year other western states followed suit. Following Populist antecedents, appearance of the new Progressive Party played an influential role in a number of states. The momentum of state-level victories resurrected old debates within the suffrage movement. Leaders like Carrie Chapman Catt, who had witnessed the debacles of the 1890s, thenceforth insisted on NAWSA's strict nonpartisanship; they adhered to this strategy all the way to 1920. But in the last decade before full national suffrage, young innovators broke with NAWSA and founded the Woman's Party to "punish the party in power" by working to defeat its candidates. Catt and her followers were appalled, insisting that such tactics would only create enemies. Alice Paul, leader of the Woman's Party, responded that "to count in an election, you do not have to be the biggest Party, you have to be simply an independent Party that will stand for one object and that cannot be diverted from that object."[47] Frances Willard would have understood. Paul's strategy was a return to the tactics of the 1880s, while Catt and NAWSA leaders shared Susan B. Anthony's disillusionment with parties after 1894.

Pressured by both wings of the suffrage movement, aware of party competition, and acknowledging women's patriotic efforts during World War I, Congress and a majority of state legislatures ratified full woman suffrage in 1920. With Democrats' deep and longstanding resistance to women's partisan activities and to suffrage, it was ironic that a Democratic president signed the bill into law. Reflecting Gilded Age precedent, however, western states were among the first to sign; in many of them women already voted. The amendment won ratification with scant support from the ex-Confederate states.[48] Old regional divisions persisted in the twentieth century. In some senses, they ran almost as deep in 1920 as they had when the Republican Party organized its first campaigns.

When Theodore Roosevelt issued his appeal in Kansas, during the centennial of John Brown's birth, he built on a partisan legacy sustained and contested over many decades. When Jane Addams seconded his nomination she also represented a partisan heritage, passed down to her by Frances Willard, J. Ellen Foster, Mary Elizabeth Lease, and thousands of others. Not only in stepping up to vote but also in voting for a party, women of the Progressive Era fulfilled an old dream. The diversity of women's opinions, loyalties, and political goals, as well as the inequality of their access to power based on differences of race, class, and region, were problems earlier generations of women would have recognized. Since Whig days, politicians had argued over "woman" as a political factor; for just as long, party loyalties had motivated and complicated women's bids for power. Even though party machinery had faded in importance, Addams echoed her predecessors in arguing that women should be enthusiastic partisans whenever "they find that they can reach the desired ends more directly through a political party." The boundary between partisanship and reform, as Addams observed, was always a "wavering line."[49]

Epilogue

Where is our Mother, the State?
—People's Party Campaign Book, *1892*

When women won full suffrage in 1920, some Americans—both women and men—hoped the new voters would transform politics by casting ballots for peace and economic and racial justice, and for candidates of moral and spiritual purity. Older hands like Susan B. Anthony and Elizabeth Cady Stanton, who did not live to see the fulfillment of their dream, would have cautioned against such optimism. American women had always been divided in their racial, economic, regional, and partisan loyalties. They had had bitter experiences with partisanship *before* they could vote; continuation of this pattern was to be expected in the new era of suffrage. Subsequent coalitions that women have built across lines of class, race, region, and nation—however temporary or partial—are achievements to celebrate. Where these fail, advocates for women's rights can take comfort in knowing that deep divisions among them are not new.

The structures of American politics have changed dramatically in the twentieth century. In addition to Progressive Era reforms, the Great Depression of 1929 produced majority support for additional measures of government activism, led by a transformed Democratic Party. Many of these initiatives built on the legacy of Gilded Age debates and policies. Union pensions, for example, provided an early model for broader forms of assistance to disabled and elderly citizens. New Deal programs for farm-price supports and aid to farmers echoed Populist ideas from the 1890s. And even though the United States has become increasingly committed to free trade, arguments about economic "protection" for wage-workers and mothers still echo in today's politics.

The growth of federal power has been influenced at each step by the work of partisan and nonpartisan women. In many contexts, women have continued to employ the rhetoric of motherhood and family to advance a variety of goals.

The history of politics from the 1840s to the Progressive Era suggests, however, that political debates have relied on ideals of both womanhood *and* manhood. If anything, manhood was even more important in winning expansions of state power. In response to appeals for masculine protection, men in power began to use government as a surrogate breadwinner, defender of female virtue, and protector of women and children in the labor market—all of which, within the family, were traditionally functions of men. Paternalism, not maternalism, may have been the driving force behind the growth of federal authority.

Some expansions of federal power were the direct result of wars—most notably the abolition of slavery, which hesitant Republicans adopted as a military measure. In terms of social welfare, the Union pension system and later equivalents, like the G.I. Bill adopted after World War II, also resulted from military mobilization. But other federal measures have borne little connection to the wars that preceded their passage. There was no direct policy connection, for example, between the Spanish-American War and the subsequent outpouring of legislation for factory inspection and Jim Crow segregation. Politicians' ability to lay claim to an aggressively masculine identity may be more important, as a prerequisite for new federal initiatives, than the specifics of the wars they fight.

In the face of growing federal power, opponents of new government programs have consistently expressed their fears by warning of threats to the family. They have returned repeatedly to gender-based attacks on their opponents as masculine women and feminine men. These stereotypes have applied not only to women's rights issues but also to others, as when Populists sought to nationalize railroads and legislate government aid to farmers. Fears about loss of male power have been inextricably linked to race, class, and regional identities: they applied not only to men's authority in patriarchal households but also to white men's superiority over black men, taxation of breadwinners' income, white middle-class men's control over urban ethnic machines, and a host of other issues. In all these cases, "unnatural" gender roles and family disorder have served as fundamental symbols of the dangers of centralized authority.

At least until the 1910s, advocates of women's political rights and of government action for economic and racial justice found it difficult to advance these projects simultaneously. During Reconstruction and in the Progressive Era, aid to freedmen and women, the destitute, the disabled, and working women relied on the leadership of aggressive men who vowed to "protect" the weak and helpless, and on women who emphasized their maternal role. Gender conservatism was thus, for many reformers, a strategy to win support for federal action to end poverty and racial injustice. Conversely, movements to advance women's rights found elitist and racist arguments to be powerfully persuasive. Movements that demanded greater class *and* gender equity—like Radical Republican suffragists and Populists—found the going tough.

These examples are a century old, and subsequent efforts at cross-class and cross-racial organizing have been more successful. But traditional ideals of manhood, womanhood, and family order persist as some of the most deep-rooted values in American politics. Conservatives still link expansions of state power to gender disorder and limitations on government with men's authority in the home. For these Americans, the political economy of family and state still seems to be a zero-sum game: state welfare programs necessarily weaken the authority of the traditional family. It is no wonder, then, that women prominently identified with activist adminstrations—like Eleanor Roosevelt and Hillary Clinton—have been attacked as "unwomanly," while liberal men have been derided for weakness and effeminacy. In their basic form, these caricatures have been in use since the era of Mary Todd Lincoln and Rutherford B. Hayes.

Attacked as corrupt and destructive to family order, the larger electoral machinery in the United States is now viewed by many Americans as the party machines came to be viewed around 1900. In conservative rhetoric, traditional family structures remain the chief repository of virtue, and government appears as an external threat rather than a responsive tool to aid both women and men. Old struggles between the state and the patriarchal household thus continue, reinvented in new contexts as each decade passes. To oppose the state, conservatives portray its supporters as undermining marriage and motherhood. To protect men's power in the home, they seek to persuade Americans that government itself is empty of virtue.

Notes

Introduction

1. *New York Tribune,* 21 Oct. 1868, 1; *National Anti-Slavery Standard,* 20 June 1868, 1; Democrat in Paula Baker, *The Moral Frameworks of Public Life* (New York, 1991), 30; *Harper's Weekly,* 12 Nov. 1892, 1082.

2. Lizzie Holmes in MaryJo Wagner, "Farms, Families, and Reform: Women in the Farmers' Alliance and Populist Party," Ph.D. diss., University of Oregon, 1986, 223.

3. Letter dated 11 February 1886, in "Woman Suffrage: Unnatural and Inexpedient" (Boston, 1894), 13, reprinted in *History of Women Microfilm* (New Haven, 1975–1977); *The Education of Henry Adams* (Boston, 1973 [1918]), 379–90, 442–48.

4. Quoted, for example, in *Chino Valley Champion,* 10 June 1892, 3; *Hancock and English Campaign Songster* (Cincinnati, 1880), 40–41.

5. Quotations from Joel H. Silbey, "The Surge of Republican Power: Partisan Antipathy, American Social Conflict, and the Coming of the Civil War," 210, and William E. Gienapp, "'Politics Seems to Enter into Everything': Political Culture in the North, 1840–1860," 37, both in Stephen E. Maizlish and John J. Kushma, eds., *Essays on American Antebellum Politics, 1840–1860* (Arlington, Tex., 1982). In recent years political historians have illuminated the religious and ethnic bases of voter loyalty. I agree with Daniel Walker Howe that the strongest approach is to combine these insights with attention to economics, recognizing that voters' loyalties and priorities often change. Howe, "The Evangelical Movement and Political Culture in the North during the Second Party System," *Journal of American History* (hereafter *JAH*) 77 (1991): 1225–26. Leading treatments of ethnocultural voting behavior in the Gilded Age include Richard Jensen, *The Winning of the Midwest: Social and Political Conflict, 1888–1896* (Chicago, 1971); Paul Kleppner, *The Third Electoral System, 1853–1892: Parties, Voters and Political Cultures* (Chapel Hill, 1979).

6. For a sweeping view of these issues, see Gerda Lerner, *The Creation of Feminist Consciousness* (New York, 1993); on the Revolution, see Linda Kerber, *Women of the Republic: Intellect and Ideology in Revolutionary America* (Chapel Hill, 1980); Mary Beth Norton, *Liberty's Daughters: The Revolutionary Experience of American Women, 1750–1800*

(Boston, 1980); and Mark E. Kann, *On the Man Question: Gender and Civic Virtue in America* (Philadelphia, 1991). On erosion of patriarchy before the Revolution, see Glenna Matthews, *The Rise of Public Woman: Woman's Power and Woman's Place in the United States, 1630–1970* (New York, 1992), 32–51.

7. Nancy A. Hewitt has traced several threads of antebellum Protestant reform, which she labels benevolent, evangelical, and ultraist. I am less interested here in doctrinal differences among these factions, and more in their common regional base and cumulative impact on national affairs. Hewitt's work shows that many women who did not participate in evangelical revivals or believe in "perfectionism" nonetheless joined reform causes. Also, as Lori D. Ginzberg observes, the "work of benevolence" long outlasted the decade of revivals and led women quickly into secular politics. Hewitt, *Women's Activism and Social Change: Rochester, New York, 1822–1872* (Ithaca, 1982); Ginzberg, *Women and the Work of Benevolence: Morality, Politics, and Class in the Nineteenth-Century United States* (New Haven, 1990). On evangelical revivals, family structure, and economics, see Nancy F. Cott, *The Bonds of Womanhood: "Woman's Sphere" in New England, 1780–1835* (New Haven, 1977), and Mary P. Ryan, *Cradle of the Middle Class: The Family in Oneida County, New York, 1790–1865* (New York, 1981).

8. *New York Herald,* 17 Oct. 1856, 1, from a rally in Poughkeepsie.

9. An excellent account of these changes and their impact is Alan Trachtenberg, *The Incorporation of America: Culture and Society in the Gilded Age* (New York, 1982).

10. On national party competition, see Kleppner, *Third Electoral System,* 298–301.

11. For alternative views identifying a separate "women's political culture" in the Gilded Age, see Michael McGerr, "Political Style and Women's Power, 1830–1930," *JAH* 77 (1990): 864–85; Paula Baker, *The Moral Frameworks of Public Life* and "The Domestication of Politics: Women and American Political Society, 1780–1920," *American Historical Review* (hereafter *AHR*) 89 (1984): 620–47; Kathryn Kish Sklar, *Florence Kelley and the Nation's Work: The Rise of Women's Political Culture, 1830–1900* (New Haven, 1995). The Kelley quotation is from Sklar, 275. I have tried to avoid the terms *political style* and *political culture* because I find them, respectively, too narrow and too broad. *Political style* does not sufficiently address the ideologies and policy goals that underlay campaign rituals. Historians are, on the other hand, invoking *political culture* both as a description of all public forums where "power is elaborated" and as an explanation of individuals' public actions. In my view, these approaches tend to reinscribe public/private distinctions or invite hopelessly broad definitions of *power* that obscure more than they explain. See, for example, the conflation of "political culture" and "public culture" in Sklar (xi–xvi, 17–18, 225–28, 301–3) and Daniel Walker Howe's suggestion that historians should "define political culture to include all struggles over power" ("The Evangelical Movement and Political Culture," 1235). Daunted by the latter proposal, I have adopted a limited definition of *power* and have described specific party ideologies, policy goals, and the identities of those who participated in electoral campaigns. By exploring the connections among these, I hope to illuminate the broader social bases and functions of politics, especially in relation to the family. For helpful definitions of *political culture,* see Lynn Hunt, *Politics, Culture, and Class in the French Revolution* (Berkeley, 1984), 10–15, and Jean H. Baker, *Affairs of Party: The Political Culture of Northern Democrats in the Mid-Nineteenth Century* (Ithaca, 1983), 11–13.

12. I have borrowed the term *female consciousness* from Nancy Cott but for somewhat different ends. I see it as a rhetorical strategy that proved useful in the service of any number of goals, from abolition of slavery to defense of high tariffs, disfranchisement of black men, and woman suffrage. By "rhetorical strategy" I do not mean to

imply that women's gender consciousness was cynically used or superficially held, merely that I have focused on its uses in partisan debate rather than its implications for women's private or inner lives. Both women's and men's public discourse in the Gilded Age was intensely gender-conscious. Americans invoked womanhood for so many contradictory purposes that it is impossible to associate an overarching "female consciousness" with any particular set of goals. I have tried to distinguish among different types of female consciousness, some based on the argument that women should obey patriarchal authority, others invoking women's moral authority as mothers, and still others using natural-rights arguments for female and male equality. Nancy F. Cott, "What's in a Name? The Limits of 'Social Feminism'; or Expanding the Vocabulary of Women's History," *JAH* 76 (1989): 826–28. The argument that female consciousness is intertwined with identities of race and class has been helpful to me here; see for example Elsa Barkley Brown, "Womanist Consciousness: Maggie Lena Walker and the Independent Order of Saint Luke," *Signs* 14 (Spring 1989), 613.

13. Robert J. Dinkin, *Before Equal Suffrage: Women in Partisan Politics from Colonial Times to 1920* (Westport, Conn., 1995), 72–73.

14. John B. Gordon in *Savannah Republican,* 15 Sept. 1868, 1; George C. Rable, *Civil Wars: Women and the Crisis of Southern Nationalism* (Urbana, 1989), 44.

15. On mugwumps and other northeastern reformers who championed independence from party, but who endorsed candidates and played active roles in campaigns, see Ari Hoogenboom, *Outlawing the Spoils: A History of the Civil Service Movement, 1865–1883* (Urbana, 1963); John G. Sproat, *"The Best Men": Liberal Reformers in the Gilded Age* (New York, 1968); Gerald W. McFarland, *Mugwumps, Morals and Politics, 1884–1920* (Amherst, Mass., 1975); and Michael E. McGerr, *The Decline of Popular Politics: The American North, 1865–1928* (New York, 1986), 42–68. Historians of the Gilded Age suffrage movement have generally characterized the AWSA as Republican and the NWSA as "independent" after 1869. Most have implied that the NWSA's choice was better for the movement. I hope to show that suffragists' party loyalties and their tactical difficulties were far more complicated. See Eleanor Flexner, *Century of Struggle: The Woman's Rights Movement in the United States* (Cambridge, Mass., 1959); Ellen Carol DuBois, *Feminism and Suffrage: The Emergence of an Independent Women's Movement in America, 1848–1869* (Ithaca, 1978).

16. On parties and political structure, see Richard M. McCormick, *The Party Period and Public Policy: American Politics from the Age of Jackson to the Progressive Era* (New York, 1986); Peter H. Argersinger, *Structure, Process, and Party: Essays in American Political History* (Armonk, N.Y., 1992). On critical elections and periodic realignment the classic works are V. O. Key, "A Theory of Critical Elections," *Journal of Politics* 17 (1955): 3–18; Walter Dean Burnham, *Critical Elections and the Mainsprings of American Politics* (New York, 1970).

17. Carrie Chapman Catt and Nettie Rogers Shuler, *Woman Suffrage and Politics: The Inner Story of the Suffrage Movement* (New York, 1923), 127, 130–1; Katharine Anthony, *Susan B. Anthony: Her Personal History and Her Era* (New York, 1954), 415.

18. Ryan, *Cradle of the Middle Class,* 190; Susan B. Anthony et al., *The History of Woman Suffrage,* vols. 1–4 (New York, 1881–1900) (hereafter *HWS*) 3: 152–53.

Chapter 1. The Political Crucible of the Civil War

1. *Mobile Register,* 29 Sept. 1868, 2; Jean Baker, *Affairs of Party,* 304; *National Anti-Slavery Standard,* 26 Sept. 1868, 2; Dinkin, *Before Equal Suffrage,* 79.

2. On republicanism and antebellum politics, see Michael F. Holt, *The Political Crisis of the 1850s* (New York, 1978); Howe, "The Evangelical Movement and Political Culture in the North," 1234–35; and in the South, J. Mills Thornton III, *Politics and Power in a Slave Society: Alabama, 1800–1860* (Baton Rouge, 1978). On gender and civic virtue, see Kerber, *Women of the Republic,* 106–10, 199–200; Ruth H. Bloch, "The Gendered Meanings of Virtue in Revolutionary America," *Signs* 13 (1987): 37–58; Matthews, *The Rise of Public Woman,* 52–71; Mary P. Ryan, *Between Banners and Ballots, 1825–1880* (Baltimore, 1990), 32–34, 52–53.

3. Cott, *Bonds of Womanhood;* Ryan, *Cradle of the Middle Class;* Carl Degler, *At Odds: Women and the Family in America from the Revolution to the Present* (New York, 1980), 26–65, 74–75. I have stressed, here, economic changes and class formation rather than revivalism and evangelical doctrine; see note 7 in the Introduction.

4. Corresponding links could be drawn outside politics: northern middle-class Protestants supplemented their family life through an "empire" of benevolent associations, while opponents voiced suspicions. Democrats seem to have consistently regarded outside institutions as threats to the primary one, the patriarchal family. On evangelical dimensions of this conflict, see Howe, "The Evangelical Movement and Political Culture," 1233–34, and Ronald P. Formisano, *The Birth of Mass Political Parties: Michigan, 1827–1861* (Princeton, 1971).

5. Dinkin, *Before Equal Suffrage,* 33. On Whig womanhood and its sources, see Elizabeth R. Varon, "Tippecanoe and the Ladies, Too: White Women and Party Politics in Antebellum Virginia," *JAH* 82 (1995): 494–521.

6. Varon, "Tippecanoe and the Ladies, Too," 497.

7. Dinkin, *Before Equal Suffrage,* 31; Lisa Severson, "Negotiating Between the Private and the Public: The Political Activity of Virginia Women during the Sectional Crisis, 1859–1861," paper in possession of the author, 23; *Crystal Springs Monitor,* 3 Aug. 1876, 1; *Portland Eastern Argus,* 30 Aug. 1880, 4. On the Whig origins of these appeals, see Varon, "Tippecanoe and the Ladies, Too," 502–3.

8. *Tallahassee Floridian,* 20 Aug. 1880, 2, and 5 Oct. 1880, 3; *Oquawka Spectator,* 15 Sept. 1880, 4.

9. On rhetorical style, see Kenneth Cmiel, *Democratic Eloquence: The Fight Over Popular Speech in Nineteenth-Century America* (New York, 1990), 61–63; Illinois voter quoted in Nicole Etcheson, "Manliness and the Political Culture of the Old Northwest, 1790–1860," *Journal of the Early Republic* 15 (1995): 71. For postbellum continuation of this style, see for example *Illinois State Journal,* 4 Aug. 1880, 2; *Bill Barlow's Budget,* 2 Nov. 1892, 2; McGerr, *Decline of Popular Politics,* 18–21.

10. Harry James Brown and Frederick D. Williams, eds., *The Diary of James A. Garfield* (East Lansing, Mich., 1981), Vol. 4, 115, 285, 291, 295, 301; W. J. Bryan to Mary Baird, 24 July 1880, William Jennings Bryan papers, Occidental College Library, Los Angeles, Calif.; Woodrow Wilson to Ellen Axson in Eleanor Wilson McAdoo, ed., *The Priceless Gift: The Love Letters of Woodrow Wilson and Ellen Axson* (New York, 1962), 75–76, 59.

11. Orators described in *Chicago Tribune,* 9 Oct. 1880, 3; *Arizona Citizen,* 18 Oct. 1880, 3; *Petersburg Index-Appeal,* 21 Oct. 1880, 4; *Cincinnati Gazette,* 6 Sept. 1880, 1; *Lynchburg Virginian,* 8 Sept. 1880, 3; pole-raisings in Jean Baker, *Affairs of Party,* 297–98; *Columbus Republican,* 9 Oct. 1888, 1; *Harrisburg Patriot,* 20 Sept. 1880, 1. On roosters and other masculine symbols, see McGerr, *Decline of Popular Politics,* 20–21. On the class connotations of bare-knuckle and gloved fighting, see Elliot J. Gorn, *The Manly Art: Bare-Knuckle Prize Fighting in America* (Ithaca, 1986), especially 46–57. I am grateful to Ben Kohl for his observations on this issue.

12. Dinkin, *Before Equal Suffrage*, 30–37, 44–55.

13. Michael Grossberg, *Governing the Hearth: Law and the Family in Nineteenth-Century America* (Chapel Hill, 1985); on colonial family ideals, see John Demos, *A Little Commonwealth: Family Life in Plymouth Colony* (New York, 1970).

14. For a brief summary of Whig policies, see Holt, *Political Crisis of the 1850s,* 34; on Whig women, Varon, "Tippecanoe, and the Ladies, Too," 504, 518; David Ross Locke, *Divers Views, Opinions, and Prophecies of Yoors Trooly Petroleum V. Nasby* (Cincinnati, 1867), 2.

15. Dinkin, *Before Equal Suffrage,* 30–33, including Democratic quotations on "dragging women in"; Varon, "Tippecanoe and the Ladies, Too." The partisan dimensions of the invitation to women were clearest in the third-party system, but Norma Basch has documented the ideological groundwork as far back as the early Jacksonian years. See Basch, "Marriage, Morals, and Politics in the Election of 1828," *JAH* 80 (1993): 890–918.

16. Dinkin, *Before Equal Suffrage,* 32–34; Varon, "Tippecanoe and the Ladies, Too."

17. *The Woman's Journal,* Boston (hereafter *WJ*), 13 Sept. 1884, 294; Abigail Scott Duniway, *Path Breaking: An Autobiographical History of the Woman Suffrage Movement in Pacific Coast States* (New York, 1971 [1914]), 5; *New Orleans Picayune,* 2 Nov. 1880, 3. See also diary entry, 3 Aug. 1888, Harriet Jane Hanson Robinson papers, Schlesinger Library, Radcliffe College, Cambridge, Mass.; Rebecca Latimer Felton, *My Memoirs of Georgia Politics* (Atlanta, 1911), 18–21. Frances Willard, Jane Addams, Florence Kelley, and other suffragists also had close relationships with fathers active in party politics. Jean Baker has noted that political awareness and party loyalties often passed from fathers to sons (*Affairs of Party,* 31–32); the cross-gender dimensions of such influence warrant more attention, as do the political influences that nineteenth-century mothers exerted on their daughters.

18. Ginzberg, *Women and the Work of Benevolence,* 98–132; anonymous Democrat in Dinkin, *Before Equal Suffrage,* 41–42.

19. Quotations in John F. Reynolds, *Testing Democracy: Electoral Behavior and Progressive Reform in New Jersey, 1880–1920* (Chapel Hill, 1988), 31; R. Hal Williams, "'Dry Bones and Dead Language': The Democratic Party," in H. Wayne Morgan, ed., *The Gilded Age* (Syracuse, 1963), 2nd ed., 130. See also Kleppner, *The Third Electoral System,* especially 98–120.

20. I am indebted here to the work of Stephanie McCurry, whose recent study illuminates the secession crisis. I see her arguments as illustrative of larger Democratic patterns, in which southern secessionists figure as an extreme example. Stephanie McCurry, *Masters of Small Worlds: Yeoman Households, Gender Relations, and the Political Culture of the Antebellum South Carolina Low Country* (New York, 1995), especially 208–304; quotation on 234. For similar views expressed by northern Democratic leader Stephen Douglas, see Jean Baker, *Affairs of Party,* 195. For northern working-class patriarchal values—among voters who were overwhelmingly Democrats—see Christine Stansell, *City of Women: Sex and Class in New York, 1789–1860* (New York, 1986), especially 20–30, 77–83.

21. Quotation from Philip Shaw Paludan, *A People's Contest: The Union and the Civil War, 1861–1865* (New York, 1988), 234 (see also 92–95, 233); Jensen, *Winning of the Midwest,* 63–69; Paul Kleppner, *The Cross of Culture: A Social Analysis of Midwestern Politics, 1850–1900* (New York, 1970), 71–91. Jensen and Kleppner explore in detail the theological agendas of various pietist and liturgical groups, from Methodists and Freewill Baptists to Episcopalians and German Lutherans. I focus here, instead, on

broad evangelical and anti-evangelical views of family order and government power, as channeled into the two-party system. Members of each coalition could share these fundamental views regardless of sect, or even if they attended no church at all.

22. Silbey, "The Surge of Republican Power," in Maizlish and Kushma, *Essays,* quotation on 217; McCurry, *Masters of Small Worlds,* 280–82.

23. Grossberg, *Governing the Hearth,* 348–49, n61, 240–41, 246; John R. Mulbern, *The Know-Nothing Party in Massachusetts* (Boston, 1990), 111; Marlene Stein Wortman, ed., *Women in American Law from Colonial Times to the New Deal* (New York, 1985), Vol. 1, 120–22, 145; McCurry, *Masters of Small Worlds,* 86–91. Massachusetts legalized interracial marriage in 1843; Iowa did so in 1851, Kansas in 1857. Because family law was left to the states, its significance in the sectional conflict of the 1850s has, I think, been underestimated.

24. McCurry, *Masters of Small Worlds,* quotation on 215; Silbey, "The Surge of Republican Power," in Maizlish and Kushma, *Essays,* 216–17.

25. Kirk H. Porter and Donald Bruce Johnson, eds., *National Party Platforms, 1840–1956* (Urbana, 1956), 27. Future Radical leader Justin Morrill of Vermont introduced antipolygamy legislation in 1856 and 1857. Democrats treated it contemptuously: amid laughter, one proposed sending it to the Committee on Naval Affairs, since sailors kept women in many ports. See *Congressional Globe,* 34th Congress, 1st and 2nd sess., 1491, 1501; 35th Congress, 1st sess., 184–85, 2114. Morrill got his revenge in 1862 when Lincoln, in signing the Morrill Act, outlawed polygamy in U.S. territories (Grossberg, *Governing the Hearth,* 123). On Republicans' anti-Mormon appeals, see Gienapp, "Politics Seem to Enter into Everything," in Maizlish and Kushma, *Essays,* 17. The local dimensions of the issue deserve further exploration. In the late 1850s both Arkansas and the Wisconsin/Michigan border witnessed sensational murder cases in which aggrieved non-Mormons killed Mormon men over the status of plural wives. These outpost Mormon communities had broken away from the main church. See Formisano, *Birth of Mass Political Parties,* 158–60, and *New York Times,* 1 June 1857, 3.

26. Silbey, "The Surge of Republican Power," in Maizlish and Kushma, *Essays,* 220; on Republicans' association of Mormonism with the "slave power" and Democrats' efforts to defend Utah from federal intrusion, see Grossberg, *Governing the Hearth,* 123–26.

27. The best assessment of the causes of the Mormon war is Norman F. Furniss, *The Mormon Conflict, 1850–1859* (New Haven, 1960), 62–94. Buchanan's intentions were never clear, and it is possible that he blundered into the fight or had other designs. Just before the conflict, however, southern Democratic leader Robert Taylor advised Buchanan, "I believe that we can supersede the Negro-Mania with the almost universal excitements of an Anti-Mormon Crusade" (74–75). On Buchanan's desire to move the Mormons to Alaska, see Philip Shriver Klein, *President James Buchanan: A Biography* (University Park, Pa., 1962), 325–26. For statements that polygamy was "the real cause" of conflict with Mormons, and for fascinating links between antipolygamy and antislavery arguments, see *New York Herald,* 4 May 1855, 8, and 3 May 1857, 1; *New York Times,* 24 Oct. 1853, 4; 26 Oct. 1853, 4 (calling also for enforcement of temperance and antiprostitution laws); 5 May 1855, 3 (comparing Mormon and slave women); and 19 Jan. 1857, 3. The latter reprinted a defense of Mormonism by "B.," who wrote: "We call slavery a domestic institution . . . ; our General Government has no power over it. Polygamy is certainly a domestic institution and is equally beyond its power. . . . We are contemplating a civil war [in Utah] . . . let us not plunge into it thoughtlessly."

28. Silbey, "The Surge of Republican Power," in Maizlish and Kushma, *Essays*, 217, 226; McCurry, *Masters of Small Worlds*, 292–94; LeeAnn Whites, "The Civil War as a Crisis in Gender," in Catherine Clinton and Nina Silber, eds., *Divided Houses: Gender and the Civil War* (New York, 1982), 9–10.

29. Ryan, *Cradle of the Middle Class*, 32; McCurry, *Masters of Small Worlds*, 232–33.

30. Holt, *Political Crisis of the 1850s*, 240–43; McCurry, *Masters of Small Worlds*, 239–304.

31. James A. Rawley, *Race and Politics: "Bleeding Kansas" and the Coming of the Civil War* (Philadelphia, 1969), 167; Paludan, *A People's Contest*, 94–95; Jean Baker, *Affairs of Party*, 227–29, 245–56.

32. *Savannah Republican*, 12 Sept. 1868, 1 and 13 Oct. 1868, 1; *Mobile Register*, 23 Oct. 1868, 1. Laura F. Edwards also makes this point in "The Disappearance of Susan Daniel and Henderson Cooper: Gender and Narratives of Political Conflict in the Reconstruction-Era South," *Feminist Studies* 22 (1996): 371.

33. *New Orleans Tribune*, 3 Nov. 1867, 1; Martha Hodes, "Wartime Dialogues on Illicit Sex: White Women and Black Men," in Clinton and Silber, eds., *Divided Houses*, 230–32; Laura Edwards, "Disappearance of Susan Daniel and Henderson Cooper." New York Democrat Samuel Tilden declared that his party "rejected black suffrage as we would reject the doctrine that an African or a Negro has a right to marry our daughter without our consent" (in Jean Baker, *Affairs of Party*, 256).

34. *New Orleans Republican* reprinted in *Charleston Free Press*, 11 April 1868, 2.

35. *Charleston Mercury*, 31 July 1868, 2; other examples, 21 Aug. 1868, 1 and 1 Sept. 1868, 4; *Mobile Register*, 23 Oct. 1868, 1; and *Savannah Republican*, 5 Oct. 1868, 2; 10 Oct. 1868, 2; and 21 Sept. 1868, 1 (the last reprinted from *New Orleans Crescent*).

36. Leonard Dinnerstein, "The Election of 1880," *History of American Presidential Elections, 1789–1968*, ed. Arthur M. Schlesinger Jr. (New York, 1971), Vol. 2, 1508; *San Francisco Examiner*, 30 Oct. 1880, 2; *Omaha Herald*, 23 Oct. 1880, 4; *Boston Globe*, 31 Oct. 1880, 5; *Montgomery Advertiser*, 16 Sept. 1880, 2; also Jean Baker, *Affairs of Party*, 253–58.

37. McCurry, *Masters of Small Worlds*, 223; Severson, "Negotiating Between the Private and the Public," 40–41. I am indebted here to Lisa Severson, a fellow graduate student at the University of Virginia, who generously shared her work on white southern women in the secession crisis.

38. Severson, "Negotiating Between the Private and Public"; Dinkin, *Before Equal Suffrage*, 53–54. On Revolutionary precedents and their political meaning, see Norton, *Liberty's Daughters*.

39. On wealth and its connections to moral vice and government corruption in Democratic thought, see Jean Baker, *Affairs of Party*, 156–58; William G. Shade, *Banks or No Banks: The Money Issue in Western Politics 1832–1865* (Detroit, 1972), especially 56–59.

40. Iver Bernstein, *The New York Draft Riots: Their Significance for American Society and Politics in the Age of the Civil War* (New York, 1990), 111; *Boston Journal*, 23 Sept. 1880, 1; *Puck*, 13 Oct. 1880, 84, 90–91; 30 June 1880, 303; 7 April 1880, 71; 24 Aug. 1880, 440–41; *Harper's Weekly*, 26 July 1884, 489; 2 Aug. 1884, 505. On links between aristocracy and effeminacy, see also E. Anthony Rotundo, *American Manhood: Transformations in Masculinity from the Revolution to the Modern Era* (New York, 1993), 270–72.

41. For quotations from the antebellum years, Rotundo, *American Manhood*, 271,

and Etcheson, "Manliness and Political Culture," 69–74; *Cleveland Penny Press,* 14 Sept. 1880, 1; on Mahone, *Charleston News and Courier,* 24 May 1884, 2. Etcheson stresses the regional roots of southern manliness in the old Northwest. I see regional, religious, and ethnic identities and partisan loyalties as mutually reinforcing by the 1850s, if not earlier. Etcheson and Rotundo do not address the partisan dimensions of conflict in earlier decades, but Etcheson notes that Abraham Lincoln, a Whig in the 1840s, found fist-fights and duels to be "ludicrous" features of campaigns and refused to fight Democratic opponents (Etcheson, 65–66). Also suggestive of partisan differences at an early date is Basch, "Marriage, Morals, and Politics."

42. *Trenton Sentinel,* 31 July 1880, 2 and 16 Oct. 1880, 2; *Cincinnati Gazette,* 6 Sept. 1880, 1; *Lynchburg Virginian,* 8 Sept. 1880, 3; on campaign violence, see for example *Indianapolis Sentinel,* 2 Aug. 1880, 1; *Oquawka Spectator,* 28 Oct. 1880, 1 and 4 Nov. 1880, 1; *Boston Globe,* 23 Oct. 1880, 3; *New York World,* 21 Oct. 1880, 1 and 24 Oct. 1880, 5.

43. In *The Journals of Alfred Doten, 1849–1903,* ed. Walter Van Tilburg Clark (Reno, 1973), 1549; notepad in Tom Watson papers, Southern Historical Collection, University of North Carolina at Chapel Hill; J. Q. Howard, *The Life, Public Services, and Selected Speeches of Governor Rutherford B. Hayes* (Cincinnati, 1876), 17. Democrats' behavior drew on regional, ethnic, and class-based customs. In the Northeast and Midwest their urban campaigns were heavily influenced by working-class constituents. In the South and West, aggressive masculinity cut across class, ethnic, and sometimes even party lines: Republicans in Nevada mining towns were not notably more temperate than Democrats. Political and social identities were, in this case as in others, mutually reinforcing.

44. Dinkin, *Before Equal Suffrage,* 58, 75–80; *New Orleans Picayune,* 2 Nov. 1880, 2. For examples of Democratic women's campaign work in the Midwest, see *Illinois State Register,* 17 Oct. 1880, 3 and 20 Oct. 1880, 1; *Indianapolis Sentinel,* 21 Aug. 1880, 2; 1 Sept. 1880, 2; 13 Sept. 1880, 5; 18 Sept. 1880, 4.

45. *Atlanta Constitution,* 15 Sept. 1880, 1.

46. *Atlanta Constitution,* 2 Oct. 1880, 1; *Tallahassee Floridian,* 5 Oct. 1880, 3 and 2 Nov. 1880, 1.

47. D. X. Junkin and Frank H. Norton, *Life of Winfield Scott Hancock: Personal, Military, and Political* (New York, 1880), 9; Frederick E. Goodrich, *Life and Public Services of Winfield Scott Hancock, Military-General, U.S.A.* (Boston, 1880), 330; John W. Forney, *Life and Military Career of Winfield Scott Hancock* (New York, 1880), 21.

48. Junkin and Norton, *Life of Hancock,* 397–98. For comparison see James D. McCabe Jr., *Life and Public Services of Horatio Seymour* (New York, 1868); Theodore Pease Cook, *Life and Public Services of Honorable Samuel J. Tilden* (New York, 1876), especially 1–8, 350; and Wilson Mason Cornell, *Life of Honorable Samuel Jones Tilden* (Boston, 1876), 22. These biographies were consistent with antebellum Democratic tradition, as represented for example in D. W. Bartlett, *Life of General Franklin Pierce* (Buffalo, 1852), 13–23.

49. Rotundo's *American Manhood* provides a partial framework for my analysis here. By concentrating on northeastern middle-class Protestant men, however, Rotundo overstates men's acceptance of the new domestic ideology, which was fiercely resisted in the South, West, and among the working class. What Rotundo identifies as the rough behavior of "boy culture" was by no means abandoned by all men at maturity. The power of marriage and work to alter "boy culture" depended on one's views of the workplace and home. Rotundo cites almost entirely the views of Whigs and Republicans (see

for example 57, 64, 71, 87, 107, 169, 172, 229–30, 247–48, 256–57, 270–71). In its campaign customs, ideology, and policy goals, the Democratic Party was a political vehicle for adult men who resisted northeastern middle-class Protestant definitions of proper male behavior. On Jacksonian manhood as a new invention see Rotundo, 10–30; on "boy culture," 31–55; on the workplace, 167–93.

50. John P. Irish quoted in Williams, "'Dry Bones and Dead Language,'" in Morgan, ed., *The Gilded Age,* 141; see also H. Wayne Morgan, *From Hayes to McKinley: National Party Politics, 1877–1896* (Syracuse, N.Y., 1969), 270, 445, 449.

51. Silbey, "The Surge of Republican Power," in Maizlish and Kushma, *Essays,* especially 221–22; Holt, *Political Crisis of the 1850s.*

52. Dinkin, *Before Equal Suffrage,* 44–48, 50–52, quotations on 51, 46.

53. Dinkin, *Before Equal Suffrage,* 45–46; Pamela Herr and Mary Lee Spence, "Introduction," *Letters of Jessie Benton Frémont* (Urbana, 1993), xvii–xxiii; Catherine Coffin Phillips, *Jessie Benton Frémont, A Woman Who Made History* (San Francisco, 1935), 210–11; James Ford Rhodes, *History of the United States from the Compromise of 1850* (New York, 1893), Vol. 2, 220–21. During the campaign both Frémonts were circumspect about their views on slavery. While in California Jessie had refused a slave offered to her as a gift and had spoken to members of an antislavery convention; see Allan Nevins, *Frémont, Pathmarker of the West* (New York, 1939), 386–87. Her political independence was particularly marked because her father was a Democrat, and she may have been the first presidential candidate's wife who was championed for her political views.

54. On the willingness of a few antebellum Republicans to consider woman suffrage, notably in Kansas and Indiana, see *HWS* (1) 186, 308–10.

55. Dinkin, *Before Equal Suffrage,* 44–45, 51; Margaret M. R. Kellow, "'For the Sake of Suffering Kansas': Lydia Maria Child, Gender, and the Politics of the 1850s," *Journal of Women's History* 5.2 (1993): 32–49; Ginzberg, *Woman and the Work of Benevolence,* 109–13; Formisano, *Birth of Mass Political Parties,* 223, 239, 272.

56. Eric Foner, *Free Soil, Free Labor, Free Men: The Ideology of the Republican Party before the Civil War* (New York, 1970), 40–72.

57. *Proceedings of the National Union Republican Convention, 20–1 May 1868* (Chicago, 1868), 67; William H. Glasson, *Federal Military Pensions in the United States* (New York, 1918), 128, 144; Megan J. McClintock, "Civil War Pensions and the Reconstruction of Union Families," *JAH* 83 (1996): 456–80; Theda Skocpol, *Protecting Soldiers and Mothers: The Political Origins of Social Policy in the United States* (Cambridge, Mass., 1992), 107–110. Like McClintock, I agree with Skocpol on the importance of the pension system as a welfare precedent, but not entirely on its gender significance. For the period 1862 to 1875, Skocpol does not distinguish between pension benefits to women and men. In later years, as she notes, the issue was complicated by the advancing age of veterans and their wives; 1890s war pensions "served for many Americans as an analogue to noncontributory old-age pensions" (132). McClintock uncovers fascinating debates in the 1870s and 1880s about pensions, dependency, and morality, but she does not examine their partisan context.

58. *New York Tribune,* 2 Oct. 1868, 1; 12 Oct. 1868, 2; 10 Oct. 1868, 1 and 8.

59. *Chicago Tribune,* 15 Oct. 1880, 1; *Warsaw Times,* 6 Oct. 1888, 2. For GOP leaders' conflation of abolition, God's will, and partisan victory, see for example *Proceedings of the Republican Convention, 1868,* 24, 50–51.

60. Grossberg, *Governing the Hearth,* 28, 134–38, 251; Laura F. Edwards, "Sexual Violence, Gender, and Reconstruction in Granville County, North Carolina," *North Carolina Historical Review* 68 (1991): 237–60; Victoria Bynum, "Reshaping the Bonds

of Womanhood: Divorce in Reconstruction North Carolina," in Clinton and Silber, eds., *Divided Houses,* 320–33. Bynum finds that looser divorce laws worked to the advantage of men, while Edwards argues that they offered limited protection to women. On the absence of miscegenation statutes in the Reconstruction constitutions of Arkansas, South Carolina, Mississippi, and Louisiana, see Charles Magnum, *The Legal Status of the Negro* (Chapel Hill, 1940), 241–42, 267–70; on the controversial nature of the issue, see Eric Foner, *Reconstruction: America's Unfinished Revolution, 1863–1877* (New York, 1988), 320–21. For local Freedmen's Bureau efforts to encourage black marriages and, in at least one case, force a white father to support his children by a former slave, see Leon F. Litwack, *Been in the Storm So Long: The Aftermath of Slavery* (New York, 1979), 233–34, 240–45. As Litwack notes, legitimization of slave marriages was an important issue to many freedwomen and men. When the Texas convention debated a measure "to declare legitimate all children born out of wedlock," a black editor declared it "the most important measure which has been introduced in the Convention" (*Freedman's Press,* 18 July 1868, 1).

61. On Republican retrenchment, see Morton Keller, *Affairs of State: Public Life in Late Nineteenth Century America* (Cambridge, Mass., 1977), 85–121; on family law in particular, Grossberg, *Governing the Hearth,* 123–26; on the disillusionment of woman suffrage activists, DuBois, *Feminism and Suffrage,* 165–66.

62. *Chicago Tribune,* 15 Oct. 1880, 1, and 14 Oct. 1880, 7; *Philadelphia Bulletin,* 27 Sept. 1880, 4; Thomas P. Cuilar, "I'm a Roaring Repeater," 1884, in Irwin Silber, *Songs America Voted By* (Harrisburg, 1971), 134.

63. *Portland Press,* 5 Sept. 1880, 3; *Benton Harbor Palladium,* 15 Oct. 1880, 2; *People's Advocate* (D.C.), 14 Aug. 1880, 1; Marlene Springer and Haskell Springer, eds., *Plains Woman: The Diary of Martha Farnsworth* (Bloomington, Ind., 1986), 19.

64. *Centralia Sentinel,* 27 Oct. 1884, 2; *New York Herald,* 24 Sept. 1880, 3; *New York Times,* 24 Sept. 1880, 1; *Topeka Tribune,* 30 Sept. 1880, 2. See also Nina Silber, "Intemperate Men, Spiteful Women, and Jefferson Davis: Northern Views of the Defeated South," *American Quarterly* 41 (1989): 620–22. Silber notes that the "northern" views she describes were largely the creation of Republicans.

65. Dinnerstein, "The Election of 1880," in Schlesinger, ed., *History of American Presidential Elections,* 1506–7; McGerr, *Decline of Popular Politics,* 143; Morgan, *From Hayes to McKinley,* 497–98, 517; sample reports in *New York Herald,* 28 Oct. 1880, 4; *Painesville Telegraph,* 14 Oct. 1880, 3; *Indianapolis Journal,* 16 Sept. 1888, 5. On the Midwest as a crucial swing region in national elections, see Jensen, *Winning of the Midwest.* The only nonveteran and non-midwesterner to win the GOP nomination was James G. Blaine of Maine, who lost to Grover Cleveland in 1884.

66. Russell B. Conwell, *The Life and Public Services of Governor Rutherford B. Hayes* (Boston, 1876), 47–49; *Our Presidential Candidates and Political Compendium* (Newark, 1880), 67.

67. Conwell, *Life and Public Services of Hayes,* 32–33; Howard, *Life, Public Services, and Speeches of Hayes,* 32–33; *Biographical Sketches of James A. Garfield and Chester A. Arthur* (New York, 1880), 17–18; Hugh Craig, *Life of James G. Blaine* (Lancaster, Penn., 1884), 43–47, 67.

68. Herr and Spence, "Introduction," in *Letters of Jessie Benton Frémont,* xvii–xxiii; Jean Baker, "Mary Todd Lincoln," in *Portraits of American Women from Settlement to the Present,* ed. G. J. Barker-Benfield and Catherine Clinton (New York, 1991), 249–55; Emily Apt Geer, *First Lady: The Life of Lucy Webb Hayes* (Kent, Ohio, 1984), 150–51, 154–55; *Puck,* 7 July 1880, 322; Lydia L. Gordon, *From Lady Washington to Mrs. Cleveland* (Boston, 1888).

69. Francis P. Weisenburger, "Lucy Ware Webb Hayes," in Edward T. Jones, ed., *Notable American Women, 1607–1950* (Cambridge, Mass., 1971), Vol. 2, 166–67; Conwell, *Life and Public Services of Hayes*, 61–63; Howard, *Life, Public Services, and Speeches of Hayes*, 27, 164; *New York Independent*, 9 Dec. 1880, 2.

70. Geer, *First Lady*, 137–38; Frances E. Willard, *Woman and Temperance* (Hartford, 1883), 256–86; Laura C. Holloway, *The Ladies of the White House* (Philadelphia, 1881), 628.

71. *Our Presidential Candidates*, 35; *Sketches of Garfield and Arthur*, 17–18; James Baird McClure, *General Garfield from the Log Cabin to the White House* (Chicago, 1881). See also advertisements in the 1884 campaign for "a most interesting account of the women of the White House . . . illustrated with superb portraits of Mrs. Washington, Mrs. Lincoln, Mrs. Grant, and Mrs. Garfield," flyers in Vincent Montgomery papers, Emory University Library, Atlanta, Georgia.

72. Conwell, *Life and Public Services of Hayes*, 321.

73. *General Garfield as a Statesman and Orator* (New York, 1880), 30; *Jingo*, 27 Aug. 1884, 13; *Concord Monitor*, 6 Oct. 1880, 1; *Portland Press*, 6 Sept. 1880, 1; *Cheyenne Sun*, 2 Nov. 1880, 4. Paula Baker notes the conflation of sexual and political concerns in overwhelmingly Republican upstate New York; *Moral Frameworks of Public Life*, 29.

74. *Leslie's Weekly*, 5 Nov. 1896, 291; *Chicago Tribune*, 29 Sept. 1880, 7; for other reports from this sample year, see *Harper's Weekly*, 11 Nov. 1876, 915; *Arkansas Gazette*, 19 Sept. 1880, 1, and 23 Oct. 1880, 1; *Montgomery Advertiser*, 27 July 1880, 2; *New Mexican*, 29 Oct. 1880, 1; *Arizona Citizen*, 30 Oct. 1880, 3; *Oregon State Journal*, 23 Oct. 1880, 3; *Yankton Press and Dakotaian*, 16 Sept. 1880, 1; *Concord Monitor*, 26 Oct. 1880, 3, and 27 Oct. 1880, 3; *New York Tribune*, 18 Oct. 1880, 4. Indiana Senator Oliver P. Morton stated in the early 1870s that "in almost every canvass in my state there are nearly as many women who attend the meetings as men" (Dinkin, *Before Equal Suffrage*, 64). Women's attendance at rallies, speeches, and barbecues, even or perhaps especially in isolated rural areas, casts doubt on Robert Dinkin's assertion that the women "active in partisan politics" were "mainly urban women of the middle and upper classes" (*Before Equal Suffrage*, 76–77). The question of who had political *influence*, based on advantages of race, wealth, or family, is separate from the question of who participated in electoral campaigns.

75. I differ here with Michael McGerr and others who argue that "men denied women . . . not only the ballot but also the experience of mass mobilization" (McGerr, "Political Style and Women's Power," 866–67; see also McGerr, *Decline of Popular Politics*, 208; Jean Baker, *Affairs of Party*, 217, 287–91; Paula Baker, *Moral Frameworks of Public Life*, 39–40). Uniformed parades, supposedly the militaristic basis for women's exclusion, were only one type of campaign event. Barbecues, picnics, speeches, and dinners were at least as frequent and popular. The formation of women's campaign marching clubs and drum corps in the Midwest suggests, also, that parades did not preclude women's presence. On "army-style" politics, see Jensen, *Winning of the Midwest*, 15–16; McGerr, *Decline of Popular Politics*, 24–26.

76. Foner, *Reconstruction*, 290–91; Julie Saville, *The Work of Reconstruction: From Slave to Wage Laborer in South Carolina, 1860–1870* (New York, 1994), 92, 169–70; Elsa Barkley Brown, "Negotiating and Transforming the Public Sphere: African American Political Life in the Transition from Slavery to Freedom," *Public Culture* 7 (1994): 118, 124; Janette Thomas Greenwood, *Bittersweet Legacy: The Black and White "Better Classes" in Charlotte, 1850–1910* (Chapel Hill, 1994), 175; see also *National Republican*, 23 Oct. 1868, 2.

77. Dinkin, *Before Equal Suffrage,* 69; Anna Julia Cooper, *A Voice from the South* (New York, 1962 [1892]), 139–40; see also Barkley Brown, "Negotiating and Transforming the Public Sphere," 124, on black women pressuring men to vote anti-Democratic in Virginia Readjuster campaigns. For Jefferson Davis quote and Republican response, see *Illinois State Journal,* 13 Sept. 1880, 2.

78. Rupert Sargent Holland, ed., *Letters and Diary of Laura M. Towne, Written from the Sea Islands of South Carolina, 1862–1884* (New York, 1969), 289; Barkley Brown, "Negotiating and Transforming the Public Sphere," 122–23; John P. Green, *Fact Stranger than Fiction: Seventy-Five Years of a Busy Life* (Cleveland, 1920), 263–65, 142–43, 145. This issue surfaced later in suffrage debates, when southern white supremacist men admitted that they had used violence to suppress black men's votes but argued they could not use the same tactic against women. Marjorie Spruill Wheeler, *New Women of the New South: The Leaders of the Woman Suffrage Movement in Southern States* (New York, 1993), 17–18.

79. I am indebted here to Barkley Brown, "Negotiating and Transforming the Public Sphere," 118–24. Contrary to her argument, though, I believe that "community" identities, as opposed to "possessive individualism," were the basis for both black and white women's partisanship, as for men's (Barkley Brown, 125 and n34). Freedmen's and women's political goals were shaped by intense race loyalty, but so were those of male and female white supremacists. The difference was not race loyalty, but black men's greater willingness to share power.

80. Barkley Brown, "Negotiating and Transforming the Public Sphere," 118–21; *Charleston Mercury,* 28 Aug. 1868, 1; for Democratic reports of the political activities of "negro wenches," see for example *Charleston Mercury,* 6 Nov. 1868, 1; *Tallahassee Floridian,* 17 July 1880, 2; epithets from *Tallahassee Floridian,* 13 Aug. 1880, 2; *Montgomery Advertiser,* 1 July 1880, 1.

81. Barkley Brown, "Negotiating and Transforming the Public Sphere," 126–35; *Letters and Diary of Laura M. Towne,* 288–89.

82. Foner, *Reconstruction,* 87–88, quotes Bayne and discusses the influence of white institutions such as the Freedmen's Bureau in enforcing gender hierarchy; *Freedmen's Press,* 1 Aug. 1868, 2 and 12 Sept. 1868, 1; *National Republican,* 3 Nov. 1868, 2. On the "politics of respectability," see Evelyn Brooks Higginbotham, *Righteous Discontent: The Women's Movement in the Black Baptist Church* (Cambridge, Mass., 1993), 185–230. Many of her insights for the years 1900–1920 hold true, I think, for earlier decades.

83. Matthew Rees, *From the Deck to the Sea: Blacks and the Republican Party* (Wakefield, N.H., 1991), 69–71; "Some Facts about the Life and Services of Benjamin Helm Bristow" (1876), 17–19, in *Pamphlets in American History Microfilm* (Sanford, N.C., 1979); *Our Presidential Candidates,* 71–72.

84. Edward A. White, "A Woman Promotes the Presidential Candidacy of Senator Allison, 1888," *Iowa Journal of History and Politics* 48 (1950): 221–46.

85. C. P. James in Geer, *First Lady,* 126; Edward White, "A Woman Promotes the Presidential Candidacy of Allison," 241; for antebellum examples, see Varon, "Tippecanoe and the Ladies, Too," 499.

Chapter 2. Suffragists, Prohibitionists, and Republicans

1. Mrs. C. F. Cunningham in *WJ,* 13 Sept. 1884, 294.

2. DuBois, *Feminism and Suffrage,* 105–61; Nell Irwin Painter, *Standing at Armageddon: The United States 1877–1919* (New York, 1987), 12–13, 30.

3. Kleppner, "The Greenback and Prohibition Parties," in Arthur M. Schlesinger, Jr., ed., *History of U.S. Political Parties* (New York, 1973), Vol. 2, 1549–84; Painter, *Standing at Armageddon,* 27–31.

4. *New York Times,* 11 June 1880, 1; Fred E. Haynes, *Third Party Movements Since the Civil War* (Iowa City, 1916), 135, 181, 504 n42; Paul L. Murphy, "Marion Todd," in Jones, ed., *Notable American Women,* Vol. 3, 469–71; Russel B. Nye, "Sarah Elizabeth Van De Vort Emery," in Jones, ed., *Notable American Women,* Vol. 1, 582–83.

5. *Our Presidential Candidates,* 98–99; Nye, "Sarah Elizabeth Van De Vort Emery," in Jones, ed., *Notable American Women,* Vol. 1, 582.

6. The best analyses of the WCTU and Prohibitionist politics are two studies by Ruth Bordin: *Woman and Temperance: The Quest for Power and Liberty* (Philadelphia, 1981) and *Frances Willard: A Biography* (Chapel Hill, 1986).

7. *Union Signal,* 2 Aug. 1888, 1; 19 July 1888, 10; 1 Nov. 1888, 2; 31 May 1888, 8.

8. *HWS* (4): xviii.

9. Emil Pocock, "Wet or Dry? The Presidential Election of 1884 in Upstate New York," *New York History* 54 (1973): 1574–90; on partisan competition after 1876, see Kleppner, *Third Electoral System,* 30.

10. For an overview, see Jack S. Blocker, Jr., *American Temperance Movements: Cycles of Reform* (Boston, 1989); on women's postbellum temperance work, see Barbara Leslie Epstein, *The Politics of Domesticity: Women, Evangelism, and Temperance in Nineteenth-Century America* (Middletown, Conn., 1981), and Bordin, *Woman and Temperance* and *Frances Willard.*

11. *Report of the International Council of Women, Assembled by the National Woman Suffrage Association* (Washington, D.C., 1888), 319.

12. Willard, *Glimpses of Fifty Years* (Chicago, 1889), 397–98. The Free Soil Party had endorsed prohibition, but as a secondary issue; see William E. Gienapp, *The Origins of the Republican Party* (New York, 1987), 44–60.

13. Bordin, *Frances Willard,* 130–35; D. Leigh Colvin, *Prohibition in the United States: A History of the Prohibition Party and of the Prohibition Movement* (New York, 1926), 110, 124, 190, 643–57; Willard, *Glimpses of Fifty Years,* 396–97, 439–40.

14. George Hall in *Union Signal,* 2 Aug. 1888 (campaign extra), 1–2; W. W. Satterlee, *The Political Prohibition Text-Book* (Minneapolis, 1883), 86, 177–79, vii, 162. Rev. J. H. Byers argued that women "are entitled to a place in the National Prohibition Party, on equal footing with the men. . . . Why should the women be excluded from the action, when they have been the main ones in formulating and perfecting the principle that underlies the action?" *Union Signal,* 24 May 1888, 3.

15. Willard, *Glimpses of Fifty Years,* 394–97, 400; Colvin, *Prohibition in the United States,* 127; *Union Signal* 12 July 1888, 11; 27 Sept. 1888, 9.

16. *Prohibition Party Campaign Text-Book* (Albion, Mich., 1896), 91.

17. Willard, *Woman and Temperance,* 338–40.

18. Willard, *Woman and Temperance,* 326–28; Bordin, *Frances Willard,* 99–100; Mrs. H. S. Lake, "Woman's Right in Government," Iowa address delivered 13 Jan. 1884, 10, in *History of Women Microfilm;* Willard in Satterlee, *Political Prohibition Text-Book,* 174.

19. Colvin, *Prohibition in the United States,* 285; Willard in Satterlee, *Political Prohibition Text-Book,* 176.

20. *Union Signal,* 31 May 1888, 5; 1 Nov. 1888, 5; 27 Sept. 1888.

21. In Satterlee, *Political Prohibition Text-Book,* 175.

22. Willard, *Woman and Temperance*, 329–33.

23. Willard, *Woman and Temperance*, 403–12.

24. Willard, *Woman and Temperance*, 333–34, 410; Michael Lewis Goldberg, "'An Army of Women,': Gender Relations and Politics in Kansas Populism, the Woman Movement, and the Republican Party, 1879–1896," Ph.D. diss., Yale University, 1992, 117–19; Robert C. Kriebel, *Where the Saints Have Trod: The Life of Helen Gougar* (West Lafayette, Ind., 1985), 87–93; Paula Baker, *Moral Frameworks of Public Life*, 47–58, 65.

25. Finley Peter Dunne in Keller, *Affairs of State*, 539; Cummings in *American Nonconformist*, 27 Sept. 1888, 3.

26. Pocock, "Wet or Dry?"; Blocker, *American Temperance Movements*, 85–93; Colvin, *Prohibition in the United States*, 145–66; Kleppner, "Greenback and Prohibition Parties," in Schlesinger, ed., *History of U.S. Political Parties*, 1574–77. Obviously Prohibitionism had its effect because of tight major-party competition, created by the resurgence of the national Democracy.

27. Kleppner, "Greenback and Prohibition Parties," in Schlesinger, ed., *History of U.S. Political Parties*, 1574–77. Prohibition Party presidential candidates won about 2.2 percent of the vote in 1888 and 1892; Frémont had captured 33 percent for the Republicans in 1856. On Republican response to Prohibitionists, see Jensen, *Winning of the Midwest*, 196–206. "General," said one Republican to third-party leader Clinton Fisk, "if I should vote for this bill it would lay me in my political grave." "Vote for it and die, then," Fisk responded, "and I will write on your tombstone, 'Blessed are the dead that die in the Lord'" (in Jensen, 200, n65).

28. Bordin, *Woman and Temperance*, 126; *Union Signal*, 7 June 1888, 8 and 1 Nov. 1888, 2. On the theme of sectional reconciliation, see also *Union Signal*, 31 May 1888, 2; 14 June 1888, 2–4; 19 July 1888, 9.

29. *Union Signal*, 21 June 1888, 8.

30. Bordin, *Frances Willard*, 130–35; Willard, *Glimpses of Fifty Years*, 402–7.

31. *Union Signal*, 24 May 1888, 4.

32. From the 1850s to the 1890s the importance of the Midwest in national politics can hardly be overstated, especially if one defines the region broadly to include the far reaches of upstate New York (along the Lakes) and western Pennsylvania—areas that, politically and socially, shared much in common with the Old Northwest. The electoral votes of Indiana, Ohio, and Illinois were desperately contested by the major parties; in addition, the region was a seedbed for new parties, including the Liberty, Free Soil, Republican, Greenback, and Prohibition movements. For this reason, Populists' inability to capture votes in the Midwest was a crucial failure. On slavery and war issues in the region, see Vernon L. Volpe, *Forlorn Hope of Freedom: The Liberty Party in the Old Northwest, 1838–1848* (Kent, Ohio, 1990); Leon Friedman, "The Democratic Party, 1860–1884," in Schlesinger, ed., *History of U.S. Political Parties*, Vol. 2, 890; Mary R. Dearing, *Veterans in Politics: The Story of the GAR* (Westport, Conn., 1974). On religious and ethnic conflict see Blocker, *American Temperance Movements*, 78–80; Kleppner, *Cross of Culture*; and Jensen, *Winning of the Midwest*.

33. For an open admission of bribery, see Dinnerstein, "Election of 1880," in Schlesinger, ed., *History of American Presidential Elections*, 1509–10; on the closeness of elections, see Kleppner, *Cross of Culture* and *Third Electoral System* and Jensen, *Winning of the Midwest*. On the Cincinnati club, see *WJ*, 18 Sept. 1880, 300; on Hazlett, *Chicago Tribune*, 29 Sept. 1880, 3, 16 Oct. 1880, 3, and 22 Oct. 1880, 2; reference to GOP campaign speaker Kate Kane in *Milwaukee Sentinel*, 30 Oct. 1880, 8. Other examples of women's campaign work: *Illinois State Journal*, 7 Oct. 1880, 3; *Benton Harbor Palladium*,

15 Oct. 1880, 3; *Indianapolis Sentinel,* 17 Aug. 1880, 1, 1 Sept. 1880, 2, and 20 Sept. 1880, 1; *Illinois State Register,* 6 Oct. 1880, 1; 17 Oct. 1880, 3 and 20 Oct. 1880, 1; *Chicago Tribune,* 7 Oct. 1880, 2, 10 Oct. 1880, 2, 15 Oct. 1880, 3.

34. *Proceedings of the Third Annual Meeting of the Non-Partisan National Woman's Christian Temperance Union, Cleveland, Ohio, 15–18 Nov., 1892* (Cleveland, 1892), 4–6, offers this breakdown of state delegates: Iowa 32, Ohio 19, Illinois 2, Indiana 1, New York 3, Maine 2, Washington D.C. 2 (one of whom was Foster, originally of Iowa), and California 1. The organization apparently had official branches in seven states, Iowa, Illinois, Ohio, Minnesota, Pennsylvania, Maine, and Vermont. Prominent leaders were from Ohio and Pennsylvania. See Frank L. Byrne, "Judith Ellen Horton Foster," in Jones, ed., *Notable American Women,* Vol. 1, 651–52; Melanie Gustafson, "Partisan Women: Gender, Politics and the Progressive Party of 1912," Ph.D. diss., New York University, 1993, 72, 79–80.

35. Byrne, "Judith Ellen Horton Foster," in Jones, ed., *Notable American Women,* Vol. 1, 651–52; Willard, *Woman and Temperance,* 321–25; Bordin, *Woman and Temperance,* 125–28. A hagiographic account, with veiled references to the first husband's alcoholism, is Elmer C. Adams and Warren Dunham Foster, "J. Ellen Foster," *Heroines of Modern Progress* (New York, 1921), especially 245, 248–54, 257–66. Foster lost two daughters, both at the age of five, one during her first marriage and one in her second. Elijah Foster adopted a six-year-old son from the first marriage, and the Fosters had a son born in 1870. Both boys lived to adulthood (Byrne, 651).

36. Byrne, "Judith Ellen Horton Foster," in Jones, ed., *Notable American Women,* Vol. 1, 651–52; Adams and Foster, "J. Ellen Foster," on her friendship with Clarkson; on Clarkson's rise in the GOP, see McGerr, *Decline of Popular Politics,* 79–80.

37. *Union Signal,* 17 May 1888, 9 and 12 July 1888, 5; Gustafson, "Partisan Women," 67; and Anna Gordon in Bordin, *Woman and Temperance,* 127. Bordin's book (125–33) provides an excellent account of the internal struggle. She rightly concludes that neither Foster's nor Willard's strategy worked in the long run, but she does not examine the larger context of partisan campaigns.

38. Mattie M. Bailey quoted in Jonathan Zimmerman, "'The Queen of the Lobby': Mary H. Hunt, Scientific Temperance, and the Dilemma of Democratic Education in America," Ph.D. diss., The Johns Hopkins University, 1993, 87; Mrs. Snell of Mississippi in *Union Signal,* 13 Nov. 1888, 5. On Foster's Republicanism as viewed by the press and regular WCTU, see Bordin, *Woman and Temperance,* 127–29; on formation of the National Women's Republican Association, *Inter-Ocean,* 29 Sept. 1888, 9, 12; Byrne, "Judith Ellen Horton Foster," 652; Dinkin, *Before Equal Suffrage,* 93–94.

39. My analysis here relies on Bordin, *Woman and Temperance,* especially 130–39, though I disagree that "logic and consistency were on Foster's side" (130). Both women had compelling reasons for advocating their opposing strategies and neither woman saw her approach win national prohibition in her lifetime. (Willard died in 1898, Foster in 1910.) Women's weaker position in politics, since they had no votes, made declarations of nonpartisanship a more important strategy for them than for men. Women seeking partisan appointments in the federal government often declared strong party loyalties and accused rivals of supporting the opposition. If dismissed for political reasons, however, many protested that they were "women who had no politics." "It is my misfortune—and not my fault," wrote one, "—that God made me a woman and that Congress has not made me a voter." See Cindy Sondik Aron, *Ladies and Gentlemen of the Civil Service: Middle-Class Workers in Victorian America* (New York, 1987), especially 117–24, 139–47.

40. DuBois, *Feminism and Suffrage,* especially 79–104, 160–202, Anthony quoted on 101; Lydia Maria Child in *National Anti-Slavery Standard,* 10 Oct. 1868, 2.

41. Dinkin, *Before Equal Suffrage,* 67–70, quotations, 68. See also *WJ* during the campaign, especially 5 Oct. 1872, 12 Oct. 1872, 2 Nov. 1872.

42. *HWS* 3: 279.

43. *WJ,* 11 Sept. 1880, 292; Duniway, *Path Breaking,* 101.

44. Satterlee, *Political Prohibition Text-Book,* viii, 155.

45. *WJ,* 9 Aug. 1884, 256 and 26 July 1884, 240.

46. *WJ,* 7 Aug. 1880, 252; 21 Aug. 1880, 268; 28 Aug. 1880, 279; Dinkin, *Before Equal Suffrage,* 70–72.

47. This statement appeared, among other places, in *WJ,* 9 Aug. 1884, 256–57, and *Woman's Exponent,* 15 Oct. 1884, 80. Mary Livermore endorsed it: *WJ,* 9 Aug. 1884, 256.

48. *WJ,* 10 July 1880, 224; 17 July 1880, 228; 21 Aug. 1880, 268; Ida Husted Harper, *The Life and Work of Susan B. Anthony* (New York, 1969 [1902]), Vol. 2, 523–54. Harper is incorrect in stating that "neither [Anthony] nor the other leading women of the country did any public work" in the presidential campaign. For Democratic loyalties, see chapter 3 of this volume, n13, on the New York group and on Caroline Dall of Boston; on California Democratic suffragist Laura DeForce Gordon, see Corinne L. Gilb, "Laura DeForce Gordon," in Jones, ed., *Notable American Women,* Vol. 2, 68–69. For the Democratic loyalties of southern white suffragists, see Wheeler, *New Women of the New South.*

49. *WJ,* 18 Sept. 1880, 300; *Illinois State Journal,* 20 Oct. 1880, 3; *Chicago Tribune,* 22 Oct. 1880, 12. Hazlett became a suffrage activist in Michigan (*HWS* 4: 763).

50. *WJ,* 17 July 1880, 232; 18 Sept. 1880, 300.

51. Harper, *Life and Work of Susan B. Anthony,* Vol. 1, 365–66, Vol. 2, 794.

52. *WJ,* 23 Aug. 1884, 272–74, 276; 13 Sept. 1884, 294–95; 4 Oct. 1884, 322; 30 Aug. 1884, 284.

53. *Union Signal,* 13 Sept. 1888, 3. Stanton wrote that the new party addressed "vital issues of equal suffrage, equal wages, temperance, arbitration for all national differences, and land for those who cultivate it"—a very broad interpretation of the Prohibition platform that spoke more to Stanton's own concerns than to the third party's priorities.

54. Duniway, *Path Breaking,* 82; Goldberg, "'An Army of Women,'" 187–92; Kreibel, *Where the Saints Have Trod,* 108–9, 113, 139–41; M. J. Thomas to May Wright Sewall, 14 Nov. 1887; Susan B. Anthony to May Wright Sewall, 8 and 17 Jan. 1890 and 9 Aug. 1898; and Susan B. Anthony to Grace Julian Clarke, 18 Dec. 1899, all in Grace Julian Clarke papers, Indiana Division, Indiana State Library, Indianapolis. Alice Judah Clarke of Vincennes reported that "a very considerable sentiment in favor of woman suffrage exists throughout the State and many well-known individuals advocate it . . . but there is so slight an organization that little opportunity is afforded for public expression or action," *HWS* 4: 617. On a similar rift in the Illinois Woman's Alliance, see Mari Jo Buhle, *Women and American Socialism, 1870–1920* (Urbana, 1981), 91–93.

55. *WJ,* 13 Sept. 1884, 294; "Democrats and Republicans," clipping dated 1888, *Woman's Tribune* scrapbook, 168, Huntington Library, San Marino, California.

56. Madeleine B. Stern, "Belva Ann Lockwood," in *We the Women: Career Firsts of Nineteenth-Century America* (New York, 1963), 224.

57. Mary B. Clay in Dinkin, *Before Equal Suffrage,* 70; *WJ,* Oct. 4, 1884, 322; Aug. 23, 1884, 269; 27 Sept. 1884, 310.

58. *WJ*, 16 Oct. 1880, 329; 4 Sept. 1880, 281.

59. *HWS* 4: xviii.

60. In DuBois, *Feminism and Suffrage*, 14.

Chapter 3. Democrats and Domestic Economics

1. Paul Leland Haworth, *The Hayes-Tilden Presidential Election of 1876* (Cleveland, 1906), 168–75; H. Wayne Morgan, "The Republican Party, 1876–1893," in Schlesinger, ed., *History of U.S. Political Parties*, Vol. 2, 1411–14.

2. Haworth, *The Hayes-Tilden Presidential Election*, 168–75; Mary Baird to William J. Bryan, 11 July 1880, William Jennings Bryan papers, Occidental College Library; Violet Blair Janin diary, 13 Nov. 1884, Janin papers, Huntington Library.

3. Caroline H. Dall to Grover Cleveland, 18 Nov. 1884, Grover Cleveland papers, Library of Congress. On reactions to the election, see also Edward L. Ayers, *The Promise of the New South: Life After Reconstruction* (New York, 1992), 47–48, and Morgan, *From Hayes to McKinley*, 231–32.

4. For elephant and donkey campaign symbols, invented in 1874 by Republican cartoonist Thomas Nast for *Harper's Weekly*, see M. B. Schnapper, *Grand Old Party: The First Hundred Years of the Republican Party, a Pictorial History* (Washington, D.C., 1955), 132–33.

5. Most helpful on the tariff issue is Joanne Reitano, *The Tariff Question in the Gilded Age: The Great Debate of 1888* (University Park, Pa., 1994); Treasury surplus figure, 2. See also Edward Stanwood, *American Tariff Controversies in the Nineteenth Century* (New York, 1903); for Cleveland's perspective, see Allan Nevins, *Grover Cleveland: A Study in Courage* (New York, 1932), 367–82.

6. Reitano, *Tariff Question in the Gilded Age*, reestablishes the tariff controversy as a crucial forum for debate over labor relations, state and federal power, and the achievement of a "just economy"; see especially chapters 2 and 4. For an influential earlier view that the sound and fury over issues like the tariff had little significance, see Matthew Josephson, *The Politicos, 1865–1896* (New York, 1938). Richard Jensen, Paul Kleppner, and other historians of ethnocultural politics tend, I think, to underestimate the urgency of economic issues in the Midwest by the late 1880s. An excellent corrective is Jeffrey Ostler, *Prairie Populism: The Fate of Agrarian Radicalism in Kansas, Nebraska, and Iowa, 1880–1892* (Lawrence, Kans., 1993). My survey of Indiana and Illinois newspapers suggests that Ostler's argument also fits those states.

7. Ginzberg, *Woman and the Work of Benevolence*, 182–83; Robert H. Bremner, "Josephine Shaw Lowell," in Jones, ed., *Notable American Women*, Vol. 2, 437–38.

8. Bremner, "Josephine Shaw Lowell," in Jones, ed., *Notable American Women*, Vol. 2, 437–38.

9. Morgan, *From Hayes to McKinley*, 214–16.

10. Morgan, *From Hayes to McKinley*, 214–16.

11. Paul F. Boller, *Presidential Campaigns* (New York, 1985), 148–49; Henry Clay Badger, *Dead-Heads Financial and Moral: The Logic of It* (Cambridge, Mass., 1884), 15–20; *Centralia Sentinel*, 19 Sept. 1884, 2.

12. *WJ*, 9 Aug. 1884, 253, 256–57; 13 Sept. 1884, 294–95; 4 Oct. 1884, 320–22; 11 Oct. 1884, 325; 18 Oct. 1884, 333; 25 Oct. 1884, 344, 352; 8 Nov. 1884, 358.

13. *Hancock Democrat*, 25 Sept. 1884, 1 and 27 Aug. 1884, 2; clipping, "Mrs. Dall on Cleveland," enclosed with letter of Caroline Dall to Grover Cleveland, 18 Nov.

1884, and confidential letter to "good friends" from Clemence S. Lozier, Delia Stewart Parnell, Susan A. King, *et al.* of New York City, 13 Oct. 1884, both in Grover Cleveland papers, Library of Congress; James Bryce, *The American Commonwealth* (New York, 1888), 173. On outsiders' attention to the debates raging in the *WJ*, see Badger, *Dead-Heads Financial and Moral*, 15–16; *Nation,* 7 Aug. 1884, 102 and 6 Nov. 184, 387; *Jingo,* 27 Aug. 1884, 13.

14. Nevins, *Grover Cleveland,* 234–52, 300; on Rose Cleveland, see also Frances Willard and Mary A. Livermore, *A Woman of the Century* (Buffalo, 1893), 183–84.

15. Nevins, *Grover Cleveland,* 302–7; Morgan, *From Hayes to McKinley,* 258–60.

16. *Public Opinion,* 5 June 1886, 141–43 (comments by *Boston Herald, Baltimore Sun, Albany Journal, St. Louis Globe-Democrat,* and others); Nevins, *Grover Cleveland,* 302–7.

17. Francis Howard Williams, *The Bride of the White House* (Philadelphia, 1886); *Tribune* quoted in *Public Opinion,* 5 June 1886, 142–43; *Judge,* 6 Aug. 1887, 8–9; Morgan, *From Hayes to McKinley,* 258–60; Nevins, *Grover Cleveland,* 302–7, 310–14.

18. Campaign references in *Omaha Republican,* 14 Oct. 1888, 9; *Hancock Democrat,* 20 Aug. 1888, 2. Frances Cleveland did suffer somewhat at the hands of Republicans; see for example the widely reprinted interview by Nellie Bly, who hinted that Washington society "cut off" the first lady (*San Francisco Chronicle,* 9 Sept. 1888, 11).

19. Herman Dieck, *The Life and Public Services of Our Great Reform President, Grover Cleveland* (Philadelphia, 1888), 181, 271–81, and frontispiece; W. U. Hensel, *Life and Public Services of Grover Cleveland* (Philadelphia, 1888), 180–201, 289; Gordon, *From Lady Washington to Mrs. Cleveland,* 376–78, 398–401, 418, 437, 442–48; Edith P. Mayo, "Campaign Appeals to Women," in Edith P. Mayo, ed., *American Material Culture: The Shape of Things Around Us* (Bowling Green, Ohio, 1984), 132–33; Roger A. Fischer, *Tippecanoe and Trinkets Too: The Material Culture of American Presidential Campaigns* (Urbana, Ill., 1888), 121–27, 130; Belva Lockwood in *Woman's News,* 31 Oct. 1888, 7.

20. Harry J. Sievers, *Benjamin Harrison, Hoosier President* (Indianapolis, 1968), 52, 55–57; Morgan, *From Hayes to McKinley,* 395, 325, 328; "Vote for Papa" campaign artifact in the Division of Political History, Museum of American History, Smithsonian Institution.

21. *New York Tribune,* 12 Feb. 1887, 1. Megan McClintock's work suggests that the federal government *was* trying to supervise widows' moral behavior. Pensions placed the GOP in a double bind: if they investigated the moral worth of each recipient, Democrats accused them of "invading the home"; if they did not, they were allowing corruption to flourish, especially since remarriage terminated benefits and some widows co-habited informally rather than lose their pensions. McClintock, "Civil War Pensions," 47–79.

22. Examples in *Inter-Ocean,* 12 Oct. 1888, 5, 25 Oct. 1888, 1 and 2, 26 Oct. 1888, 2; *Franklin Democrat* (town of Franklin), 2 Nov. 1888, 1; *Illinois State Register,* 11 Oct. 1888, 4; *Evansville Journal,* 12 Oct. 1888, 1, and 14 Oct. 1888, 2; *Goshen News,* 19 Oct. 1888, 1; *Illinois State Journal,* 9 Oct. 1888, 4, and 11 Oct. 1888, 4; *Centralia Sentinel,* 16 Oct. 1888, 2.

23. In Nevins, *Grover Cleveland,* 426; see also Dinkin, *Before Equal Suffrage,* 93–94.

24. *Los Angeles Times,* 29 Oct. 1888, 2; Gilb, "Laura DeForce Gordon," 68–69; *Cheyenne Leader,* 5 Oct. 1892, 3; *Logansport Pharos,* 1 Nov. 1888, 2; *WJ,* 6 Oct. 1888, 318.

25. Dinkin, *Before Equal Suffrage,* 98.

26. *New York Herald,* 3 July 1892, 15; 28 Sept. 1892, 5; and 4 Oct. 1892, 6; George Harmon Knoles, *The Presidential Campaign and Election of 1892* (Palo Alto, 1942).

27. I am indebted here and in the following paragraphs to McGerr, *Decline of Popular Politics.* McGerr offers an excellent assessment of the class bases of the new political style, but he focuses only on men's campaign work and almost entirely on the Northeast.

28. *New York Tribune,* 14 Dec. 1887, 2; *Baltimore Sun,* 4 July 1888, 1 and 4; 5 July 1888, 1.

29. For regional representation in 1892, still weighted heavily toward the Northeast, see *New York Post,* 4 Oct. 1892, 3. In many areas old rituals persisted for another decade; see sample events in *Illinois State Register,* 11 Oct. 1888, 1 and 4, 13 Oct. 1896, 3; *Columbus Herald,* 5 Nov. 1888, 15 Oct. 1892, 1; *San Francisco Chronicle,* 23 Sept. 1888, 15–16; *Birmingham State Herald,* 19 July 1896, 1. On the South: *Leslie's,* 15 Sept. 1888, 117. On the new clubs' regional base see also *The National League of Republican Clubs* (New York, 1889). Some allegedly permanent clubs disbanded after the campaign (for example in Wisconsin; *National League,* 35). McGerr notes that rural areas spurned the educational pamphlets sent by party headquarters and demanded cash payments for parades and brass bands (McGerr, *Decline of Popular Politics,* 60–62, 78–80, 96, 99).

30. *Boston Globe,* 2 Oct. 1888, 3; *Warsaw Times,* 15 Oct. 1892, 2.

31. *Abstract of the Eleventh Census: 1890* (Washington, D.C., 1896), 58; I have classified all men of unknown age as thirty-six or older. William Allen White, "The Confederate Colonel as a Political Issue: From a Young Republican's Point of View," William A. Phillips, "The Young Crowd," and C. S. Finch, "A Response to 'The Young Crowd,'" *Agora* 3 (1893): 30, 261, 322–28. See also *Judge,* 10 Dec. 1892, 431; *Omaha Republican,* 4 Nov. 1888, 1. By the 1890s millions of new immigrants, irrespective of age, also created challenges for party leaders. This issue is most ably covered by Gwendolyn Mink, *Old Labor and New Immigrants in American Political Development: Union, Party, and State, 1875–1920* (Ithaca, 1986).

32. F. J. Loudin to John Patterson Green, 1 Dec. 1896, John Patterson Green papers, Western Reserve Historical Society, Cleveland, Ohio; Cooper, *A Voice from the South,* 139–40; see also Rees, *From the Deck to the Sea.* On age-of-consent debates, see David J. Pivar, *Purity Crusade: Sexual Morality and Social Control, 1868–1900* (Westport, Conn., 1973), 145–46; on generational divisions, see Rotundo, *American Manhood,* 233–35. I am indebted here and in the next paragraph to McGerr, *Decline of Popular Politics.*

33. Black in McGerr, *Decline of Popular Politics,* 90; Clarkson in *WJ,* 24 Sept. 1892, 310.

34. *Puck,* 15 Sept. 1880, 21 and 29 Oct. 1884, 131; see also *Leslie's,* 4 Oct. 1884, 101 and 103, 15 Sept. 1888, 71 and 73.

35. "Old-fashioned" used in *Centralia Sentinel,* 31 Oct. 1888, 1; *Warsaw Times,* 6 Oct. 1888, 2; *Detroit Free Press,* 21 Oct. 1888, 5; *Vincennes Commercial,* 11 Oct. 1888, 2. Pole raisings in *Warsaw Times,* 24 Oct. 1892, 3; *Franklin Democrat* (Brookville), 2 Nov. 1888, 2; *Franklin Democrat* (town of Franklin), 11 Oct. 1888, 3; on portraits, *Brookville American,* 25 Oct. 1888, 3, and *Columbus Republican,* 1 Nov. 1888, 2; quotation from *White County Democrat,* 7 Oct. 1892, 1.

36. Reitano, *Tariff Debate in the Gilded Age,* 89–95; J. Richard Piper, "Party Realignment and Congressional Change: Issue Dimensions and Priorities in the U.S. House of Representatives, 1871–1893," *American Politics Quarterly* 11 (1983): 472; Nevins, *Grover Cleveland,* 367–82.

37. Marjorie Housepian Dobkin, ed., *The Making of a Feminist: Early Journals and Letters of M. Carey Thomas* (Kent, Ohio, 1979), 230–31; clipping of undated speech (1888?), Harriet Jane Hanson Robinson papers, Schlesinger Library, Radcliffe College. The Democratic Party did not advocate free trade, but a lower tariff "for revenue only." Free traders saw this as a step in the right direction. For background on the issue, see McGerr, *Decline of Popular Politics,* 59–63.

38. My analysis here differs from that of Richard Jensen (*Winning of the Midwest,* 89–149), Paul Kleppner (*Cross of Culture,* 130–78), and others who argue that ethnocultural issues, especially anti-liquor crusades and debates over funding for Catholic schools, were the primary factors affecting voters between 1888 and 1893. Such issues were undoubtedly influential in some states, but a debate over school funding in Wisconsin cannot explain why, in 1890, Republicans lost half their 18 House seats in New York, 4 out of 5 in Minnesota, and every seat they held in Maryland (4), Missouri (2), New Hampshire (2), and West Virginia (2). The catastrophe was national, and leaders of both parties (excluding McKinley, for obvious reasons) ascribed it to growing economic distress, which Democrats blamed on the tariff. Historians have long seen Populists as the first agents of economic discontent; in *Prairie Populism* Jeffrey Ostler makes a persuasive case that economics was key in the Midwest and that Democrats led the first attack on tariffs and trusts (47–53). For election results, see Kenneth C. Martis, *Historical Atlas of Political Parties in the United States Congress, 1789–1989* (New York, 1989), 143–45; contemporary views in *New York Times,* 8 Nov. 1890, 1, 9 Nov. 1890, 1, and 19 Nov. 1890, 5; *Public Opinion,* 8 Nov. 1890, 97–100, 15 Nov. 1890, 123–24. Ethnic and religious conflict did play a role in some states, as did the Lodge Elections bill, or "force bill," which I address in chapter 6.

39. *Columbus Herald,* 3 Nov. 1888, 2; also *White County Democrat,* 23 Sept. 1892, 4; *Vincennes Sun,* 1 Nov. 1892, 3; *Lynchburg Virginian,* 4 Oct. 1888, 1, and 13 Oct. 1888, 1. On Democrats' consumer focus, see also Tom Terrill, *The Tariff, Politics, and American Foreign Policy, 1874–1901* (Westport, Conn., 1973), 118–20, 185–86, though Terrill discounts the success of a strategy I believe was effective until 1893.

40. *Boston Globe,* 22 Oct. 1888, 4; *New York Post,* 26 Oct. 1888, 11. A description of the same cartoon appears in *Lynchburg Virginian,* 29 Oct. 1888, 2. Mills in Reitano, *Tariff Question in the Gilded Age,* 21–22.

41. For an excellent discussion of this trend, see chapter 1, "Urban Women and the Emergence of Shopping," in Elaine S. Abelson, *When Ladies go A-Thieving: Middle-Class Shoplifters in the Victorian Department Store* (New York, 1989), 13–41.

42. *Hancock Democrat,* 11 Oct. 1888, 1; *New York Post,* 7 Oct. 1892, 5; Morgan, *William McKinley and his America* (Syracuse, 1963), 148; R. Hal Williams, *Years of Decision: American Politics in the 1890s* (New York, 1978), 44–45. On women in the workforce, see Alice Kessler-Harris, *Out to Work: A History of Wage-Earning Women in the United States* (New York, 1982), 122–23.

43. *Vincennes Sun,* 1 Nov. 1892, 3; *Indianapolis Sentinel,* 25 Oct. 1888, 1; also *Lynchburg Virginian,* 20 Sept. 1888, 2. The *Sentinel* cartoon was a rough copy from *Puck,* 10 Oct. 1888, 97.

44. *Hancock Democrat,* 13 Oct. 1892, 2, and 20 Aug. 1888, 2; *Columbus Herald,* 3 Nov. 1892, 2.

45. *Illinois State Register,* 9 Oct. 1888, 2; *Lynchburg Virginian,* 4 Oct. 1888, 3; *Louisville Courier-Journal,* 23 Sept. 1888, 3, and 24 Sept. 1888, 2.

46. *Hancock Democrat,* 22 Nov. 1888, 2.

47. Dinkin, *Before Equal Suffrage,* 98.

48. *Lynchburg Virginian*, 9 Oct. 1888, 2.

49. Peabody in *WJ*, 22 Nov. 1890, 369; *Woman's Tribune* scrapbook, Huntington Library. See also William Everett in *WJ*, 8 Nov. 1890, 355; Morgan, *From Hayes to McKinley*, 241. The furor over "shopping women" may say more about politicians' fears than about women's real priorities. Recently, though, Kristi Andersen cites intriguing evidence that in the 1920s a higher percentage of women than men voted for tariff reduction. Commentators of that decade argued that women voted from their experiences as consumers. Kristi Andersen, *After Suffrage: Women in Partisan and Electoral Politics before the New Deal* (Chicago, 1996), 159–60.

50. *Philadelphia Record* reprinted in *New York World*, 31 Oct. 1892, 1; *New York World*, 6 Nov. 1892, 35, and 21 May 1898, 5. I thank Kristin Hoganson for sharing the last citation. Thomas Reed, an advocate of woman suffrage, believed that lack of suffrage rights prompted women to exercise forms of indirect political leverage that were detrimental to the republic. Reed's motives in blaming "shopping women" for his party's defeat may thus have been complex. See Samuel W. McCall, *Life of Thomas Brackett Reed* (Boston, 1914), 100–2, 242; William A. Robinson, *Thomas B. Reed, Parliamentarian* (New York, 1930), 241.

51. Abelson, *When Ladies Go A-Thieving*, 28–31, 36–39; William Leach, *Land of Desire: Merchants, Power, and the Rise of a New American Culture* (New York, 1993), 5–6, 20–24, 31.

52. *South-Bend Tribune*, 23 Oct. 1888, 1.

53. In McGerr, *Decline of Popular Politics*, 79–80.

Chapter 4. The Gospel of St. Republican

1. *Inter-Ocean*, 29 Sept. 1888, 9.

2. On Prohibitionists' appropriation of the Republican term, see Willard, *Glimpses of Fifty Years*, 401.

3. Rhodes, *History of the United States*, Vol. 2, 220–21, 485; *WJ*, 8 Nov. 1884, 364.

4. *Concord Monitor*, 25 Oct. 1880, 1, and 22 Sept. 1880, 3; Joseph B. Foraker, campaign speech in *Notes of a Busy Life* (Cincinnati, 1916), Vol. 1, 281–83.

5. *New York Tribune*, 5 Oct. 1887, 2; *New York Times*, 9 Oct. 1888, 4; *Hancock Democrat*, 20 Aug. 1888, 2.

6. *New York Press*, 19 July 1888, 7; for a typical interview with Carrie Harrison, *Indianapolis Journal*, 16 Sept. 1888, 5.

7. Reitano, *Tariff Question in the Gilded Age*, 73–82, 93–94, 98–101.

8. *Chino Valley Champion*, 12 Oct. 1888, 3; *Evansville Journal*, 4 Oct. 1888, 5; Giles B. Stebbins, *The American Protectionist's Manual* (Detroit, 1883), 2–3, 12.

9. *South-Bend Tribune*, 23 Oct. 1888, 1; 24 Oct. 1888, 1; 1 Nov. 1888, 4.

10. *New York Press*, 16 Aug. 1888, 4; Reitano, *Tariff Question in the Gilded Age*, 79–80, 122, 20 (latter on the "harlot of free trade"); on Singer women, *South-Bend Tribune*, 20 Oct. 1888, 8. Other appeals to working women in *Logansport Journal*, 14 Oct. 1888, 2; *Woman's News*, 10 Oct. 1888, 7.

11. Stebbins, *American Protectionist's Manual*, 145–46, 131.

12. *Indianapolis Journal*, 16 Sept. 1888, 9; reprinted widely.

13. *Columbus Republican*, 17 Oct. 1888, 2; *South-Bend Tribune*, 31 Oct. 1888, 2 and 6 Oct. 1888, 6; *San Francisco Chronicle*, 16 Sept. 1888, 8. I differ here with Gwendolyn Mink, who argues that ethnic and religious concerns were foremost in the 1880s, and

Republicans crafted appeals to new immigrants after 1896. On the contrary, national struggles between a nativist-labor coalition among Democrats (and, in my view, Populists) and a more elite, pro-immigration, pro-cheap-labor GOP had roots in the tariff arguments of the late 1880s. Mink, *Old Labor and New Immigrants*, 113–57.

14. Quotations in this and the following two paragraphs, except as noted, are from McKay's article, reprinted in *Minneapolis Tribune*, 5 Oct. 1892, 1; *Centralia Sentinel*, 11, 12, and 14 Oct. 1892, 3 in each case; *Los Angeles Times*, 11 Oct. 1892, 9–12; Nathaniel McKay, *Free Trade Toilers* (New York, [1892]), campaign pamphlet in Division of Political History, Museum of American History, Smithsonian Institution. For other repetitions of the same theme, see *New York Times*, 17 Sept. 1888, 4; *New York Tribune*, 22 Sept. 1888, 2; William P. Frye, *What Senator Frye Saw in Europe* (Boston, [1888]), 9–13; and *Cuba Patriot*, N.Y., cited in Paula Baker, *Moral Frameworks of Public Life*, 27.

15. Sklar, *Florence Kelley*, 111.

16. Jensen, *Winning of the Midwest*, 190–200, though I would not—as Jensen does—characterize the Prohibitionists as "fanatics."

17. Bordin, *Woman and Temperance*, 128.

18. *Woman's News*, 31 Oct. 1888, 4; *New York World*, 23 Oct. 1892, 35; Equal Rights platform in Belva Lockwood papers, Division of Political History, Museum of American History, Smithsonian Institution.

19. *Goshen News*, 10 Oct. 1888, 1; *Inter-Ocean*, 4 Nov. 1888, 2; *Centralia Sentinel*, 6 Oct. 1888, 4, 17 Oct. 1888, 2, and 5 Nov. 1888, 1; *Indianapolis Journal*, 16 Sept. 1888, 9; *Illinois State Register*, 11 Oct. 1888, 4.

20. *Omaha Republican*, 3 Oct. 1888, 4; 14 Oct. 1888, 7; 19 Oct. 1888, 1; 28 Oct. 1888, 1; and 2 Nov. 1888, 1; *Omaha Herald*, 4 Nov. 1888, 2–3; *WJ*, 15 Sept. 1888, 294; *Columbus Republican*, 10 Oct. 1888, 4 and 18 Oct. 1888, 1; *Goshen News*, 10 Oct. 1888. On the midwestern origins of Nebraska settlers, see Bradley H. Baltensperger, *Nebraska: A Geography* (Boulder, 1985), 71. On the campaign in Indiana, see Robert F. Wesser, "The Election of 1888," in Schlesinger, ed., *History of American Presidential Elections*, Vol. 2, 1648.

21. *Inter-Ocean*, 12 Oct. 1888, 5, and 4 Nov. 1888, 2.

22. In McGerr, *Decline of Popular Politics*, 79, and *WJ*, 24 Sept. 1892, 310.

23. *New York Times*, 18 Oct. 1888, 4.

24. On Foster's visit, see Adams and Foster, "J. Ellen Foster," 248–54; *Leslie's*, 1 Oct. 1896, 218. On the Primrose League, see Janet Henderson Robb, *The Primrose League, 1883–1906* (New York, 1942); membership figures, 228. Foster's essays on the Irish economy are in J. Ellen Foster, *The Crime Against Ireland* (Boston, 1888), and reflect her interlocking views on temperance and protective tariffs. Her arrangement with the *Journal* and the quick publication of her report suggest that GOP managers sponsored her trip.

25. Dinkin, *Before Equal Suffrage*, 94; on Rockefeller's gifts, see *Proceedings of the Third Annual Meeting of the NPWCTU*, 56.

26. Willard, *Glimpses of Fifty Years*, 438–39; Dinkin, *Before Equal Suffrage*, 94–95; *Providence Journal*, 25 Oct. 1888, 6.

27. *Providence Journal*, 25 Oct. 1888, 6; *New York Press*, 13 Oct. 1888, 3.

28. Dinkin, *Before Equal Suffrage*, 94; *New York Press*, 13 Oct. 1888, 3; *Lynchburg Virginian*, 20 Sept. 1888, 3. On press attitudes toward Foster, see Bordin, *Woman and Temperance*, 129.

29. Willard, *Glimpses of Fifty Years*, 438–39.

30. *Providence Journal,* 25 Oct. 1888, 6.

31. *Proceedings of the Third Annual Meeting of the NPWCTU,* 17–18.

32. *Inter-Ocean,* 29 Sept. 1888, 9; on Anthony's GOP speaking engagements, see *WJ,* 17 Sept. 1892, 300, and 5 Nov. 1892, 358; Dinkin, *Before Equal Suffrage,* 72.

33. *Inter-Ocean,* 29 Sept. 1888, 9 and 12; *Omaha Republican,* 15 Oct. 1888, 2; Adams and Foster, "J. Ellen Foster," 266–68; *Columbus Republican,* 4 Nov. 1892, 3.

34. *Columbus Republican,* 4 Nov. 1892, 3.

35. *Pueblo Chieftain,* 24 Oct. 1894, 8; *Providence Journal,* 25 Oct. 1888, 6; *New York Press,* 3 Sept. 1888, 2.

36. On Foster's appearance in the Senate, *Lynchburg Virginian,* 20 Sept. 1888, 2; *Los Angeles Times,* 29 Oct. 1888, 4; Tupper in *Columbus Republican,* 4 Nov. 1892, 3.

37. *Warsaw Times,* 19 Oct. 1892, 4 and 25 Oct. 1892, 4; *Logansport Journal,* 25 Oct. 1892, 4.

38. Petitions to the House of Representatives, 51A (1889–1891), 23.3–23.4, especially boxes 145–47, National Archives. Petition files for a number of years contain thousands of signatures from textile operatives in Massachusetts, Connecticut, Rhode Island, and Pennsylvania.

39. June Cunningham Croly, *The History of the Woman's Club Movement in America* (New York, 1898), documents political debates in many nonpartisan women's clubs; see for example 248, 292, 310, 324, 343–44, 449–54, 519–22, 555–56, 584, 602–4, 735–39, 793–94, 816–19, 911, 1070, 1139. A good, brief analysis of the class bases of nonpartisan woman's clubs is Suzanne Lebsock, "Women and American Politics, 1880–1920," in Louise A. Tilly and Patricia Gurin, eds., *Women, Politics, and Change* (New York, 1990), 41–44. See also Karen J. Blair, *The Clubwoman as Feminist: True Womanhood Redefined, 1868–1914* (New York, 1980), 12–13, 57–68, 98, 118; Anne Firor Scott, *Natural Allies: Women's Associations in American History* (Urbana, Ill., 1991), 141–58. On the activities of Republican women's clubs, Kate M. Bostwick, "Women's Political Clubs," *Monthly Illustrator* 13 (1896): 304–8; *Seattle Post-Intelligencer,* 12 Oct. 1896, 2; "Minutes of the Woman's Republican Association of Alfred Center, New York," Woman's Club papers, Alfred University Library, Alfred, New York.

40. Painter, *Standing at Armageddon,* 44–50, 110–25; Ostler, *Prairie Populism,* 47–53, 82–83.

41. *New York Press,* 2 Sept. 1888, 11; 4 Oct. 1888, 2; 21 Oct. 1888, 2; *Woman's News,* 31 Oct. 1888, 4.

Chapter 5. Populism

1. For comparison of the Midwest and Plains, see Ostler, *Prairie Populism;* the best recent synthesis is Robert C. McMath, Jr., *American Populism: A Social History, 1877–1898* (New York, 1993).

2. Dennis Sven Nordin, *Rich Harvest: A History of the Grange, 1867–1900* (Jackson, Miss., 1974), 123–25, 114–15; Donald B. Marti, *Women of the Grange: Mutuality and Sisterhood in Rural America, 1866–1920* (Westport, Conn., 1991), 29–31, 55–69.

3. McMath, *American Populism,* 83–107; Ayers, *Promise of the New South,* 215–19. For an interpretation emphasizing Alliance activities outside party politics, see Lawrence Goodwyn, *Democratic Promise: The Populist Moment in America* (New York, 1976). The Alliance was actually four organizations: the southern-based Farmers' Alliance and Industrial Union, the Colored Farmers' National Alliance, and on the Great Plains, the National Farmers' Alliance and the Northwestern Alliance. Though they

tried to cooperate, they underwent confusing disputes and name changes (for example, in 1889 the Dakota and Kansas Alliances joined the Southern Alliance, which renamed itself the National Alliance). I have discussed tensions within the movement without naming the separate organizations involved.

4. McMath, *American Populism*, 132, 166; Ayers, *Promise of the New South*, 252–56; on Kansas economics, Goldberg, "'An Army of Women,'" 77–81, 196–97.

5. On women's rights and domestic rhetoric in the Knights of Labor, see Susan Levine, "Labor's True Woman: Domesticity and Equal Rights in the Knights of Labor," *JAH* 70 (1983), especially 328–32; on women's office holding in the Grange, see Marti, *Women of the Grange*, 19–31, 107–23.

6. Sklar, *Florence Kelley*, 124–32, on the Socialist Labor Party of the United States; McMath, *American Populism*, 145, 190–91. As McMath observes, the labor-Populist alliance was most successful in Chicago. Illinois Democratic governor John P. Altgeld cooperated with socialist women in Chicago and appointed Florence Kelley as the state's first factory inspector.

7. Marion Todd, *The Protective Tariff Delusion* (Battle Creek, Mich., 1886); Pauline Adams and Emma S. Thornton, *A Populist Assault: Sarah E. Van De Vort Emery on American Democracy, 1862–1895* (Bowling Green, Ohio, 1982), chapters 2–3; Wagner, "Farms, Families, and Reform," 85–86, 103–7.

8. The Ocala demands and Omaha platform appear in John D. Hicks, *The Populist Revolt: A History of the Farmer's Alliance and the People's Party* (Minneapolis, 1931), 431, 443; see also McMath, *American Populism*, 167–69; Wagner, "Farms, Families, and Reform," 85–86, 103–4. For an overview of the financial issues at stake, see Walter T. K. Nugent, "Money, Politics, and Society: The Currency Question," in Morgan, ed., *The Gilded Age*, 109–28.

9. Hicks, *Populist Revolt*, 167, 241; on the Kansas campaign, see McMath, *American Populism*, 153; *Texas Populist Campaign Book* (Dallas, 1898), 24–25, 28.

10. Adams and Thornton, *A Populist Assault*, 82–83; Mary A. Hobart, *A Scientific Exposure of the Errors in Our Monetary System* (Seattle, 1891), 76; *The Farmer's Voice* reprinted in Chester McArthur Destler, *American Radicalism, 1865–1901: Essays and Documents* (New York, 1972), 75; McMath, *American Populism*, 152; see also *Coxey's Sound Money*, 27 Aug. 1896, 3 and 1 Oct. 1896, 1; *The Alliance and Labor Songster* (New York, 1975 [1891]), 53, 55, 73.

11. Lease in Hicks, *Populist Revolt*, 160; Todd in Wagner, "Farms, Families, and Reform," 86; *People's Advocate* (Ga.), 18 May 1893, 3. Other references by leading Populists in James B. Weaver, *A Call to Action* (New York, 1974 [1892]), 369–72; Thomas E. Watson, *The People's Party Campaign Book, 1892* (New York, 1975 [1892]), 219; Julie Roy Jeffrey, "Women in the Southern Farmer's Alliance: A Reconsideration of the Role and Status of Women in the Late Nineteenth Century South," *Feminist Studies* 3 (1975), 81–84; Goldberg, "'An Army of Women,'" 232; Bruce Palmer, *Man Over Money: The Southern Populist Critique of American Capitalism* (Chapel Hill, 1980), 135, 200–1.

12. Ignatius Donnelly, *Caesar's Column: A Story of the Twentieth Century* (Cambridge, Mass., 1960 [1890]); Adams and Thornton, *A Populist Assault*, 68–69; Todd, *Protective Tariff Delusion*, 17, 104. A helpful analysis of Donnelly's novel *The Golden Bottle* (1892) appears in Buhle, *Women and American Socialism*, 85.

13. Frances Allen in Wagner, "Farms, Families, and Reform," 72; *American Nonconformist*, 5 Feb. 1891, 8, and 12 March 1891, 8; see also Wagner, 71, 110–12.

14. Lois Waisbrooker, *Helen Harlow's Vow* (Boston, 1870); George Noyes Miller, *The Strike of a Sex* (Chicago, 1891), quotation from 101. Populists promoted other

works of fiction that drew links between sexual and class oppression; see for example Helen Hunt Gardener's *Pray You Sir, Whose Daughter?* (Boston, 1892) and Helen Winslow's *Salome Shepard, Reformer* (Boston, 1893).

15. Adams and Thornton, *A Populist Assault,* 42–43; Todd, *Protective Tariff Delusion;* also Wagner, "Farms, Families, and Reform," 62–130, for an overview of Populist women's political thought. On Donnelly and Harvey, see Hicks, *Populist Revolt,* 340–42.

16. Diggs in Wagner, "Farms, Families, and Reform," 273; *Boulder Camera,* 28 Oct. 1894, 2; *Grand Valley Star-Times,* 11 Nov. 1893, 1; *Rocky Mountain News,* 5 Nov. 1894, 1. On women and Colorado Populism, see James E. Wright, *The Politics of Populism: Dissent in Colorado* (New Haven, 1974), 190–204.

17. *People's Journal,* 28 Oct. 1892 and 12 Aug. 1892, 1; *Leadville Herald Democrat,* 31 Oct. 1894, 1; sample appeals for "Katie [etc.] and the babies" in *Texas Advance,* 21 July 1894, 14; Wagner, "Farms, Families, and Reform," 223; Goldberg, "'An Army of Women,'" 265; Ayers, *Promise of the New South,* 262.

18. In Goldberg, "'An Army of Women,'" 265.

19. Todd, *Pizarro and John Sherman* (Chicago, 1891), 11–14; Weaver, *A Call to Action,* 226–29.

20. Anonymous fragment to Bishop W. A. Candler, Warren Aikin Candler papers, Emory University Library; Bordin, *Frances Willard,* 147–48, 159.

21. Bordin, *Woman and Temperance,* 131–32, and *Frances Willard,* 175–89; McMath, *American Populism,* 160, 170; Wagner, "Farms, Families, and Reform," 257–60.

22. Adams and Thornton, *A Populist Assault,* 63; other quotations and the substance of my analysis here are drawn from Goldberg, "'An Army of Women,'" 281–90.

23. Jeffrey, "Women in the Southern Farmers' Alliance," 76–77, 85; McMath, *American Populism,* 125–26; Barton C. Shaw, *The Wool-Hat Boys: Georgia's Populist Party* (Baton Rouge, 1984), 176–77; McMath, *Populist Vanguard: A History of the Southern Farmers' Alliance* (Chapel Hill, 1975), 67–69. Complete records of Alliance membership are not available, but in the North Carolina record book of 1890, 44 percent of suballiances reported no female members and 23 percent reported a small number (1–3). MaryJo Wagner finds somewhat higher figures in Nebraska, where women constituted about 31 percent of total membership; in a random survey of eight Kansas suballiances (1890), Michael Goldberg finds female membership averaging 35 percent, with no suballiance recording less than 20 percent women. North Carolina Farmers' Alliance Book, Leonidas L. Polk papers, Southern Historical Collection, University of North Carolina at Chapel Hill; Wagner, "Farms, Families, and Reform," 48–51; Goldberg, "'An Army of Women,'" 210.

24. Jeffrey, "Women in the Southern Farmers' Alliance," 82–83.

25. Rebecca Felton, "Address at McRae," 1899, and "Address before Farmers' Congress" and "Farmers' Wives and their Needs" (both undated), Rebecca Latimer Felton papers, University of Georgia Library, Athens.

26. Shaw, *Wool-Hat Boys,* 176–78; Ayers, *Promise of the New South,* 233–34; William DuBose Sheldon, *Populism in the Old Dominion: Virginia Farm Politics 1865–1900* (Gloucester, Mass., 1967), 8n. Annie Diggs reported that southern Populist women "never venture upon the platform," though there may have been exceptions in Texas and Arkansas. Diggs, "The Women in the Alliance Movement," *Arena,* July 1892, 163.

27. Otis in Wagner, "Farms, Families, and Reform," 147–49; Goldberg, "'An Army of Women,'" 262–64; Marilyn Dell Brady, "Populism and Feminism in a News-

paper by and for Women of the Kansas Farmers' Alliance, 1891–1894," *Kansas History* 7 (1984/85): 286–88.

28. Diggs, "Women in the Alliance Movement," 161; Brady, "Populism and Feminism," 288–90; Lizzie Holmes in Wagner, "Farms, Families, and Reform," 136, n97.

29. Lindsley in Nyle H. Miller, Edgar Langsdorf, and Robert W. Richmond, eds., *Kansas in Newspapers* (Topeka, 1963), 121; Jane Taylor Nelsen, ed., *A Prairie Populist: The Memoirs of Luna Kellie* (Iowa City, 1992), 136. See also Goldberg, "'An Army of Women,'" 302–3.

30. Mrs. S. V. P. Johnson to Leonidas L. Polk from Shaw, Kansas, 1 April 1892, Leonidas L. Polk papers, Southern Historical Collection, University of North Carolina at Chapel Hill; Goldberg, "'An Army of Women,'" 212–13.

31. Diggs in Goldberg, "'An Army of Women,'" 312; Eva McDonald Valesh interview, Columbia University Oral History Project, Part 1 (New York, 1952), 38.

32. Historians have generally argued that the move from Alliance to Populist politics marginalized women and that for this reason, women viewed it suspiciously. It is true that women could not vote for state and national offices outside Colorado, but the decline in western women's partisan activities does not seem to have occurred until 1895 or later, as a result of fusion with Democrats and the party's general exhaustion and decline. There is little evidence that Alliance women themselves viewed the move into politics as detrimental to their interests, either as women or as Populists. For women ardently in favor of the new party, see Annie Diggs, "Women in the Alliance Movement," 163; Goldberg, "'An Army of Women,'" 257, 265–67, 300–1; Wagner, "Farms, Families, and Reform," 115, 253, 267–69; Jeffrey, "Women in the Southern Farmers' Alliance," 80; Buhle, *Women and American Socialism,* 82–83. For arguments that Alliance women were excluded from party politics, see for example McMath, *American Populism,* 127, Goldberg, 300–10, and Wagner, 264–68.

33. Buhle, *Women and American Socialism,* 82–83; Marti, *Women of the Grange,* 19–31, 107–23.

34. Levine, "Labor's True Woman," 325–26; Jonathan Garlock, *Guide to the Local Assemblies of the Knights of Labor* (Westport, Conn., 1982); Diggs, "Women in the Alliance Movement," 165–67, 172–75; Margaret Kolb Holden, "The Rise and Fall of Oregon Populism: Legal Theory, Political Culture, and Public Policy, 1868–1895," Ph.D. diss., University of Virginia, 1993, 492; Willard and Livermore, *A Woman of the Century,* 239; Brady, "Populism and Feminism," 281; Valesh interview, Columbia Oral History Project, 11–19.

35. Goldberg, "'An Army of Women,'" 274–75; Wagner, "Farms, Families, and Reform," 19–35; Valesh interview, Columbia Oral History Project, 38; Thomas A. Clinch, *Urban Populism and Free Silver in Montana* (Missoula, Mont., 1970), 53–54, 84, 170; Worth Robert Miller, *Oklahoma Populism: A History of the People's Party in the Oklahoma Territory* (Norman, Okla., 1987), 52–53.

36. William Allen White in Goldberg, "'An Army of Women,'" 269–70; *Silver Standard,* 30 July 1892, 2; *Journals of Alfred Doten,* 1825; *Atlanta Constitution,* 22 Sept. 1892, 1; *Atlanta Journal,* 22 Sept. 1892, 1.

37. Hicks, *Populist Revolt,* 167–70, 261, 286; Diggs, "Women in the Alliance Movement," 164–65; Holden, "Rise and Fall of Oregon Populism," 490–92, 500; Goldberg, "'An Army of Women,'" 217–19; Roscoe C. Martin, *The People's Party in Texas: A Study in Third Party Politics* (Austin, 1933), 146–47, 167, 171–72; Wagner, "Farms, Families, and Reform," 60, 268–70. The history of women's campaign work for

the major parties, as explored by Elizabeth Varon, Robert Dinkin, and others, revises the standard view of Populism as uniquely family centered. For the latter argument, see for example Ostler, *Prairie Populism*, 108–10, Williams, *Years of Decision*, 47–50, and Goldberg, "'An Army of Women,'" 217–20.

38. *Denver Times*, 27 Oct. 1894, 11; *Boulder Camera*, 8 Oct. 1894, 1, and 4 Nov. 1894, 1; *Greeley Tribune*, 27 Sept. 1894, 7. As Suzanne Lebsock suggests, mixed-gender organizing strategies may have been more common among economic groups in which "women were engaged in production with men in the family unit," such as farm families (Lebsock, "Women and American Politics," 62, n64). Other factors were, however, at least as important. White farm women in Vermont, Kansas, and North Carolina were all part of productive "family units" but they played very different roles in politics; the same could be said for Democratic and Populist farm women in the West and black and white farm women in the South. In addition, Populist women and men apparently formed joint campaign clubs in Colorado mining towns, where work was extremely sex-segregated. Single-sex organizing was a clear preference among urban Republican women who did not work for wages, but Populists like Annie Diggs came from the same background and moved easily into organizing with men. I view the willingness of men in a given political project to share power, and women's commitment to demanding it, as key factors (themselves, of course, products of many influences).

39. McMath, *American Populism*, 168; Wagner, "Farms, Families, and Reform," 158, 221–24, 263–64, 270, 300; *Woman's Tribune*, 6 Aug. 1892, 164; *Washington Post*, 5 July 1892, 1. I cannot find a full list of delegates to the Omaha convention, and women may also have represented other states.

40. *WJ*, 20 Oct. 1894, 330–31; *HWS* 4: 595; Clinch, *Urban Populism and Free Silver*, 53–54; Phoebe Reeve, "Colorado Women Legislators," *Modern World*, April 1907, 208; *Rocky Mountain News*, 5 Nov. 1894, 1; also Wright, *Politics of Populism*, 190–204, and Wagner, "Farms, Families, and Reform," 270, 288–89.

41. Anonymous Populist in Goldberg, "'An Army of Women,'" 355.

42. *WJ*, 5 Nov. 1892, 358, and 3 Nov. 1894, 354; *HWS* 4: 477, 590, 617, 801, 809; McMath, *American Populism*, 171; on Kansas, Goldberg, "'An Army of Women,'" 290–93, and Peter H. Argersinger, ed., *Populism and Politics: William Alfred Peffer and the People's Party* (Lexington, Ky., 1974), 127–29.

43. Wagner, "Farms, Families, and Reform," 258–62, analyzes the struggle at St. Louis and includes the quotations used here.

44. *Rocky Ford Enterprise*, 2 Nov. 1893, 2; *Silver Standard*, 7 Oct. 1893, 2, and 4 Nov. 1893, 2; Beverly Beeton, *Women Vote in the West: The Woman Suffrage Movement, 1869–1896* (New York, 1986), 108, 111–13, 116–35. Woman suffrage also passed in Utah in 1896, though this was not a new victory. The territory had approved full woman suffrage in 1873, only to have anti-Mormon Republican congressmen override the measure; Utah managed to reintroduce woman suffrage with statehood in 1896. Few residents of the state were Populists, but like Colorado and Idaho voters they believed they were besieged by external forces on the basis of a single issue, in this case Mormonism. In addition to Beeton's book, see Joan Smyth Iversen, "A Debate on the American Home: The Antipolygamy Controversy, 1880–1890," in John C. Fout and Maura Shaw Tantillo, eds., *American Sexual Politics: Sex, Gender, and Race Since the Civil War* (Chicago, 1990), 123–40.

45. H. M. Bebyner to Davis Waite, 22 Sept. 1894, Davis Waite papers, Colorado State Archives, Denver; *Denver News*, 17 Oct., 1894, 2, and 18 Oct. 1894, 2; *Georgetown Courier*,

13 Oct. 1894, 2; on Republicans, *Leadville Herald Democrat,* 3 Nov. 1894, 6; *Colorado Miner,* 25 Aug. 1894, 1; *Denver Times,* 16 and 17 Oct. 1894, 4 in each case; *Pueblo Chieftain,* 23 Oct. 1894, 2.

46. *Denver Times,* 27 Oct. 1894, 11; *WJ,* 8 Sept. 1894, 284, 22 Sept. 1894, 297, and 10 Nov. 1894, 353–54; Reeve, "Colorado Woman Legislators," 208; *Denver Road,* 20 Oct. 1894, 8, and 3 Nov. 1894, 8; *Rocky Mountain News,* 7 Oct. 1894, 3.

47. W. E. Rohde to Davis Waite, 8 Nov. 1894, S. D. Caffried to Waite, 1 Nov. 1894, and Phila Bliven to Waite, 9 Nov. 1894, all in Davis Waite papers, Colorado State Archives; Wagner, "Farms, Families, and Reform," 290–91; *Boulder Camera,* 7 Nov. 1894, 1. The best analysis of the election and women's role in it is Wright, *Politics of Populism,* especially 198–200.

48. Wagner, "Farms, Families, and Reform" covers this debate in depth; quotations from 267, 257, 262–63.

49. *Woman's Tribune* in Wagner, "Farms, Families, and Reform," 229; *WJ,* 17 Sept. 1892, 300; 5 Nov. 1892, 358; 14 July 1894, 217 and 221; 28 July 1894, 236; and 17 Nov. 1894, 364; on Anthony's Republican speeches in Kansas, see *Girard Press,* 13 Oct. 1892, *Newton Kansan,* 11 Oct. 1892, *Leavenworth Times,* 21 Oct. 1892, all clippings reprinted in Patricia G. Holland and Ann D. Gordon, eds., *The Papers of Elizabeth Cady Stanton and Susan B. Anthony* (microfilm), (Wilmington, Del., 1991).

50. Valesh interview, Columbia Oral History Project, 60–61; C. N. Churchill, *Active Footsteps* (Colorado Springs, 1909), 214. On the Republican leanings of middle-class women's clubs in the towns and cities, see also Blair, *Clubwoman as Feminist,* 95, 110.

51. Except as noted, quotations and analysis in the following paragraphs are drawn from Michael Lewis Goldberg's excellent treatment in "'An Army of Women,'" 326–60. On the partisan intensity of the campaign, see Anna Howard Shaw and Elizabeth Jordan, *The Story of a Pioneer* (New York, 1915), 252.

52. On Johns and the Topeka Populists, see Wilda D. Smith, "A Half Century of Struggle: Gaining Woman Suffrage in Kansas," *Kansas History* 4 (1981): 90–91.

53. Harper, *Life and Work of Susan B. Anthony,* vol. 1, 792–94.

54. Smith, "Half-Century of Struggle," 90–92; Wagner, "Farms, Families, and Reform," 285–86, 343–44; *WJ,* 30 June 1894, 204 and 14 July 1894, 40–41.

55. Sarah Thurston, an officer of the Kansas Equal Suffrage Association, examined returns from 75 of 105 counties and reported that suffrage votes were distributed as follows: 14 percent of Democrats, 38.5 percent of Republicans, 54 percent of Populists, and 80 percent of Prohibitionists (Goldberg, "'An Army of Women,'" 373).

56. Goldberg, "'An Army of Women,'" 376, 381.

57. Harper, *Life and Works of Susan B. Anthony,* Vol. 1, 870–86.

58. Susan B. Anthony to Jessie Anthony, n.d., Anthony Family papers, and Anthony to Clara Bewick Colby, 26 July 1896, Clara Bewick Colby papers, both in Huntington Library; Harper, *Life and Works of Susan B. Anthony,* Vol. 1, 885–86. On Anthony's efforts to foster a nonpartisan strategy, see also *San Francisco Examiner,* clippings from July 1896, *San Francisco Post,* 14 Aug. 1896, and *Marin County Journal,* 24 Sept. 1896 in Susan B. Anthony scrapbook #25, Rare Book Division, Library of Congress. The tone differs markedly from her Kansas speeches of 1892.

59. Diary entry for 12 May 1896, Susan B. Anthony papers, Schlesinger Library, Radcliffe College.

Chapter 6. Redemption

1. Charles Hoffman, *The Depression of the Nineties: An Economic History* (Westport, Conn., 1970), 63–71, 97–110, 258–63.

2. See chapter 3, note 38.

3. Samuel T. McSeveney, *The Politics of Depression: Political Behavior in the Northeast, 1893–1896* (New York, 1972), 32–162; Kleppner, *Third Electoral System,* 366–67. Political historians have long identified 1896 as a realigning election; see Burnham, *Critical Elections and the Mainsprings of American Politics.*

4. On Lloyd, Willard, and Kelley's support for the Populist Party in 1894 and disillusionment by 1896, see Sklar, *Florence Kelley,* 274–76. Two New Yorkers who moved in the same direction, from Republican backgrounds, were Josephine Shaw Lowell and William Dean Howells; Julia Ward Howe of Boston also identified herself by the 1890s with Christian Socialism and Bellamyite Nationalism. See Buhle, *Women and American Socialism,* 78–81.

5. Cecilia O'Neill to Davis Waite, 1 Nov. 1893, Davis Waite papers, Colorado State Archives.

6. *New York World,* 21 Sept. 1896, 3; *Pueblo Chieftain,* 24 Oct. 1894, 8.

7. *Philadelphia Times* in *Public Opinion,* 6 Aug. 1896, 168. Richard Slotkin has traced these themes back to John Hay's *The Breadwinners* and other Republican efforts to appropriate the image of frontier lawmen; Nell Painter stresses the importance of the Paris Commune and the Great Railway Strike as foci of middle-class fears in the 1870s. In a broad sense, as these authors suggest, class anxieties over anarchism and communism grew in fits and starts over the course of the Gilded Age, intensified by crises like the depression of the 1870s and the Haymarket affair. In national electoral politics, though, use of law-and-order rhetoric appeared more suddenly and dramatically in response to Populism. Painter, *Standing at Armageddon,* 17–23; Richard Slotkin, *The Fatal Environment: The Myth of the Frontier in the Age of Industrialization, 1800–1890* (New York, 1985), 462–63, 512–15.

8. George T. Winston, "The Relation of the Whites to the Negroes," *Annals of the American Academy of Political and Social Science* 18 (1901): 113–14.

9. *Chicago Tribune,* 3 July 1892, 1–2; also Ostler, *Prairie Populism,* 129.

10. Reda Davis, *California Women: A Guide to their Politics, 1885–1911* (San Francisco, 1967), 86; clippings in H. E. Taubeneck papers, American Heritage Center, University of Wyoming, Laramie; *Judge,* 6 Nov. 1896, 312.

11. Clipping from *Philadelphia Public Ledger,* 15 March 1897, and letter from Annie Haines Barton of Mt. Ephraim, N.J., to Martha Conine, 16 March 1897, Martha A. Bushnell Conine papers, Denver Public Library.

12. White in Hicks, *Populist Revolt,* 374; *WJ,* 5 Nov. 1892, 358; Goldberg, "'An Army of Women,'" 268, 276, 295; *Harper's Weekly,* 6 Oct. 1900, 950.

13. Goldberg, "'An Army of Women,'" 268–71; Barton Shaw, *Wool Hat Boys,* 68; Wagner, "Farms, Families, and Reform," 24, 226. On Lease, see also *Atlanta Constitution,* 21 Sept. 1892, 1; Ostler, *Prairie Populism,* 129.

14. *Leslie's,* 25 Aug. 1892, 141.

15. On portrayals of women who were active in the labor movement and in strikes, see Levine, "Labor's True Woman," 326–27; Meredith Tax, *The Rising of the Women: Feminist Solidarity and Class Conflict, 1880–1917* (New York, 1980), 40, 50–51, 220–21; for an example from the bitter Pullman strike, see *Chicago Tribune,* 21 July 1894, 1.

16. Jenkins in *Woman's Exponent*, 1 July 1892, 7; Foster in *Proceedings of the Tenth Republican National Convention* (Minneapolis, 1892), 91–92.

17. *Greeley Sun*, 6 Oct. 1894, 5 and 3 Nov. 1894, 8; *Leadville Herald Democrat*, 21 Oct. 1894, 6; *Pueblo Chieftain*, 20 Oct. 1894, 3; Populist quote from *Grand Valley Star Times*, 3 Nov. 1894, 3.

18. *Pueblo Chieftain*, 24 Oct. 1894, 8; *Denver Times*, 27 Oct. 1894, 11.

19. *Aspen Sun* quoted in *Georgetown Courier*, 13 Oct. 1894, 2; C. W. Judkins to Celia Waite, 24 Aug. 1894, Davis Waite papers, Colorado State Archives; *Denver Times*, 27 Oct. 1894, 11.

20. For analysis of the election, see Wright, *Politics of Populism*, 190–204; quotations from *Colorado Miner*, 10 Nov. 1894, 2; *Greeley Sun*, 10 Nov. 1894, 4; earlier Populist doubts expressed by *Rocky Mountain News*, quoted in *WJ*, 18 Aug. 1894, 257.

21. *Pueblo Chieftain*, 21 Oct. 1894, 4, and 3 Nov. 1894, 2; *Rocky Mountain News*, 2 Sept. 1896, 4; Joseph G. Brown, *The History of Equal Suffrage in Colorado, 1868–1898* (Denver, 1898), 37–41.

22. On Parkhurst's crusade, see Paul Boyer, *Urban Masses and Moral Order in America, 1829–1920* (Cambridge, Mass., 1978), 162–67; on its early phase, see *WJ*, 1 Nov. 1894, 348–49; on Parkhurst and Schieren, *New York Times*, 25 Sept. 1894, 9 and 26 Sept. 1894, 2. S. Sara Monoson, "The Lady and the Tiger: Women's Electoral Activism in New York City Before Suffrage," *Journal of Women's History* 2.2 (1990): 100–35, is also helpful in identifying the campaigners. Monoson mentions only the Women's Municipal League, not the Women's Republican Association. The reform crusade obviously served Republican interests, but not all its supporters were Republicans; anti-Tammany sentiment also fit the emerging pattern of antipartisanship (see chapter 8).

23. *New York Times*, 5 Oct. 1894, 8; 6 Oct. 1894, 8; 11 Oct. 1894, 9; 13 Oct. 1894, 9.

24. *New York Times*, 25 Oct. 1894, 9; 26 Oct. 1894, 3; 27 Oct. 1894, 5; 30 Oct. 1894, 3. Whether they had full, partial, or no suffrage rights, women around the country showed a keen interest in national economic policy. In Chicago, where women were mobilizing to vote for university trustees, Republican Florence McCartney Worthington announced to one largely female audience, "I cannot recall a time when women have had to band themselves together so long in advance of winter to take care of the poor. Women, I think, can tell something about tariff legislation by results" (*Chicago Tribune*, 12 Oct. 1894, 5).

25. *New York Times*, 14 Oct. 1894, 4, 20 Oct. 1894, 9, 25 Oct. 1894, 9, 31 Oct. 1894, 5, and 1 Nov. 1894, 5; *New York Tribune*, 26 Oct. 1894, 3; *Review of Reviews*, Dec. 1895, 649–50.

26. Monoson, "The Lady and the Tiger," 115–23; William L. Riordan, *Plunkitt of Tammany Hall*, ed. Arthur Mann (New York, 1963 [1905]), xxii, 17–20.

27. *Chicago Tribune*, 19 Oct. 1894, 12; *Los Angeles Times*, 18 Oct. 1894, 4; *Boston Herald* comments reprinted in *Chicago Times*, 2 Nov. 1894, 4; entry for 7 Nov. 1894, Katherine Johnstone Brinley Wharton diary, Pennsylvania Historical Society, Philadelphia.

28. On the complexities of the 1896 campaign I have relied especially on Morgan, *William McKinley and His America*, 225–45; Morgan, *From Hayes to McKinley*, 486–520; and Williams, *Years of Decision*, 97–127. On the Populists, see McMath, *American Populism*, 201–6; Watson quoted on 201.

29. *Public Opinion*, 10 Sept. 1896, 325, and 13 Aug. 1896, 200; "Good Reading for Sound Money Democrats. Hon. W. Bourke Cockran's Speech at Madison Square

Garden, Aug. 18, 1896," 9, pamphlet in Western Reserve Historical Society.

30. *Harper's Weekly* in *Public Opinion*, 25 Oct. 1894, 712, *Philadelphia Record* in *Public Opinion*, 6 Aug. 1896, 165; see also 4 Oct. 1894, 642. *New York Tribune*, 26 Sept. 1896, 12, and 6 Sept. 1896, 3.

31. *Campaign Text Book of the Democratic Party of the United States for the Presidential Election of 1888* (New York, 1888), 8; *New York World*, 13 Aug. 1896, 2. On connections between proposals for tariff reduction and for a progressive income tax as a revenue source and "sop to the Populists," proposed by some Democrats in 1893, see Walter LaFeber, *The New Empire: An Interpretation of American Expansion, 1860–1898* (Ithaca, 1963), 164–66. Not all Democrats went along with the income tax plank, but many did; for a typical defense, see *Raleigh News and Observer*, 6 Sept. 1896, 2.

32. *Public Opinion*, 17 Sept. 1896, 361; *New York Tribune*, 6 Sept. 1896, 3; on the "anarchy plank," see for example the *Tribune*, 10 Sept. 1896, 6, 12 Sept. 1896, 1, and 25 Sept. 1896, 14.

33. *Public Opinion*, 4 Oct. 1894, 640; *Inter-Ocean*, 2 Nov. 1896, 2; Hay, "The Platform of Anarchy: An Address to the Students of Western Reserve University, Cleveland, Oct. 6, 1896," 24, Western Reserve Historical Society; Thomas B. Reed, "The Safe Pathway of Experience," *North American Review*, Oct. 1896, 387.

34. Andrew White, "Some Practical Lessons of the Recent Campaign," *Forum*, Dec. 1896, 415; *Public Opinion*, 9 July 1892, 320–21 and 6 Aug. 1896, 167–68; *El Dorado Republican* quoted in Goldberg, "'An Army of Women,'" 254; *Los Angeles Times*, 23 Oct. 1894, 1.

35. *New York Times*, 25 Sept. 1896, 4; *Public Opinion*, 10 Sept. 1896, 326–27; *Nation*, 15 Oct. 1896, 379; *Seattle Post-Intelligencer*, 16 Oct. 1896, 1; *Leslie's*, 15 Oct. 1896, 242.

36. Williams, *Years of Decision*, 107–8; Andrew White, "Encouragement in the Present Crisis," *Forum*, Sept. 1896, 18; *Philadelphia Times* in Dinkin, *Before Equal Suffrage*, 100; see also *Century*, Oct. 1896, 954, and "Democratic Opinion," Republican broadside in Division of Political History, Museum of American History, Smithsonian Institution.

37. Ostler, *Prairie Populism*, 126; *Los Angeles Times*, 9 Oct. 1894, 3.

38. *St. Louis Globe-Democrat*, 12 July 1896, 2; *Boston Globe*, 3 Sept. 1896, 3; *Inter-Ocean*, 14 July 1896, 1; untitled address dated 1896, Addie Melvina Billings papers, Schlesinger Library, Radcliffe College. On free silver as an "infatuation" or "coquette," see also *Leslie's*, 14 June 1896, 412; *Nation* quoted in Morgan, *William McKinley and His America*, 216; Henry Clews's Republican broadside, 24 May 1896, Division of Political History, Museum of American History, Smithsonian Institution.

39. "Facts for Old Soldiers," 1896 Republican pamphlet, 6, Western Reserve Historical Society; *St. Paul Pioneer Press*, 9 Oct. 1896.

40. Stanley P. Hirshson, *Farewell to the Bloody Shirt: Northern Republicans and the Southern Negro, 1877–1893* (Gloucester, Mass., 1968), 211–14, 226–46; Ayers, *Promise of the New South*, 50–51.

41. J. Morgan Kousser, *The Shaping of Southern Politics: Suffrage Restriction and the Establishment of the One-Party South, 1880–1910* (New Haven, 1974), 29–33, 34–38. Bryan also won the border states of Missouri and Tennessee, but not Kentucky; see William Jennings Bryan, *The First Battle: A Story of the Campaign of 1896* (Chicago, 1896), 610–11.

42. On Democratic fears and Republican and Populist achievements in North Carolina—including greater support for charitable institutions and introduction of black history into the schools—see Ayers, *Promise of the New South*, 290–304.

43. Watson in McMath, *American Populism*, 173; Ayers, *Promise of the New South*, 272–73.

44. Maurice Thompson, "The Court of Judge Lynch," *Lippincott's*, Aug. 1899, 258; Frederick Douglass, "Lynch Law in the South," *North American Review*, July 1892, 19; E. E. Hoss, "Lynch Law and the Southern Press," *Independent*, 1 Feb. 1894, 2; L. W. Zwisohn in *New York Tribune*, 10 July 1903, 9.

45. W. Cabell Bruce, "Lynch Law in the South," *North American Review*, Sept. 1892, 379; *New York Tribune*, 12 Aug. 1903, 6.

46. *Outlook*, 28 June 1902, 533; *Harper's Weekly*, 29 Aug. 1903, 1395–96; Winthrop D. Sheldon, "Shall Lynching Be Suppressed, and How?" *Arena*, Sept. 1906, 227–28; see also David J. Brewer, "Plain Words on the Crime of Lynching," *Leslie's*, 20 Aug. 1903, 182, in which he argued that "men would disgrace their manhood" if they did not seek to avenge interracial rape, and that "if a few lynchings had put a stop to the offense, society might have condoned such breaches of its law"—a remarkable argument from a Supreme Court Justice.

47. *WJ*, 22 Sept. 1900, 296; Frederick Douglass, "The Lesson of the Hour," in Philip S. Foner, ed., *Life and Writings of Frederick Douglass* (New York, 1955), Vol. 4, 502–3; on the rape myth and its psychological roots, see also Joel Williamson's interpretation in *A Rage for Order: Black/White Relations in the American South Since Emancipation* (New York, 1986), 117–51.

48. Wells's major works are reprinted in *On Lynching* (New York, 1969); see also Wells, "Lynching and the Excuse for It," *Independent*, 16 May 1901, 1134; Sheldon, "Shall Lynching Be Suppressed?" 226; Clarence H. Poe, "Lynching: A Southern View," *Atlantic Monthly*, Feb. 1904, 156. A similar view is expressed in Thomas Nelson Page, "The Lynching of Negroes—Its Cause and Prevention," *North American Review*, Jan. 1904, 36.

49. Myrta Lockett Avary, *Dixie After the War* (New York, 1906), 377; Elizabeth Avery Meriwether (under the pseudonym George Edmonds), *Facts and Falsehoods Concerning the War on the South, 1861–1865* (Memphis, 1904), 231, 265–71; see also Kathleen Berkeley, "Elizabeth Avery Meriwether, 'An Advocate for Her Sex': Feminism and Conservatism in the Post-Civil War South," *Tennessee Historical Quarterly* 43 (1984): 390–407. For comments similar to Meriwether's from a professional historian, see Walter L. Fleming, *Civil War and Reconstruction in Alabama* (New York, 1949 [1905]), 762. The causes of lynching were complicated and localized; for differing interpretations, see Ayers, *Promise of the New South*, 156–59 and 495–97; Williamson, *A Rage for Order*; George C. Wright, *Racial Violence in Kentucky, 1865–1940: Lynchings, Mob Rule, and "Legal Lynchings"* (Baton Rouge, 1990); and Fitzhugh Brundage, *Lynching in the New South: Georgia and Virginia, 1880–1930* (Urbana, 1993). My emphasis here is not on lynching, but on the larger discourse over "the new Negro crime," which I believe bore a stronger relationship to Democratic ideology than to specific, local acts of racial violence.

50. Henderson M. Somerville, "Some Co-operative Causes of Negro Lynching," *North American Review*, Oct. 1903, 510; Page, "The Lynching of Negroes," 45; Georgia newspaper in Ayers, *Vengeance and Justice: Crime and Punishment in the Nineteenth-Century South* (New York, 1984), 339.

51. "Democracy vs. Radicalism, Hand-book of North Carolina Politics for 1888," 98–100, in Coulter Pamphlet Collection, University of Georgia Library; Francis Butler Simkins, *Pitchfork Ben Tillman, South Carolinian* (Baton Rouge, 1944), 225.

52. *Birmingham State Herald*, 27 May 1896, 4; 7 June 1896, 1–2, 10; 7 July 1896, 3.

53. The course of this campaign dispute can be traced in the *Atlanta Constitution,* 3 Sept. 1896, 8; 7 Sept. 1896, 6; 9 Sept. 1896, 3; 12 Sept. 1896, 3; 20 Sept. 1896, 18; 23 Sept. 1896, 6; 2 Oct. 1896, 5; 3 Oct. 1896, 5.

54. Josie Southall Bowen to Julia, 10 Nov. 1888, in Southall and Bowen papers, and memoir in Thomas W. Clawson papers, both in Southern Historical Collection, University of North Carolina at Chapel Hill; *Raleigh News and Observer,* 23 Oct. 1896, 4; Eric Anderson, *Race and Politics in North Carolina 1872–1901: The Black Second* (Baton Rouge, 1981), 244, 251; Gilmore, "Gender and Jim Crow: Women and the Politics of White Supremacy in North Carolina, 1896–1920," Ph.D. diss., University of North Carolina at Chapel Hill, 1992, 198–200.

55. George Rountree, "Memorandum of My Personal Recollection of the Election of 1898," 2–6, in Henry George Connor papers, Southern Historical Collection, University of North Carolina at Chapel Hill. See also Jane Cronly, "Account of the Race Riot at Wilmington," Cronly papers, Duke University Library, Durham, N.C.

56. Wheeler, *New Women of the New South,* 18–19; *Raleigh News and Observer,* 28 Sept. 1898, 1; Greenwood, *Bittersweet Legacy,* 208.

57. Wheeler, *New Women of the New South,* 18–19; Greenwood, *Bittersweet Legacy,* 190, 209; Rebecca C. Wood to Alfred Moore Waddell, 26 Oct. 1898, Alfred Moore Waddell papers, Southern Historical Collection, University of North Carolina at Chapel Hill.

58. Thad Jones Jr. to Marion Butler, 1 Nov. 1898, and D. M. Hobbs to Marion Butler, 10 Nov. 1898, both in Marion Butler papers, and Mrs. Henry George Connor to "Kate," 13 Nov. 1898, Connor papers, all in Southern Historical Collection, University of North Carolina at Chapel Hill.

59. Cronly, "Account of the Race Riot," 5, Cronly papers, Duke University Library.

60. Clawson memoir, 2, 5, and "exhibit A," Clawson papers, Southern Historical Collection, University of North Carolina at Chapel Hill.

61. Cronly, "Account of the Race Riot," 3, Cronly papers, Duke University Library; Ayers, *Promise of the New South,* 302–4.

62. R. H. Thomson to Alfred Moore Waddell, 11 Nov. 1898, Waddell papers, Southern Historical Collection, University of North Carolina at Chapel Hill.

63. Charles Crowe, "Racial Violence and Social Reform: Origins of the Atlanta Riot of 1906," *Journal of Negro History* 53 (1968): 249–50, 243; Dewey W. Grantham, Jr., *Hoke Smith and the Politics of the New South* (Baton Rouge, 1958), 142; Williamson, *Rage for Order,* 143–47.

64. Clippings dated 23 and 24 Sept. 1906 in scrapbook on the riot, James M. Griggs papers, Southern Historical Collection, University of North Carolina at Chapel Hill.

65. Winston, "Relation of the Whites to the Negroes," 106, 113–14.

66. Fanny M. Preston, "The South Yet in the Saddle," *Independent,* 1 Feb. 1894, 2; Mrs. L. H. Harris, "A Southern Woman's View," *Independent,* 18 May 1899, 1355.

67. *Report of the Proceedings and Debates of the Constitutional Convention, State of Virginia . . . June 12, 1901 to June 26, 1902* (Richmond, 1906), 2999–3002; *Official Proceedings of the Constitutional Convention of the State of Alabama, May 21, 1901 to September 3, 1901* (Montgomery, 1901), days 53, 54, 57, 58.

68. On Ely and other controversies over socialism, see Mary O. Furner, *Advocacy and Objectivity: A Crisis in the Professionalization of American Social Science, 1865–1905* (Lexington, Ky., 1975), 150–58; on the South, Ayers, *Promise of the New South,* 423–25.

69. On the impact of disfranchisement, see Gilmore, "Gender and Jim Crow," chapter 6.

70. Burnham, *Critical Elections and the Mainsprings of American Politics*, 74–75; Argersinger, "'A Place on the Ballot': Fusion Politics and Antifusion Laws," in *Structure, Process, and Party*, 150–71.

71. Fulton Cutting quoted in Monoson, "The Lady and the Tiger," 118.

Chapter 7. New Parameters of Power

1. Catt in *WJ*, 20 Oct. 1900, 338; on suffrage laws, see state-by-state listings in *HWS* 4; populations calculated from *Abstract of the Eleventh Census*, 10.

2. Jenkins in *Cheyenne Leader*, 23 July 1920, from clipping in Woman Suffrage file, American Heritage Center, University of Wyoming. States and territories in which women's extensive elected office holding preceded suffrage for those offices included California, Illinois, Iowa, Kentucky, Maine, Massachusetts, Montana, Nebraska, Nevada, New York, Oklahoma, Rhode Island, and Wisconsin; see *HWS* 4: 506, 605–6, 623, 635, 674, 693, 747, 799, 808, 814, 890, 903, 916, 978–79, 992–93.

3. *Silver Standard*, 16 Oct. 1897, 2, and 30 Oct. 1897, 3; on Colorado and Idaho generally, see *WJ*, 20 Oct. 1894, 330–31 and *HWS* 4: 594.

4. *Silver Standard*, 12 Oct. 1895, 3, and 26 Oct. 1895, 3; "Sarah Christie Stevens: A Minnesota Farm Woman in Politics," in Gerda Lerner, ed., *The Female Experience: An American Documentary* (Indianapolis, 1977), 361–62; Paula Baker, *Moral Frameworks of Public Life*, 76–78.

5. From state-by-state accounts in *HWS* 4, especially 463, 506, 551, 561, 636, 657, 675, 779, 799, 890, 979.

6. Pettey quoted in Gilmore, "Gender and Jim Crow," 49–50; *Boston Post*, 16 Oct. 1896, 2, and *WJ*, 29 Oct. 1896, on the Sound Money League; on the Silver League, see *Illinois State Register*, 30 Oct. 1896, 2, 1 Nov. 1896, 2, and Bryan, *The First Battle*, 603, 616. Other examples of women's 1896 campaign work are in *Leslie's*, 1 Oct. 1896, 218, and 12 Nov. 1896, 310–11; Bostwick, "Women's Political Clubs," 304–8; *Omaha World Herald*, 11 Oct. 1896, 2, and 26 Oct. 1896, 5; *Seattle Post-Intelligencer*, 12 Oct. 1896, 2, 15 Oct. 1896, 2, and 27 Oct. 1896, 3; Dinkin, *Before Equal Suffrage*, 97–98.

7. *HWS* 4: xviii.

8. Polly Wells Kaufman, *Boston Women and City School Politics, 1872–1905* (New York, 1994); on Wells, see 103, 116; on registration, 139–58 (only 725 women registered prior to the intensely partisan 1888 campaign); on events after 1905, including strong opposition to Democratic committee member Julia Harrington Duff, see 258–61, 271–72. As Kaufman notes, suffragists' pro-Republican activities in the 1890s "could not have helped but convince the public that women suffragists were synonymous with Republicans, anti-Catholics, and Prohibitionists" (196).

9. *Silver Standard*, 26 Oct. 1895, 2; *Los Angeles Times*, 24 Oct. 1894, 4, 28 Oct. 1894, 3, 4 Nov. 1894, 6 Nov. 1894, 4, and election returns on 9 Nov. 1894, 2.

10. *Chicago Tribune*, 7 Oct. 1894, 33; see also 11 Oct. 1894, 3, and 31 Oct. 1894, 2. Populists did not nominate a woman for university trustee, but chose a woman for state superintendent of schools, an office for which women could not yet vote (same page as quotation).

11. *Chicago Tribune*, 3 Oct. 1894, 5; 7 Oct. 1894, 3; 24 Oct. 1894, 1; and 27 Oct. 1894, 3.

12. *Chicago Times,* 5 Nov. 1894, 4, 7 (see also quotes from *Detroit Tribune, Philadelphia Enquirer,* and others on these pages).

13. *Seattle Post-Intelligencer* (reprinted from *St. Louis Mirror*), 1 Nov. 1896, 22.

14. Elta Matheson, "Since Maw Went Into Politics," *Omaha World-Herald,* 4 Nov. 1900, 20.

15. *New York Times,* 25 Sept. 1894, 9, and 11 Oct. 1894, 9; *New York Tribune,* 24 Oct. 1894, 9.

16. Helen Kendrick Johnson, *Woman and the Republic: A Survey of the Woman-Suffrage Movement in the United States and a Discussion of the Claims and Arguments of its Foremost Advocates* (New York, 1913 [1897]); for quotations in this and the following paragraphs, see 31–33, 94–95, 98–102, 206–8, 290, 314–15. On the book's public reception, see 364–68 (reprinted reviews) and Manuela Thurner, "'Better Citizens Without the Ballot': American Antisuffrage Women and Their Rationale during the Progressive Era," *Journal of Women's History* 5.1 (1993): 36.

17. *Harper's Weekly,* 6 Oct. 1900, 950; Beeton, *Women Vote in the West,* 78; *Portland Oregonian,* 12 Nov. 1898, and *Official Proceedings of the Constitutional Convention of Alabama,* day 52. The Alabama delegate was confused about which states had had Populist administrations (only Colorado) and which had enfranchised women (not New Mexico).

18. William Phillips in Goldberg, "'An Army of Women,'" 295; *Philadelphia Press* in *Public Opinion,* 15 Nov. 1894, 787; Dinkin, *Before Equal Suffrage,* 100.

19. Dinkin, *Before Equal Suffrage,* 100; W. E. H. Lecky in *Public Opinion,* 6 Aug. 1896, 176.

20. On the doldrums, see Katharine Anthony, *Susan B. Anthony,* 415; Catt and Shuler, *Woman Suffrage and Politics,* 127, 130–31.

21. Crowe, "Racial Violence and Social Reform," 249–50, 243.

22. Richard B. Sherman, *The Republican Party and Black America from McKinley to Hoover* (Charlottesville, 1973), 63–64; *Congressional Record,* 57th Congress, 2nd sess., 2562; William F. Holmes, *White Chief: James K. Vardaman* (Baton Rouge, 1970), 105.

23. Raymond Arsenault, *Wild Ass of the Ozarks: Jeff Davis and the Social Bases of Southern Politics* (Philadelphis, 1984), 146, 205–6; R. D. W. Connor and Clarence Poe, *Life and Speeches of Charles Brantley Aycock* (Garden City, N.Y., 1912), 229–30; Simkins, *Pitchfork Ben Tillman,* 397.

24. Page, "The Lynching of Negroes," 38; Maurice Thompson, "The Court of Judge Lynch," *Lippincott's,* Aug. 1899, 258; Atticus G. Haygood, "The Black Shadow in the South," *Forum,* Oct. 1893, 168; William Hayne Levell, "On Lynching in the South," *Outlook,* 16 Nov. 1901, 732.

25. J. T. Graves in *Baltimore Sun,* scrapbook, James M. Griggs papers, Southern Historical Collection, University of North Carolina at Chapel Hill; A. A. Clarke in *New York Tribune,* 3 July 1903, 9. The link between rape stories and fear of white women's autonomy is made by Jacquelin Dowd Hall, *Revolt Against Chivalry: Jessie Daniel Ames and the Women's Campaign Against Lynching* (New York, 1979), 153, and Wheeler, *New Women of the New South,* 240–41.

26. *HWS* 2: 162; Grossberg, *Governing the Hearth,* 296.

27. Journal entry for 11 Jan. 1896, Leonora O'Reilly papers, Schlesinger Library, Radcliffe College; Kellie, *A Prairie Populist,* 144–45.

28. Goldberg, "'An Army of Women,'" 383–85.

29. Gilmore, "Gender and Jim Crow," chapter 6. As Eileen Boris observes, "black women were usually fighting the state, rather than courting it"; Boris, "The Power of

Motherhood: Black and White Activist Women Redefine the 'Political,'" in Seth Koven and Sonya Michel, eds., *Mothers of a New World: Maternalist Politics and the Origins of Welfare States* (New York, 1993), 213.

30. Mary Church Terrell, "Lynching from a Negro's Point of View," *North American Review*, June 1904, 862. On white women's later anti-lynching efforts see Hall, *Revolt Against Chivalry;* on white women's support for lynching, Williamson, *A Rage for Order*, 125–26.

31. Roosevelt, "Annual Address to Congress, 1906," in William H. Harbaugh, ed., *The Writings of Theodore Roosevelt* (Indianapolis, 1967), 207; for context see Sherman, *The Republican Party and Black America*, 65–66; C. Vann Woodward, *Origins of the New South* (Baton Rouge, 1951), 463–66.

32. Wells, "A Red Record," in *On Lynching*, 84, 89.

33. Anthony in Alfreda M. Duster, ed., *Crusade for Justice: The Autobiography of Ida B. Wells* (Chicago, 1970), 229–30; Blackwell in *WJ*, 13 Oct. 1900, 324.

34. *New York Tribune*, 6 Aug. 1899, 12, and 15 Sept. 1900, 11; *Boston Globe*, 16 Sept. 1900, 3. On Jewett's Republican loyalties see her letter to Mark Hanna, 10 Nov. 1900, in congratulations albums, Mark Hanna papers, Western Reserve Historical Society. The Baker case exposed deep rifts between black and white anti-lynching campaigners: black leaders in Boston vigorously opposed Jewett's effort to remove the Bakers, wanting Mrs. Baker to testify at a South Carolina trial. Convictions never resulted. I. D. Barnett, "The Baker Family," *Colored American Magazine*, May 1900, 10–13.

35. *WJ*, 29 Sept. 1900, 309, on Jacksonville; on the WCTU, support for schools, public hygiene campaigns, and other reform work accomplished by southern women in the Progressive Era, see William A. Link, *The Paradox of Southern Progressivism, 1880–1930* (Chapel Hill, 1992); Mary Martha Thomas, *The New Woman in Alabama: Social Reforms and Suffrage, 1890–1920* (Tuscaloosa, 1992); Gilmore, "Gender and Jim Crow."

36. On the Aycocks and their predecessors: *WJ*, 20 Oct. 1898, 336, Oliver H. Orr, Jr., *Charles Brantley Aycock* (Chapel Hill, 1961), 37, 202, and Gilmore, "Gender and Jim Crow," 328–29; on other states, Link, *The Paradox of Southern Progressivism*, 134–40.

37. My argument here relies on Wheeler, *New Women of the New South;* on Kentucky see *HWS* 4: 674–75; on New Orleans, *WJ*, 18 March 1899, 88, 15 April 1899, 120, and 6 May 1899, 143.

38. Warren A. Candler to Mrs. J. E. Silbey, 2 May 1892, Warren Aiken Candler papers, and "Minutes of the Eleventh Annual Convention, WCTU of Georgia" (1893), 14, in Georgia WCTU papers, both in Emory University Library; *Atlanta Constitution*, 18 June 1897, 2, 19 June 1897, 9, and 27 June 1897, 13.

39. *WJ*, 22 Sept. 1900, 304, 3 Nov. 1900, 345 and 352, and Dinkin, *Before Equal Suffrage*, 110–11, all on Foster's work in the West; on NWRA funding and visibility between 1897 and 1910, Harper, *Life and Work of Susan B. Anthony*, Vol. 2, 1215, and Gustafson, "Partisan Women," 156; on lack of artifacts, Mayo, "Campaign Appeals to Women," 132–35.

40. *Chicago Tribune*, 6 Oct. 1894, 5, and 7 Nov. 1894, 4; *New York Times*, 3 Nov. 1894, 5; *Woman Voter* (Denver) quoted in *WJ*, 15 Sept. 1894, 290; *Rocky Mountain News*, 4 Nov. 1894, 1; *Boulder Camera*, 7 Nov. 1894, 1.

41. *Denver Times* reprinted in *WJ*, 13 Oct. 1894, 323; *Chicago Tribune*, 12 Oct. 1894, 5; see also, for example, *New York Times*, 3 Nov. 1894, 5; *Rock Springs Miner*, 2 Nov. 1896, 1.

42. *Denver Times,* 14 Jan. 1895, 8.

43. Roosevelt in McGerr, *Decline of Popular Politics,* 145; Mrs. Elroy Avery in Joseph P. Smith, ed., *McKinley, The People's Choice* (Canton, Ohio, 1896), 42–44.

44. In keeping with the Midwest's long tradition of women's campaign participation, the Postum contest was covered most prominently in midwestern newspapers. See, for example, *Minneapolis Journal,* 17 Oct. 1896, 8, and *Indianapolis Sentinel,* 17 Oct. 1896, 5, 4 Nov. 1896, 5, and 11 Nov. 1896, 6.

45. Brown, *History of Equal Suffrage in Colorado,* 27–29, 37–41.

46. Reeve, "Colorado Woman Legislators," 207–11; *Denver Times,* 19 Jan. 1895, 4, and 23 Jan. 1895, 6; David Boyd to Jesse House from Denver, 19 January 1895, David Boyd papers, Denver Public Library.

47. *Denver Times,* 18 Jan. 1895, 4.

48. Reeve, "Colorado Woman Legislators," 208–10; *HWS* 4: 953; clippings in Martha A. Bushnell Conine papers, Denver Public Library.

Chapter 8. Progressives and Protection

1. *Harper's Weekly,* 12 Nov. 1892, 1082; *Omaha World-Herald,* 4 Nov. 1900, 20; Richard Hofstadter, "The Citizen and the Machine," in *The Age of Reform* (New York, 1955), 257–71; Robert H. Wiebe, *The Search for Order, 1877–1920* (New York, 1967), especially 60–63, 128–30. On the earlier roots of antiparty thought, see McCormick, "Antiparty Thought in the Gilded Age," in *The Party Period and Public Policy,* 228–61.

2. Sklar, *Florence Kelley,* 286–315; Willard and WCTU's decision for nonpartisanship in Bordin, *Woman and Temperance,* 133–35.

3. On the suffrage movement, see for example Katharine Anthony, *Susan B. Anthony,* 415; Catt and Shuler, *Woman Suffrage and Politics,* 127, 130–31; on urban reformers, Wiebe, *The Search for Order,* 153–79; on middle-class urbanites' sense that they were losing ground to political bosses who did not share their interests, see also Boyer, *Urban Masses and Moral Order,* especially 162–90.

4. On links between businessmen and politicians, McCormick, *Party Period and Public Policy,* 311–56; on disillusionment with politics more generally, Wiebe, *The Search for Order,* and Leon Epstein, *Political Parties in the American Mold* (Madison, 1986).

5. Epstein, *Political Parties in the American Mold,* on the need to "instill within the parties a new sense of purpose" (7).

6. On new communities of shared faith, especially settlement houses, I am indebted to Sklar, *Florence Kelley.*

7. *New York Times,* 20 Oct. 1894, 4, and 3 Nov. 1894, 4; *Nation,* 15 Oct. 1896, 282; Thomas B. Reed, "The Safe Pathway of Experience," *North American Review,* Oct. 1896, 389–92; White, "Some Practical Lessons," 415; *Public Opinion,* 6 Aug. 1896, 167–69; "Democratic Opinion," Republican broadside in Division of Political History, Museum of American History, Smithsonian Institution.

8. LaFeber, *The New Empire,* especially 300–11, 333–416; Morgan, *William McKinley and His America,* 326–78.

9. LaFeber, *The New Empire,* 326–406, on the decision for war; LaFeber emphasizes McKinley's concern for workers, and the search for overseas markets, while I focus more here on the regional and racial dimensions of pro-war sentiment. On these issues, see Gerald Linderman, *The Mirror of War: American Society and the Spanish-American War* (Ann Arbor, Mich., 1974), especially chapter 5.

10. Morgan, *William McKinley,* 329–78, 499–501; Williams, *Years of Decision,* 138–42.

11. Nina Silber, *The Romance of Reunion: Northerners and the South, 1865–1900* (Chapel Hill, 1993); John Pettigrew, "'The Soldier's Faith': Turn-of-the-Century Memory of the Civil War and the Emergence of Modern American Nationalism," *Journal of Contemporary History* 31 (1996): 49–73.

12. On the cultural dimensions of expansion, see Emily S. Rosenberg, *Spreading the American Dream: American Economic and Cultural Expansion, 1980–1945* (New York: Hill and Wang), especially "Capitalists, Christians, Cowboys, 1890–1912," 14–37. See also Wiebe, *The Search for Order*, 224–55.

13. William Henry Harbaugh, *Power and Responsibility: The Life and Times of Theodore Roosevelt* (New York, 1961), 93–109, 143–44, 149–55; on Roosevelt's exploits in Cuba, Edmund Morris, *The Rise of Theodore Roosevelt* (New York, 1979), 629–30, and Linderman, *Mirror of War*, 91–113.

14. Roosevelt, "The Manly Virtues and Practical Politics," *Forum*, July 1894, 551–57; Henry Herzberg, "Remedies for Political Evils," and William B. Chisholm, "The Social Pressure in Politics," both in *American Magazine of Civics*, May 1895, 479–82 and 454, respectively.

15. John Hay and Elihu Root, "The Republican Party: A Party Fit to Govern," (1904), pamphlet in Division of Political History, Museum of American History, Smithsonian Institution; on campaign tactics, McGerr, *Decline of Popular Politics*, 149–55, and Robert J. Dinkin, *Campaigning in America: A History of Election Practices* (New York, 1989), 118–21.

16. *Theodore Roosevelt: An Autobiography* (New York, 1919), 176–84; Robert J. Thomson, "A Square Deal for Everyone: What Theodore Roosevelt Stands For" (1904), pamphlet in Division of Political History, Museum of American History, Smithsonian Institution; Albert Shaw, *A Cartoon History of Roosevelt's Career* (New York, 1910); McGerr, *Decline of Popular Politics*, 145. Roosevelt represented in the political arena a number of broader social trends. The popularity of sports accompanied a new fascination with the West and a plethora of novels featuring cowboys, gunfighters, and Klondike men. On these changes, see John Higham, "The Reorientation of American Culture in the 1890s," in *Writing American History: Essays on Modern Scholarship* (Bloomington, Ind., 1970), 73–102, and Rotundo, *American Manhood*, chapter 10.

17. *Theodore Roosevelt*, 176–84; Roosevelt, "The Strenuous Life," speech before the Hamilton Club of Chicago, 10 April 1899, in *The Strenuous Life: Essays and Addresses* (New York, 1901), 3–4.

18. "The Hero as Politician," in Theodore P. Greene, *America's Heroes: The Changing Models of Success in American Magazines* (New York, 1970), 232–82, quotations from 232, 240.

19. Quotations from *Portland Oregonian, Seattle Post-Intelligencer, Boston Advertiser* and others in *Public Opinion*, 16 July 1892, 345–46.

20. Harbaugh, *Power and Responsibility*, 166–81. As Harbaugh makes clear, Roosevelt was a forceful president prone to sweeping aside the objections and worries of businessmen or members of his own administration. There are interesting parallels between his domestic and foreign policy decisions. In a 1902 dispute between Venezuela, Germany, and Great Britain, Roosevelt insisted on negotiation among the parties and backed his demand with the threat of force; he succeeded in securing arbitration. Five years later the United States intervened in the Dominican Republic and ran the country's customs office as a receivership—the same action Roosevelt had threatened to apply to anthracite mines (Harbaugh, 191–97).

21. Painter, *Standing at Armageddon*, 249–67, 270–71 (the latter on Debs).

22. Douglass, "The Lesson of the Hour," 504; Ayers, in *Promise of the New South,* 140, quotes the *Times-Democrat* and makes the broader argument about gender and segregation I have built upon here.

23. Vernon Lane Wharton, "Jim Crow Laws and Miscegenation," in Joel Williamson, ed., *The Origins of Segregation* (Boston, 1968), 14–17; C. Vann Woodward, *The Strange Career of Jim Crow* (New York, 1955), 99. See also Ayers, *Promise of the New South,* 139; George M. Frederickson, *The Black Image in the White Mind* (New York, 1971), 219, 221.

24. Grossberg, *Governing the Hearth,* 138–39, 140–44, 247; *HWS* 4: 24–72; Keller, *Affairs of State,* 471–72.

25. *Washington Wife: The Journal of Ellen Maury Slayden, 1897–1919* (New York, 1962), 14, 18; Judith Papachristou, "American Women and Foreign Policy, 1898–1905: Exploring Gender in Diplomatic History," *Diplomatic History* 14 (1990): 493–509. Papachristou sees a "distinct female perspective" which was anti-war, but she notes that a great majority of women who wrote to the *WJ* were pro-war (498). The WCTU opposed the war because "nothing increases intemperance like war," and because they viewed war itself as a type of "intoxication" (499–501).

26. Papachristou, "American Women and Foreign Policy," 499; Adams and Foster, "J. Ellen Foster," 272–78; Boswell's obituary in *New York Times,* 6 Jan. 1942, 23.

27. *Domestic Science Bulletin,* Dec. 1906, 2; Adams and Foster, "J. Ellen Foster," 272–78; Francis Warren to William McKinley, 13 Feb. 1897, Francis E. Warren papers, American Heritage Center, University of Wyoming; on Foster's work in the West, *WJ,* 22 Sept. 1900, 304; 3 Nov. 1900, 345 and 352; and 17 Nov. 1900, 361.

28. *South-Bend Tribune,* 31 Oct. 1896, 6; Bostwick, "Women's Political Clubs," 304–8; see also Croly, *History of the Woman's Club Movement,* 248, 343–44, 445, 519.

29. Diary entries for 28 Oct. 1896 and 31 Oct. 1900, Harriet Hanson Robinson papers, Schlesinger Library, Radcliffe College; *WJ,* 10 Nov. 1900, 360.

30. Zimmerman, "'The Queen of the Lobby,'" provides an excellent account of Hunt's strategy and its success.

31. Kathryn Kish Sklar, "Hull House in the 1890s: A Community of Women Reformers," *Signs* 10 (1985): 658–77. On Addams and her father, see Anne Firor Scott, "Jane Addams," in Jones, ed., *Notable American Women,* Vol. 1, 16–17. On Addams's early loyalty to her father's high-tariff views, see also Allen F. Davis, *American Heroine: The Life and Legend of Jane Addams* (New York, 1973), 35. On Kelley's youthful role as a political confidante to her father, Congressman William Kelley of Philadelphia, see Sklar, *Florence Kelley,* 27–49. Kelley recalled in her autobiography her father's "never-failing, flowing interest in the misfortunes of defenseless women and children. . . . To my generation, other measures commended themselves and became my burning concern; but Father's charge had been to meet the issues of the ensuing decades with such light as might be ours." Kathryn Kish Sklar, ed., *The Autobiography of Florence Kelley* (Chicago, 1986), 24. On other Progressive women whose fathers were leading Republicans, see Kristie Miller, *Ruth Hanna McCormick: A Life in Politics, 1880–1944* (Albuquerque, N.M., 1992); James P. Louis, "Mary Garrett Hay," and Phillip R. Shriver, "Harriet Taylor Upton," both in Jones, ed., *Notable American Women,* Vol. 2, 163–65, and Vol. 3, 501–2, respectively. On women and socialism, see Gustafson, "Partisan Women," 350–51; for an in-depth study of California, see Sherry Katz, "Dual Commitments: Feminism, Socialism, and Women's Political Activism in California, 1890–1920," Ph.D. diss., University of California at Los Angeles, 1991.

32. I differ here with historians who describe "maternalism" as a new and effective

political identity and strategy for women in the Progressive Era. I agree, rather, with Lisa D. Brush that "maternalism is feminism for hard times"—a rhetorical fallback position in which women, forced on the defensive, revert to arguments based on motherhood and women's "natural" moral superiority. Brush, "Love, Toil, and Trouble: Motherhood and Feminist Politics," *Signs* 21 (1996): 429–54. Also useful have been Eileen Boris, "Reconstructing the 'Family': Women, Progressive Reform, and the Problem of Social Control," in Noralee Frankel and Nancy S. Dye, eds., *Gender, Class, Race, and Reform in the Progressive Era* (Lexington, Ky., 1991), 73–86; and Felicia Kornbluh, "The New Literature on Gender and the Welfare State: The U.S. Case," *Feminist Studies* 22 (1996): 171–97. For alternative views of maternalism, see Skocpol, *Protecting Soldiers and Mothers;* and Kathryn Kish Sklar, "The Historical Foundations of Women's Power in the Creation of the American Welfare State, 1830–1930," and Sonya Michel, "The Limits of Maternalism: Policies Toward American Wage-Earning Mothers During the Progressive Era," both in Koven and Michel, *Mothers of a New World,* 43–93 and 277–320, respectively; Molly Ladd-Taylor, "Toward Defining Maternalism in U.S. History," *Journal of Women's History* 5.2 (1993): 110–13.

33. Skocpol, *Protecting Soldiers and Mothers,* 382–423, Kelley quoted on 408; Boris, "Reconstructing the 'Family,'" notes the complexity of the conflict between men and women who both wielded "paternal" and "maternal" arguments. On family-wage arguments among women reformers, see Linda Gordon, *Pitied But Not Entitled: Single Mothers and the History of Welfare* (New York, 1994), 56–59.

34. Skocpol, *Protecting Soldiers and Mothers,* 424–79. I am building on Skocpol's work here and agree with her that emergence of the Progressive Party was a key factor in the success of mothers' pensions (456–65). I am less inclined to agree that American women's "remarkable kind of maternalist political consciousness" was an effective Progressive Era innovation (529).

35. On the shift in suffrage rhetoric, see Aileen Kraditor, *Ideas of the Woman Suffrage Movement, 1890–1920* (New York, 1965), 43–74; Dorr quoted in Skocpol, *Protecting Soldiers and Mothers,* 340.

36. Scott, *Natural Allies,* 141–47; Ruth Rosen, *The Lost Sisterhood: Prostitution in America, 1900–1918* (Baltimore, 1982), 14–68; on prohibition, Blocker, *American Temperance Movements,* 114–32.

37. Eileen Boris, *Home to Work: Motherhood and the Politics of Industrial Homework in the United States* (New York, 1994), 85–93.

38. Mrs. Frank O. Immler, "Woman's Natural Debarments from Political Service: A Reply," *American Magazine of Civics,* March 1896, 277. On professional women, Robyn Muncy, *Creating a Female Dominion in American Reform, 1890–1935* (New York, 1991); Gordon, *Pitied But Not Entitled,* 67–108.

39. Gilmore, *Gender and Jim Crow;* Eileen Boris, "The Power of Motherhood: Black and White Activist Women Redefine the 'Political,'" in Koven and Michel, *Mothers of a New World,* 213–45; on the politics of respectability and class divisions among African-American women, see Anne Neis Kaupfer, "'Toward a Tenderer Humanity and a Nobler Womanhood': African-American Women's Clubs in Chicago, 1890 to 1920," *Journal of Women's History* 7.3 (1995): 58–76, Higginbotham, *Righteous Discontent.*

40. Harbaugh, *Power and Responsibility,* 391–92.

41. Harbaugh, *Power and Responsibility,* 390–92.

42. Gustafson, "Partisan Women," 97–146, 207–11, 224–25, Addams quoted on 210.

43. Gustafson, "Partisan Women," 147–97, 246–47, 262–67.

44. Muncy, *Creating a Female Dominion,* emphasizes the role of professional women in lobbying at the federal level for change; Skocpol, *Protecting Soldiers and Mothers,* focuses more on electoral contexts. I agree with both on the influence of the Progressive Party as an immediate spur to new legislation, and in fact would place even more stress on the partisan context rather than on the effectiveness of "maternalist" rhetoric.

45. Skocpol, *Protecting Soldiers and Mothers;* Wiebe, *The Search for Order,* 218–22.

46. Peter Odegard, *Pressure Politics: The Story of the Anti-Saloon League* (New York, 1966).

47. Nancy F. Cott, *The Grounding of Modern Feminism* (New Haven, 1987), chapter 2, Paul quoted on 54.

48. See, for example, the dramatically regional U.S. map in Beeton, *Women Vote in the West,* 155. Of the 15 full-suffrage states before 1918, 13 were west of the Mississippi and none were in the former Confederacy (with the arguable exception of Oklahoma, which was a territory during the Civil War). Only Texas, Arkansas, Tennessee, and Kentucky ratified the Nineteenth Amendment: see Anne Firor Scott, *The Southern Lady: From Pedestal to Politics, 1830–1930* (Chicago, 1970), 184. On post-suffrage politics, see Andersen, *After Suffrage;* Cott, *The Grounding of Modern Feminism.*

49. Quoted in Gustafson, "Partisan Women," 210, 208.

Selected References

Location of Newspapers Cited

Newspapers are not listed if their titles identify them with a city and state (*Lynchburg Virginian, Tallahassee Floridian*) or with New York, Boston, Philadelphia, Baltimore, Atlanta, New Orleans, Chicago, Minneapolis, Indianapolis, Denver, San Francisco, Los Angeles, or Seattle.

American Nonconformist and Kansas Industrial Liberator, Winfield, Kansas
Arizona Citizen, Tucson
Arkansas Gazette, Little Rock
Benton Harbor Palladium, Michigan
Bill Barlow's Budget, Douglas, Wyoming
Birmingham State Herald, Alabama
Boulder Camera, Colorado
Brookville American, Indiana
Centralia Sentinel, Illinois
Charleston Free Press, South Carolina
Charleston Mercury, South Carolina
Charleston News and Courier, South Carolina
Cheyenne Leader, Wyoming
Cheyenne Sun, Wyoming
Chino Valley Champion, Chino, California
Cincinnati Gazette, Ohio
Cleveland Penny Press, Ohio
Colorado Miner, Georgetown
Columbus Herald, Indiana
Columbus Republican, Indiana
Concord Monitor, New Hampshire
Crystal Springs Monitor, Mississippi

Detroit Free Press, Michigan
Evansville Journal, Indiana
Franklin Democrat, Brookville, Franklin Co., Indiana
Franklin Democrat, Franklin, Johnson Co., Indiana
Freedman's Press, Austin, Texas
Georgetown Courier, Colorado
Goshen News, Indiana
Grand Valley Star Times, Grand Junction, Colorado
Greeley Sun, Colorado
Greeley Tribune, Colorado
Hancock Democrat, Greenfield, Indiana
Harrisburg Patriot, Pennsylvania
Illinois State Register, Springfield
Illinois State Journal, Springfield
Inter-Ocean, Chicago
Jackson Clarion-Ledger, Mississippi
Leadville Herald Democrat, Colorado
Logansport Journal, Indiana
Logansport Pharos, Indiana
Louisville Courier-Journal, Kentucky
Milwaukee Sentinel, Wisconsin
Mobile Register, Alabama
Montgomery Advertiser, Alabama
National Republican, Augusta, Georgia
New Mexican, Santa Fe
Omaha Herald and *World-Herald*, Nebraska
Omaha Republican, Nebraska
Oquawka Spectator, Illinois
Oregon State Journal, Eugene
Painesville Telegraph, Ohio
People's Advocate, Crawfordville, Georgia
People's Advocate, Washington, D.C.
People's Journal, Lampasas, Texas
Petersburg Index-Appeal, Virginia
Portland Eastern Argus, Maine
Portland Press, Maine
Providence Journal, Rhode Island
Pueblo Chieftain, Colorado
Raleigh News and Observer, North Carolina
Rock Springs Miner, Wyoming
Rocky Ford Enterprise, Colorado
Rocky Mountain News, Denver
St. Paul Pioneer Press, Minnesota
Savannah Republican, Georgia
Silver Standard, Silver Plume, Colorado
South-Bend Tribune, Indiana
Topeka Tribune, Kansas
Trenton Sentinel, New Jersey
Union Signal, Evanston, Illinois

Vincennes Commercial, Indiana
Vincennes Sun, Indiana
Warsaw Times, Indiana
White County Democrat, Monticello, Indiana
Woman's Exponent, Salt Lake City, Utah
Woman's News, Indianapolis
WJ (Woman's Journal), Boston
Woman's Tribune, Beatrice, Nebraska
Yankton Press and Dakotaian, Dakota Territory

Selected References

Abelson, Elaine S. *When Ladies Go A-Thieving: Middle-Class Shoplifters in the Victorian Department Store*. New York, 1989. 13–41.

Abstract of the Eleventh Census: 1890. Washington, D.C., 1896.

Adams, Elmer C., and Warren Dunham Foster. *Heroines of Modern Progress*. New York, 1921.

Adams, Pauline, and Emma S. Thornton. *A Populist Assault: Sarah E. Van De Vort Emery on American Democracy, 1862–1895*. Bowling Green, Ohio, 1982.

Andersen, Kristi. *After Suffrage: Women in Partisan and Electoral Politics before the New Deal*. Chicago, 1996.

Anthony, Katharine. *Susan B. Anthony: Her Personal History and Her Era*. New York, 1954.

Anthony, Susan B. et al., eds. *The History of Woman Suffrage (HWS)*. Vols. 1–4. New York, 1881–1900.

Argersinger, Peter H. *Structure, Process, and Party: Essays in American Political History*. Armonk, N.Y., 1992.

Aron, Cindy Sondik. *Ladies and Gentlemen of the Civil Service: Middle-Class Workers in Victorian America*. New York, 1987.

Ayers, Edward L. *The Promise of the New South: Life After Reconstruction*. New York, 1992.

Badger, Henry Clay. *Dead-Heads Financial and Moral: The Logic of It*. Cambridge, Mass., 1884.

Baker, Jean H. *Affairs of Party: The Political Culture of Northern Democrats in the Mid-Nineteenth Century*. Ithaca, N.Y., 1983.

Baker, Paula. "The Domestication of Politics: Women and American Political Society, 1780–1920." *American Historical Review* 89 (1984): 620–47.

———. *The Moral Frameworks of Public Life: Gender, Politics, and the State in Rural New York, 1870–1930*. New York, 1991.

Barkley Brown, Elsa. "Negotiating and Transforming the Public Sphere: African American Political Life in the Transition from Slavery to Freedom." *Public Culture* 7 (1994): 107–46.

Basch, Norma. "Marriage, Morals, and Politics in the Election of 1828." *Journal of American History* 80 (1993): 890–918.

Beeton, Beverly. *Women Vote in the West: The Woman Suffrage Movement, 1869–1896*. New York, 1986.

Blair, Karen J. *The Clubwoman as Feminist: True Womanhood Redefined, 1868–1914*. New York, 1980.

Blocker, Jack S. Jr. *American Temperance Movements: Cycles of Reform*. Boston, 1989.

Bordin, Ruth. *Frances Willard: A Biography*. Chapel Hill, N.C., 1986.

————. *Woman and Temperance: The Quest for Power and Liberty.* 1981. 2nd ed. New Brunswick, N.J., 1990.

Boris, Eileen. "Reconstructing the 'Family': Women, Progressive Reform, and the Problem of Social Control." In *Gender, Class, Race, and Reform in the Progressive Era,* Noralee Frankel and Nancy S. Dye, eds. Lexington, Ky., 1991. 73–86.

Bostwick, Kate M. "Women's Political Clubs." *Monthly Illustrator* 13 (1896): 304–8.

Boyer, Paul. *The Urban Masses and Moral Order in America, 1820–1920.* Cambridge, Mass., 1978.

Brady, Marilyn Dell. "Populism and Feminism in a Newspaper by and for Women of the Kansas Farmers' Alliance, 1891–1894." *Kansas History* 7 (1984/1985): 280–90.

Brown, Joseph G. *The History of Equal Suffrage in Colorado, 1868–1898.* Denver, 1898.

Bryan, William Jennings. *The First Battle: A Story of the Campaign of 1896.* Chicago, 1896.

Buhle, Mari Jo. *Women and American Socialism, 1870–1920.* Urbana, Ill., 1981.

Burnham, Walter Dean, ed. *Critical Elections and the Mainsprings of American Politics.* New York, 1970.

Clinch, Thomas A. *Urban Populism and Free Silver in Montana.* Missoula, Mont., 1970.

Clinton, Catherine, and Nina Silber, eds. *Divided Houses: Gender and the Civil War.* New York, 1992.

Colvin, D. Leigh. *Prohibition in the United States: A History of the Prohibition Party and of the Prohibition Movement.* New York, 1926.

Conwell, Russell H. *Life and Public Services of Governor Rutherford B. Hayes.* Boston, 1876.

Cooper, Anna Julia. *A Voice from the South.* New York, 1892/1962.

Cott, Nancy F. *The Bonds of Womanhood: "Woman's Sphere" in New England, 1780–1835.* New Haven, Conn., 1977.

————. *The Grounding of Modern Feminism.* New Haven, Conn., 1987.

Croly, June Cunningham. *The History of the Woman's Club Movement in America.* New York, 1898.

Diggs, Annie. "The Women in the Alliance Movement." *Arena,* July 1892, 160–79.

Dinkin, Robert J. *Before Equal Suffrage: Women in Partisan Politics from Colonial Times to 1920.* Westport, Conn., 1995.

Doten, Alfred. *The Journals of Alfred Doten, 1849–1903,* Walter Van Tilburg Clark, ed. Reno, Nev., 1973.

Douglass, Frederick. "The Lesson of the Hour." In *The Life and Writings of Frederick Douglass,* Philip S. Foner, ed. Vol. 4. New York, 1955.

DuBois, Ellen Carol. *Feminism and Suffrage: The Emergence of an Independent Women's Rights Movement in America, 1848–1869.* Ithaca, N.Y., 1978.

Duniway, Abigail Scott. *Path Breaking: An Autobiographical History of the Woman Suffrage Movement in Pacific Coast States.* New York, 1914/1971.

Edwards, Laura F. "The Disappearance of Susan Daniel and Henderson Cooper: Gender and Narratives of Political Conflict in the Reconstruction-Era South." *Feminist Studies* 22 (1996): 363–86.

Etcheson, Nicole. "Manliness and the Political Culture of the Old Northwest." *Journal of the Early Republic* 15 (1995): 59–77.

Foner, Eric. *Reconstruction: America's Unfinished Revolution, 1863–1877.* New York, 1988.

Formisano, Ronald P. *The Birth of Mass Political Parties.* Princeton, N.J., 1971.

Geer, Emily Apt. *First Lady: The Life of Lucy Webb Hayes*. Kent, Ohio, 1984.

Gilmore, Glenda Elizabeth. "Gender and Jim Crow: Women and the Politics of White Supremacy in North Carolina, 1896–1920." Ph.D. diss., University of North Carolina at Chapel Hill, 1992.

Ginzberg, Lori D. *Women and the Work of Benevolence: Morality, Politics, and Class in the Nineteenth-Century United States*. New Haven, Conn., 1990.

Goldberg, Michael Lewis. "'An Army of Women': Gender Relations and Politics in Kansas Populism, the Woman Movement, and the Republican Party, 1879–1896." Ph.D. diss., Yale University, 1992.

Gordon, Linda. *Pitied But Not Entitled: Single Mothers and the History of Welfare*. New York, 1994.

Gordon, Lydia L. *From Lady Washington to Mrs. Cleveland*. Boston, 1888.

Greenwood, Janette Thomas. *Bittersweet Legacy: The Black and White "Better Classes" in Charlotte, 1850–1910*. Chapel Hill, N.C., 1994.

Grossberg, Michael. *Governing the Hearth: Law and the Family in Nineteenth-Century America*. Chapel Hill, N.C., 1985.

Gustafson, Melanie Susan. "Partisan Women: Gender, Politics, and the Progressive Party of 1912." Ph.D. diss., New York University, 1993.

Hall, Jacquelyn Dowd. *Revolt Against Chivalry: Jessie Daniel Ames and the Women's Campaign Against Lynching*. New York, 1979.

Harbaugh, William Henry. *Power and Responsibility: The Life and Times of Theodore Roosevelt*. New York, 1961.

Haworth, Paul. *The Hayes-Tilden Presidential Election of 1876*. Cleveland, 1906.

Herr, Pamela, and Mary Lee Spence. "Introduction." *Letters of Jessie Benton Frémont*. Urbana, Ill., 1993.

Hicks, John D. *The Populist Revolt: A History of the Farmers' Alliance and the People's Party*. Minneapolis, 1931.

Higginbotham, Evelyn Brooks. *Righteous Discontent: The Women's Movement in the Black Baptist Church*. Cambridge, Mass., 1993.

Holden, Margaret Kolb. "The Rise and Fall of Oregon Populism: Legal Theory, Political Culture, and Public Policy, 1869–1895." Ph.D. diss., University of Virginia, 1993.

Holt, Michael F. *The Political Crisis of the 1850s*. New York, 1978.

Howard, J. Q. *The Life, Public Services, and Selected Speeches of Rutherford B. Hayes*. Cincinnati, Ohio, 1876.

Howe, Daniel Walker. "The Evangelical Movement and Political Culture in the North during the Second Party System." *Journal of American History* 77 (1991): 1216–39.

Jeffrey, Julie Roy. "Women in the Southern Farmers' Alliance: A Reconsideration of the Role and Status of Women in the Late Nineteenth-Century South." *Feminist Studies* 3 (1975): 72–91.

Jensen, Richard. *The Winning of the Midwest: Social and Political Conflict, 1888–1896*. Chicago, 1971.

Jones, Edward T., ed. *Notable American Women, 1607–1950*. Cambridge, Mass., 1971.

Keller, Morton. *Affairs of State: Public Life in Late Nineteenth Century America*. Cambridge, Mass., 1977.

Kellie, Luna E. *A Prairie Populist: The Memoirs of Luna Kellie*. Ed. Jane Taylor Nelson. Iowa City, 1992.

Kleppner, Paul. *The Cross of Culture: A Social Analysis of Midwestern Politics, 1850–1900*. New York, 1970.

————. *The Third Electoral System, 1853–1892: Parties, Voters, and Political Cultures.* Chapel Hill, N.C., 1979.

Koven, Seth, and Sonya Michel, eds. *Mothers of a New World: Maternalist Politics and the Origins of Welfare States.* New York, 1993.

Kreibel, Robert C. *Where the Saints Have Trod: The Life of Helen Gougar.* West Lafayette, Ind., 1985.

LaFeber, Walter. *The New Empire: An Interpretation of American Expansion, 1860–1898.* Ithaca, N.Y., 1963.

Lebsock, Suzanne. "Women and American Politics, 1880–1920." In *Women, Politics, and Change,* Louise A. Tilly and Patricia Gurin, eds. New York, 1990. 35–62.

Levine, Susan. "Labor's True Woman: Domesticity and Equal Rights in the Knights of Labor," *Journal of American History* 70 (1983): 323–39.

Link, William A. *The Paradox of Southern Progressivism, 1880–1930.* Chapel Hill, N.C., 1992.

Maizlish, Stephen E., and John J. Kushma, eds. *Essays on American Antebellum Politics, 1840–1860.* Arlington, Tex., 1982.

Marti, Donald B. *Women of the Grange: Mutuality and Sisterhood in Rural America, 1866–1920.* Westport, Conn., 1991.

Matthews, Glenna. *The Rise of Public Woman: Woman's Power and Woman's Place in the United States, 1630–1970.* New York, 1992.

Mayo, Edith. "Campaign Appeals to Women." In *American Material Culture: The Shape of Things Around Us,* Edith P. Mayo, ed. Bowling Green, Ohio, 1984. 128–48.

McClintock, Megan J. "Civil War Pensions and the Reconstruction of Union Families." *Journal of American History* 83 (1996): 456-80.

McCormick, Richard L. *The Party Period and Public Policy: American Politics from the Age of Jackson to the Progressive Era.* New York, 1986.

McCurry, Stephanie. *Masters of Small Worlds: Yeoman Households, Gender Relations, and the Political Culture of the Antebellum South Carolina Low Country.* New York, 1995.

McGerr, Michael. *The Decline of Popular Politics: The American North, 1865–1928.* New York, 1986.

————. "Political Style and Women's Power, 1830–1930," *Journal of American History* 77 (1990): 864–85.

McMath, Robert C. Jr. *American Populism: A Social History, 1877–1898.* New York, 1993.

Mink, Gwendolyn. *Old Labor and New Immigrants in American Political Development: Union, Party, and State, 1875–1920.* Ithaca, N.Y., 1986.

Monoson, S. Sara. "The Lady and the Tiger: Women's Electoral Activism in New York City Before Suffrage." *Journal of Women's History* 2.2 (1990): 100–135.

Morgan, H. Wayne. *From Hayes to McKinley: National Party Politics, 1877–1896.* Syracuse, N.Y., 1969.

————, ed. *The Gilded Age,* 2nd ed. Syracuse, N.Y., 1963.

————. *William McKinley and His America.* Syracuse, N.Y., 1963.

Muncy, Robyn. *Creating a Female Dominion in American Reform, 1890–1935.* New York, 1991.

Nevins, Allan. *Grover Cleveland: A Study in Courage.* New York, 1932.

Norton, Mary Beth. *Liberty's Daughters: The Revolutionary Experience of American Women, 1750–1800.* Boston, 1980.

Official Proceedings of the Constitutional Convention of the State of Alabama, May 21, 1901 to September 3, 1901. Montgomery, Ala., 1901.

Ostler, Jeffrey. *Prairie Populism: The Fate of Agrarian Radicalism in Kansas, Nebraska, and Iowa, 1880–1892*. Lawrence, Kans., 1993.

Our Presidential Candidates and Political Compendium. Newark, N.J., 1880.

Painter, Nell Irwin. *Standing at Armageddon: The United States, 1877–1919*. New York, 1987.

Paludin, Philip. *A People's Contest: The Union and the Civil War, 1861–1865*. New York, 1988.

Pocock, Emil. "Wet or Dry? The Presidential Election of 1884 in Upstate New York." *New York History* 54 (1973): 174–90.

Proceedings of the National Union Republican Convention, 20–1 May, 1868. Chicago, 1868.

Proceedings of the Third Annual Meeting of the Non-Partisan National Woman's Christian Temperance Union, Cleveland, Ohio, 15–18 Nov. 1892. Cleveland, 1892.

Rees, Matthew. *From the Deck to the Sea: Blacks and the Republican Party*. Wakefield, N.H., 1991.

Reeve, Phoebe. "Colorado Woman Legislators." *The Modern World*, April 1907, 206–11.

Reitano, Joanne. *The Tariff Question in the Gilded Age: The Great Debate of 1888*. University Park, Pa., 1994.

Report of the International Council of Women, Assembled by the National Woman Suffrage Association, Washington, D.C., 1888.

Rhodes, James Ford. *The History of the United States from the Compromise of 1850*, Vol. 2. New York, 1893.

Roosevelt, Theodore. *Theodore Roosevelt: An Autobiography*. New York, 1919.

Rotundo, E. Anthony. *American Manhood: Transformations in Masculinity from the Revolution to the Modern Era*. New York, 1993.

Ryan, Mary P. *Cradle of the Middle Class: The Family in Oneida County, New York, 1790–1865*. New York, 1981.

Satterlee, W. W. *The Political Prohibition Text-Book*. Minneapolis, Minn., 1883.

Schlesinger, Arthur M. Jr., ed. *History of American Presidential Elections*. New York, 1971.
———. *History of U.S. Political Parties*. New York, 1973.

Scott, Anne Firor. *Natural Allies: Women's Associations in American History*. Urbana, Ill., 1991.

Sheldon, Winthrop. "Shall Lynching Be Suppressed, and How?" *Arena*, Sept. 1906, 225–33.

Shaw, Barton C. *The Wool-Hat Boys: Georgia's Populist Party*. Baton Rouge, La., 1984.

Sherman, Richard B. *The Republican Party and Black America from McKinley to Hoover*. Charlottesville, Va., 1973.

Simkins, Francis Butler. *Pitchfork Ben Tillman, South Carolinian*. Baton Rouge, La., 1944.

Sklar, Kathryn Kish. *Florence Kelley and the Nation's Work: The Rise of Women's Political Culture, 1830–1900*. New Haven, Conn., 1995.

Skocpol, Theda. *Protecting Soldiers and Mothers: The Political Origins of Social Policy in the United States*. Cambridge, Mass., 1992.

Smith, Wilda D. "A Half Century of Struggle: Gaining Woman Suffrage in Kansas." *Kansas History* 4 (1981): 74–95.

Stebbins, Giles B. *The American Protectionist's Manual*. Detroit, 1883.

Todd, Marion. *The Protective Tariff Delusion*. Battle Creek, Mich., 1886.

Towne, Laura M. *Letters and Diary of Laura M. Towne, Written from the Sea Islands of South Carolina, 1862–1884*, Rupert Sargent Holland, ed. New York, 1969.

Varon, Elizabeth R. "Tippecanoe and the Ladies, Too: White Women and Party Politics in Antebellum Virginia," *Journal of American History* 82 (1995): 494–521.

Wagner, MaryJo. "Farms, Families, and Reform: Women in the Farmers' Alliance and Populist Party." Ph.D. diss., University of Oregon, 1986.

Weaver, James B. *A Call to Action*. New York, 1974.

Wells, Ida B. *On Lynching. 1892–1895*. New York, 1969.

Wheeler, Marjorie Spruill. *New Women of the New South: The Leaders of the Woman Suffrage Movement in the Southern States*. New York, 1993.

White, Andrew. "Some Practical Lessons of the Recent Campaign." *Forum*, Dec. 1896, 414–22.

Wiebe, Robert H. *The Search for Order, 1877–1920*. New York, 1967.

Willard, Frances E. *Glimpses of Fifty Years*. Chicago, 1889.

———. *Woman and Temperance*. Hartford, Conn., 1883.

Willard, Frances E., and Mary A. Livermore. *A Woman of the Century*. Buffalo, N.Y., 1893.

Williams, R. Hal. *Years of Decision: American Politics in the 1890s*. New York, 1978.

Williamson, Joel. *A Rage for Order: Black/White Relations in the American South Since Emancipation*. New York, 1986.

Winston, George T. "The Relation of the Whites to the Negroes." *Annals of the American Academy of Political and Social Sciences* 18 (1901): 105–18.

Wright, James E. *The Politics of Populism: Dissent in Colorado*. New Haven, Conn., 1974.

Zimmerman, Jonathan. "'The Queen of the Lobby': Mary H. Hunt, Scientific Temperance, and the Dilemma of Democratic Education in America." Ph.D. diss., The Johns Hopkins University, 1993.

Index